Axi:Ome

INVISIBLE

Axi:Ome INVISIBLE

Sung Ho Kim
Heather Woofter

Novato, CA

ACKNOWLEDGMENTS

Sung Ho Kim and Heather Woofter

The making of this book was possible thanks to the generous support and collaboration of many people. We thank them for their enthusiasm and dedication in compiling these projects. First and foremost, we are indebted to the Axi:Ome team, who have devoted vision and talent to our practice. We thank Jae Bum Byun, Cassandra Cook, and Jaymon Diaz for their energy and dedication as project coordinators and mentors to young design team members. Their sharing of techniques and wisdom promoted a tangible consistency across time. Also, our gratitude to Ji Hoon Kim for two decades of collaboration and for advancing Axi:Ome of Korea. We thank Becca Leffell Koren for her infallible design sense and ability to visualize our intentions through the book's beautifully crafted and layered systems. Michelle L. Hauk has been a paramount collaborator whose editing brought unity in concept, structure to the book, and voice to visual narratives.

We are most grateful to our mentor Nader Tehrani for supporting us over the years as we navigated the conflicts between the academic and professional fields of practice. Thank you also to Alan Balfour for his contribution and support; his humor and shared experiences continue to guide us on our academic journeys. We are also forever thankful to Eric Mumford for his friendship and for lending historical insights that contextualized St. Louis. We are indebted to Jennifer Yoos for her support and friendship on numerous levels and stand strengthened by her encouragement. Thank you to Jesse Reiser and Nanako Umemoto for their inspiration and resilience. Within their practice, we also thank Julian Harake for his expert essay craftsmanship in collaboration with Nanako and Jesse.

Thank you to Nancy and Aaron Novack for giving us their love and embracing us into their lives, and to Emily Pulitzer, whom we consider family. We greatly appreciate Young Hie and David Kromme for their kindhearted support, and we are indebted to Nancy and Ken Kranzberg for always being proud of us. Thank you to Gia Daskalakis, Jeff Clark, and Aris, Andes, Eco, and Emily Daskalakis-Perez for their love.

We are grateful to our many St. Louis friends for filling our lives with joy: Mary Jane and Mike Baughman, Marie-Helene Bernard, Susan Bower and Steven Leet, Cindy Branheimer, Adrienne Davis, Antonio and Kirven Douthit-Boyd, Bobby Duffy and Marty Kaplan, Peggy Guest, Christine Jacobs and Hank Weber, Marilee Keys and Bruce Lindsey, JoAnna LaSala and Karen Tokarz, Lesley Laskey, Magda and Adrian Luchini, Lisa Melandri, Melissa and John Carlo Pilot, Bella Sanevich and Brad Fogel, Bob Sears, Phoebe and Steve Smith, Devora Tulcensky, Melissa and Enrique Von Rohr, and Jessica Willingham and David Dankmyer.

We would also like to express special thanks to Cynthia and Ben Weese for their mentorship and for bringing us to St. Louis, and to Adelaide Donnelly for sharing her positive energy with us adopted "pals."

Thanks also goes to our friends at Washington University in St. Louis, who shared their talents and brought the school together, with special mention to Chandler Ahrens, Julie Bauer, Wyly Brown, Ram Dixit, Eric Ellingsen, Catalina Freixas and Pablo Moyano, Bob Hansman, Derek Hoeferlin, Phil Holden, Petra Kempf, Zeuler Lima, Emiliano Lopez Matas, Gay Lorberbaum, Allison Mendez and Jonathan Stitelman, Monica Rivera, Constance Vale, Kelley Van Dyck Murphy, Kotch Voraakhom, Michael Willis, and Hongxi Yin. Furthermore, we could only survive the day-to-day demands of the school with the cheer and intelligence of Ellen Bailey, AnnaMarie Bliss, and Audrey Treece—thank you!

Design projects are only possible with caring and dedicated clients. We will forever express gratitude to our many collaborators for their strength and vision. Thanks to Tim Eby and Larry Eisenberg, Jack Galmiche, Rebekha Hager and Jamison Ford, Brandyn Jones, and Kelly Pollock and Catherine Wermert.

Thank you to our many design friends with whom we shared friendship and support, with special mention to Manuel Bailo, Stella Betts and David Leven, Lawrence Blough, Craig Borum, Laura Briggs and Jonathan Knowles, Elena Canovas, Luis Carranza, Dennis Crompton, Jeff Day, Arindam Dutta, Alan Gordon, Erik Hemingway, Ron Henderson, Dorothee Imbert and Andrew Cruse, Jamie Kolker, Todd Leong, Mimi Locher, Jennifer Maigret, Carl Miller, Patricia Olynyk, Maurizio Sabini, Pia Sarpaneva, Nasrine Seraji, Richard Sommer, Carol Strohecker, Adam Whiton, Lynnette Widder, Bryant Yeh, and Yun Kyu Yi.

This book would not have been possible without support and funding from our Sam and Marilyn Fox Professorship and Raymond E. Maritz Professorship endowments from Washington University in St. Louis. In addition, we received a generous grant from the Korean Timber Cluster Association and faculty development funding from the Kent State University College of Architecture and Environmental Design.

Special thanks to Dean Carmon Colangelo for his support during our twenty-plus years at Washington University in St. Louis. We are also grateful to President Jay Hartzell and Provost Sharon L. Wood of the University of Texas in Austin and Dean Mark Mistur of Kent State University College of Architecture and Environmental Design for supporting our new adventures in Austin and Cleveland.

Words cannot express enough gratitude to our family for their patience and encouragement. To Evan for his creativity and resilience; to our mothers Cynthia and Min Ja for giving us love; to our sister Sung Hee, brother-in-law Paul, and niece Ashley. Thank you.

This book is dedicated to our fathers, whom we greatly miss, David and Sin Jang; to Greg, who left us too young; and to our dear friend Paul Donnelly for his kindness.

St.Louis
Public Radio
90.7 KWMU

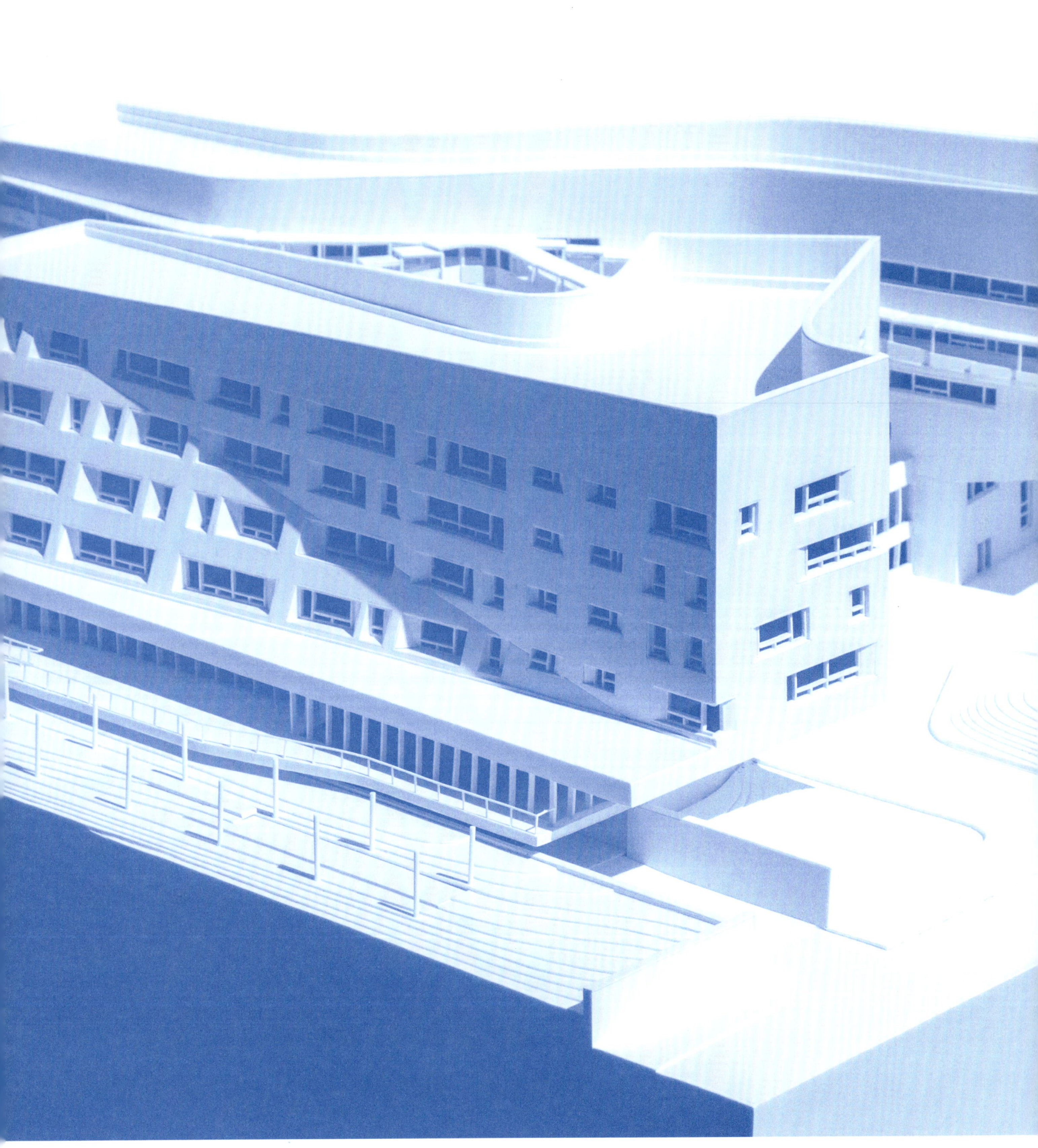

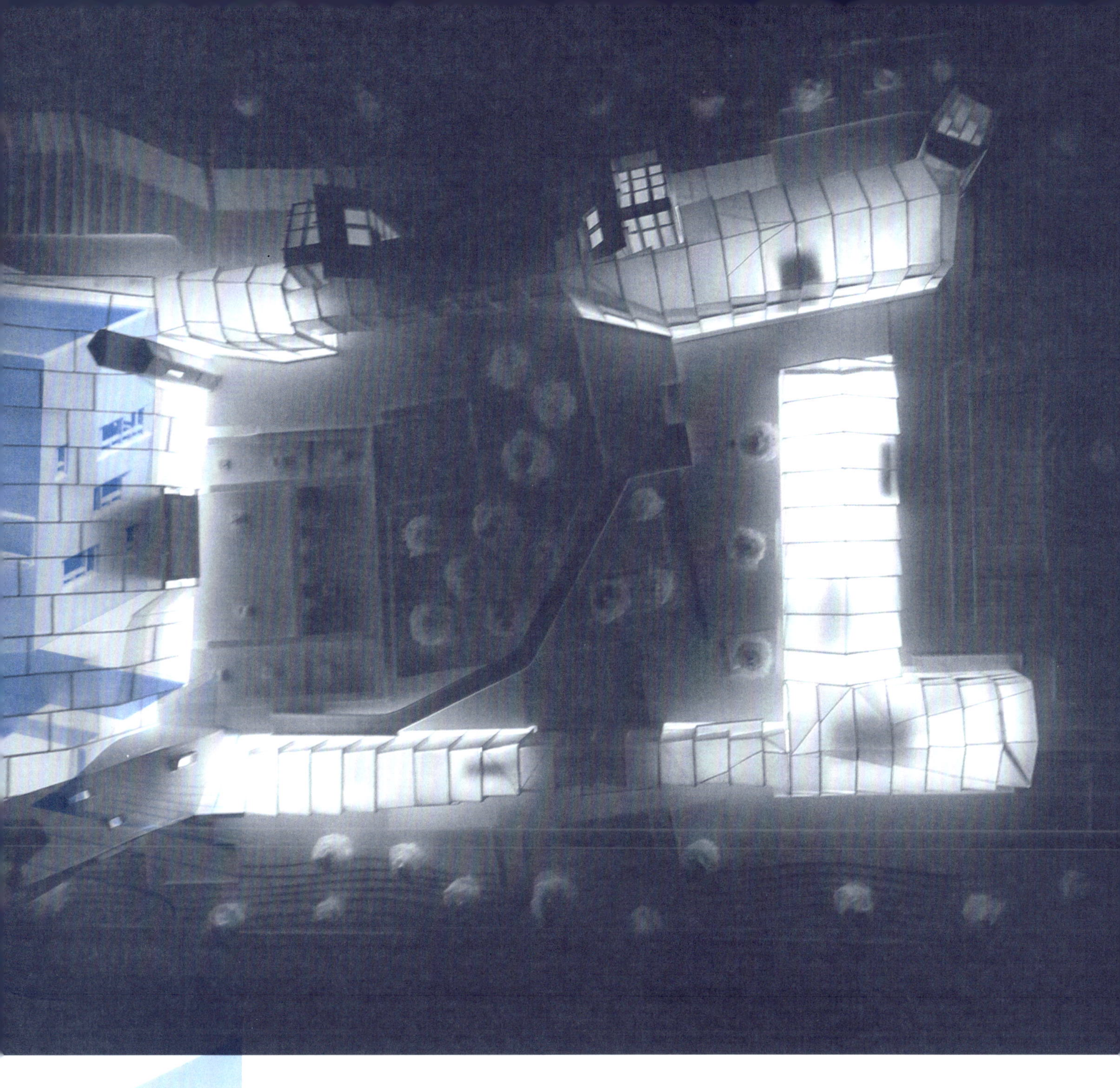

PREFACE

TRANSITIONS

Nader Tehrani

Led by Heather Woofter and Sung Ho Kim, Axi:Ome is characterized by a number of salient features laid out lovingly in this book. With a concurrent commitment to the academy and professional practice, the couple disentangles the traditional oppositions they have inherited from generations past. Having tinkered with core pedagogies from the bottom-up for over two decades, more recently starting with Woofter's leadership at Washington University in St. Louis, the pair has turned their attention to building a school of thought that attends to the broader top-down issues that characterize current thinking—among them the climate crisis, social equity, and the decolonization of the curriculum. To say that these two individuals have created a culture within St. Louis and WashU would be an understatement. It is important to underscore the idea that they did not merely go through the motions of academic procedures; they served as catalysts, advocates, and partners to colleagues, students, and faculty alike. Having known both for some time, I come to this introduction with ample bias. Sung Ho Kim was, in effect, my first student ever, and Heather Woofter a trusted advisor at MIT, where we undertook a serious revision of our core pedagogies in the undergraduate program in 2010. For these reasons, I cannot hide the personal or disciplinary affinities that I share with them.

First, theirs is a commitment to an architectural process that is inexhaustible. The sheer volume of work Axi:Ome has produced since its early years, most of which cannot be included in this publication, is a testament to Woofter and Kim's infinite thirst for speculation, exploration, and experimentation. If we are taught, conventionally, to give primacy to quality over quantity, they demonstrate that the quantity required by *iteration* is possibly the only guarantor of critical inquiry. Volume serves not as an end but as a means to research, test, and probe with the kind of curiosity we wish unto our students. In their work, this sensibility has persisted as an ethic now for decades. The combination of competitions, commissions, and self-propelled research has created an archive, a body of work layered with themes, techniques, and scales that offers views into their thinking from multiple perspectives.

Beyond such tenacity, their work maintains a thematic consistency, which, in the early years, maintained purity through its isolation from the construction industry, and which has now been further enriched by its engagement with patronage and the building trades alike. If their early work was maniacal in its fidelity to the model, both virtual and physical, Axi:Ome's allegiance to the means and methods of fabrication has helped translate that ethic to another scale. In essence, the bridge they build between representation and actuality has a dual function: to construct models as a projective device used to imagine a world that might yet be, but also to delve deeply into the means and methods of each trade to radicalize how construction details help form that reality.

Woofter and Kim's compositional sensibilities reveal another red thread that binds their projects together; in the name of creating a public realm, their affinity for connectivity, transparency, and continuity takes on both material and visual resonance. Though certain programs require spatial autonomy, their dominant *modus operandi* has been to overcome typological compartmentalization. In its place, we find fluid figures, seamless spatial extensions, and mutable surfaces that seek to blur the boundaries between inside and outside, challenging the strict programmatic delineation of one function over another. It is important to note that although patronage has allowed them to engage in robust construction, the evolution toward professional engagement has also tamed and framed their penchant for fluidity into smaller parcels, sometimes disallowing the mono-material bias they displayed in earlier years. Indeed, their predisposition towards self-similar organizational systems, single materials aggregations, and unitized construction displays a desire to bring rationality to the mass-customized while at the same time, seeks to demonstrate the sophistication that is born out of distinguishing the fundamental differences between surfaces that are walked upon, surfaces that shelter, and surfaces that insulate. In this sense, their linguistic bias towards the project of continuity has always maintained a steadfast commitment to tectonic and programmatic disciplines, something lost to many who share similar sensibilities.

Lodged within these new projects is another revealing story; beyond the professional commitments Axi:Ome holds towards the audiences it serves, Woofter and Kim also maintain a commitment to their buildings as pedagogical tools. In this vein, their commitment to developing exemplary projects serves a didactic function; these buildings teach by revealing what might otherwise remain dormant and by inviting varied audiences to enter their work, no matter their backgrounds. The senses are called upon in their full capacity to embody certain ideas and to allow architecture to speak through the experiences that these designers help frame. Teaching through building while building a pedagogical practice, Axi:Ome is now at a critical moment. Drawing upon well-established professional skills in everyday practice, their practice is a commitment to advancing a discipline in need of agency. This next phase of engagement will set the stage for a larger set of projects through which their thesis might be gauged.[1]

1 Since this introduction was written, both Woofter and Kim have taken on new leadership positions, respectively, at the University of Texas in Austin and Kent State University. Needless to say, this sways the challenges that loom for such a collaboration, at once extending their commitments to a new generation of academics while also reinforcing the necessary resilience of a mobile practice. The boldness of this move cannot be understated, nor undervalued, as invariably it stands to define the next ten years of Axi:Ome.

PROJECT INDEX

2002

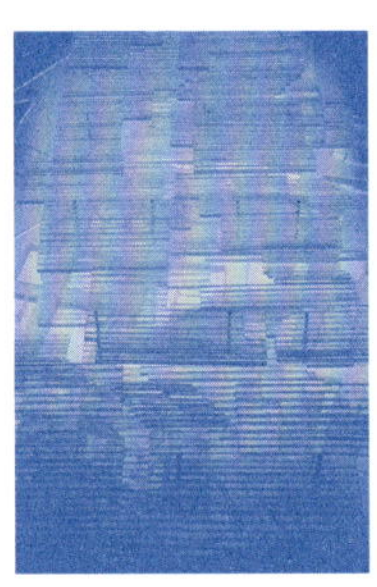

2002
Multi-Level Master Plan
Taipei, Taiwan

2002
Parallel Church
Rangsit, Thailand

2002
Keliher House
Weymouth, MA

2002
Sandol Church
Pinebrook, NJ

2002
Opera House
Oslo, Norway

2002
Jaguar Dealership
Aleppo, Syria

2003

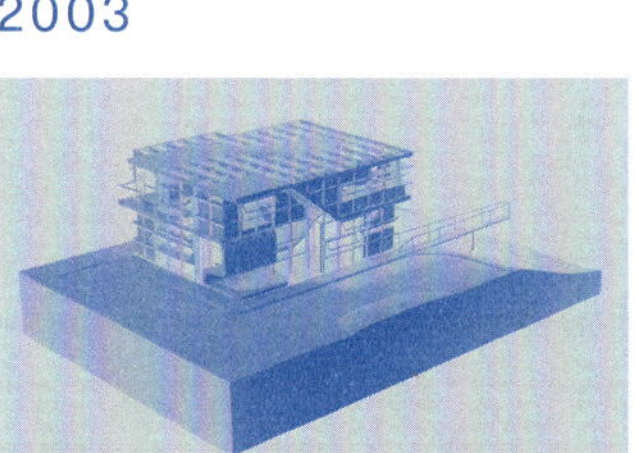

2003
Book House
Narragansett, RI

2003
Admotiv Headquarters Tower
Bangkok, Thailand

2003
Via Frontier
Daly City, CA

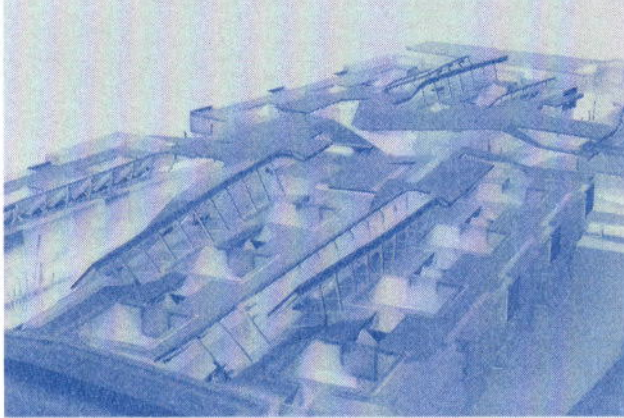
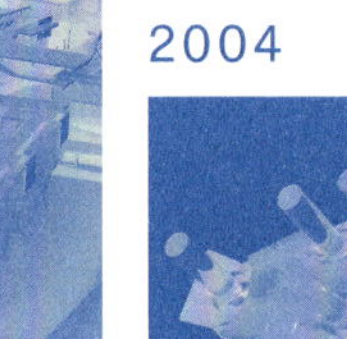

2003
Aomori Housing
Aomori, Japan

2004

2004
Osaka Master Plan
Osaka, Japan

2004
Noguchi Table Research

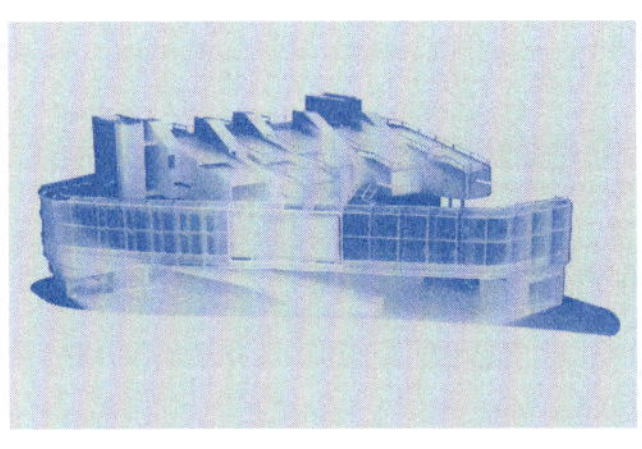

2004
Media Arcade
St. Louis, MO

2004
Slavery Memorial
Nantes, France

2004
Moscow Hotel
Moscow, Russia

2005

2005
Secret Stage Set
St. Louis, MO

2005
Glass House
Catawba Valley, VA

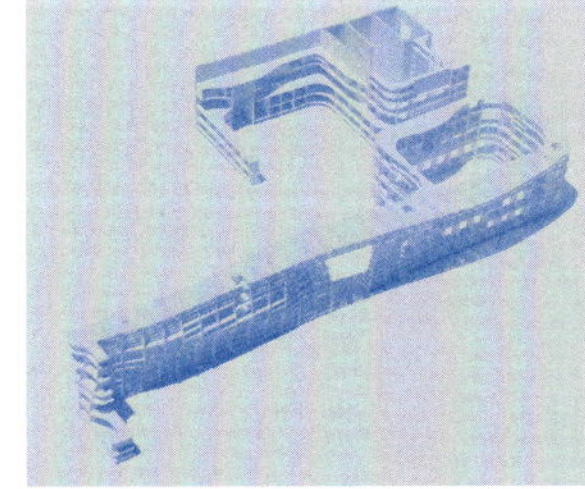

2005
Locust Office
St. Louis, MO

2005
Amonte House
Town and Country, MO

2006

2006
Women's Shelter
St. Louis, MO

2006
Urban Gallery I
St. Louis, MO

2008

2008
Fablab Furniture
St. Louis, MO

2009
Per For Mance Installation
St. Louis, MO

2010

2010
Terra Garden Towers
Bangkok, Thailand

2011
Orchid Tower
Taichung, Taiwan

2006
Urban Gallery II
St. Louis, MO

2008
Metabolic City Installation
St. Louis, MO

2009
UMSL in Grand Center
St. Louis, MO

2010
Urban Mirage
Incheon, South Korea

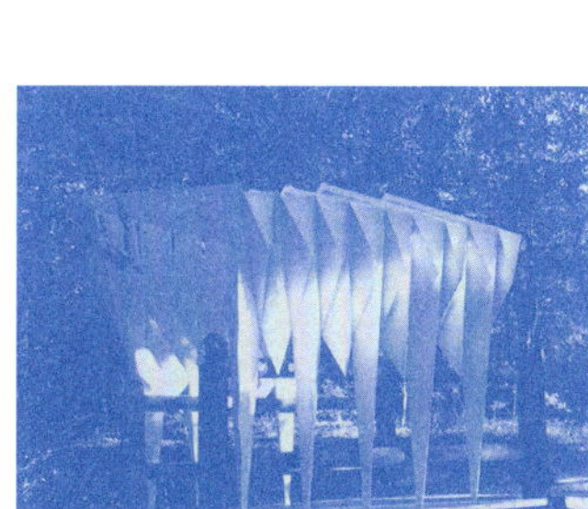

2011
Folded Bridge Installation
St. Louis, MO

2007

2007
Soulard Office
St. Louis, MO

2008
Carbon Tower
Dubai, UAE

2009
Media Plaza
St. Louis, MO

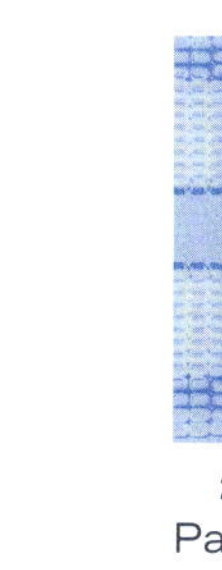

2010
Prism Tower
Winston Salem, NC

2011
Volume Formation Research

2007
Fablab Furniture
St. Louis, MO

2009

2009
Nine Networks
St. Louis, MO

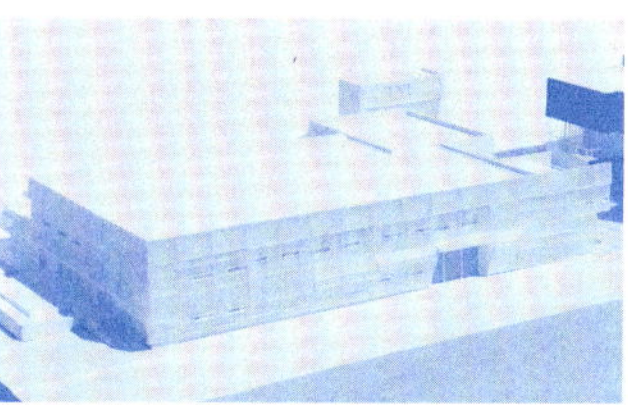

2009
KETC Skin
St. Louis, MO

2011

2011
Pattern Formation Research

2012

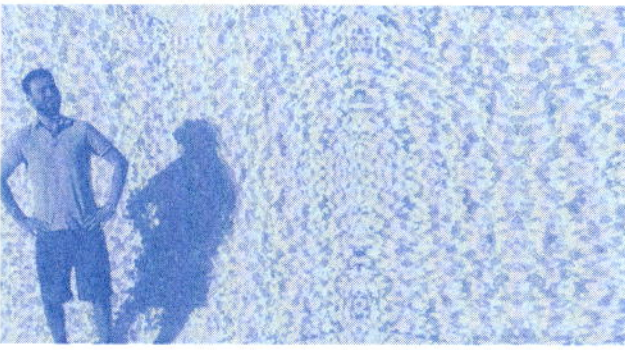

2012
Projection Terrain I
Los Angeles, CA

PROJECT INDEX

2012
Cineplex
Belleville, IL

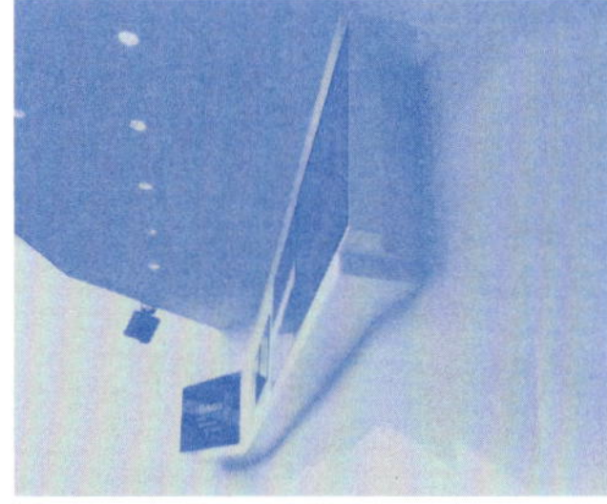

2012
Stay Tuned
St. Louis, MO

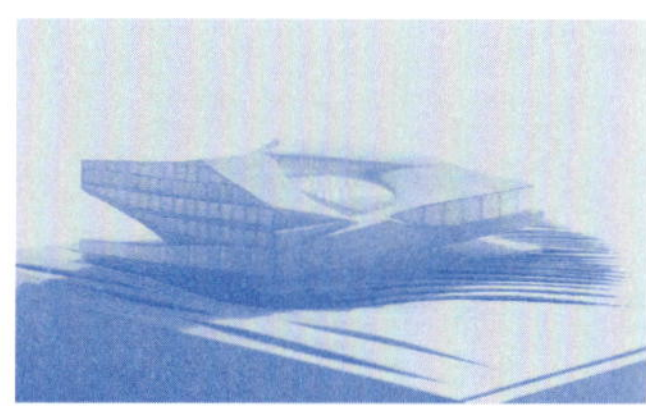

2012
Kedi
Jincheon, South Korea

2012
Flexi Glass Research

2013

2013
KETC Renovation
St. Louis, MO

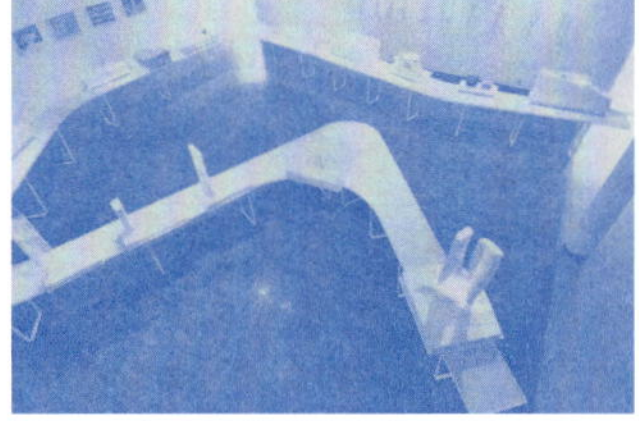

2013
Between Research and Practice Installation
Charlotte, NC

2013
Adult Day Care
Ridge Park, NJ

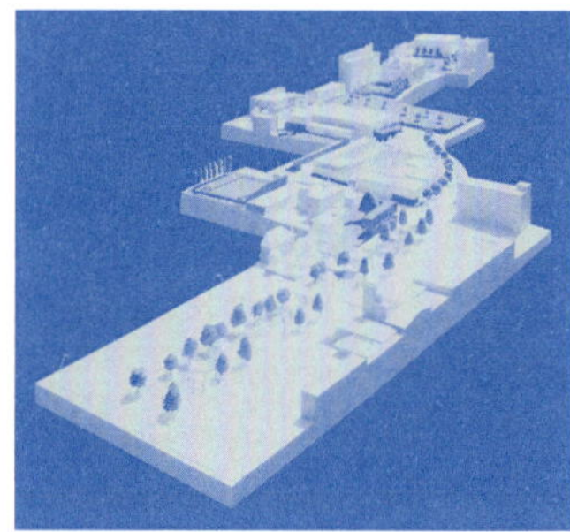

2013
Artwalk
St. Louis, MO

2013
Urban Forest
Shanghai, China

2014

2014
Box House
Seoul, South Korea

2014
Pulitzer Signage
St. Louis, MO

2014
Han House
St. Louis, MO

2015

2015
COCA Expansion I
St. Louis, MO

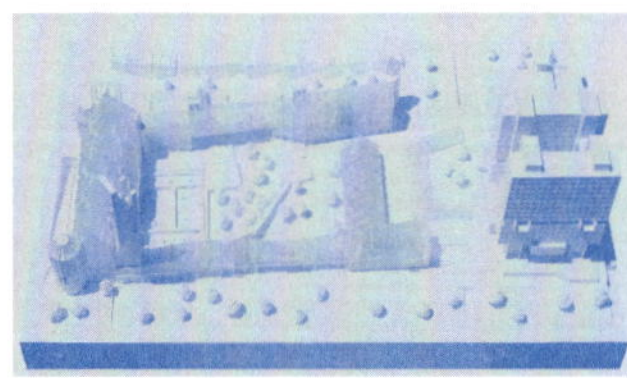

2015
Crystal Armature
Kaliningrad, Russia

2015
V9 Digital
St. Louis, MO

2016

2016
Roofscape Haus
Jecheon, South Korea

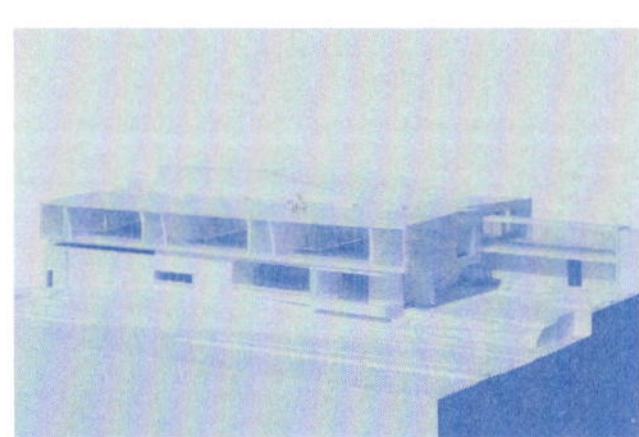

2016
COCA Expansion II
St. Louis, MO

2016
COCA Parking
St. Louis, MO

2016
Floating Pool
New Providence, Bahamas

2016
Elevated Ground
New Providence, Bahamas

2016
Micro Housing I
Jecheon, South Korea

2017
Olive Street Redevelopment
St. Louis, MO

2019
Fence
Jecheon, South Korea

2021
wUNDERland Stage Set
St. Louis, MO

2023

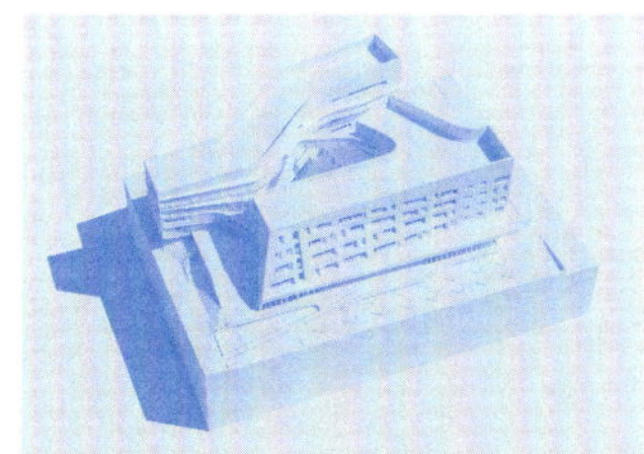

2023
Silverlake International High School
Hangzhou, China

2016
Micro Housing II
Jecheon, South Korea

2018

2018
Silver Tower
Chicago, IL

2020

2020
COCA Expansion III
St. Louis, MO

2022

2022
Jack Galmiche Memorial
St. Louis, MO

2023
Maison Feline
St. Louis, MO

2017

2017
Wolfner Redevelopment
St. Louis, MO

2018
Ferry Terminal
Seoul, South Korea

2021

2021
Projection Terrain II
St. Petersburg, Russia

2022
Lens Bridge and Urban Deck
St. Louis, MO

2023
Northwood Residence
St. Louis, MO

2017
Nine Network Master Plan
St. Louis, MO

2019

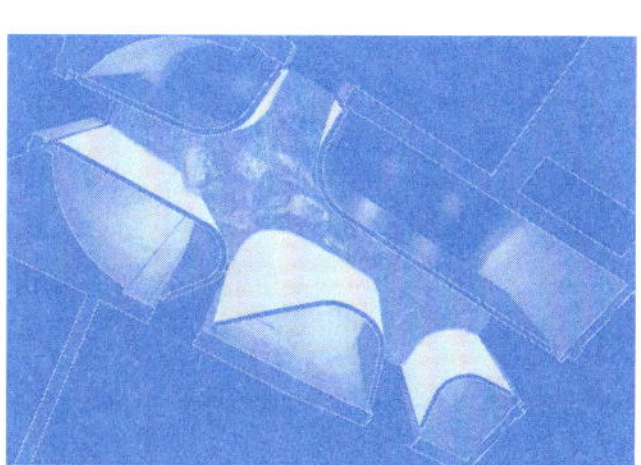

2019
Klepto Genic Chamber
Venice, Italy

2021
Stratiffications Scapes
Kafountine, Senegal

2022
Little Dancer Stage Set
St. Louis, MO

2023
Factory
Jecheon, South Korea

Sung Ho Kim and Heather Woofter

Over the last several years, we have been engaged in an exploration of the *invisible* in our design practice. Our conviction is less to explore the perceptual disappearance of architecture; rather, we seek more to develop a critical understanding of the subordination of the author's voice when complex forces arising from site, culture, and context come to bear on design inquiry. In turn, through the invisible we propose a responsive architectural practice, one with the capacity to meet the ever-shifting specificities of each project and realize their latent potentialities. Although we view architecture as a central force in the environment, it cannot intervene as a singular actor. Within our current social and environmental context, it is necessary to interrogate the impact of architecture as a physical presence that shapes and is shaped by its surrounding ecosystems and communities. This means that we endeavor to integrate each project into its unique landscapes and urban conditions in order to bring life to architecture. In the Olive Street Redevelopment project, for example, we reimagined how a set of three abandoned buildings could be repurposed as an energizer of a thriving ecosystem. In referencing the specificities of individual places, our projects are an homage to the landscape.

In our practice, we experiment with the generative aspects of design evolution that engage architecture as a mechanism with which to read and calibrate the landscape. This approach demands that building projects better exploit spatial practices within the environment it influences. The events we create through our designs reinforce, and even strengthen, the existing social and ecological characteristics of a specific community. The Kafountine, Senegal Secondary School draws on community knowledge to empower people in developing artisanal and industrial skills through the direct participation of village members in the building-making process. Lens Bridge, meanwhile, develops from the ecological qualities of its site, providing infrastructure that channels and filters rainwater and auto-derived pollutants into retention gardens. Such processes enable us to expand the scope of what architecture is through our design and research practices. At the same time, our theoretical approach, centered on the ecology of place, calls for a commitment to exploring the domain of knowledge within the discipline of architecture. We believe that architecture must offer an antidote to the global and local problems that arise when the built environment is disengaged from the social and biological ecosystems from which it springs.

We investigate the notions of timelessness in both research and practice, treating architectural form not as something static, but as a phenomenon that emerges from the convergence of past, present, and future. Place, which is shaped by human intervention in the landscape, arises in the now, from the unique perspective of those who observe and act upon a particular location at a specific moment in time. But what differentiates place from a mere position in space is that it is at once layered with traces of what came before and the potential for what might come to be after. Place comes into existence through the formation of meaning, which is generated in the present through its conversation with past and future.

Our practice is defined by thematic explorations centered around lightness, transparency, luminosity, and gravity. We challenge the boundaries of these concepts in order to expand the ways in which architecture can engage directly with its context. Light, for example, has a quality of tangible presence. Light is but one element of sensorial experience, illuminating architectural forms, amplifying sensations of openness, and regulating the temperature of the air. Our practice uses such elements to subtly shape sensorial and atmospheric experience, using light, material, space, and ground to create conditions that invite particular ways of feeling and inhabiting space. The atmospheric experience of architecture that arises from our speculative inquiries into the nature of light, material, and mass grounds our projects within their contextual fields, balancing the presence of illusion and reality.

Design is the tool through which architects engage with perception: it shapes how we perceive the world and delineates what we see and what we do not. Atmospheric conditions in architecture materialize from formal operations that penetrate vision and produce bridges between memory and visual phenomena such as the layering of transparencies. We are inspired by Merleau-Ponty's notion of art, literature, and music as explorations of the invisible. For Merleau-Ponty, the invisible refers to the observation of everyday phenomena that are often overlooked or mistranslated through ordinary perception (Merleau-Ponty 1968, 246–48). In this conceptualization, the invisible is a fabric of intuitive construction, one that is charged by a latent condition of visibility. Architecture deploys atmospheric, formal, and spatial effects as a means of organizing latent phenomena.

By engaging with the invisible, our practice seeks to reimagine the visual and aesthetic languages of architecture as tools of communication and connection. It is through the invisible that we discover and articulate the continuities between buildings and their sites, strengthen the relationship between architecture and the communities to which it belongs, and make visible the convergences between past, present, and future. We believe that as the field of architecture tackles the challenges of technological production, it risks losing the sensitivity and sympathy born of human experience and the beauty born of heart and sweat. We must take a more humanistic approach, marrying the visual with the invisible—the social, cultural, and biological biography of a place—so that we, as architects, can model a sensitive practice rooted in human endeavor.

References

Merleau-Ponty, Maurice. 1968. *The Visible and the Invisible: Followed by Working Notes*. Edited by Claude Lefort. Translated by Alphonso Lingis. Evanston: Northwestern University Press.

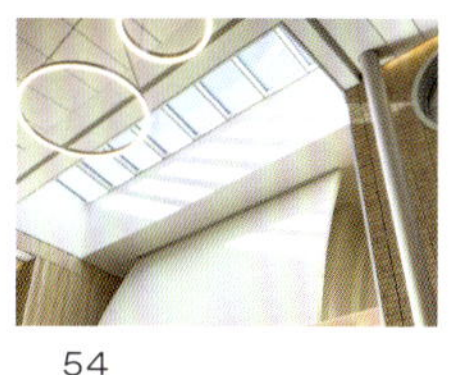
54

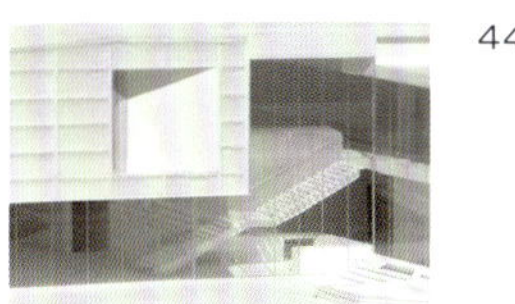
44

INVISIBLE WITHIN SOCIAL AND CULTURAL CONTEXT

74

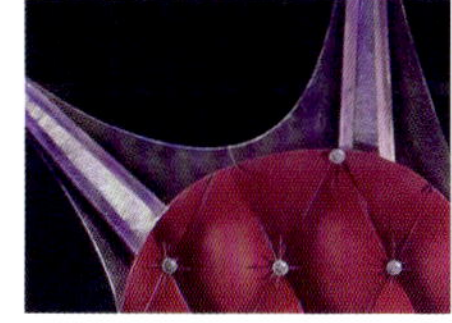
82

88
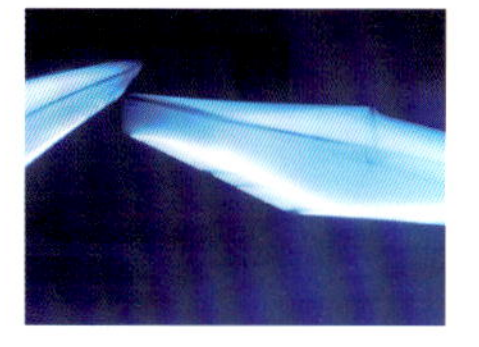

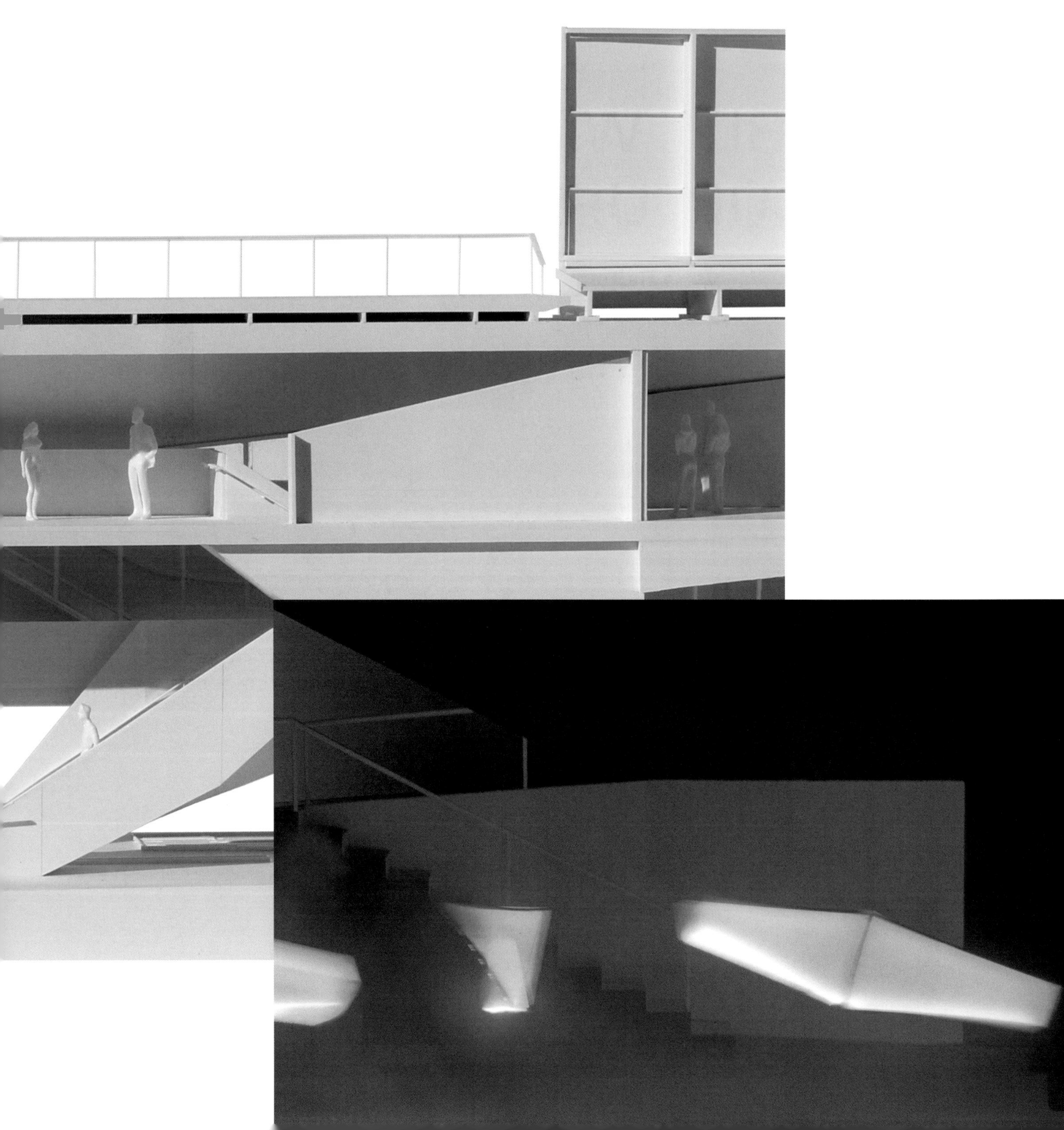

WITHIN SOCIAL AND CULTURAL CONTEXT

Alan Balfour

When approached from the parking lot across the street, COCA's new facade is elegant, polite, and gives no indication that it is an addition. It does, however, share the site with what was once the B'nai Amoona Synagogue—one of the last works by the revered German architect Erich Mendelsohn (1887–1953)—which was transformed after the congregation departed in 1986 into COCA, the Center of Creative Arts. (Although it sits in the heart of University City, this is a community-funded institution with no connection to Washington University in St. Louis.) The subtle modeling of its surfaces, muted colors, and what appears to be dancers behind the great window on the upper floor, quietly express COCA's function as a place of performance. The entrance, formed in the space between the old and the new, feels exactly right, the new enhancing and balancing the old. Two raised pavilions flank each end of the Mendelsohn wing, one now defining the entrance, the other marking the end of the block. In earlier iterations of the design, before the site was drastically reduced, Axi:Ome had conceived of the space between the addition and the Mendelsohn complex as a generous courtyard; however, in my view, the resulting compression of the site strengthens the relationship between old and new. (A remnant of the courtyard is present in the form of a slim wedge of grass above the entrance.) The thrusting roof of the former synagogue visible in the distance suggests something dramatic in its interior. Taken as a whole, the old and new structures, which together form the new north elevation, present planes and masses in satisfying balance—a distant echo of the composition Mendelsohn achieved in the De la Warr Pavilion (1935).

This is a place designed for creativity and performance and should be judged thus. Left to explore on an early spring evening, I found myself at ease and intrigued. Sweeping through the entrance doors and past the welcoming committee at the front desk, I stood beneath a swirl of circular lights (echoes of Mendelsohn) in a delightful entrance hall, itself a performance space with stepped seating facing the entryway. The sound of youthful voices drew me behind a reception desk, which led to a charmingly small room where very young children marched back and forward singing "It's a Small World After All." The entrance hall fully occupies the connection between the Mendelsohn complex and the new addition, with all the new facilities to the left of the hall. Continuing up a short flight of steps, the hall becomes the foyer of the theater, which has seating for 450 and a balcony. It is an exquisitely proportioned volume, dark and subdued, enhanced by golden wooden panels that flank the stage. The theater is sufficiently well-equipped to support professional performances. I entered quietly, trying not to be noticed by the older boys and girls aggressively rehearsing to a hip-hop beat.

The upper-level balcony looks across to the Mendelsohn complex, past the swirl of circular lights. I followed it to the front of the building to the vast light-filled dance studios whose windows dominate the street elevation. Ballet classes were in session as I walked past young women pirouetting and doing pliés along a wall of mirrors. Large soft chairs invite passersby to watch. A wedge cut into the wall at the end of the corridor, mysteriously named Sadie and Sachi's Pocket, offers a view of University City to all. Everywhere, the architecture is essential yet unobtrusive.

Axi:Ome's addition gently reveals a key element of Mendelsohn's design: within a framed opening at the south end of the entrance hall appears the tail-end of a light spine at the center of the curved roof of what had once been the temple. Through a doorway marked Staenberg Performance Lab, I entered what had once been the community center of the B'nai Amoona Congregation, where I was greeted by an eager group of eight-year-olds rehearsing for what promised to be a very lively performance of *Diamonds Are a Girl's Best Friend*. Until the arrival of the new theater, the former temple had served as the stage for all COCA performances, a use that once necessitated major alterations to the space, but not the structure. Acoustic panels and stage lights were suspended from the ceiling, and, by necessity, the great west-facing window had been blinkered. These additions remain and they distract from experiencing the space as Mendelsohn imagined it. Fortunately, they can now be removed and in the not-too-distant future, the original space may be restored so that it can once again capture and be transformed by the late afternoon sun.

The result is a new COCA formed from two distinct realities, the new sympathetically scaled to the old. Apart from the thrusting roof of the original temple, Mendelsohn's architecture is surprisingly restrained, which allows the new north façade to convincingly accommodate the Mendelsohn wing. Meanwhile, the much-photographed west façade of the Mendelsohn design, with its great sweeping skylight, remains essentially unchanged.

Erich Mendelsohn

As the architect Erich Mendelsohn began to work on the design of a modest synagogue in St. Louis, Missouri, he was beset by regrets and his continual struggle to find work since arriving in the United States in 1941. In 1930, he had been celebrated as one of the great visionaries of German architecture, but this ended with sudden force when Hitler became German Chancellor in January of 1933—within months his name had been struck from the list of German architects. He practiced with some success in England between 1934 and 1936, during which time he was invited and then moved to Palestine. His friendship with Chaim Weizmann, the future president of Israel, and his favorable reception by the British administration, led him to believe that he was uniquely capable of shaping the built landscape of the new Jewish homeland. He received a few significant commissions, but by 1940, his rudeness and arrogance had made him unpopular with the leaders of the Jewish community. A lack of work and the threat of the war in Europe spreading to the Middle East led him to leave for the United States in 1941. He was never able to understand why his intense vision for the architecture of a Jewish Palestine had been rejected.

Once in the United States, Mendelsohn's major concern was to find work. From 1941 until 1946, he toured the country giving lectures and setting up exhibitions of his work, hoping to be given a commission—all to no avail. He applied for teaching positions in New York and California, with no success. He was also seriously considered for the deanship of the School of Architecture at Washington University in St. Louis but was not offered the position. It was, however, his lecture and exhibition in St. Louis that led to the commission to design a synagogue for B'nai Amoona, a leading conservative Jewish congregation in the city.[1]

In a drawing by Erich Mendelsohn made in California in 1946, Mendelsohn made his first attempt to give form to the concept of a synagogue. Mendelsohn's drawings are very small, no more than the size of a letter. There is a direct relationship between their structure and the muscles of his wrist and hand. They not only seek to express tension but are created out of it. Mendelsohn viewed these drawings in different ways. He recognized that they were physical gestures, their small size determined by the limits of a wrist at rest. The manner of their execution, their size, and their spareness are important to their quality. Though brief, these rendered gestures distilled for him the essence of architecture. They are moments held in time and space.

1 When Mendelsohn arrived in London in 1934, the Architectural Association (AA) School gave him a generous welcome, which included invited lectures and an exhibition of his work. When I was the director of the AA in 1993, I met his daughter, Ester Joseph, who wanted to discuss a possible exhibition. I offered full support, but nothing came of it. However, we did spend an hour or so discussing her father. I gave her a copy of my book *Berlin: The Politics of Order* (1990) in which Mendelsohn's last Berlin project, Columbus Haus, plays a heroic if tragic role. She said he had loved London, but that the last ten years of his life spent in the United States had been the most difficult. Mendelsohn had become a British citizen in 1939 but wrote later that he despised the English.

There is firm concentration in the making of Mendelsohn's drawings. The hand dances in arabesques across the page, leaving behind forms shaped by the passage of movement and by the words "B'nai Amoona," which imbue the space with the mythical potential of a new world. Each vignette is intense and deliberate. The impressions in the architect's mind are fleeting, demanding that the drawings be executed quickly. The viewpoint is always the same—set at eye level some distance from the object, the ground in between remaining undefined. The sketches are confident and fluid, effortless productions of a clear intention. There is a direct relationship between the speed and strength of the physical gesture and the symbolism of the image. Mendelsohn is fifty-six years old. He has produced similar drawings for over thirty years. He experiences them in his mind as he experiences music. So habitual has the process become that when an idea is complete or when a drawing satisfies, he gives it a final flourish—an arc or a circle—to isolate and enhance it.[2]

Mendelsohn was born in Allanstein, East Prussia (now Poland), in 1887 and raised in an affluent merchant family. He first studied economics at the University of Munich and then, between 1908 and 1910, architecture at Berlin's Technische Hochschulle. He rode a wave of exceptional fortune through all the post-war chaos in Germany to become, by the end of the 1920s, Berlin's most successful modernist architect. Mendelsohn served on the front line in the First World War and from the trenches produced a series of very small and intense drawings depicting his vision for architecture, apocalyptic drawings in the mood of expressionism with the character of living organisms. They were exhibited in Berlin where colleagues of Albert Einstein saw in them a spiritual affinity with their scientific work. In 1919, he was commissioned to design the Einstein Tower in Potsdam, a Prussian state facility for research in astrophysical phenomena arising from Einstein's theory of relativity. The building was designed to present a new order that would, in Mendelsohn's imagination, transcend the cultural destruction wrought by the war.

Not untouched by Nietzsche, Mendelsohn saw himself as a solitary genius. He is reported to have told his assistants on several occasions, "When God created the world he had no associates, so why should I?" (Von Eckardt 1960, 16). Another favorite expression of his was, "Would you have asked Beethoven for the Seventh Symphony when he was ready to create the Ninth? All I'll say is you'll get a Mendelsohn!" (23). He rejected

2 The material on Mendelsohn used in this essay is drawn from two of my books: *Berlin: The Politics of Order*, published by Rizzoli in 1990, in which Mendelsohn's last Berlin project, Columbus Haus plays a tragic role in the destruction of the city; and *The Walls of Jerusalem*, published by Wiley Blackwell in 2019, which discusses Mendelsohn's years in Palestine.

any notion of the decline of the West and believed profoundly in the sacred character of the new world and in his role as its prophet. "Expressing the power of an age has always been the task for art," he wrote in 1924 (Beyer 1967, 68). Giving physical expression to the relativity of space and time became the mission of his architecture.

Beginning in the mid-1920s, his reputation established, Mendelsohn produced a series of designs for commercial and industrial buildings that epitomized the brilliant surge of energy that had jolted Germany out of cultural stagnation. He had become a public figure whose words and designs aimed to recharge the nation. For the opening of his Schocken Department Store in Nuremberg in 1926 he delivered an epic poem in which he proclaimed that "to want to deny our [modern] way of life is self-deception, it is pitiful and cowardly" (Beyer 1967, 94).

Mendelsohn's last and most powerful project in Berlin, Columbus Haus, was built on Potsdamer Platz, at the very center of Berlin within sight of Hitler's Reich Chancellery. It was completed in 1932, just before Hitler became German Chancellor on January 30, 1933. Shortly thereafter, Mendelsohn and his family left Germany forever. In his memoir, he wrote, "The day Hitler takes over, March 1933. I am forty-five years old. The door to the European continent closes behind me" (Rapaport 2009).[3] In exile, he was deeply concerned with the fate of Columbus Haus. He knew that the building had been seized by Hitler's government but mistakenly believed that it had been used as a prison during the first period of Jewish persecution.[4] He was dead before it was finally destroyed in 1960; its fate would have greatly saddened him.

In 1932, Mendelsohn settled and formed a practice in England where he built several projects, the foremost among them being the De La Warr Pavilion on England's south coast. In 1934, Chaim Weizmann commissioned him to design a house twelve miles south of Tel Aviv, and for the next five years he would divide his time between England and Palestine. (Weizmann would become the first president of Israel in 1947.) His practice continued until 1936, when he bought a home and opened an office in Jerusalem. Within a few months, Mendelsohn was reunited with his most important client from Germany, Zalman Schocken, for whom he had designed several celebrated department stores, a family home, and a library for his extensive and invaluable rare book collection.

3 Mendelsohn's complete correspondence can be found in the Erich and Luise Mendelsohn Papers, 1894 – 1992, held at the Getty Research Institute, Special Collections.

4 Mendelsohn knew that Columbus Haus had suffered in the bombing, yet, while all the masonry building had been reduced to rubble, he was pleased that its structure had survived. The building was partially restored in the next decade; however, it lay directly in the path of Russia's brutal division of the city in 1961 and was slowly destroyed as Germany divided into East and West.

Mendelsohn began to consider settling permanently in Palestine: "Is not our place here?... I am resolved to remain here. Every day I come to regard the people in the fields, even the towns' people, a little more as my brothers," he wrote in a letter to his wife in December 1934 (Rapaport 2009). He believed he had a unique role to play: "What the country needs most is creative people. They alone will once more win respect and honor for our name" (Rapaport 2009). He believed he could be a guiding spirit. He dreamed of designing all the major buildings for this emerging Jewish homeland and outlined a plan for what he called "Artistic Zionism."

This cathartic urge to make public the intentions behind his intense vision for the future of the "National Home" found its full expression in a pamphlet he wrote and published in Jerusalem in 1940, titled *Palestine and the World of Tomorrow*. This is one of several texts in which Mendelsohn called for a union between Islam and Judaism in building this new world. He could not have been unaware of how inflammatory this was to so many Zionists. His wife Luise later wrote, "He made himself very unpopular in Palestine with this brochure, but... Eric was not a diplomat, and it was his whole personality to say what he thought was right. It did not make life easier for him, or for me" (Hoffman 2016, 121).

Mendelsohn's largest and, in his mind, most important project for the future of Palestine was the design of the Hadassah Medical Center. This engaged him from 1936 to 1939, three of the most frustrating and depressing years of his professional life. The project was overseen by and funds managed through New York, where there was continual interference and costs were cut at every opportunity. For Mendelsohn, the greatest offense was the refusal to pay what he believed was a fair fee.

With war threatening the Middle East, Mendelsohn made the difficult journey with his family from Palestine to the United States where he settled in 1941. While working on the design for the synagogue in St. Louis in 1947, he wrote to the head of the Hadassah Medical Center offering to return to the new nation of Israel and resume work on the complex. The reply from Jerusalem was blunt and harsh:

> It is up to you to reconcile those two parties, namely, Jewish Palestine and Mendelsohn. The reconciliation may take place when Mendelsohn humbly comes to Palestine as many thousands have done before and many thousands dream of doing now... I should be extremely sorry to see that what I mistook for your sincere desire to return to Palestine was conditioned by the number of projects which you might or might not be asked to undertake. That, my dear Eric, is a peculiar Zionism with which I personally can have nothing to do (Hoffman 2016, 122).

The B'nai Amoona Synagogue

When Mendelson began to consider the design of the B'nai Amoona Synagogue, he knew he was doing so at a time when Jewish communities across the U.S. were concerned with modernizing the form of the temple. In a formative article in the March 1947 issue of the Jewish monthly magazine *Commentary* titled, "The Problem of Synagogue Architecture: Creating a Style Expressive of America," architect and art historian, Rachel Wischnitzer-Bernstein, considered this issue in careful detail:

> Exponents of the progressive camp, such as Ely Jacques Kahn and Percival Goodman, strongly advocate a frank display of new design in plan and elevations. They vigorously oppose all sorts of period trappings, whether Neo-Gothic, Romanesque, or Moorish. The main objection to the historicizing styles is not, however, that they express conservatism, but that they were artificially established mostly by Christian architects who adopted them as models on the basis of their own very limited knowledge of the Jewish background (Wischnitzer-Bernstein 1947, 240).

Wischnitzer-Bernstein concludes with what sounds like a challenge to Mendelsohn:

> As I write this, many communities are planning to remodel or build synagogues or social centers. A social center incorporating a synagogue is to be built in Cleveland and a new synagogue in St. Louis. Eric Mendelsohn, known from his buildings in Palestine and England as well as for brilliant achievements in Germany, has been entrusted with both projects.
>
> In St. Louis the synagogue will be set in a typical environment, which includes a Neo-Gothic Catholic church, a revivalist-Renaissance Methodist church, and an Egyptian Masonic Temple. No one today expects the architect to add another "period piece" to this 19th-century décor, and the problem requires daring. But respect for the given situation is also required. A 20th-century solution is necessary that will, nevertheless, harmonize with the surroundings.
>
> Granted the necessity for tact, Mr. Mendelsohn will still have to make some bold departures; and it is precisely here that he will need the understanding and cooperation of the Jewish community. What Mr. Mendelsohn produces may supply at least a partial indication of the future of American synagogue architecture (Wischnitzer-Bernstein 1947, 241).

As he had throughout his creative life, Mendelsohn believed he was uniquely placed to respond, although he had never designed a synagogue himself.[5] He also recognized that he was in competition with Kahn and Goodman, not only in

5 He had designed a chapel for a Hebrew cemetery in Konigsberg, which was destroyed in the war.

producing the concept for the modern synagogue but also for commissions.[6] In the June 1947 issue of *Commentary*, Kahn, Paul Goodman (Percival's bother), and Mendelsohn replied under the title "Creating a Modern Synagogue Style," each offering their position of the modern synagogue. Under the subtitle "In the Spirit of Our Age" Mendelsohn described his intentions:

> Temples should reject in their interiors the mystifying darkness of an illiterate time and should place their faith in the light of day. The House of God should either be an inspiring place for festive occasions that lift up the heart of man, or an animated gathering place for a fellowship warming men's thoughts and intentions by the fire of the divine word given forth from altar and pulpit right in their midst (Landsberger et al. 1947, 541).

This is an apt description for B'nai Amoona, which expresses the idea that temples should "place their faith in the light of day" with its great curved, light-catching roof and enormous skylight, which seizes the sun with geometries reminiscent of the Einstein Tower as it scans the cosmos. Mendelsohn continues:

> If, however, the needs and limitations of the community are seriously appraised, the site carefully chosen, the geographic and climatic factors thoroughly evaluated, and contemporary building methods boldly and surely employed, the result is bound to be stimulating and sincere—a visual proof that we Jews are full participants in this momentous period of America's history (Landsberger et al. 1947, 542).

All the above are present in the simple plans and basic structures of B'nai Amoona. He continues:

> It is a period that demands centers of worship where the spirit of the Bible is no ancient mirage but a living truth, where Jehovah is not a distant king but our guide and companion (Landsberger et al. 1947, 542).

There is an echo of this proposition in Bruno Zevi's 1974 speech, "Hebraism and Concept of Space-Time in Art," in which Zevi offers a revealing contrast between Jewish and Christian classical views of being human and places Mendelsohn's concept within Hebraic tradition and culture:

> Hebraism is a concept of time, that, while the divinities of other peoples are associated with places and things, the God of Israel is a god of events and that Jewish life, nourished by the Book, is permeated history, that is, with a time-related consciousness of human tasks ... Hebraism

6 I worked on a research project with Percival Goodman in the early 1960s, who, by then, had become the dominant architect of the modern synagogue on the East Coast.

cannot be reduced from any point of view to the concept of space. At the root core, the very Hebraic idea of God denies it (Zevi 1974, 155).

Given this reading, the temple hall of B'nai Amoona can be seen as framing the event of gathering in the sun's changing light over time. On the crucial differences between the Jewish and Greek views of man, Zevi writes, "the Greek ideal represents the human being as an absolute, above history, beyond time . . . the human type, indeed the prototype," for the Jewish people (Zevi 1974, 157). Man is defined by the dynamics of daily living. And so it was with the St. Louis Synagogue: apart from the soaring roof of the temple hall seizing the light, this is a simple arrangement of assembly rooms, classrooms, a library, and a nursery around an open courtyard.

Mendelsohn developed the design for B'nai Amoona in his California office. He made several journeys back to St. Louis and argued with the building committee as costs soared from an initially modest budget. But the work was completed, and the synagogue opened in 1950. In a letter to his wife at the completion of the work, Mendelson wrote, "the inside is exactly as I envisioned it, light–day and night–perfect" (James-Chakraborty 2000, 44). While in failing health, he conceived and built three more synagogues all exploring different forms of the modern synagogue. He died from cancer in 1953. He was 66.

Mendelson ended his essay from over seventy years ago by stating that the period "demands temples that will bear witness to man's material achievements and, at the same time, symbolize our spiritual renascence. This question no architect can pass upon, but the answer will be recorded in the pages of history now being written" (Landsberger et al. 1947, 542). Given that the temple ceased to be a place of worship almost forty years ago, there remains one question that cannot be easily answered but can be experienced: to what degree does this carefully conceived metaphysical structure—Mendelsohn's concept of the temple—continue to "symbolize spiritual renascence?" Does its significant form transcend its original intention?

References

Beyer, Oskar ed. 1967. *Erich Mendelsohn: Letters of an Architect.* London: Abelard-Schuman.

James-Chakraborty, Kathleen. 2000. *In the Spirit of Our Age: Eric Mendelsohn's B'Nai Amoona Synagogue.* St. Louis: Missouri Historical Society Press.

Hoffmann, Adina. 2016. *Till We Have Built Jerusalem: Architects of a New City.* New York: Farrar, Straus and Giroux.

Landsberger, Franz, Ely Jacques Kahn, Eric Mendelsohn, Percival Goodman, and Paul Goodman. 1947. "Creating a Modern Synagogue Style: A Discussion." *Commentary 3*, no. 000006 (June): 537 – 44.

Rapaport, Raquel. 2009. "Blood and Space, Race and Three Dimensions! Letters of an Architect Revisited." *Bezalel*, no. 14 (September): N.p. https://journal.bezalel.ac.il/en/protocol/article/3652.

Von Eckardt, Wolf. 1960. *Erich Mendelsohn.* New York: George Braziller.

Wischnitzer-Bernstein, Rachel. 1947. "The Problem of Synagogue Architecture." *Commentary 3*, no. 000003 (March): 233 – 41.

Zevi, Bruno. 1974. "Hebraism and the Concept of Space-Time in Art." In *Bruno Zevi: On Modern Architecture*, edited by Andrea Oppenheimer Dean, 155 – 66. New York: Rizzoli.

Site St. Louis, MO, United States | Status Schematic Design | Program Cultural | Client Center of Creative Arts

COCA EXPANSION II

The Center of Creative Arts (COCA) Expansion II is an addition and renovation of a modernist synagogue designed by Erich Mendelsohn for the B'Nai Amoona congregation and completed in 1950. The expansion embraces the values and resonates with the architectural expressionism of Mendelsohn's vision for modernism. This includes the use of authentic details, original materials, the articulation of a strong relationship between interior and exterior, well-lit and proportioned spaces, and the economic use of materials to express egalitarian ideals. In this project, individuals and programs are as important as a thoughtfully constructed building. The design integrates programmatic spaces of various sizes together, including several interdisciplinary arts programs, a new theater, and a black box. The structure of the courtyard creates an opportunity for interior and exterior performances and furnishes multiple types of performance and educational classroom spaces.

At COCA, the landscape acts as a staging space between nature and the built environment while angled glass curtain walls create reflective surfaces and respond to the acoustical performances of the dance studios. A chromatic staircase serves various programmatic functions and stands as a beacon in the open public space. Metallic curtains flow through the entrance and multi-functional theater to provide both privacy and noise control. The design strategy creates flexibility and invites young artists to embrace architecture as a stage set for inspiration.

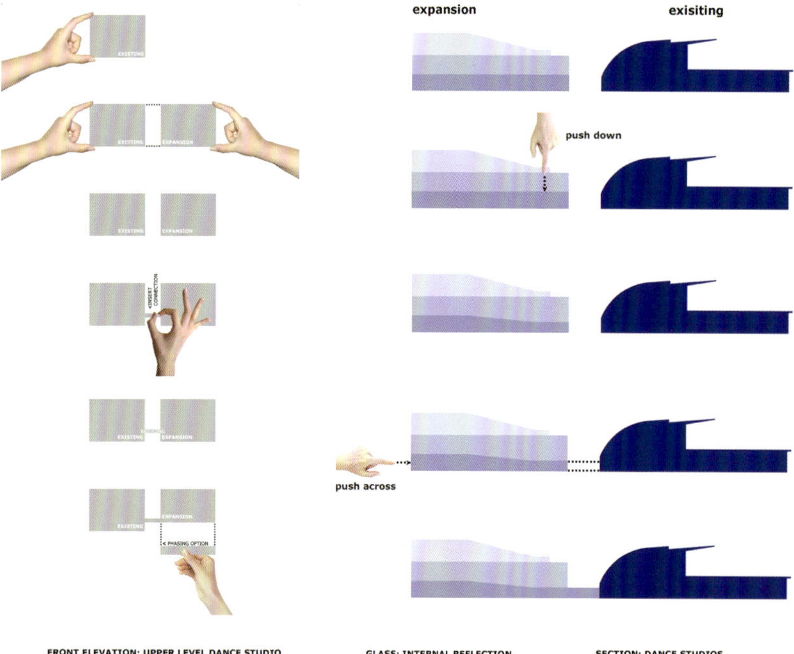

Conceptual massing diagram (left),
Conceptual figure diagram (right)

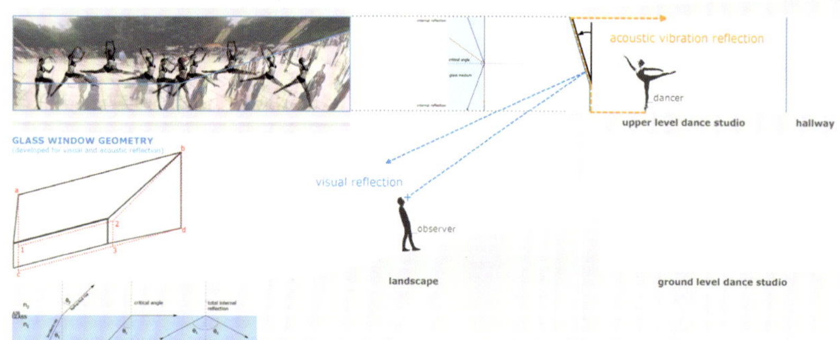

Glass curtain wall diagram

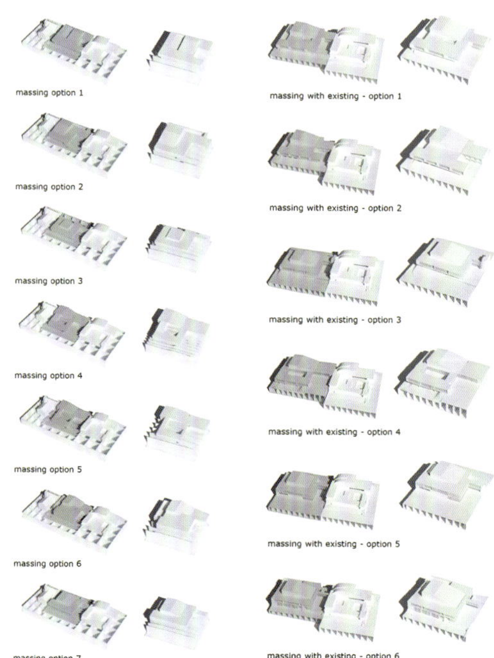

1/32" = 1' scale massing model index (left),
1/16" = 1' scale massing model index (right)

South elevation

North elevation

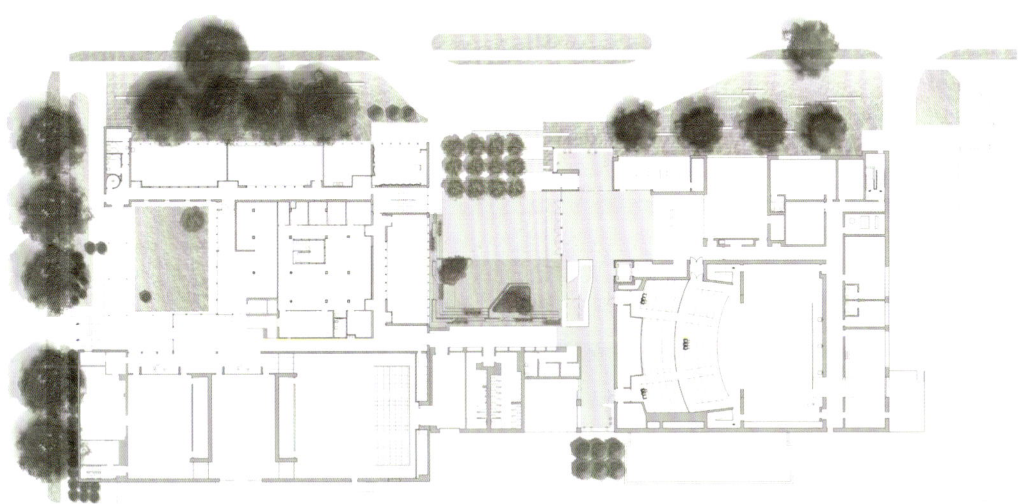

First-floor plan

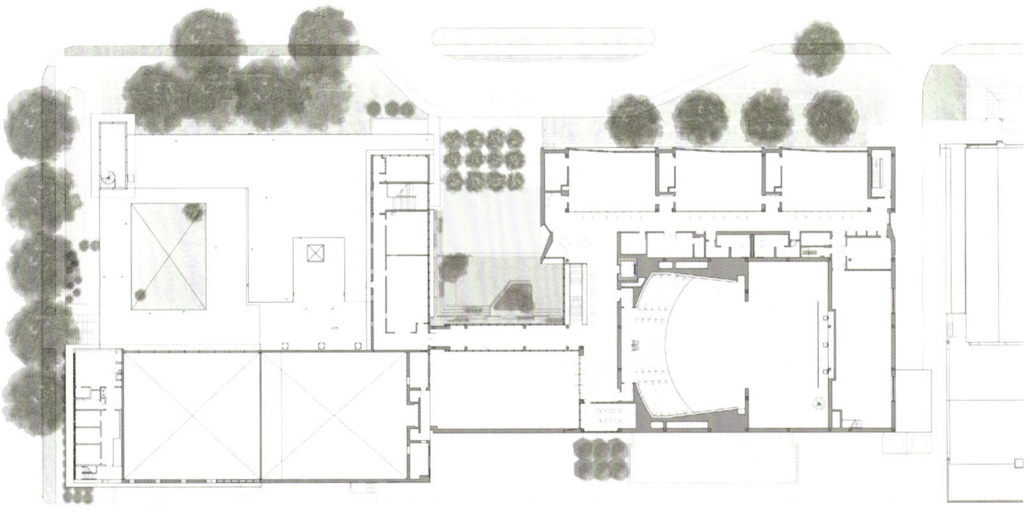

Second-floor plan

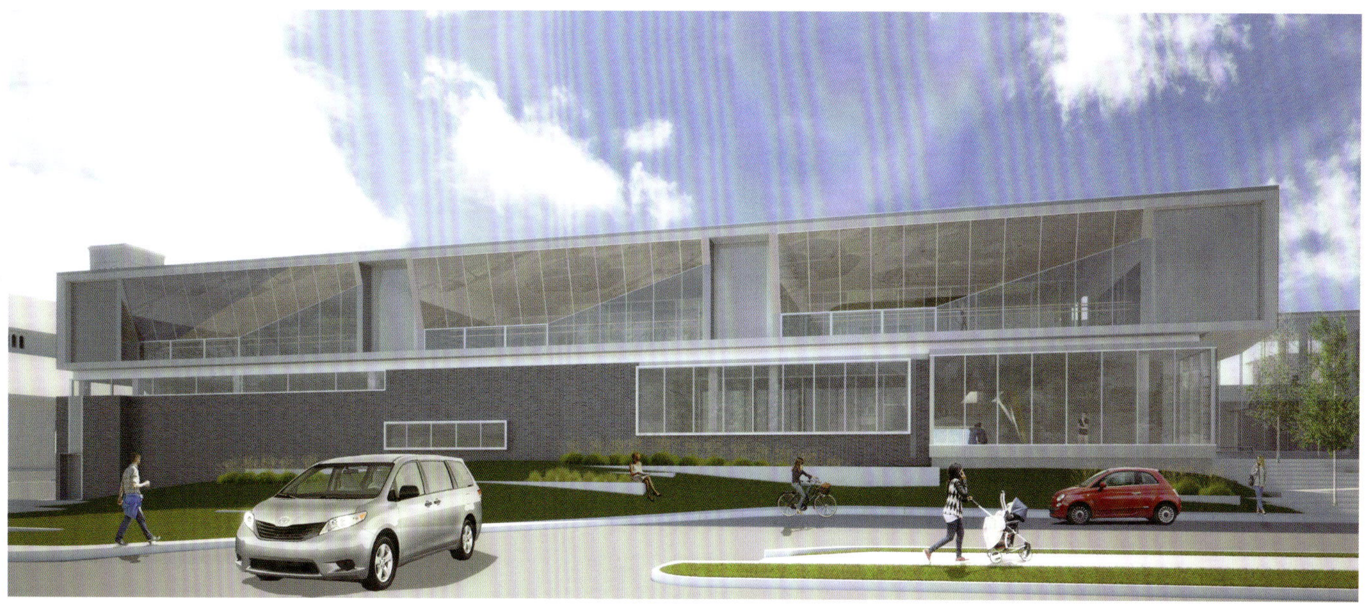

Detail model with theater roof removed

COCA

Site St. Louis, MO, United States

Status Built

Program Cultural

Client Center of Creative Arts

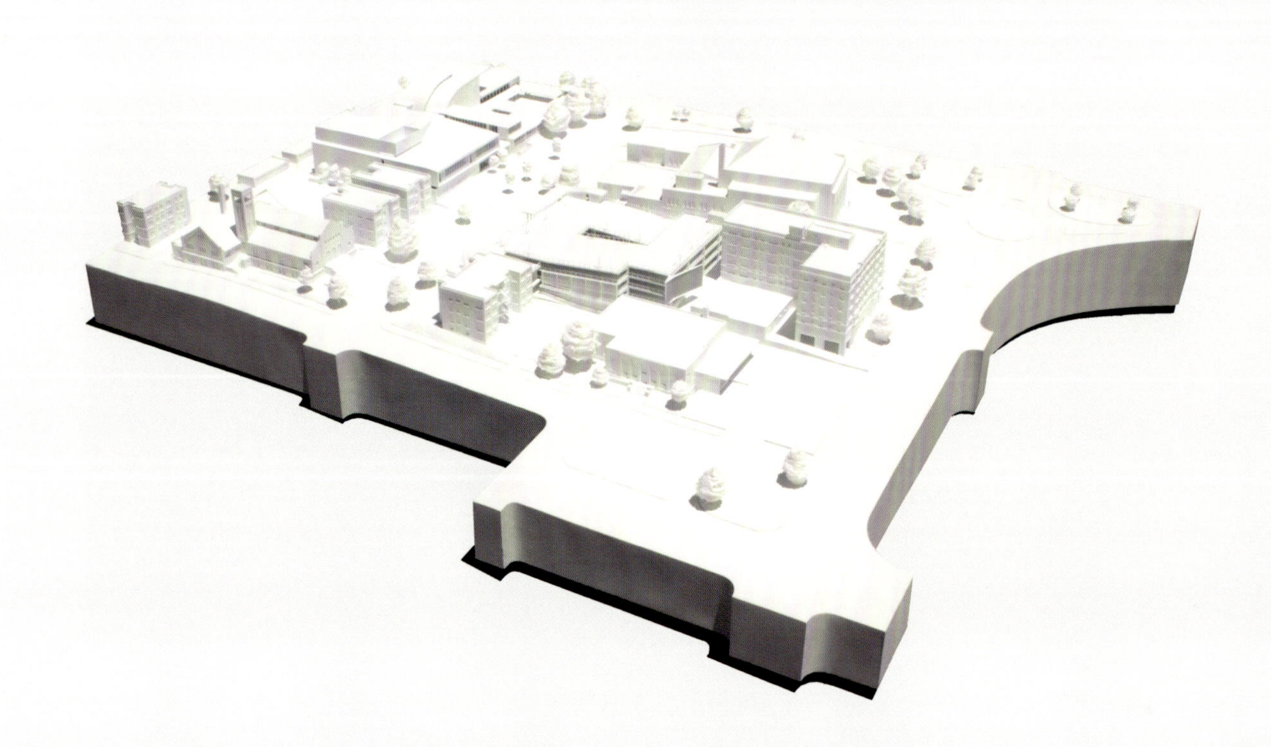

COCA EXPANSION III

COCA Expansion III is a 58,000-square-foot addition to Erich Mendelsohn's modernist synagogue. In Mendelsohn's original plans, educational spaces are located across the garden from the assembly spaces. In the garden's interior was a library and kindergarten, a space framed by light and with views of the natural surroundings that placed children at the center of the design. Rather than romanticize the machine, Mendelsohn expressed materiality through the spiritual qualities of light. These basic principles guided our interpretation of the proposed renovation, a protected campus with natural and social spaces organized around a second-level landscape situated between the existing building and the new addition. Inspired by Mendelsohn's concept that man's public life is central to architecture, we designed COCA to reflect its role as an institutional anchor; its substantial building mass, driven by the scale of the theater space, is carefully integrated into the adjoining residential neighborhood.

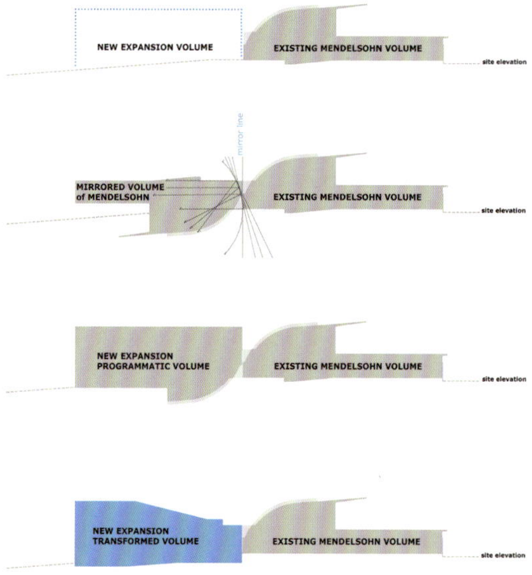

NEW EXPANSION VOLUME
EXISTING MENDELSOHN VOLUME
site elevation

mirror line
MIRRORED VOLUME of MENDELSOHN
EXISTING MENDELSOHN VOLUME
site elevation

NEW EXPANSION PROGRAMMATIC VOLUME
EXISTING MENDELSOHN VOLUME
site elevation

NEW EXPANSION TRANSFORMED VOLUME
EXISTING MENDELSOHN VOLUME
site elevation

Conceptual figure diagram

Detail massing diagram

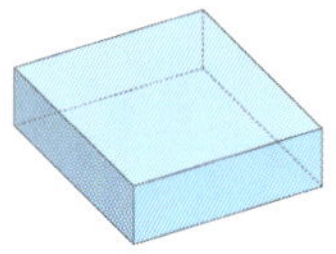

Massing

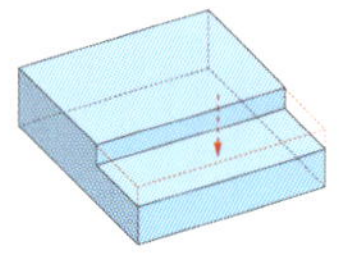

Push

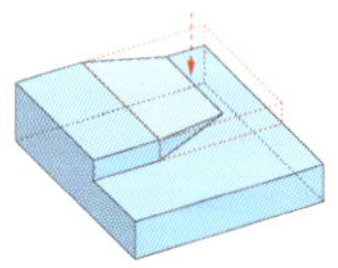

Angle

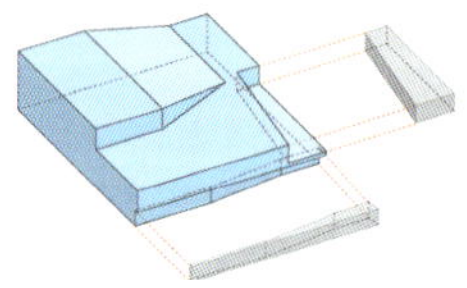

Subtract

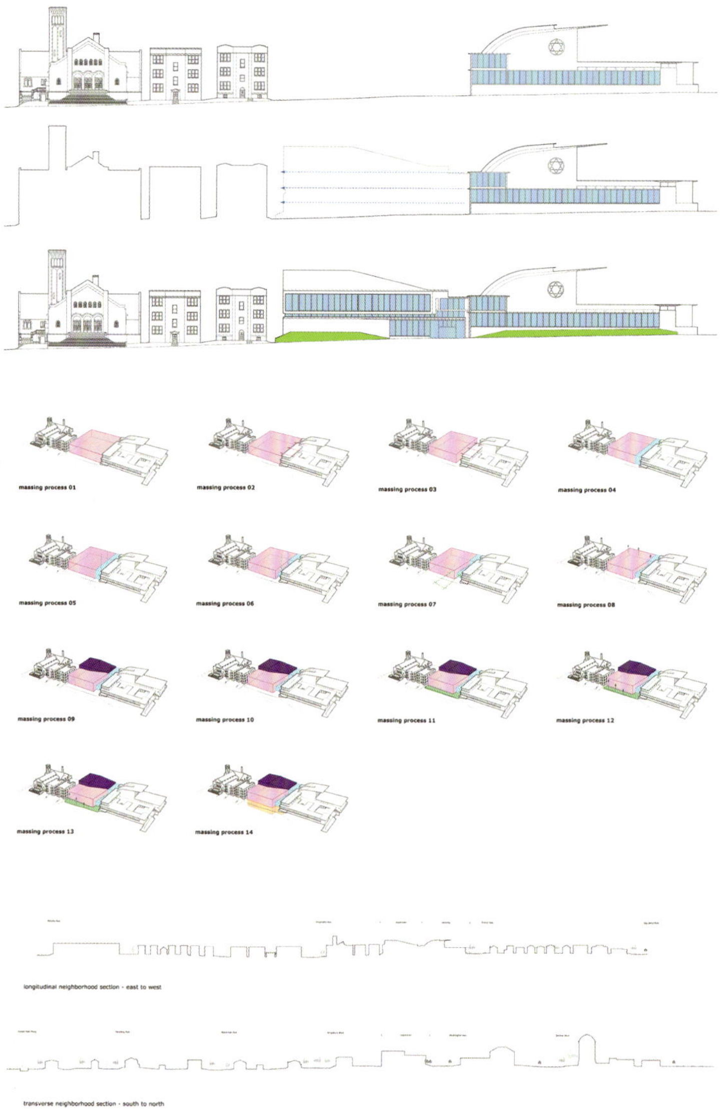

massing process 01
massing process 02
massing process 03
massing process 04
massing process 05
massing process 06
massing process 07
massing process 08
massing process 09
massing process 10
massing process 11
massing process 12
massing process 13
massing process 14

longitudinal neighborhood section - east to west

transverse neighborhood section - south to north

Context transferral diagram (top), massing elevation diagrams (center), site context sectional diagrams (bottom)

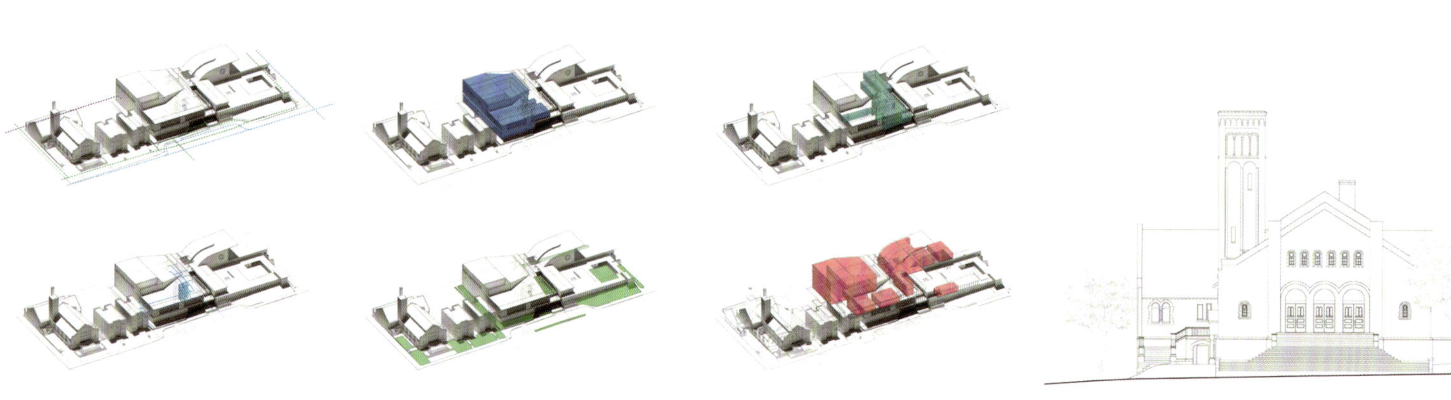

Design performance diagrams

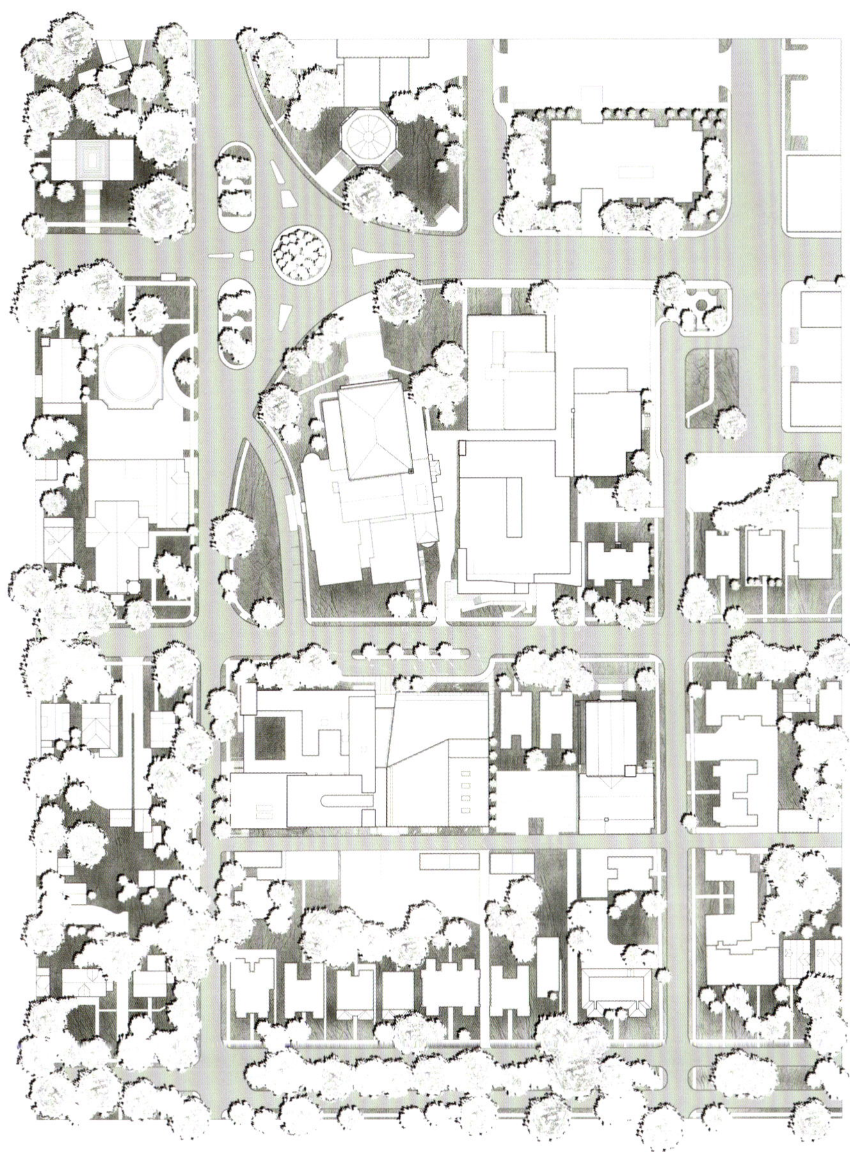

Site plan

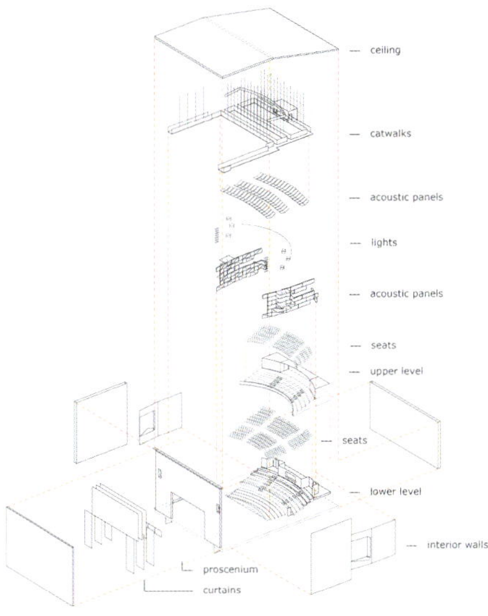

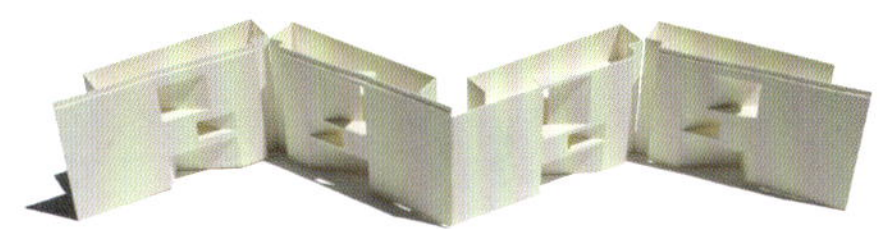

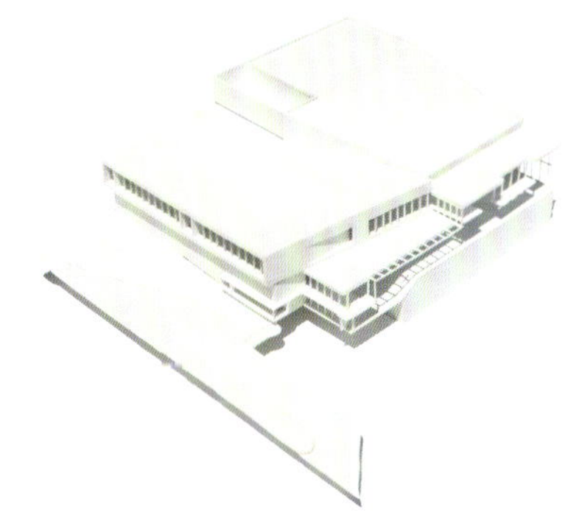

Exploded theater axon diagram, unfolded theater wall model, massing study model (top to bottom)

North elevation with site context

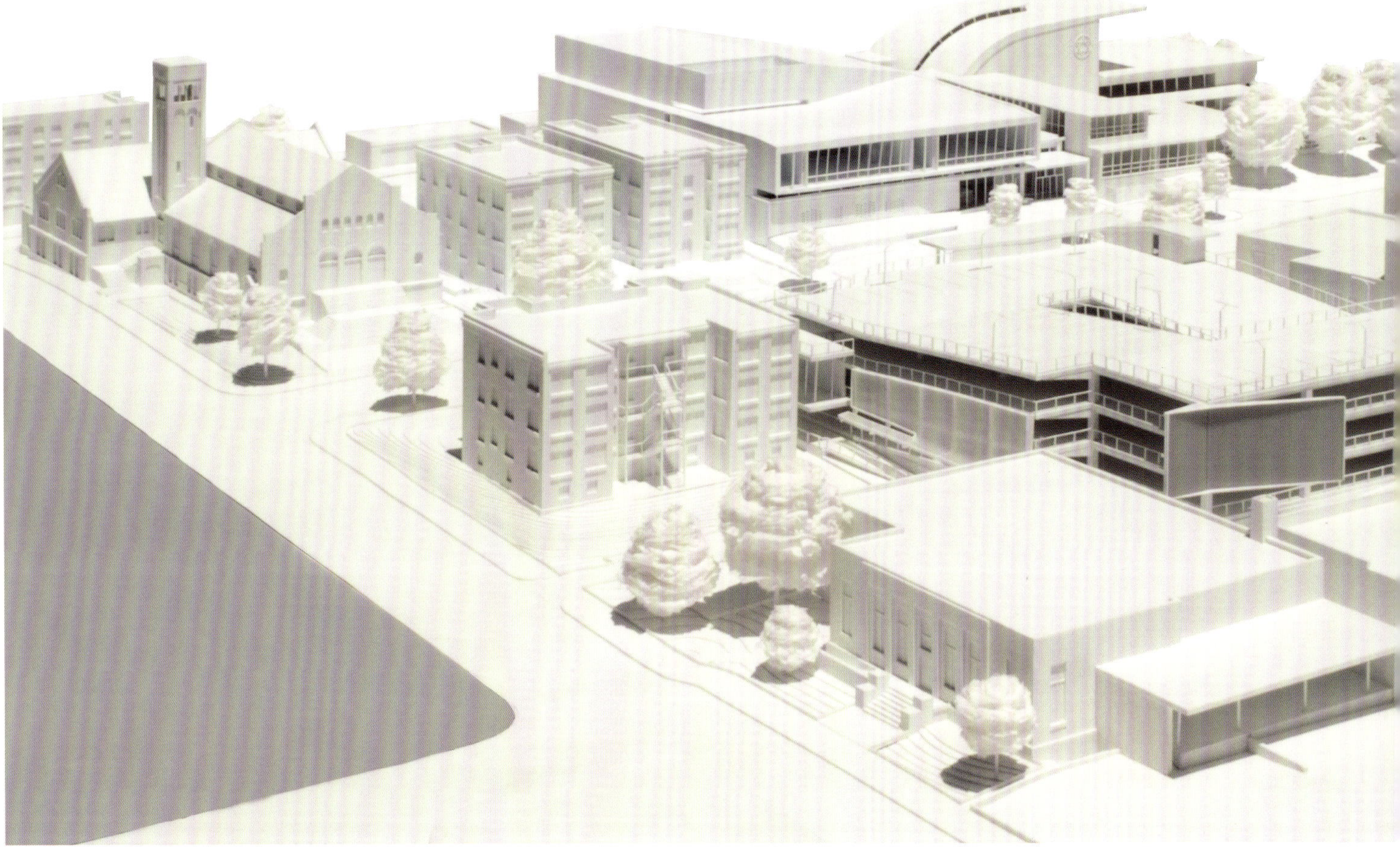

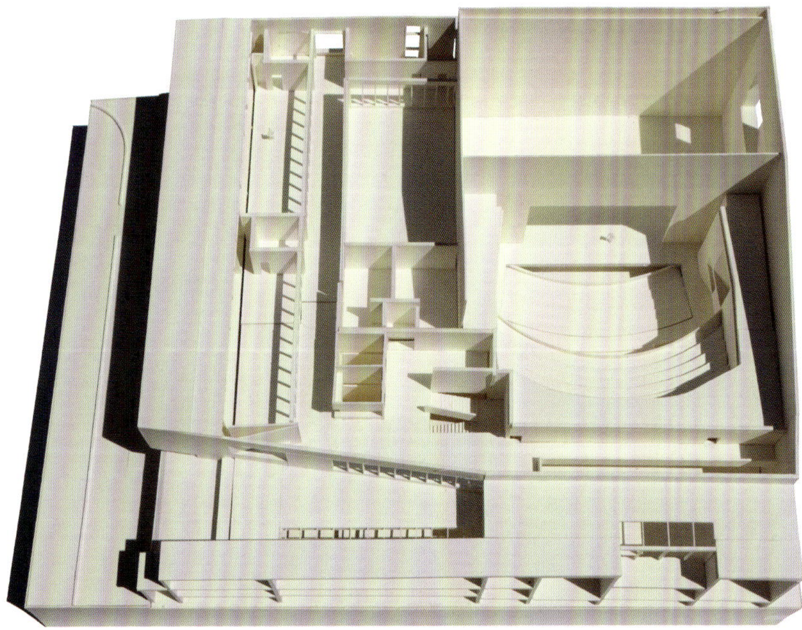

Detail model with second-floor roof removed

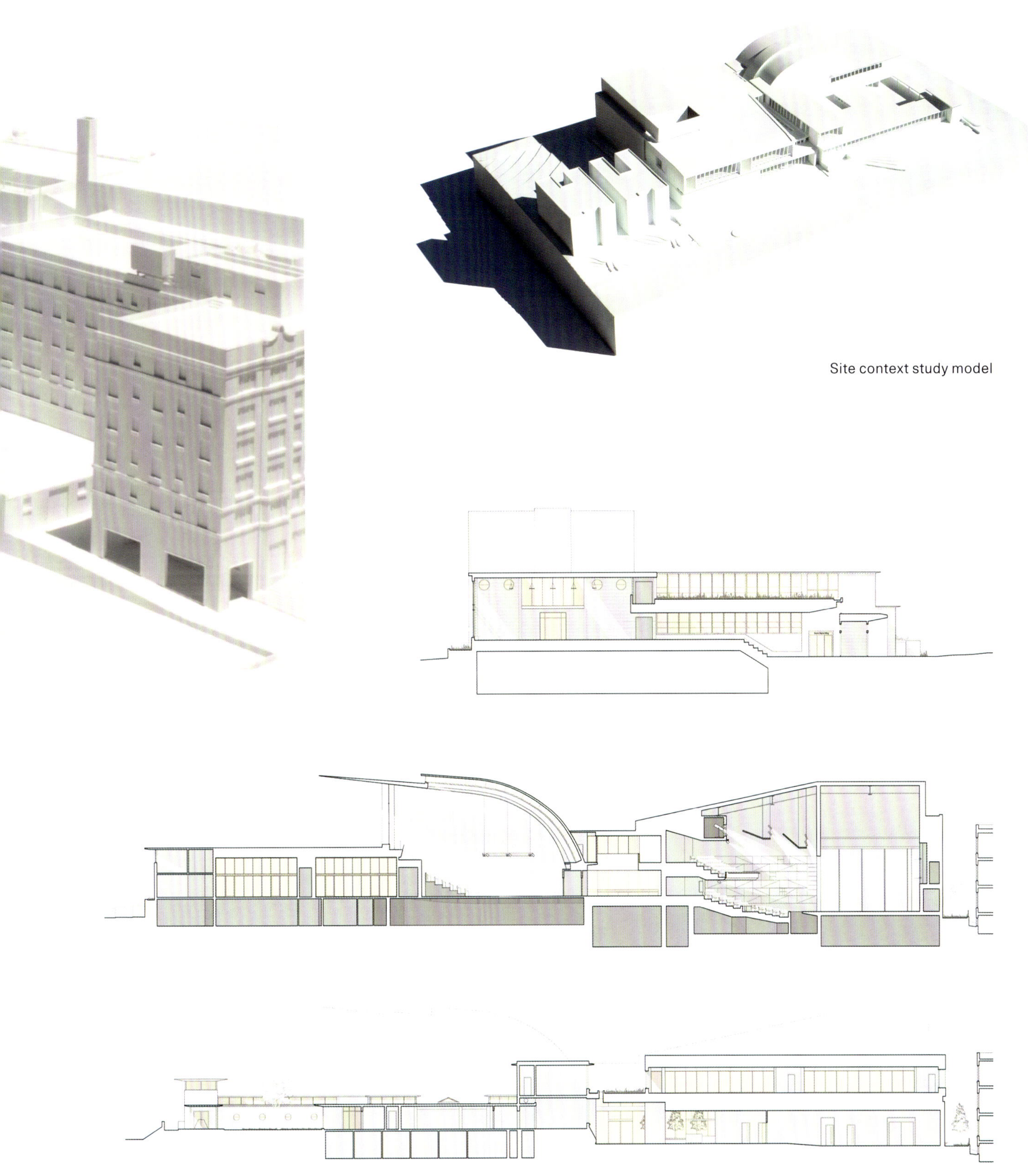

Site context study model

Transverse section through public spaces (top), longitudinal section through theaters (center), longitudinal section through studios (bottom)

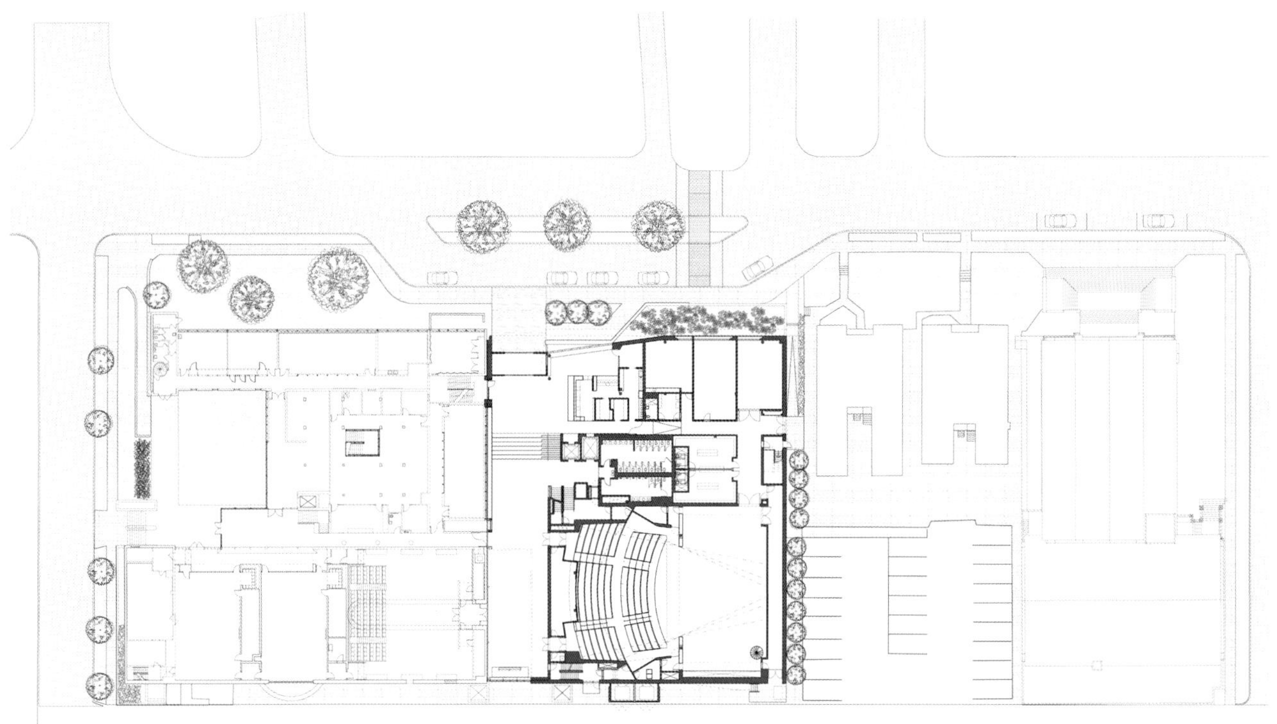

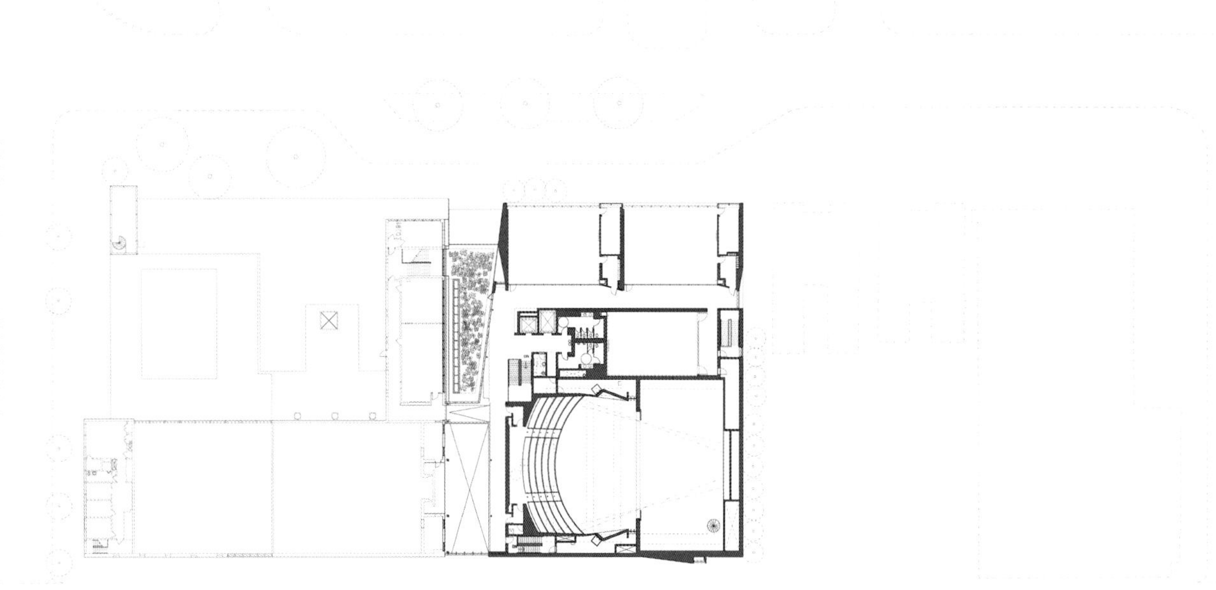

First-floor plan (above), second-floor plan (below)

Holman Family Amphitheatre

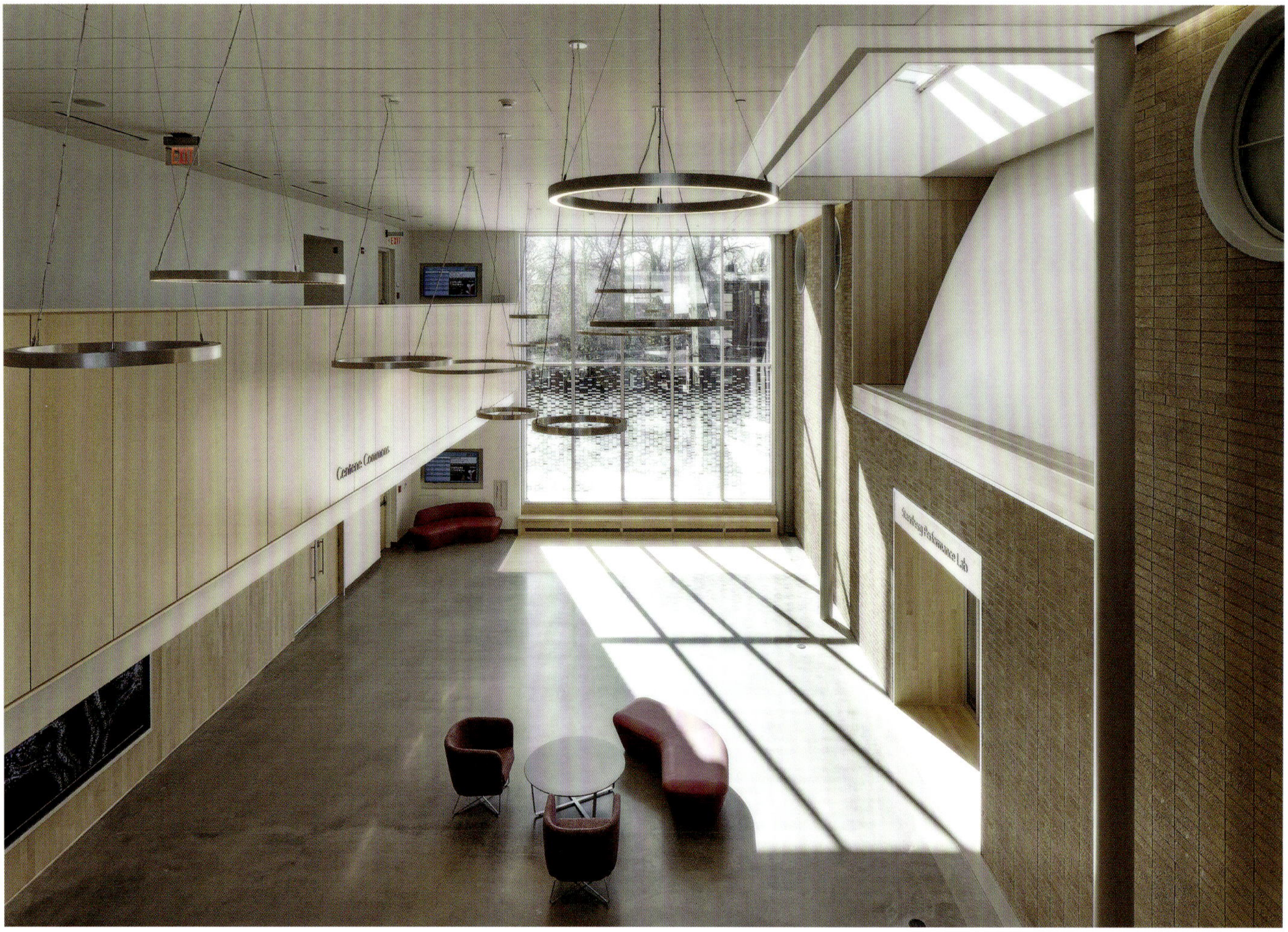
Centene Commons
Sternberg Performance Lab

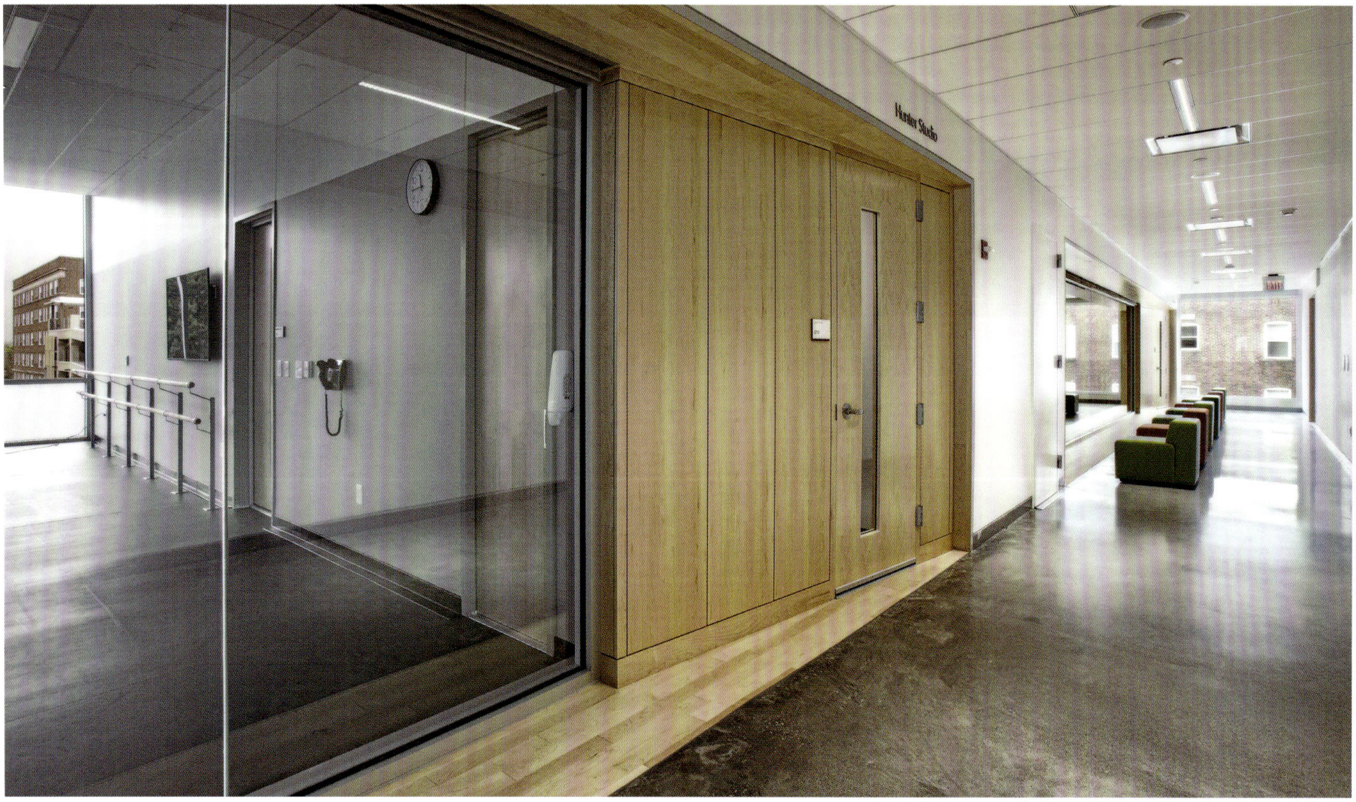
Hunter Studio

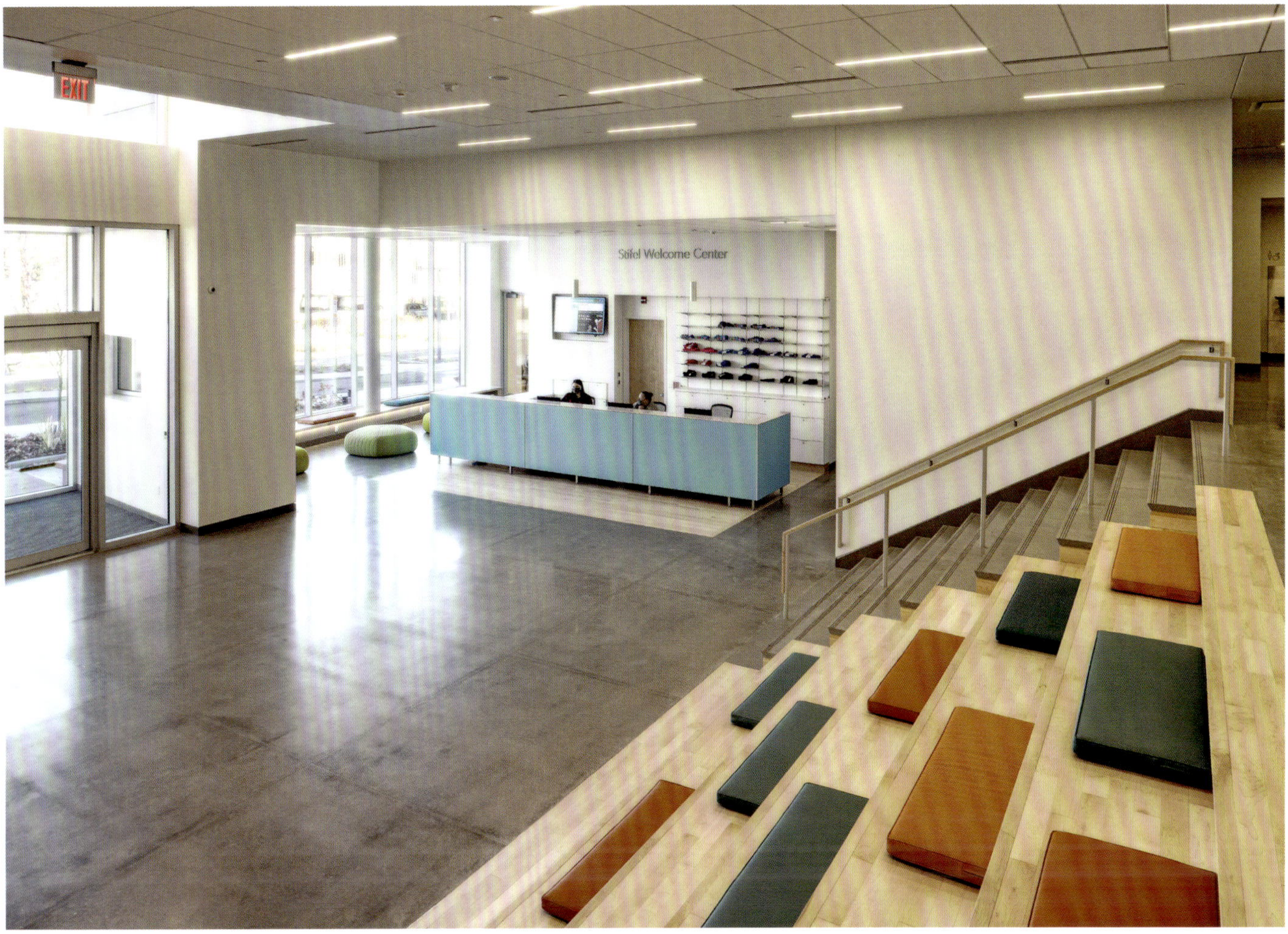
EXIT
Stifel Welcome Center

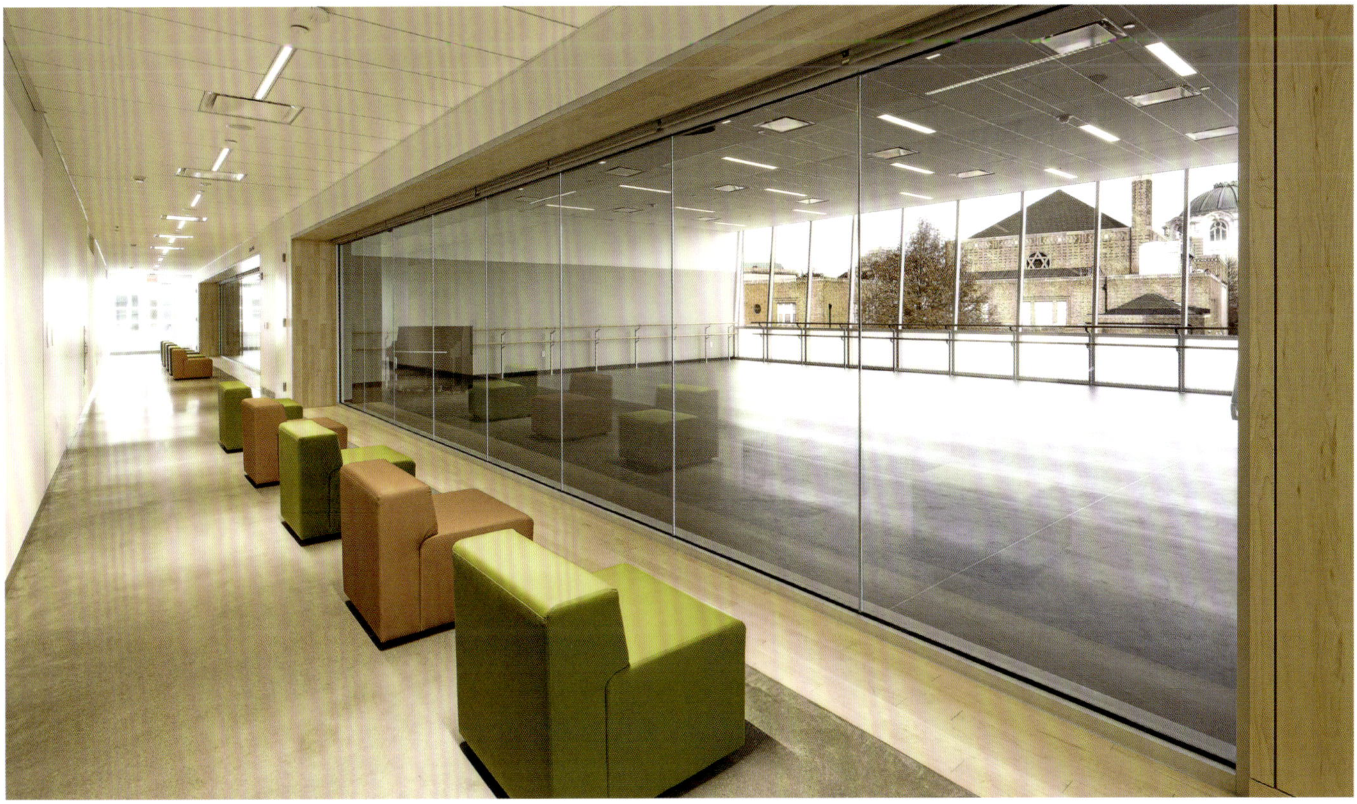

Ferring East Wing

COCA

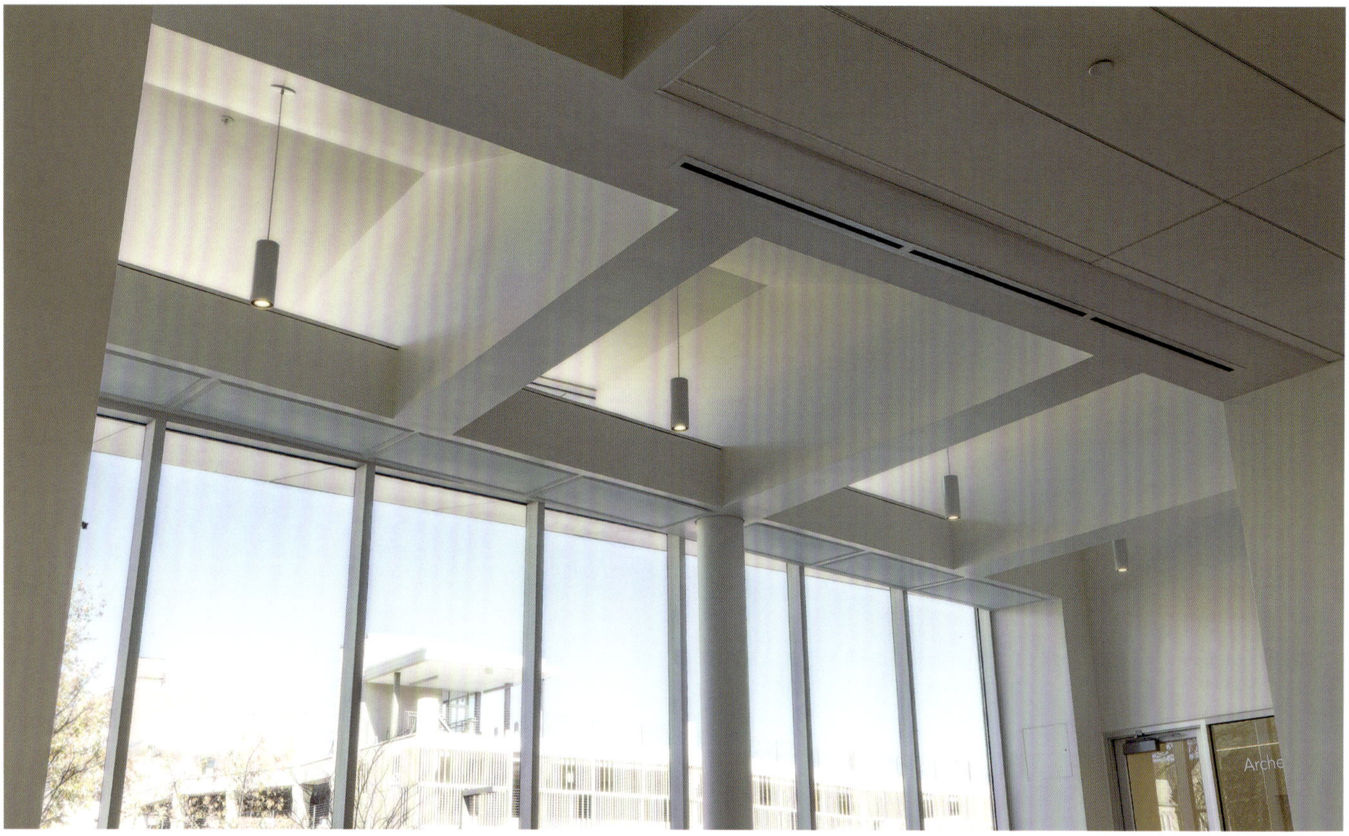
Arche

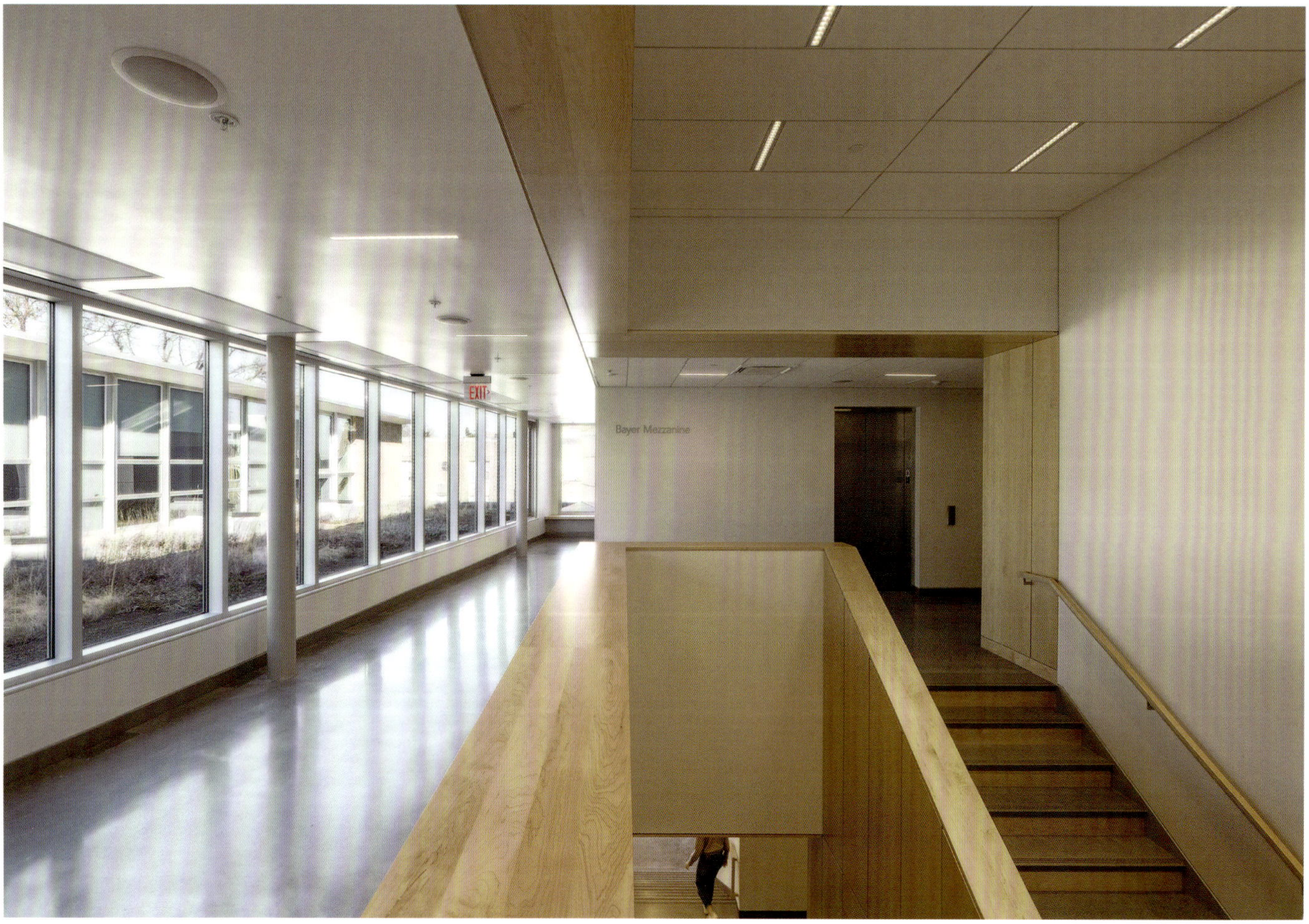
EXIT
Bayer Mezzanine

BOX OFFICE
RECEPTION

See things differently.
Donor Name Wing

Berges Theater

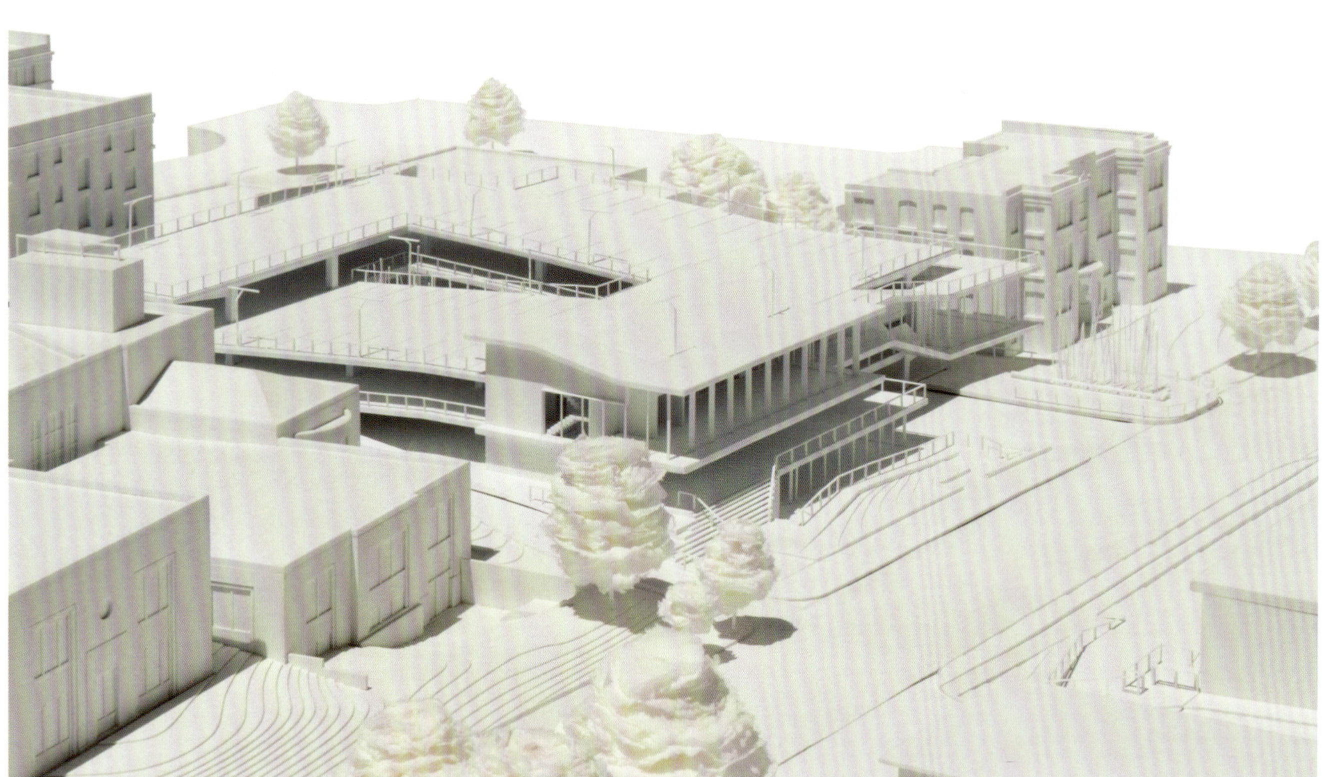

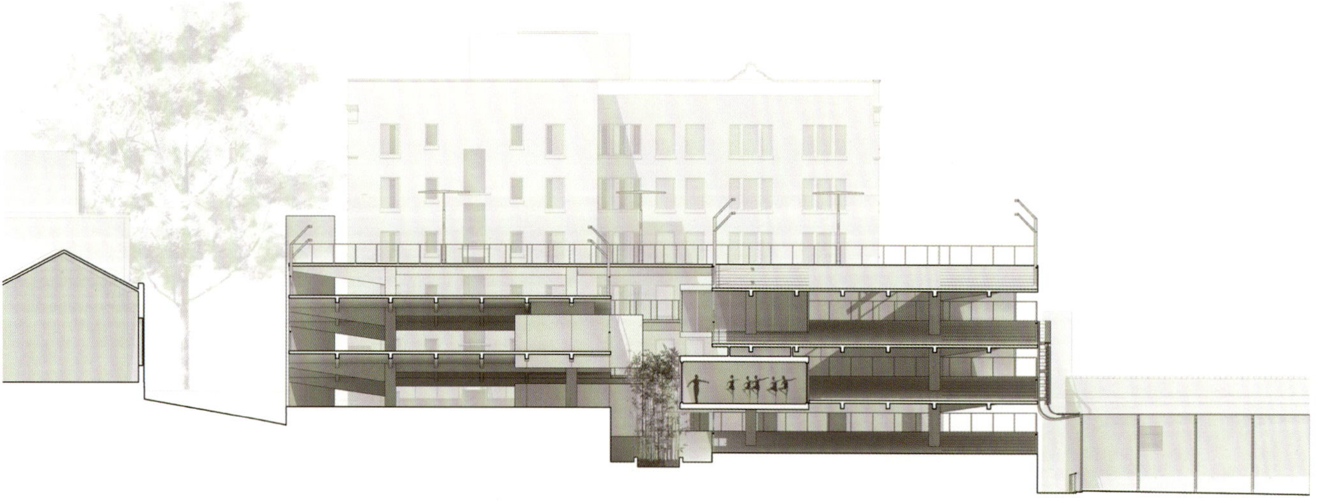

Site model (above), transverse section (below)

Site St. Louis, MO, United States

Status Conceptual Design

Program Cultural · Educational

Client Center of Creative Arts

COCA PARKING

Designed as an urban beacon situated between Delmar and Washington Avenues, the COCA Parking Garage connects urban and visual corridors to visually raise public awareness of COCA's new performing arts campus. It is developed as an extension of the streetscape with programmatic volumes inserted into the parking garage to create space not only for public parking but for a café as well as hybrid events from the performance school. The design strategy seeks to expand the elevated and layered grounds as they loop up and through street-like events and green spaces, inviting new kinds of urban experiences. As architecture, this infrastructural facility blends urban space and landscape to produce a new form of neighborhood platform that brings the public together with the institution.

Massing models

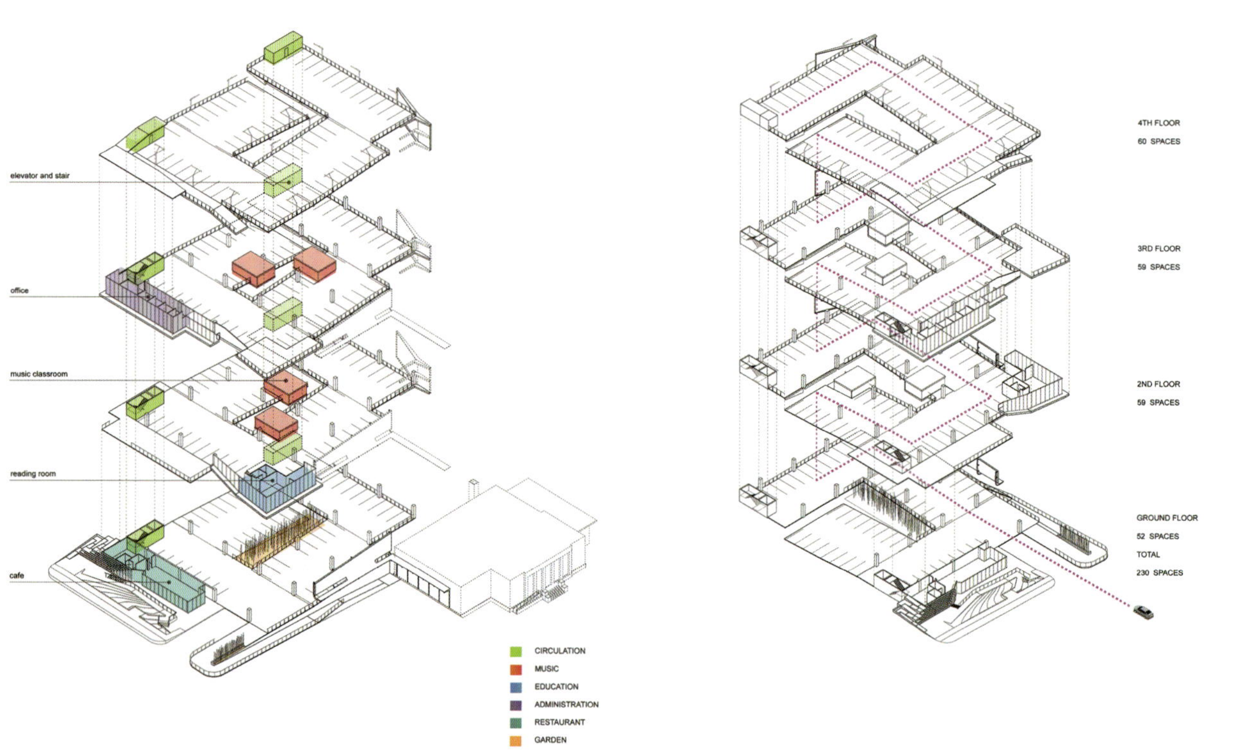

Exploded programmatic axon

Exploded parking axon

South elevation

East elevation

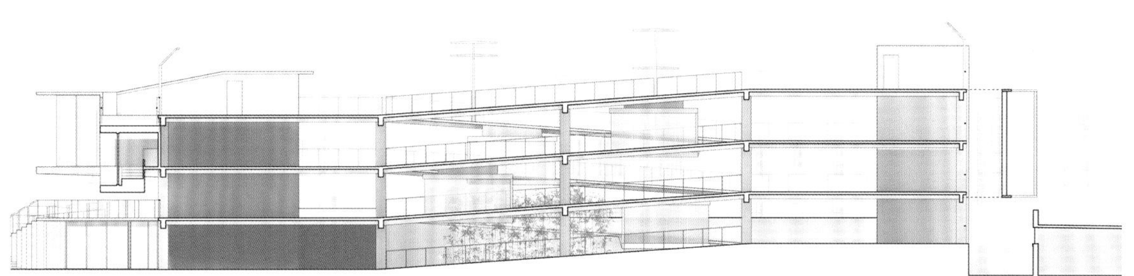

Longitudinal section

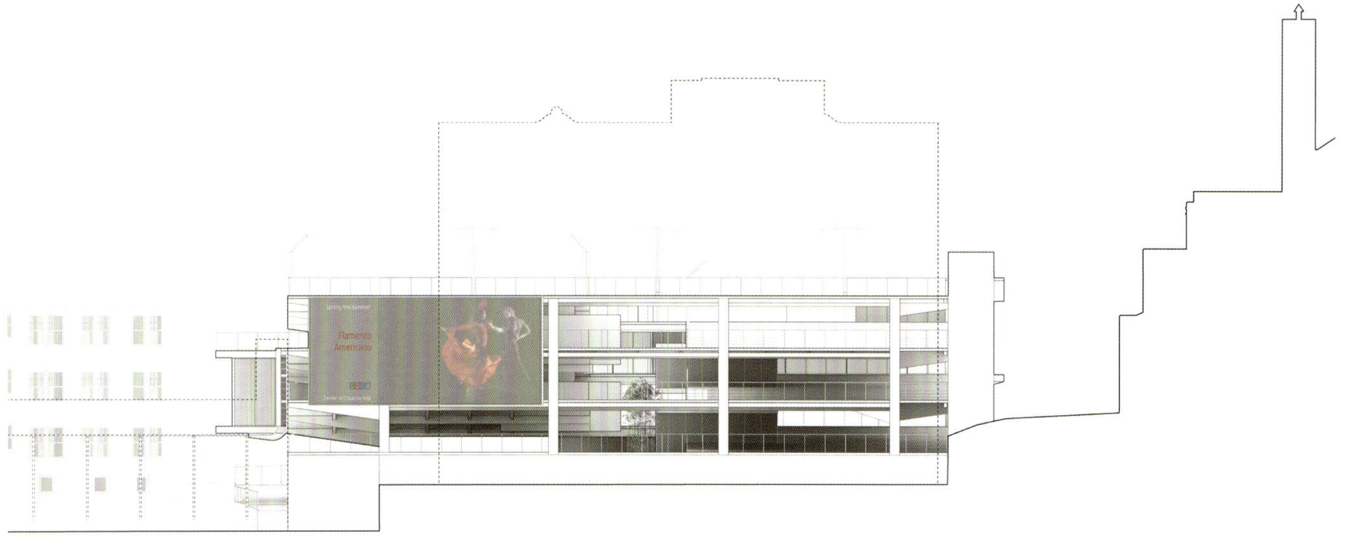

North elevation

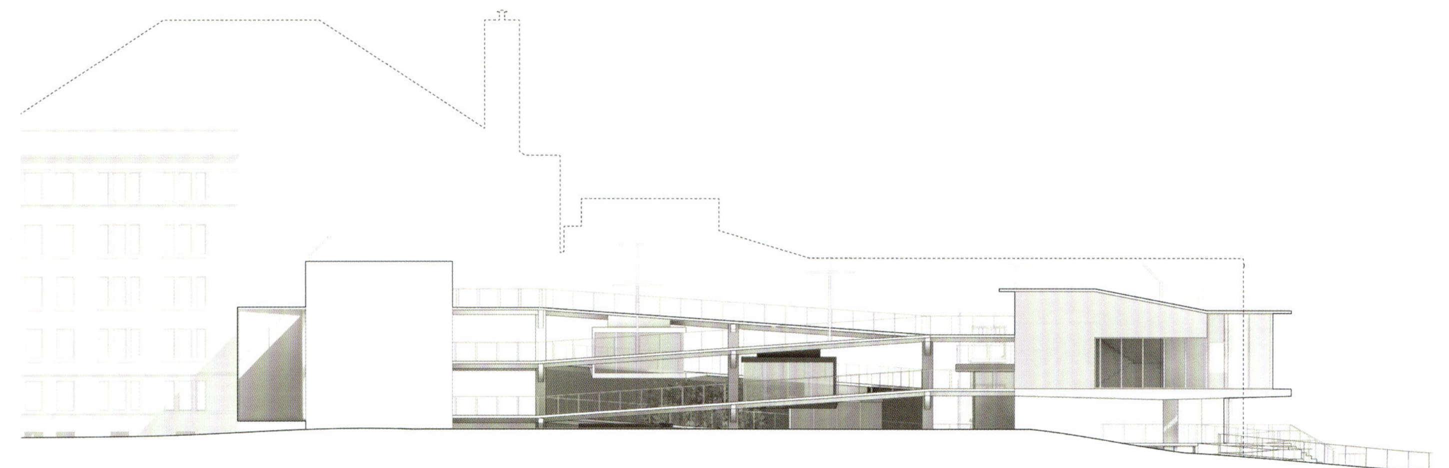

West elevation

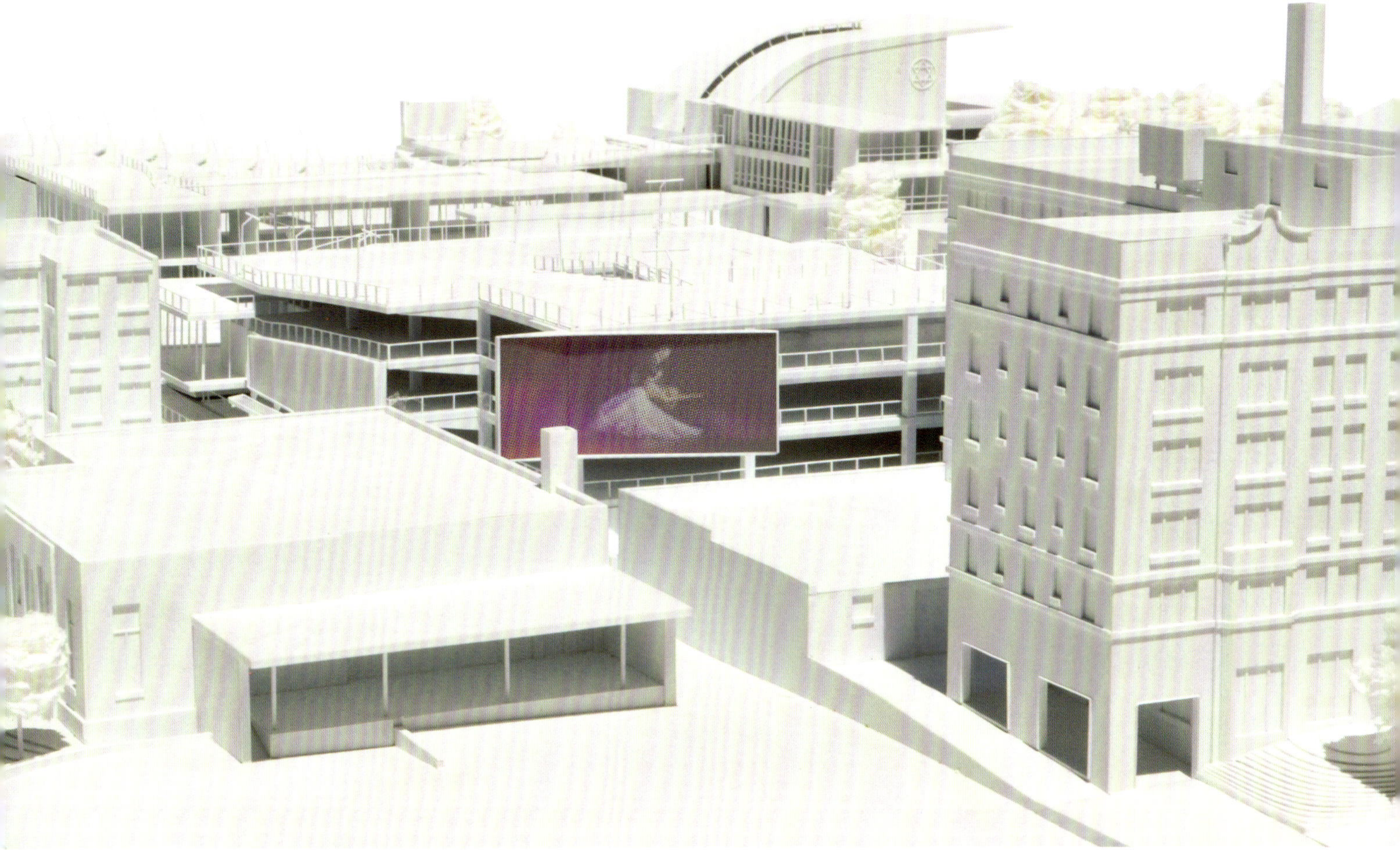

Washington University in St. Louis
PARKING

B1
B2

Washington University in St. Louis

Client Center of Creative Arts

Program Installation

Status Built

Site St. Louis, MO, United States

Mad Hatter store elevations and plan

WUNDERLAND STAGE SET

wUNDERland Stage Set was inspired by Alice in Wonderland syndrome, a neurological disorder from which patients perceive parts of their body to be transforming in size and misperceive the scale and distance of objects in time and space. The author of the eponymous *Alice in Wonderland*, Lewis Carroll (1832 – 1893), suffered from it but it was not until 1955 that the English psychiatrist John Todd would discover the disease.

Axi:Ome designed *wUNDERland* Stage Set for Redd Williams, the artistic director of hip-hop at COCA, to give architectural form to his contemporary vision of *Alice in Wonderland* through the lens of hip-hop dance and music. *wUNDERland* demanded a high artistic standard in local community performance production. This project demonstrated the collaborative spirit of the community, utilizing digital fabrication as the main tool to realize the expansive vision for the performance. A key goal of the project was to build the entire set design with minimal budget and maximum construction.

The design for the stage set arranges mushrooms and flowers in the foreground, along with a proscenium arch designed to alter perceptions of scale and gravity and bring the audience into a world of fantasy and wonder. Other major stage set props—wBed, wTable, Forest Lines, Cat Cages, Mad Hatter Store, Giant Mad Hat, Jabberwocky, and Red Queen's Throne—were designed to enhance the choreography and the expressive movements of the dancers.

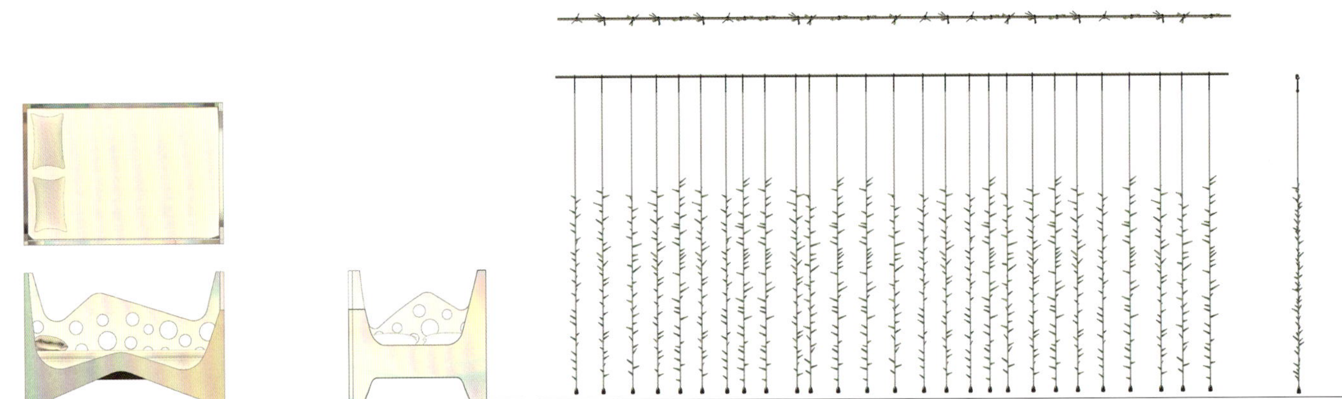

wBed plan and elevations

Forest line plan and elevations

Proscenium plan and elevations

Plan and elevations

Flowers

Mushroom

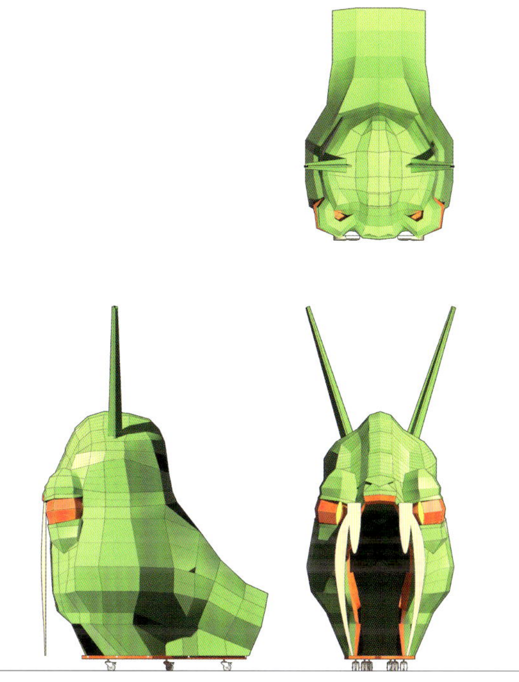

Jabberwocky

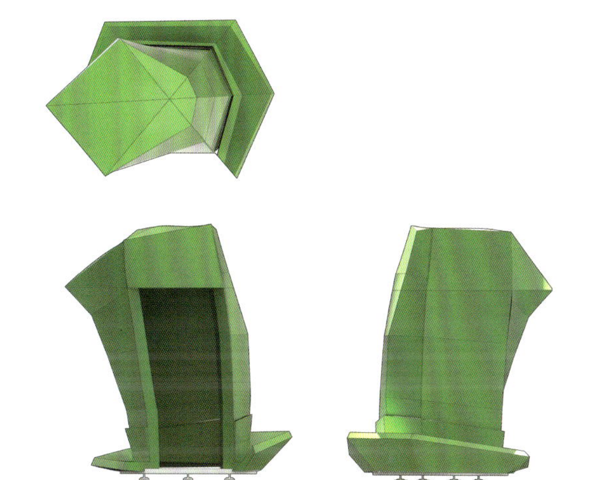

Grand Mad Hat

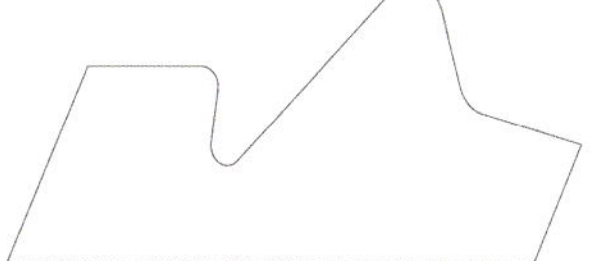

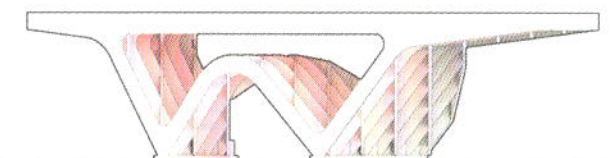

wTable plan and elevations

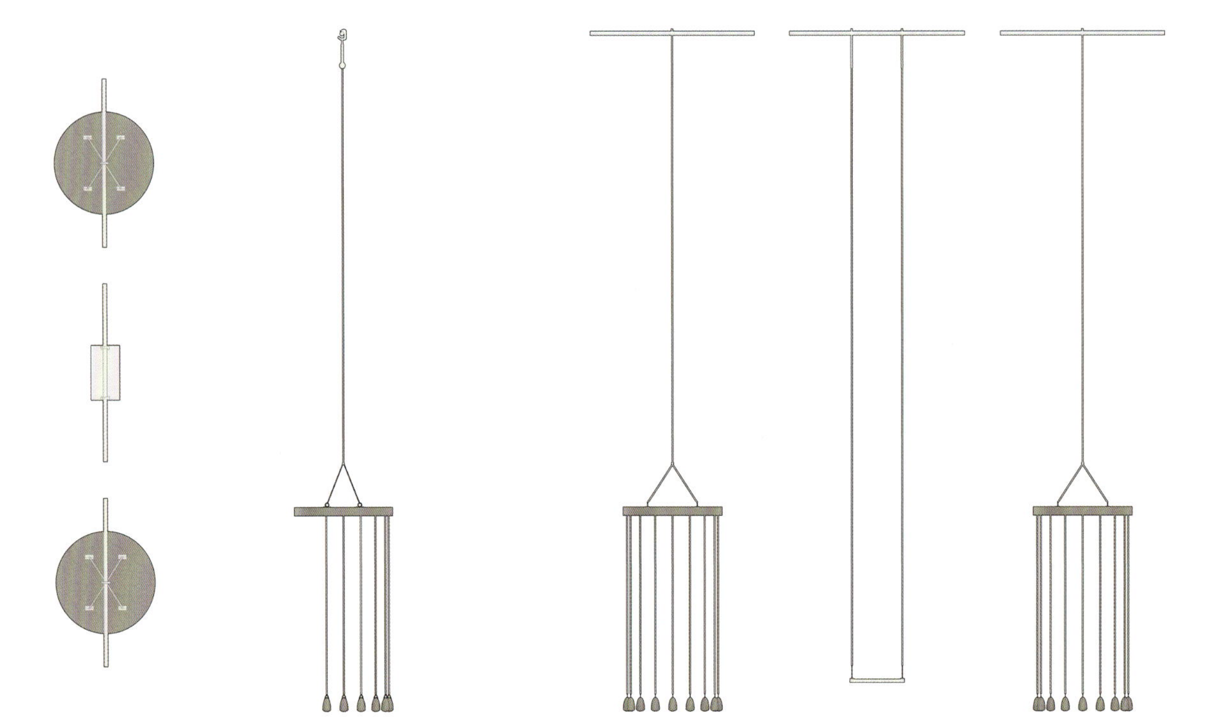

Cat cages plan and elevations

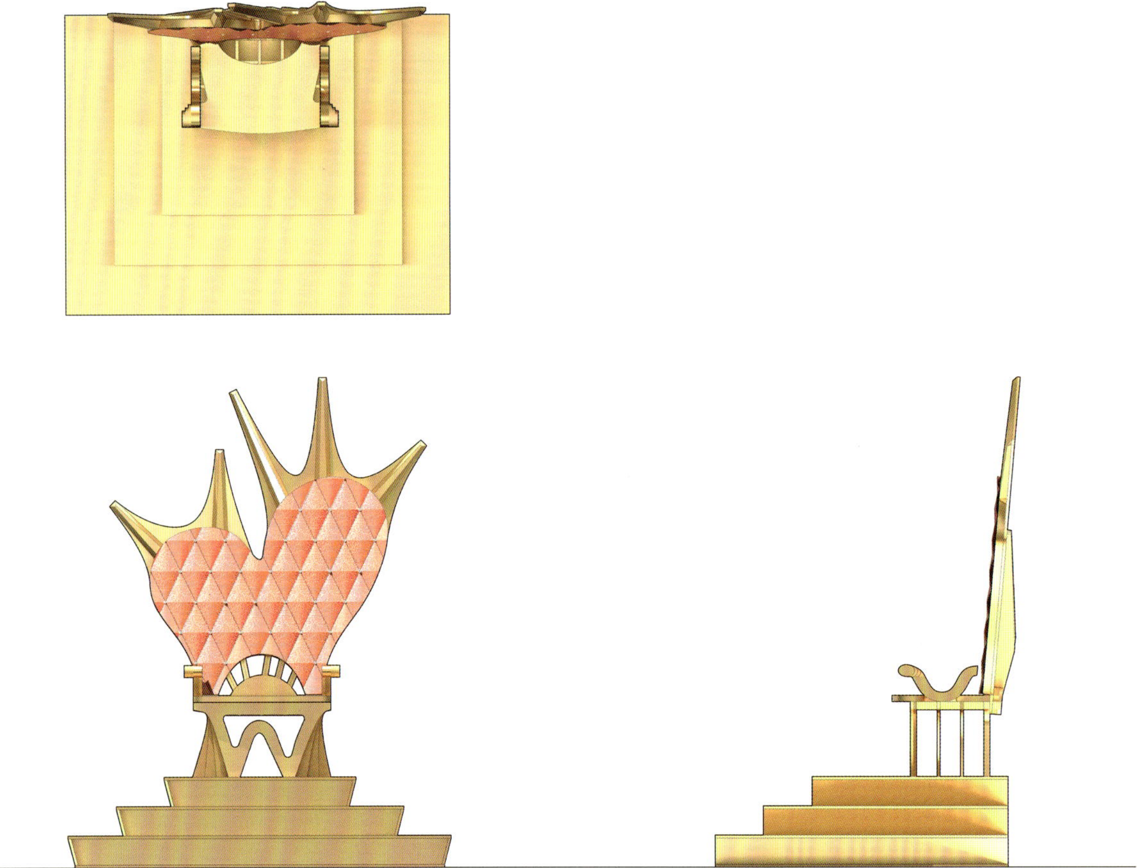

Red Queen's throne plan and elevations

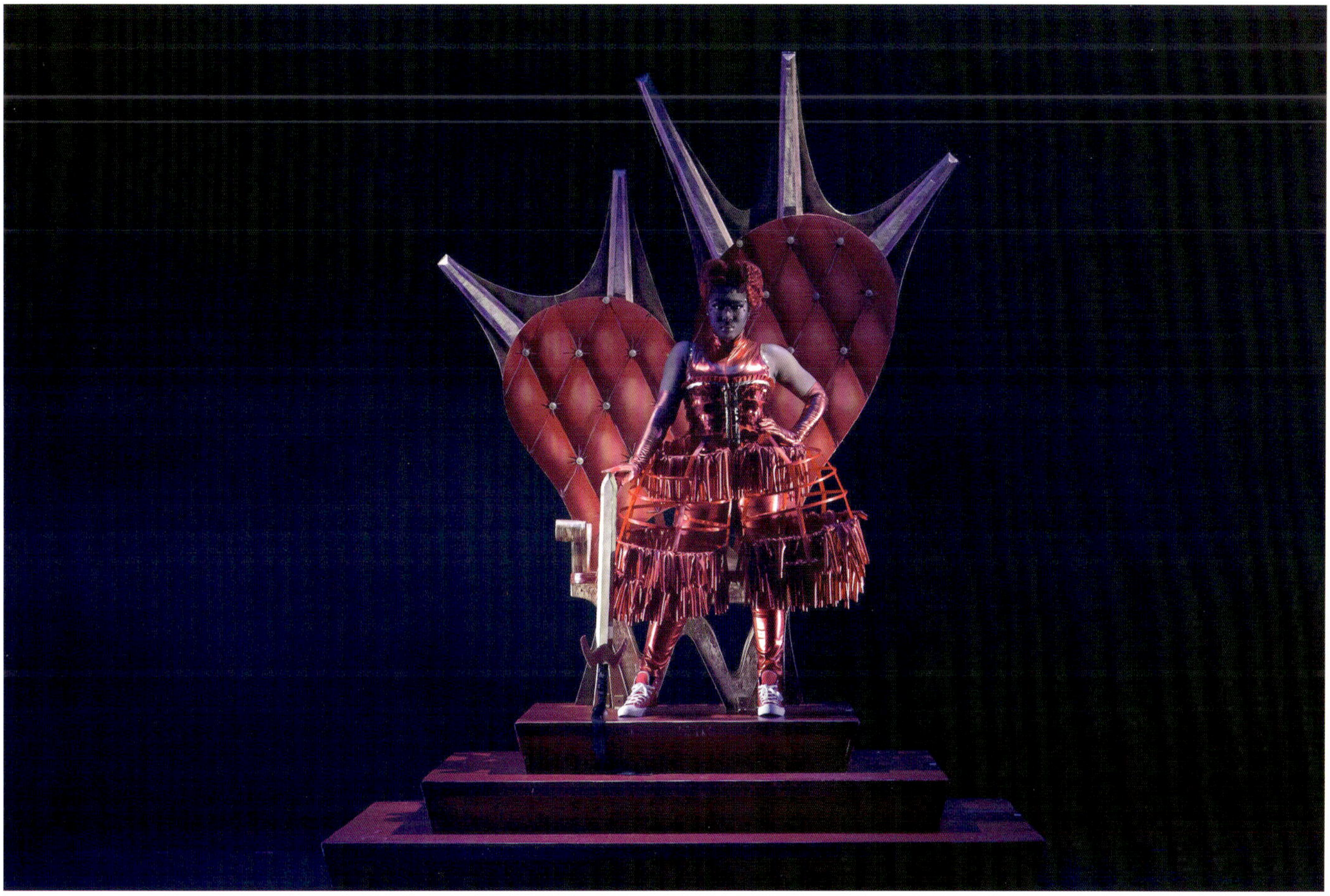

Site St. Louis, MO, United States

Status Built

Program Installation

Client Center of Creative Arts

LITTLE DANCER STAGE SET

Axi:Ome designed *The Little Dancer* Stage Set for Kevin Jenkins, a renowned choreographer who served as creative director for *The Little Dancer: Moments in Time*, a classical ballet performed by COCA's Ballet Eclectica. The set design alters the layers of the performance environment and breaks the scale between the ground, ramp, and staircases through the convergence of motion and time.

The Little Dancer Stage Set is influenced by Benesh Movement Notation and Labanotation, as well as the choreography of movement and space on the stage. Mappings of the movements of dancers define an architectural space. The set connects dance theory and language to create an interface between spatial and formal expression in the discipline of space-making.

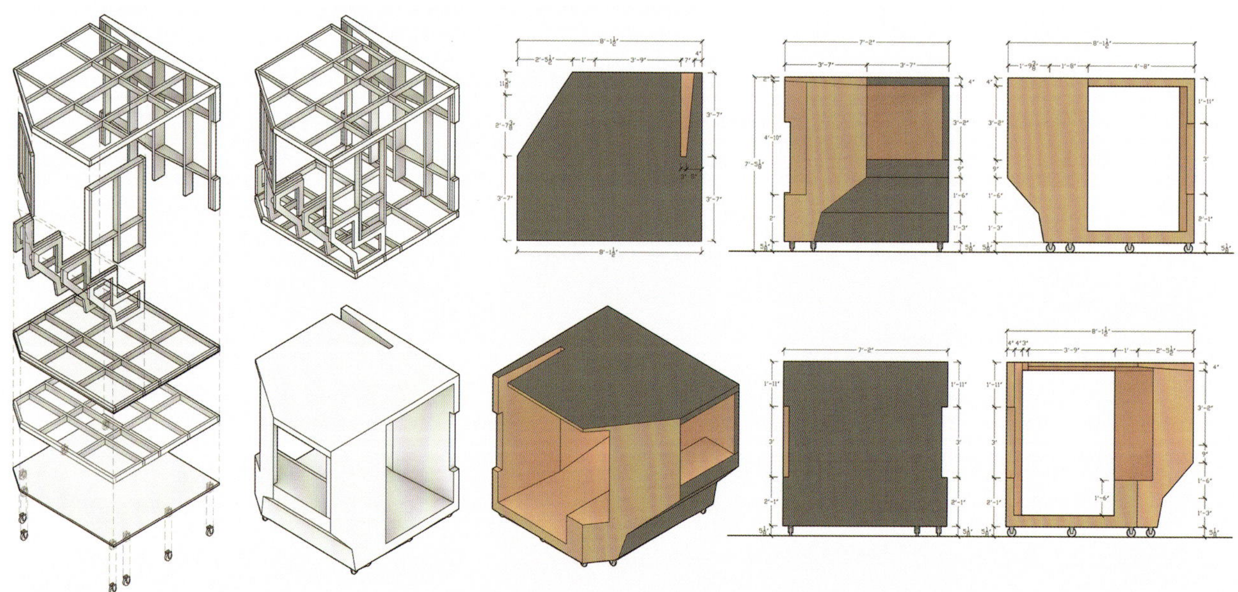

Floating room

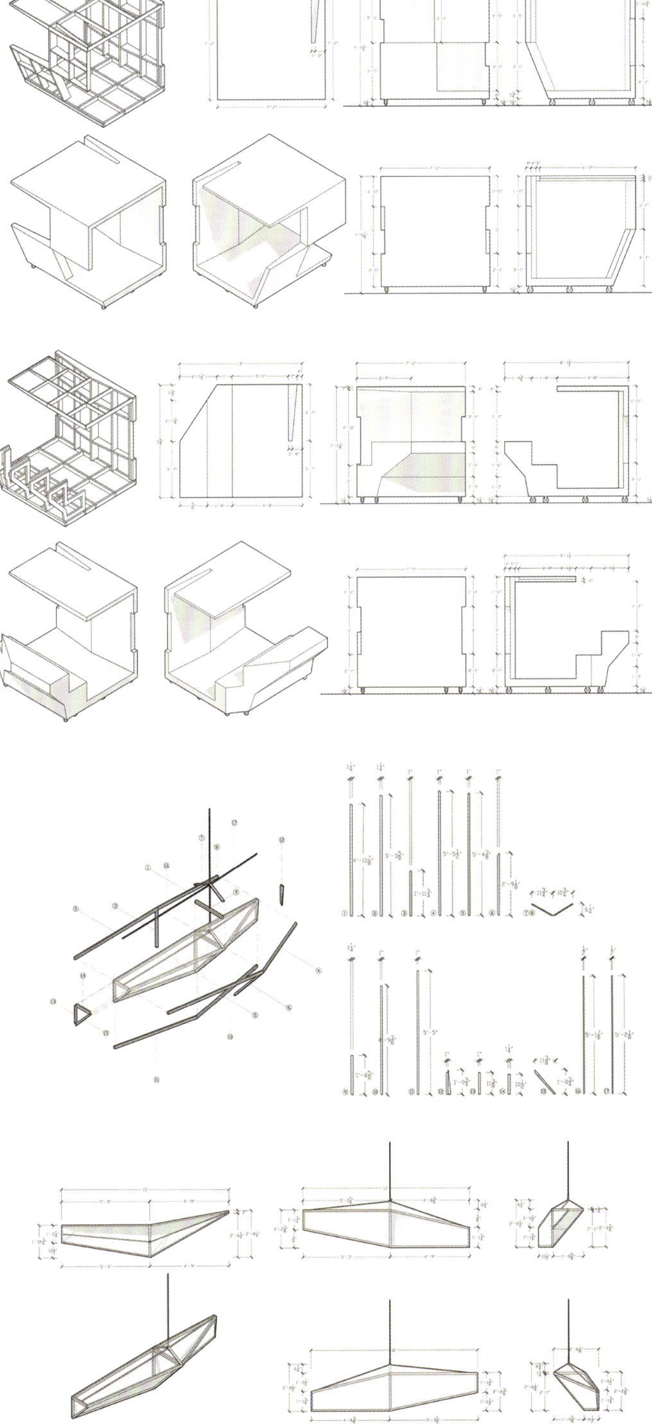

Floating rooms studies, cloud construction diagram, cloud (top to bottom)

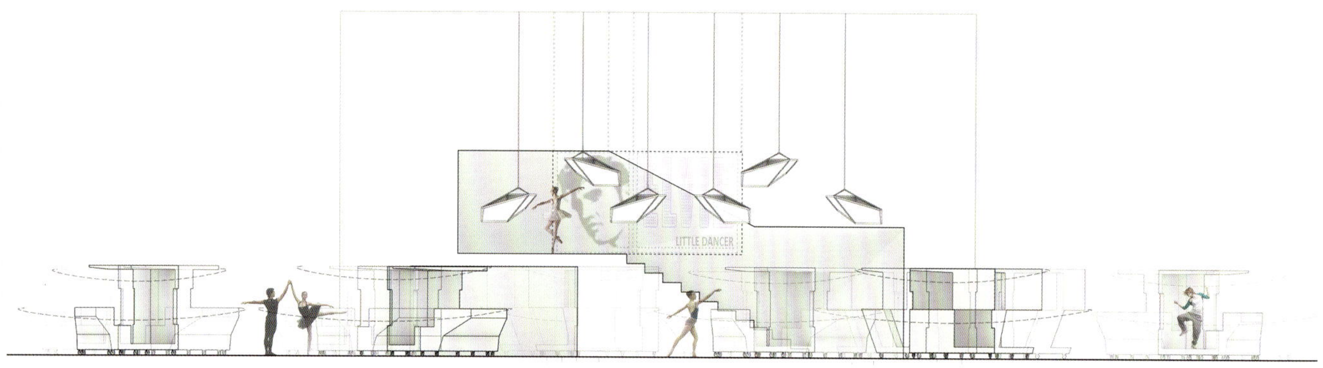

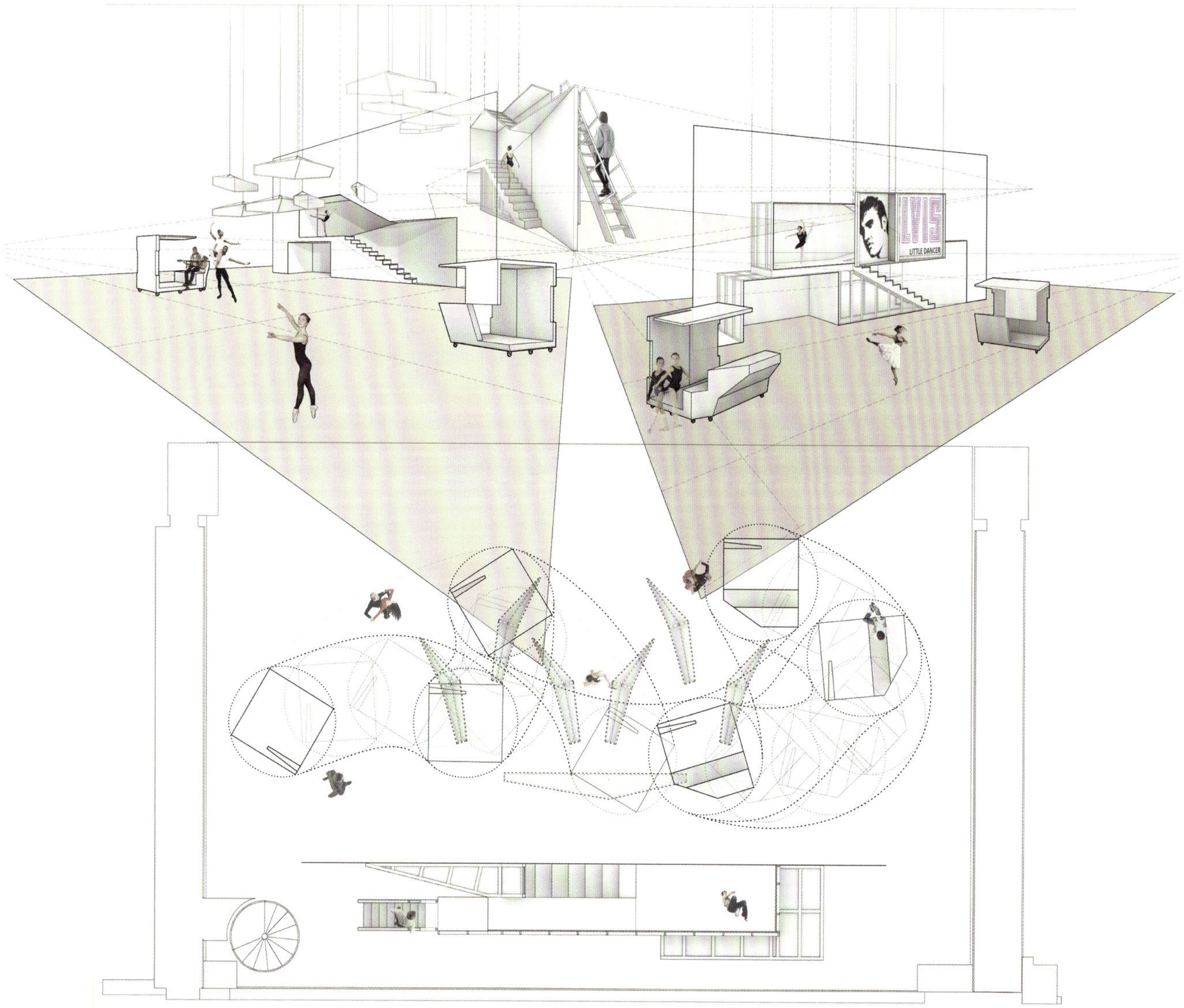

Dance notation diagrams

100

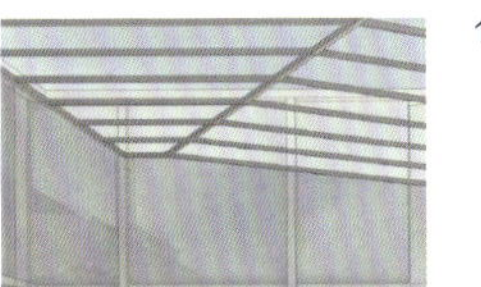
106

INVISIBLE WITHIN REGIONAL AND URBAN CONDITIONS

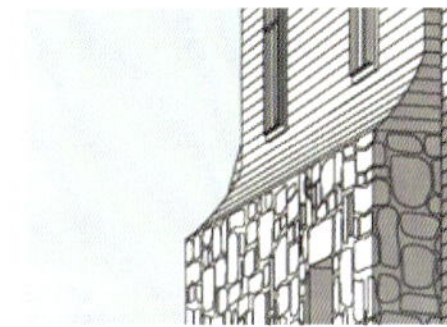
124

132

158

186

166

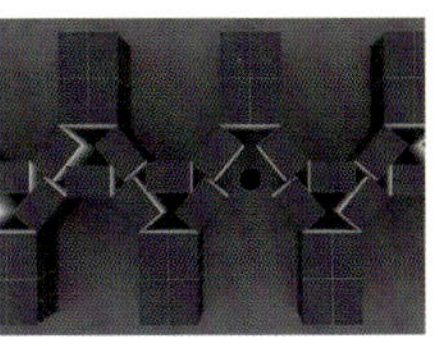
196

MONSANTO
COMMUNITY EDUCATION

WITHIN REGIONAL AND URBAN CONDITIONS

Eric Mumford

Since their arrival in St. Louis in the early 2000s to teach architectural design at Washington University, joining a distinguished group of faculty who over the years have included Buckminster Fuller, Gyo Obata, Aldo van-Eyck, Balkrishna Doshi, Ben and Cynthia Weese, and Hans Hollein, the partners of Axi:Ome have also sought to realize their architectural ideas in built projects. While they did not attempt to grow their internationally-oriented firm and compete with successful local practices, they were nonetheless able to balance their teaching with thought-provoking professional activities in the city and its nearby suburbs. Among these are a series of both built and unbuilt projects for the Midtown area of the city, which is located some seven kilometers (4.5 miles) west of downtown with its well-known Gateway Arch sited on the Mississippi River, as well as some residential work.

Midtown St. Louis was developed as a "second downtown" office and commercial center in the 1920s when the city was still among the ten largest in the United States, a world industrial center, and a major regional rail center. Midtown was where northbound and southbound streetcar lines crossed, and its many churches, theaters, and medical offices once served the entire region. This period has left a significant architectural legacy of extraordinary theaters and other historic buildings, which includes the Isaac H. Lionberger House by H.H. Richardson (1886), Tadao Ando's Pulitzer Arts Foundation (2001), and the home since 1968 of the St. Louis Symphony, Powell Hall, which will soon have an addition by Snøhetta. Midtown is also just north of the large campus of St. Louis University (SLU), which moved to its current location in 1898 and covers over ten blocks near I-64, the organizing east-west arterial highway that links the city to its more affluent western suburbs.

After the city began to racially desegregate in the 1960s as a result of Federal Civil Rights legislation—which occurred around the same time that the region's once extensive streetcar system was removed—Midtown lost many of its previous reasons for existence, as its medical and entertainment facilities moved farther west.

Successful efforts, many of which are still ongoing, were made by local cultural institutions to reuse many of its theaters and other buildings, and eventually, some new residential and institutional development followed. These new uses respond to the complex social dynamics of the area, which is directly adjacent to North St. Louis, a historically disadvantaged and racially segregated part of the city which continues to lose businesses and population to nearby suburban areas.

Not long after their arrival, Axi:Ome was commissioned by Grand Center and other mostly "invisible" non-profit organizations to propose creative urban interventions intended to improve urban vitality and social inclusion. These include their innovative unbuilt Artwalk project (2013) and their UMSL at Grand Center (2009) building for the local National Public Radio station, in partnership with the St. Louis branch of the University of Missouri. Their more recent memorial to Jack Galmiche, the late CEO and president of the local Public Television Station (PBS), KETC, is also part of these efforts, which include work by other architects and designers as well.

Another project commissioned by Jack Galmiche was the V9 commercial space proposal. This was part of Galmiche's vision of making KETC a national center for digitizing old news videotapes, which would have created a usable digital archive and an important future archival resource for historians. As is typical in their work, Axi:Ome solved both the technical processing issues and produced a design proposal that was materially and experientially rich, yet did not require a large budget. It was part of a series of design interventions that they proposed for the relatively undistinguished existing two-story KETC building, built in the 1980s, to make it more publicly accessible. This included a new entrance and lobby, public spaces, a café, and more places for community-related programs. Their most recent addition was a new usable canopy facing the plaza between it and UMSL at Grand Center, a welcome gesture in the typically very hot and sunny climate of St. Louis between June and September.

Just west of these works is the area of Axi:Ome's Olive Street Master Plan, which covered the same area as the On Olive development currently under construction, the block of Olive St. east of Vandeventer. The Pulitzer Arts Foundation eventually commissioned the Mexican architect Tatiana Bilbao for a master plan for the area, a residential development with multiple individual brick houses to be designed by various architects chosen by design competition, along with several apartment buildings, with one on Vandeventer to be designed by Michael Maltzan.

Central to these developments is a small former library building, the Wolfner Library for the Blind. Axi:Ome produced different reuse schemes for the project, one to simply reuse it as a public library branch, one as some new housing units built within the vacant shell, and one as an ecology center and children's park. Like the nearby shell of the Spring Church at 620 North Spring Street, which has been stabilized by the Pulitzer Arts Foundation, Axi:Ome's scheme proposed stabilizing the ruins of the Wolfner Library as a place of outdoor gathering and events. Their design also sought to use design to call the attention of the children's groups visiting the site to its subtle natural features and microclimatic aspects, including the patterns of birds, bees, insects, and plant growth, typical of many vacant lots in the area. They proposed to use the existing walls for outdoor movie projection and suggested rainwater collection gutters, grooved concrete walls for growing plants, and glass boxes that glow in the dark to create a sense of place that related to the invisible forces of nature and to the human legal and social frameworks that have shaped the conditions on this site.

Some similar design intentions are also visible in Axi:Ome's Lens Bridge project, adjacent to the City Foundry (2021), where the local architects the Lawrence Group have successfully designed and developed the reuse of an old industrial plant as a mixed-use food court and shopping complex, which is also near the SLU campus. Here the urban design challenge was a completely different one than at the Wolfner Library, but the project also alluded to the need to respond to a variety of partly invisible natural conditions, as well as to the practical issues of creating a pedestrian crossing under an elevated interstate highway. A design for this bridge by Marlon Blackwell is part of the city-wide Brickline Greenway project as well. A key aspect was the idea of the pedestrian bridge as an urban gateway visible from I-64 to motorists entering the city. To carry the runoff from the highway, in their proposal Axi:Ome designed a series of gutters leading to retention ponds, where the water would be naturally cleaned, surrounded by remediating plantings. Open space on the site also included a community pool and recreation center, in a part of the city where these will be much needed if density increases with new residential and other development.

These projects, all in the Midtown area of the city, demonstrate this firm's commitment to using innovative architectural and landscape design strategies to improve urban living in what can be still a harsh and depressing environment with little pedestrian street life, often characterized by extensive car-oriented paved areas, many of which are also currently underutilized.

Within the more typical regional framework of small firm practice is Axi:Ome's residential rehab work. One, the unbuilt Han house renovation, involved responding to the invisible forces of historic preservation in an older residential area. They were commissioned to renovate an existing nineteenth-century wood-framed Shingle Style house, which is surrounded by three-story 1920s brick apartment buildings. The clients asked for a new kitchen and rear addition, and the architects also proposed an open sleeping porch and new landscaping for the site. Much of the design work involved field documentation of the complex existing conditions typical of historic houses, as well as correctly responding to the preservation requirements for the new elements on the exterior.

Another residential project was the Northwood renovation, which involved turning the lower two units of a three-story apartment building into a single dwelling. Local requirements did not permit alterations to the building's 1920s brick exterior, but the interior spaces and wood structure were entirely transformed. After demolishing the existing series of relatively small, box-like rooms in the two apartments, Axi:Ome created a large open-plan ground floor similar to those often found in new American residential construction, with a large new kitchen and several ample bathrooms, all expertly detailed and organized. Built-in wood and plexiglass screens modulate the light at the main internal staircase, and it, along with various other built-in furniture, acts as an armature for the necessary new plumbing and ventilation systems. Residential requirements of a different kind—for cats—shaped the conceptual design of the Maison Feline project. Here Axi:Ome's skill as architects is once again evident.

Using conceptual frameworks concerned with the interdependence of humans with natural systems drawn from R. Buckminster Fuller's "spaceship earth" (Fuller 1981, 55) and other modern design theorists—as well as some drawn from East Asian cultures—Axi:Ome's work moves beyond the entirely visually-organized and human-centered perspectival approaches of the Renaissance. They articulate through architectural design various recent science-based efforts to incorporate invisible environmental and phenomenological issues into their built projects and landscape proposals. Although many of their project sites are in places with difficult histories of segregation, violence, and abandonment, their work seeks to provide optimistic future scenarios where power is more accountable and responsible and where long-term natural resource considerations are taken into account. These approaches have informed their teaching of architecture students at Washington University as well, where they maintained a clear focus on the defining aspects of both the discipline and profession of Architecture within the Sam Fox School of Design & Visual Arts. They are aware that architecture in this sense may itself be becoming invisible, as many of its practices, techniques, and ways of seeing have increasingly become part of a general global digital design culture, where architecture is often understood to be, as Reiser, Umemoto, and Harake write in the epilogue of this book, "little more than the power structures and material resources which bring it into being" (345).

The projects shown here both demonstrate these design and pedagogical intentions, as well as some of the difficulties of their realization, in the contemporary North American urban environment of St. Louis.

References Fuller, R. Buckminster, with Kiyoshi Kuromiya. 1981. *Critical Path*. New York: St. Martin's Press.

Site St. Louis, MO, United States

Status Schematic Design

Program Commercial

Client KETC/Nine Network

V9 DIGITAL

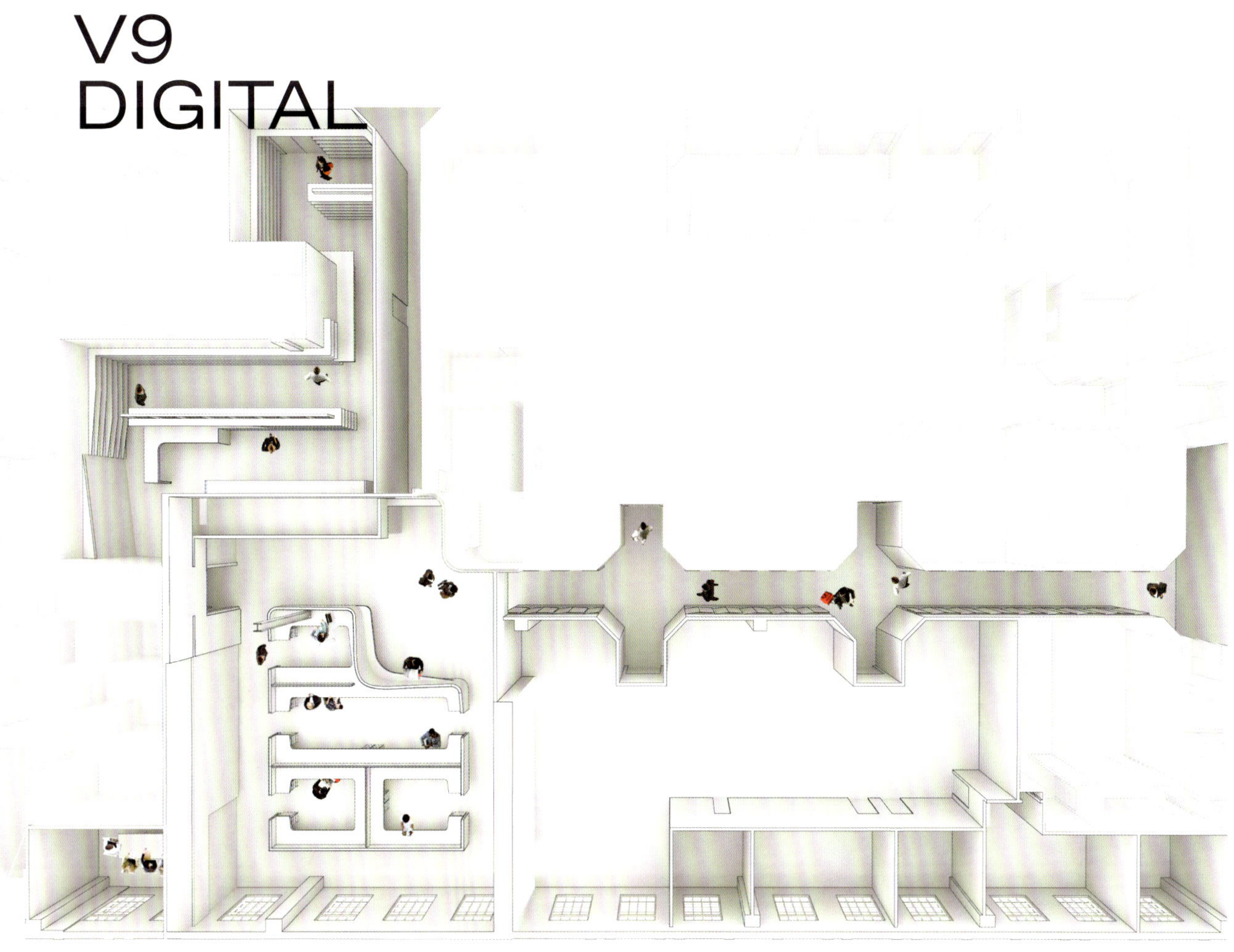

V9 Digital, an independent digital processing company, develops outdated film and video archives within the facilities of Nine Network. Here, an investigation into the light spectrum transforms the spatial construction of the architecture by articulating various wavelengths of light from smooth (analog) to striated (digital) along the interior corridors. The difference between analog and digital signal waves is that analog waves are smooth and continuous while digital waves are stepping, square, discrete, and have a finite set of possible values. This lighting strategy heightens the experience of the transition from public to private and from fluid to grid organizations.

Transparent glass walls create visual depth and openness in order to display the technology and the processes of the facilities. V9 Digital is a space that merges optical and spatial effects as it unfolds to reveal the history of technology and media.

South perspectival section

North perspectival section

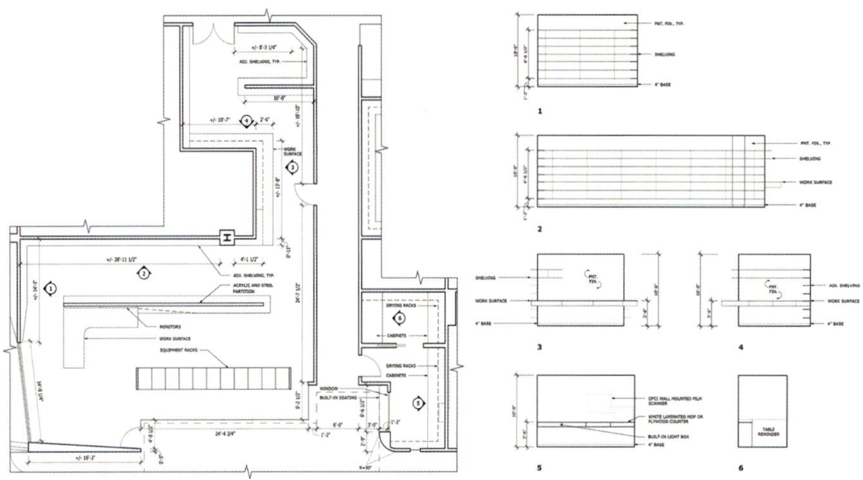
Rackroom and storage plan and elevations

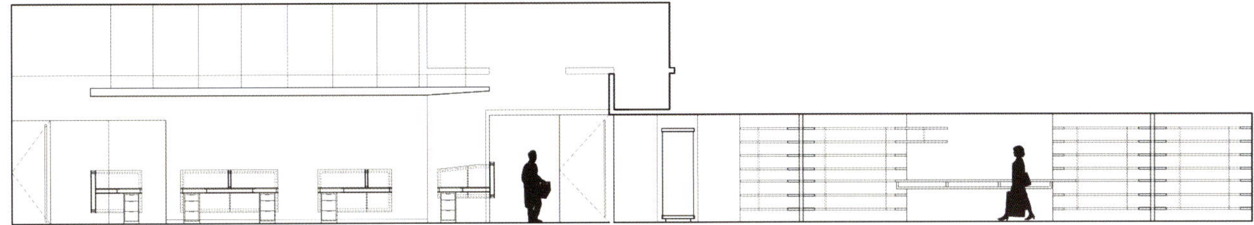

Workroom and rackroom section

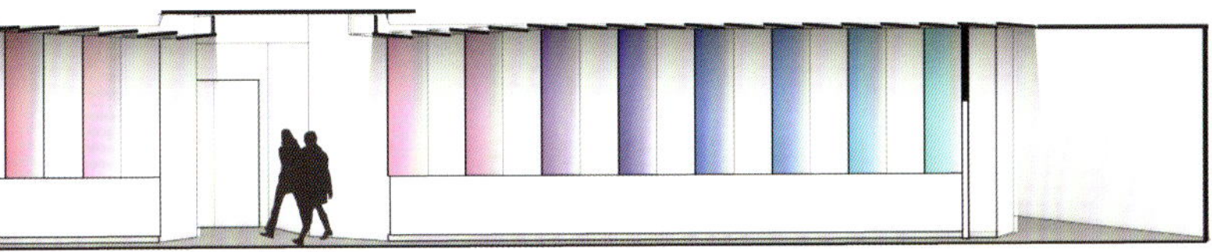

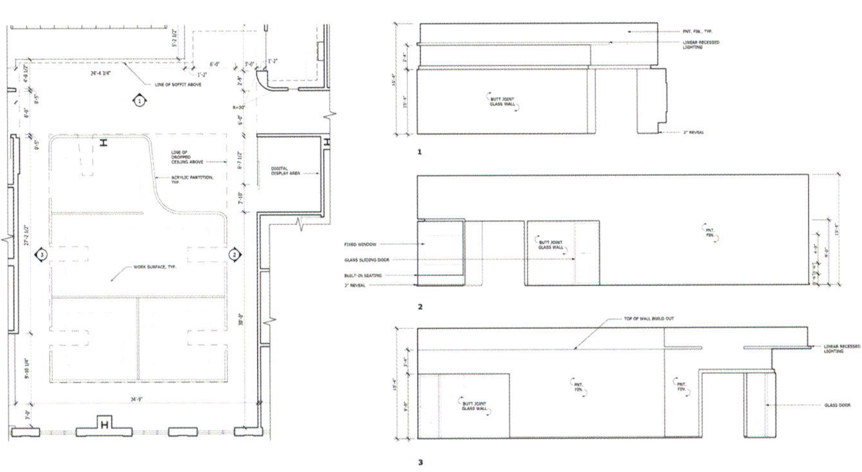

Workroom plan and elevations

V9 DIGITAL

CONFERENCE ROOM

Site St. Louis, MO, United States

Status Schematic Design

Program Cultural

Client KETC/Nine Network

NINE NETWORK MASTER PLAN

Nine Network is a nonprofit public media organization located in the Grand Center district of St. Louis. Its late CEO, Jack Galmiche, envisioned Nine Network as an organization that would become an integral part of St. Louis by serving, engaging, and energizing the members of the community as a forerunner of public media innovation.

Galmiche selected Axi:Ome in 2009 to design a 4,500-square-foot multi-functional space to house their community outreach forums, innovative education sessions, and local media production work. The Nine Center was the first of many projects upon which Axi:Ome has collaborated with the Nine Network.

In 2017, Galmiche asked Axi:Ome to design a 3,500-square-foot space for V9 Digital, a newly-formed media digitization and preservation organization under the Nine Network umbrella. After completing the schematic design for V9 Digital, he requested Axi:Ome to visualize the entirety of the Nine Network building in a conceptual master plan, including the adjacent parking lot. The purpose was to explore different possibilities and ways of engaging the community through architectural intervention while supporting the shifting internal work culture as the organization focused on becoming an innovator in public media.

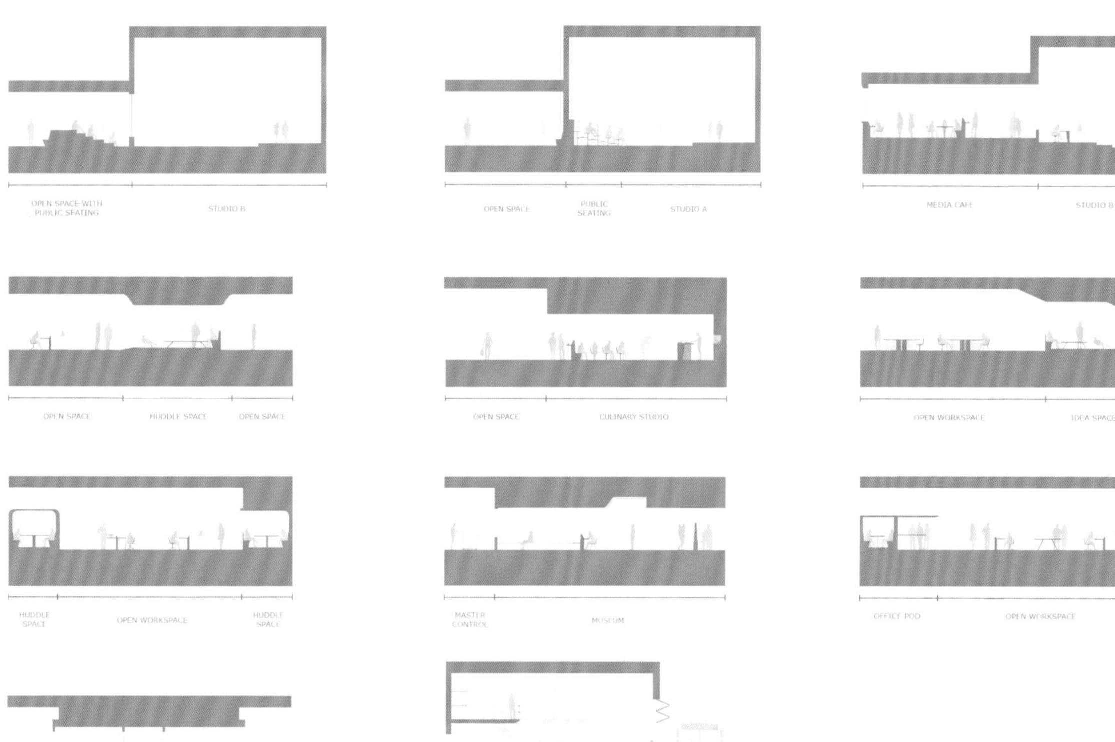

Interior program diagram

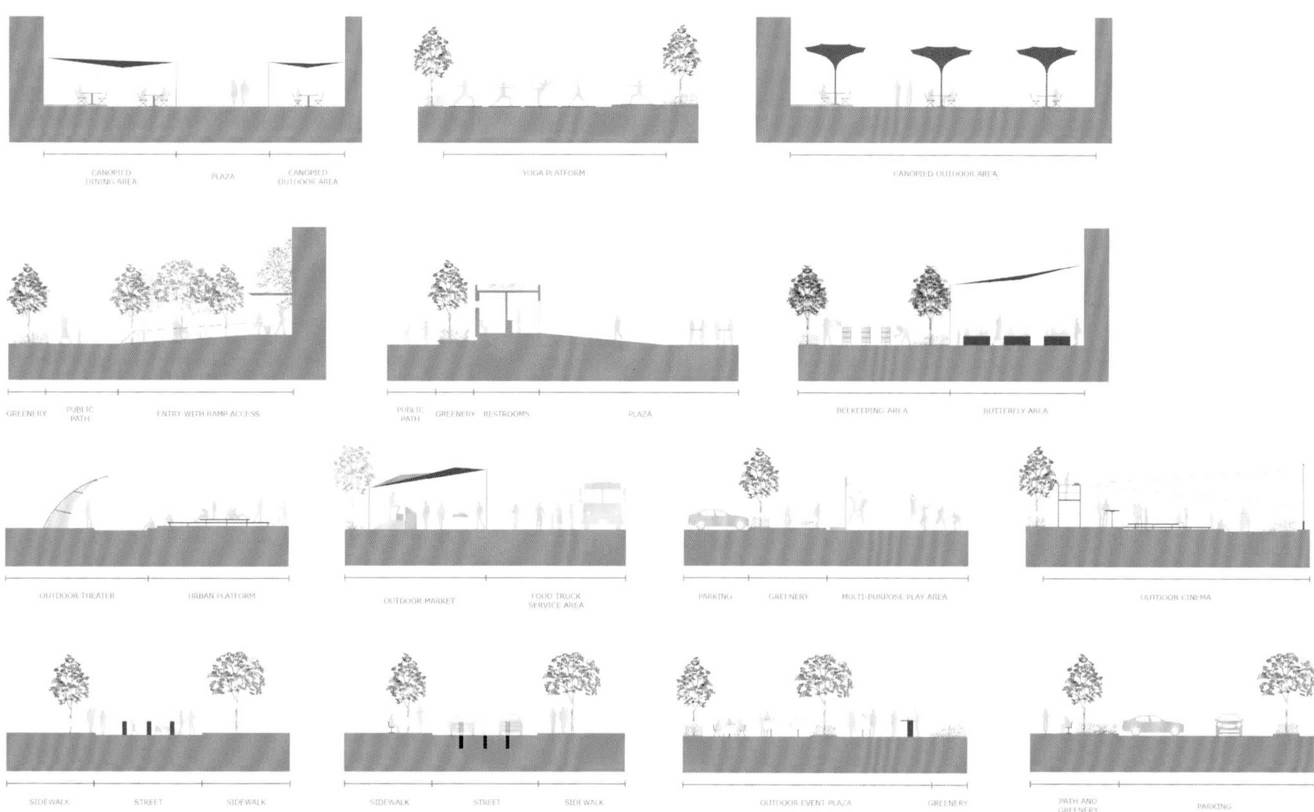

Exterior program diagrams

Storage processing diagrams

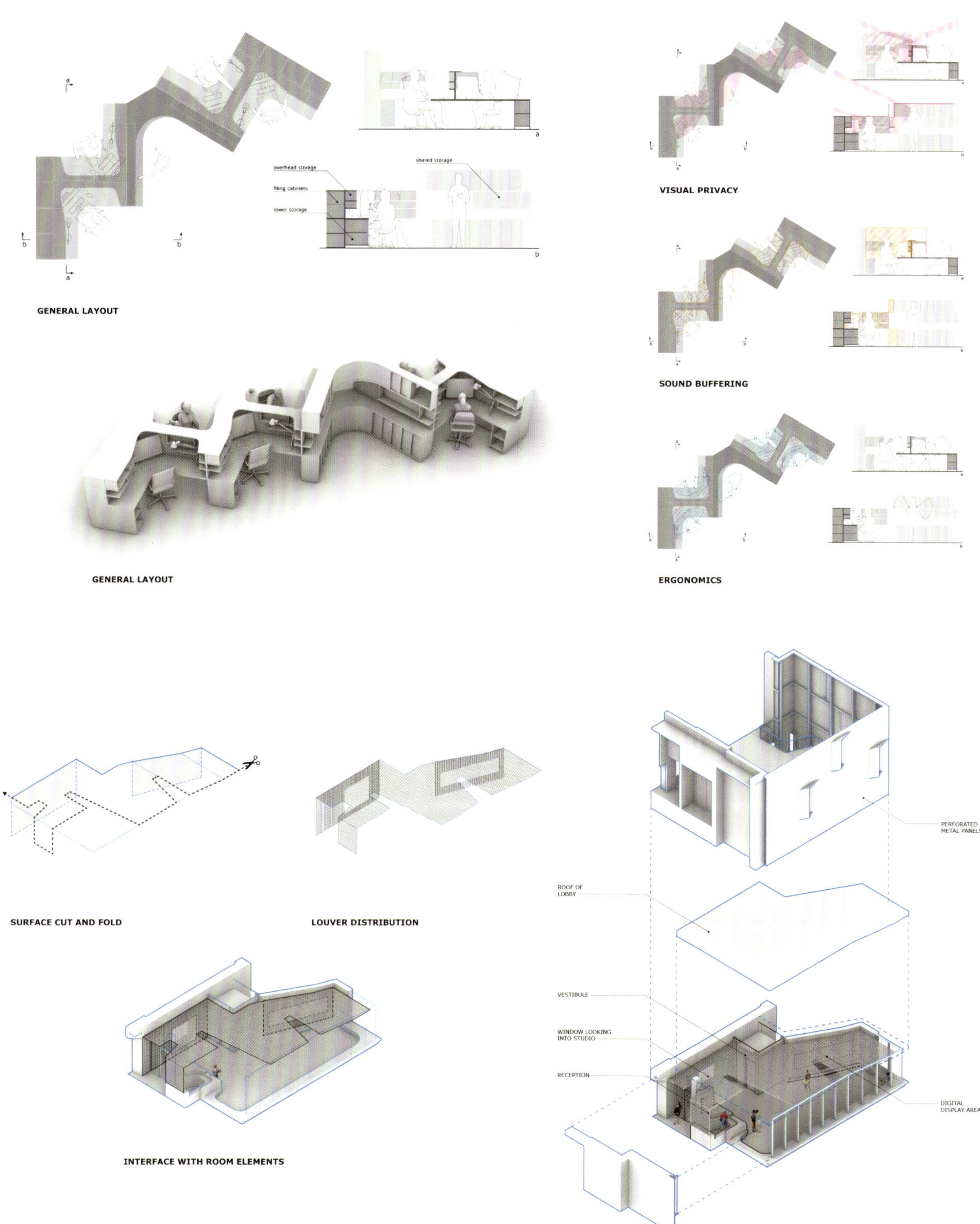

Work station diagrams (above), Nine Network entry lobby and public patio diagrams (below)

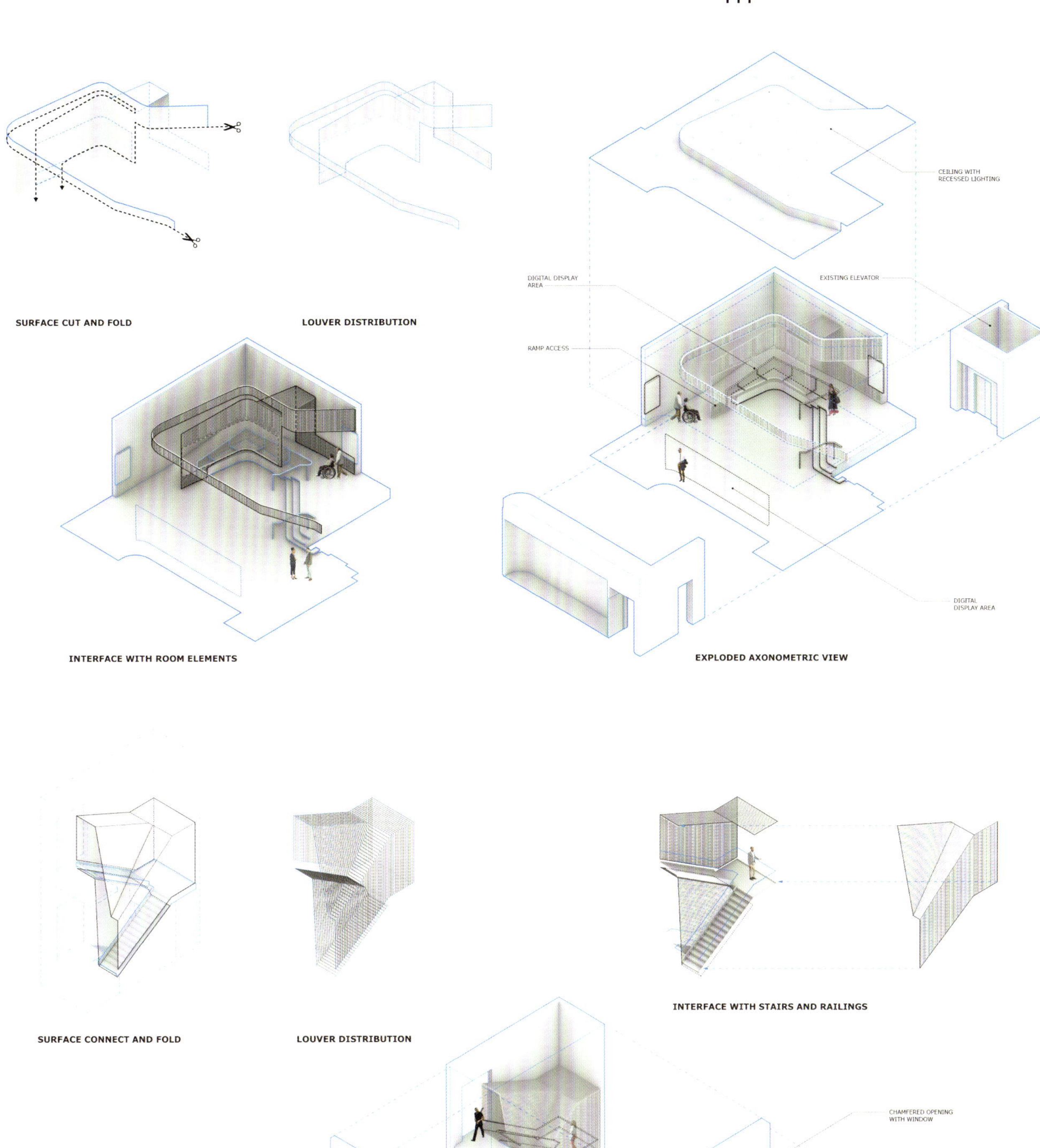

Media exhibition diagrams (above), public stairs diagrams (below)

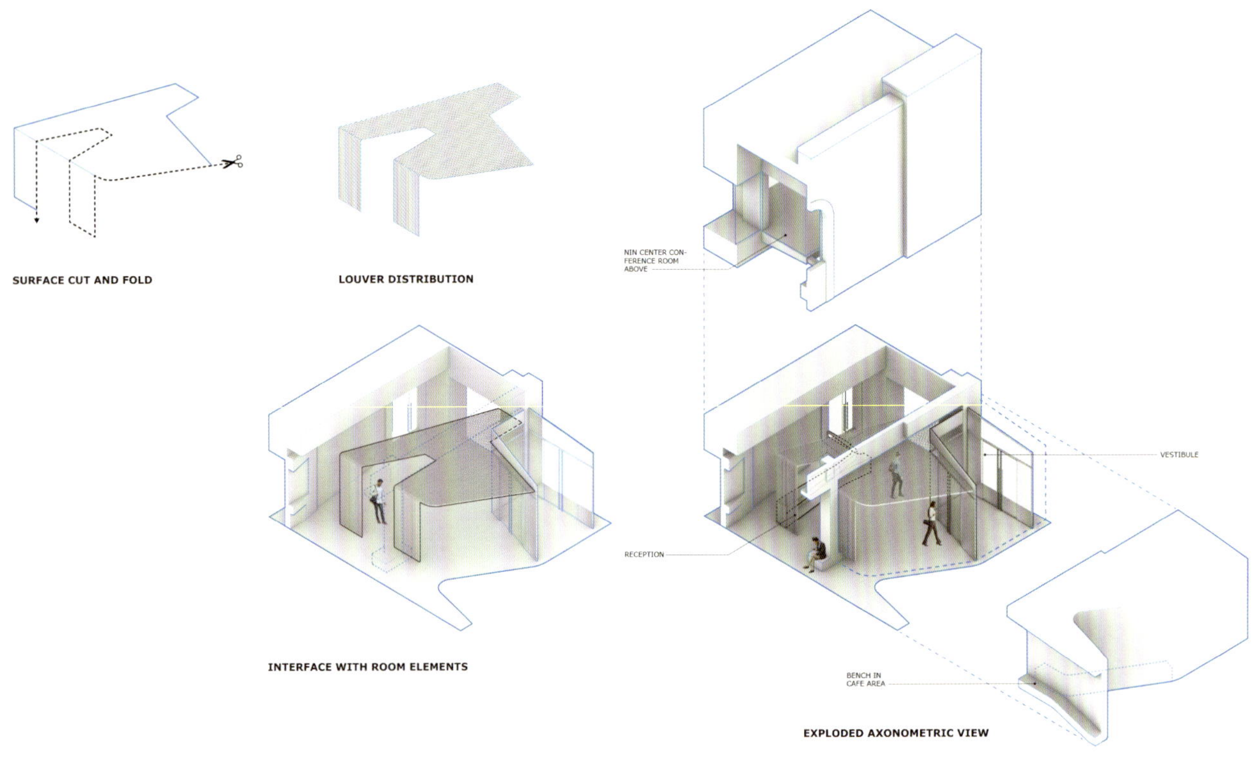

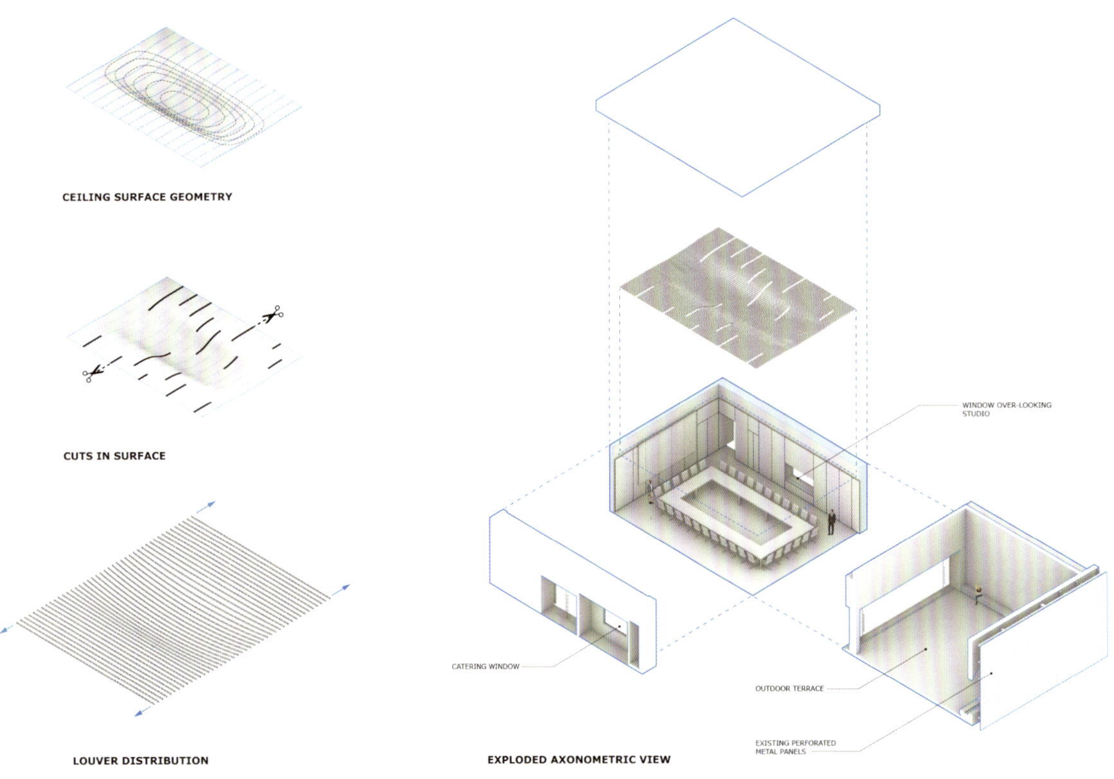

V9 entry lobby diagrams (above), board room diagrams (below)

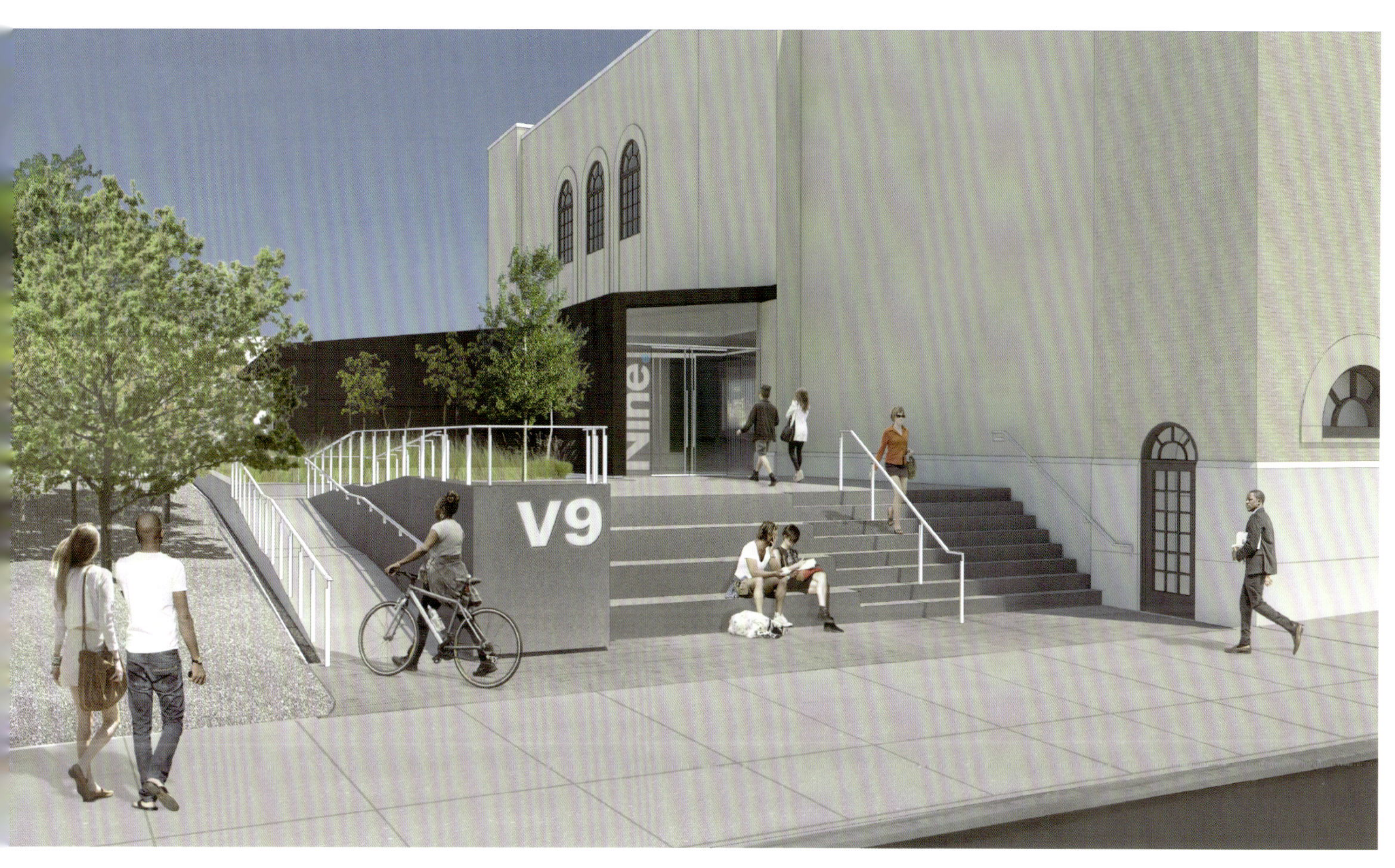
Nine
V9

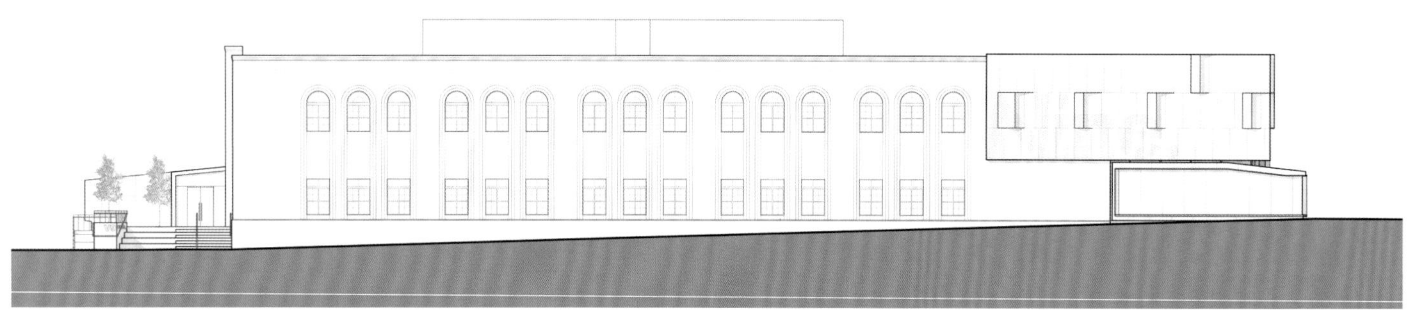

South elevation

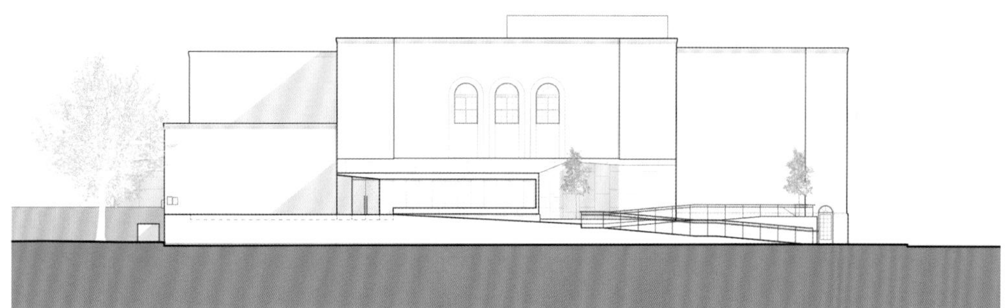

West elevation

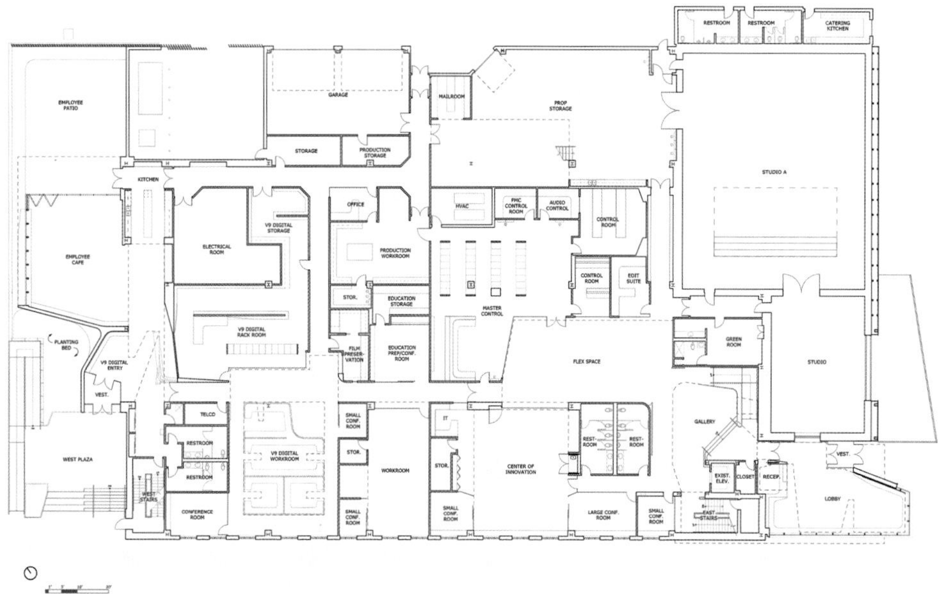

First-floor plan

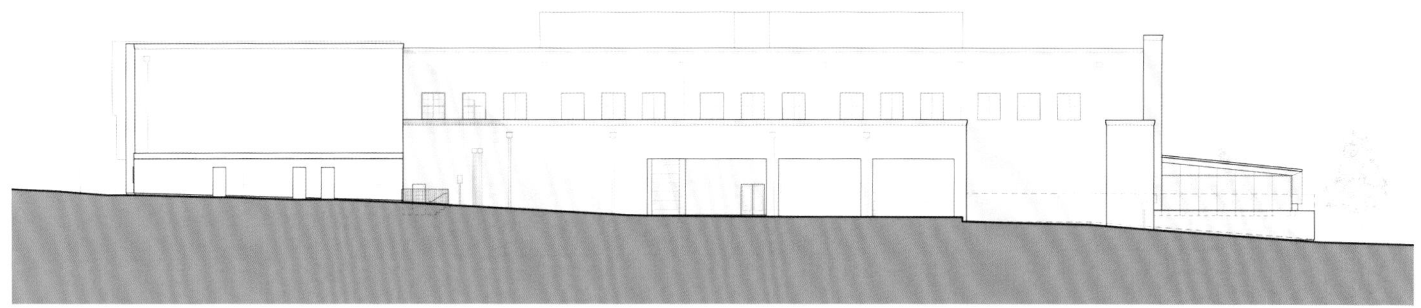

North elevation

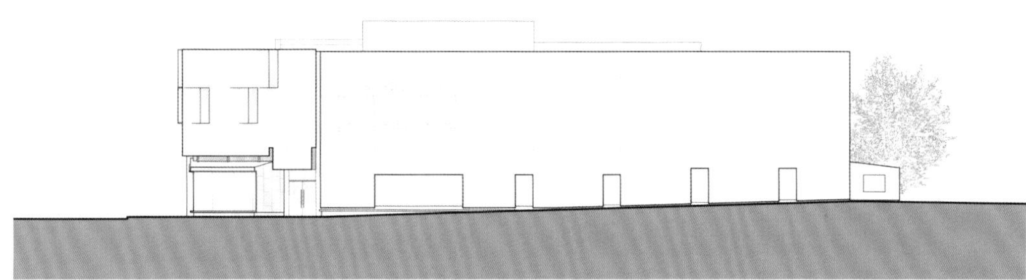

East elevation

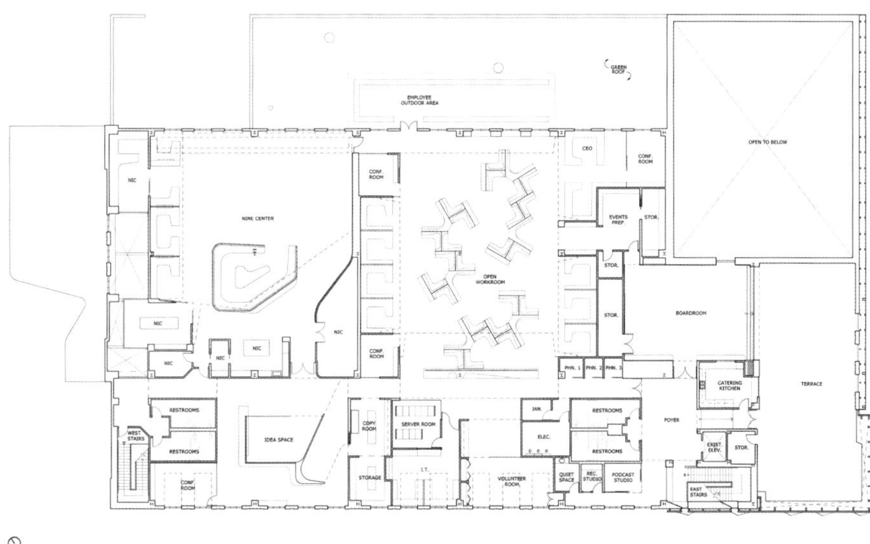

Second-floor plan

Nine.

line.

TERRACE

Nine.

Nine.
Nine.

Site	St. Louis, MO, United States	Status	Schematic Design	Program	Residential	Client	Han and Yang Family

HAN HOUSE

Transverse section

This residential project explores the financial and architectural implications of the federal Historic Preservation Tax Incentive program in St. Louis. The design required a modest expansion based on historical research, which resulted in a sleeping porch added to the late eighteenth-century structure that typified a common St. Louis residential building typology. The strategy aims to transform the current building plans, which have been altered over time, into ones that meet the new owner's twenty-first-century programmatic needs.

Historical research diagrams

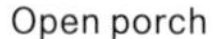
Open porch

Open porch

Sleeping porch

Infill railings

Fenestration/enclosure

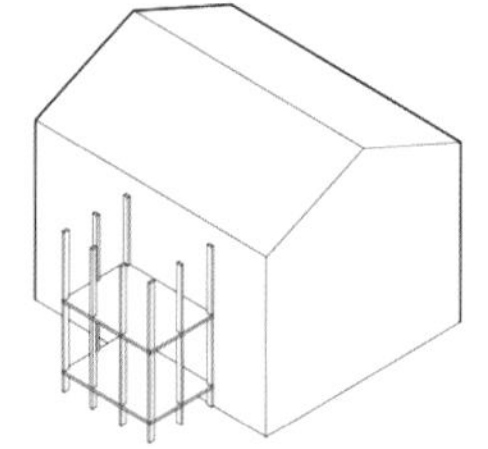
Posts

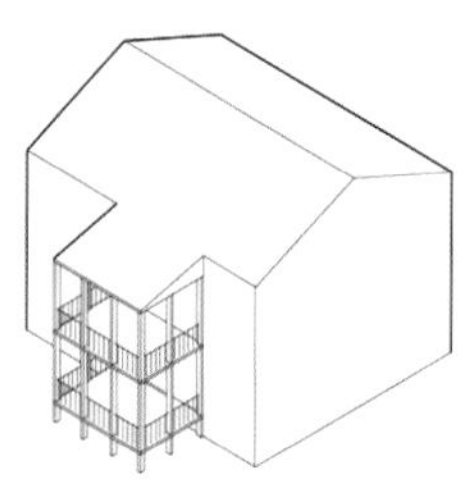
Roof and railings

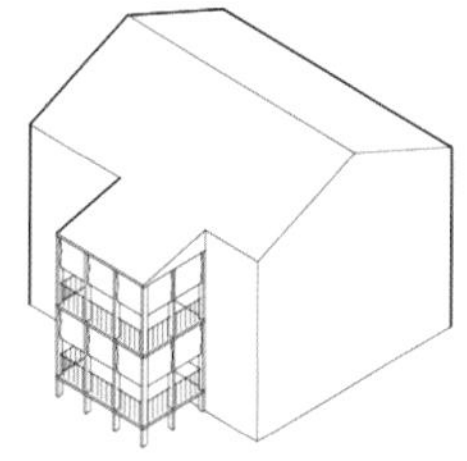
Curtains and blinds

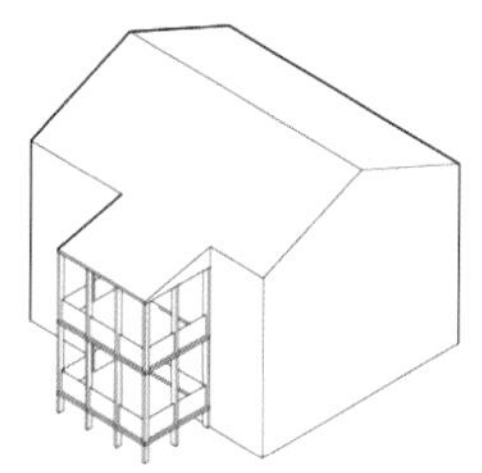
Infill railings

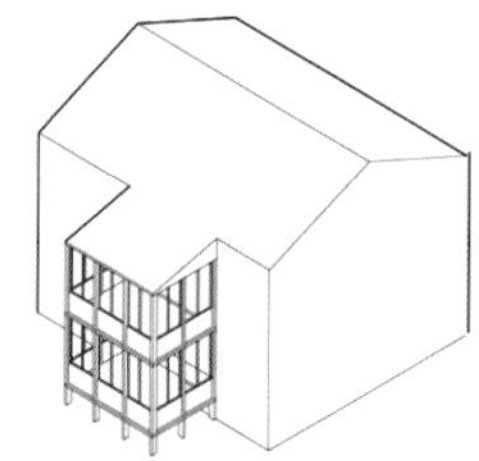
Windows

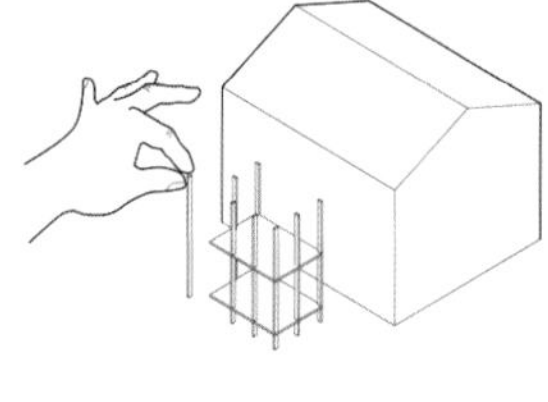
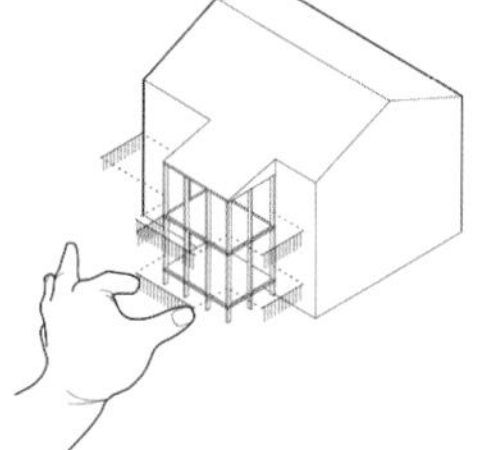
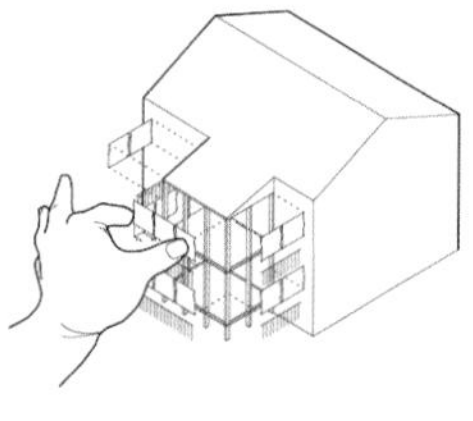
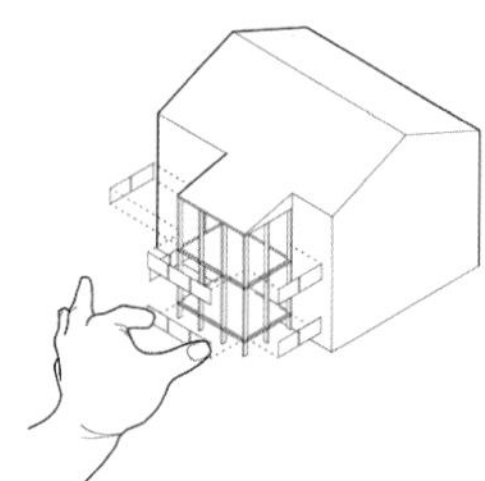
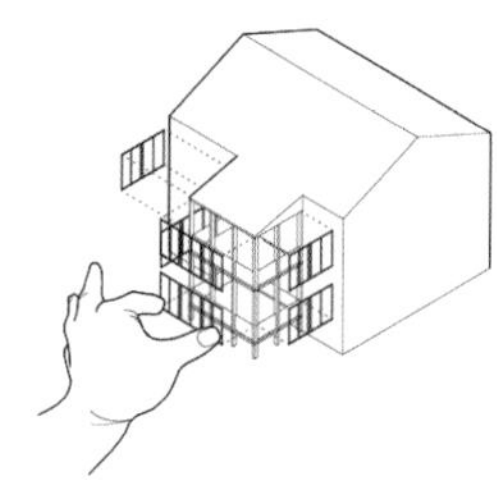

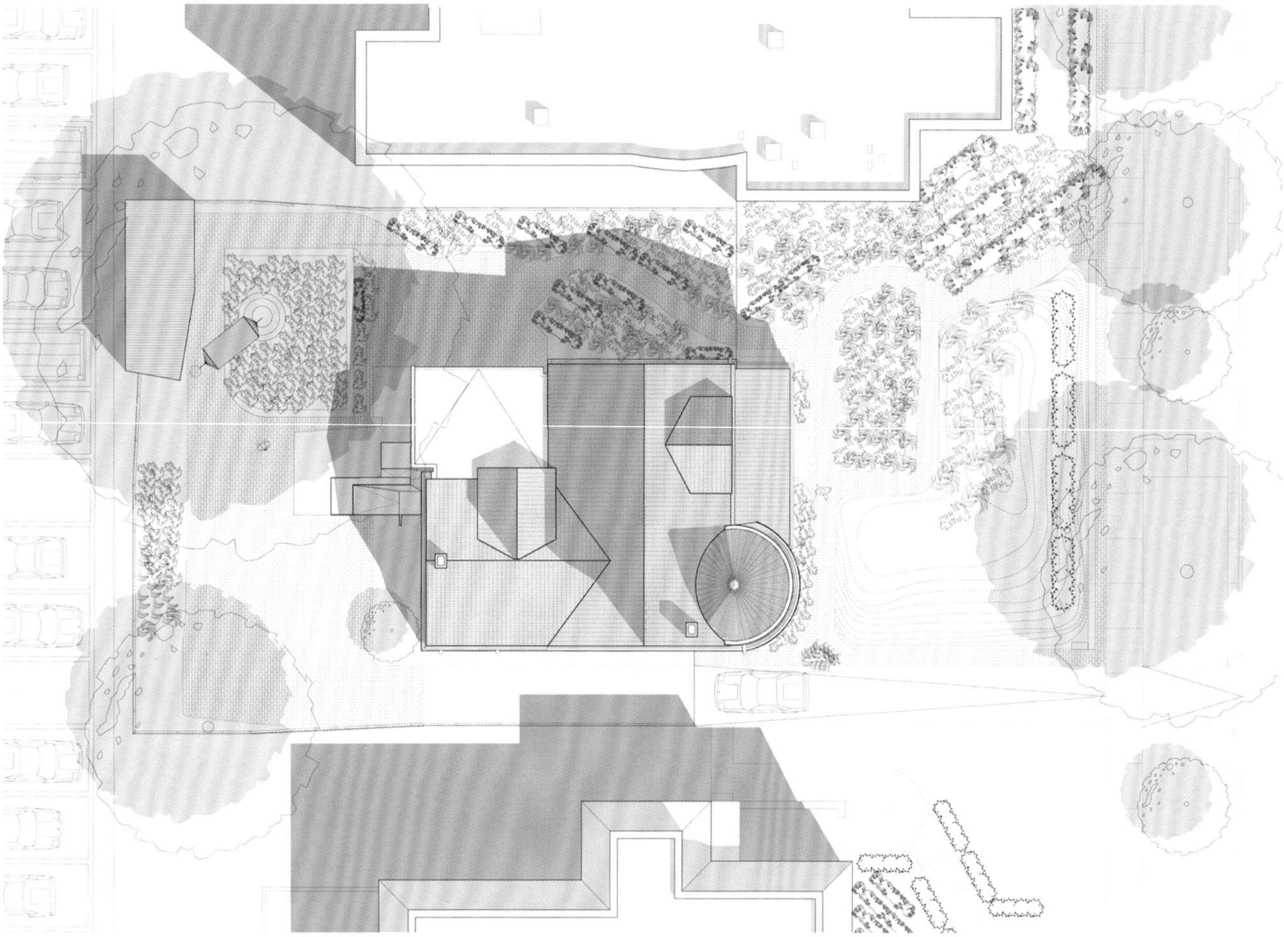

Site plan

North elevation

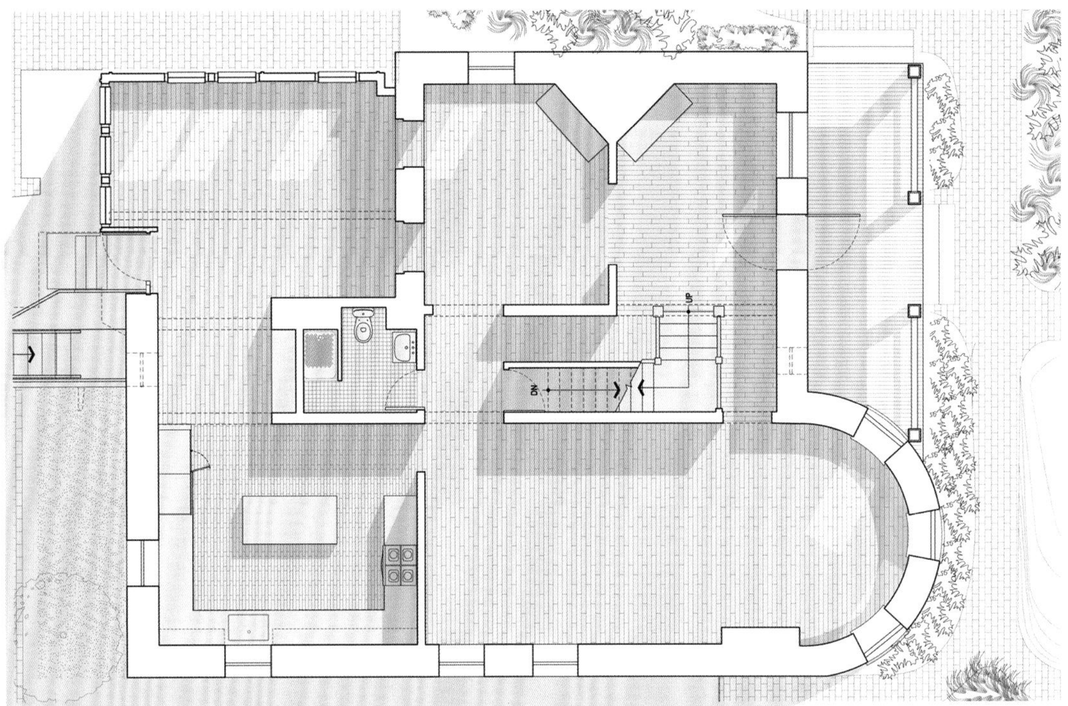

First-floor plan

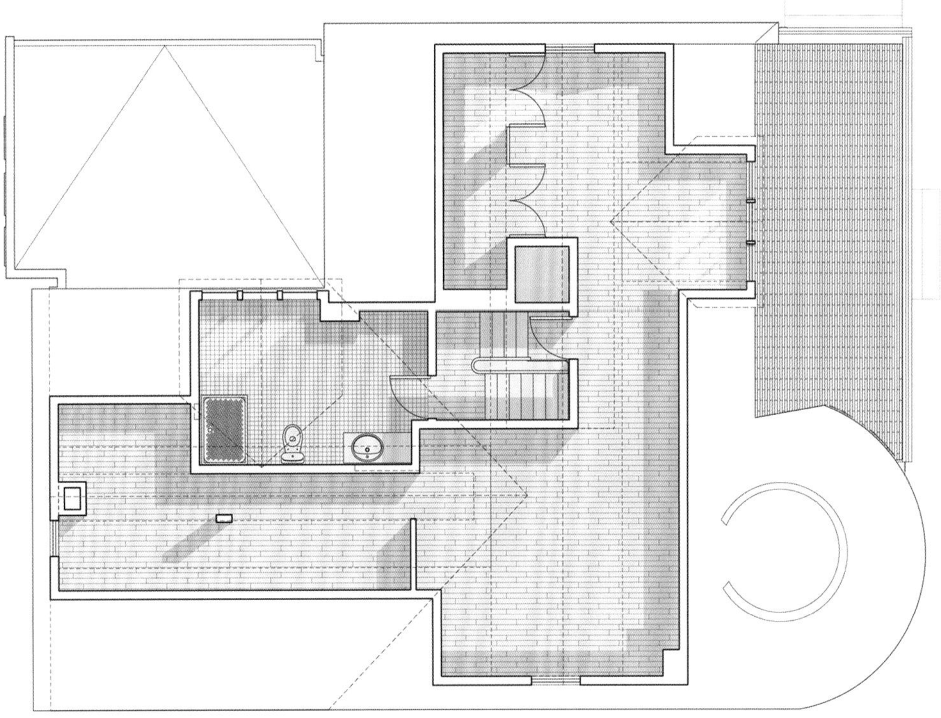

Second-floor plan

East elevation

Longitudinal section

West elevation

South elevation

Site St. Louis, MO, United States

Status Conceptual Design

Program Commercial · Cultural · Residential

Client Olive West Development

OLIVE STREET REDEVELOPMENT

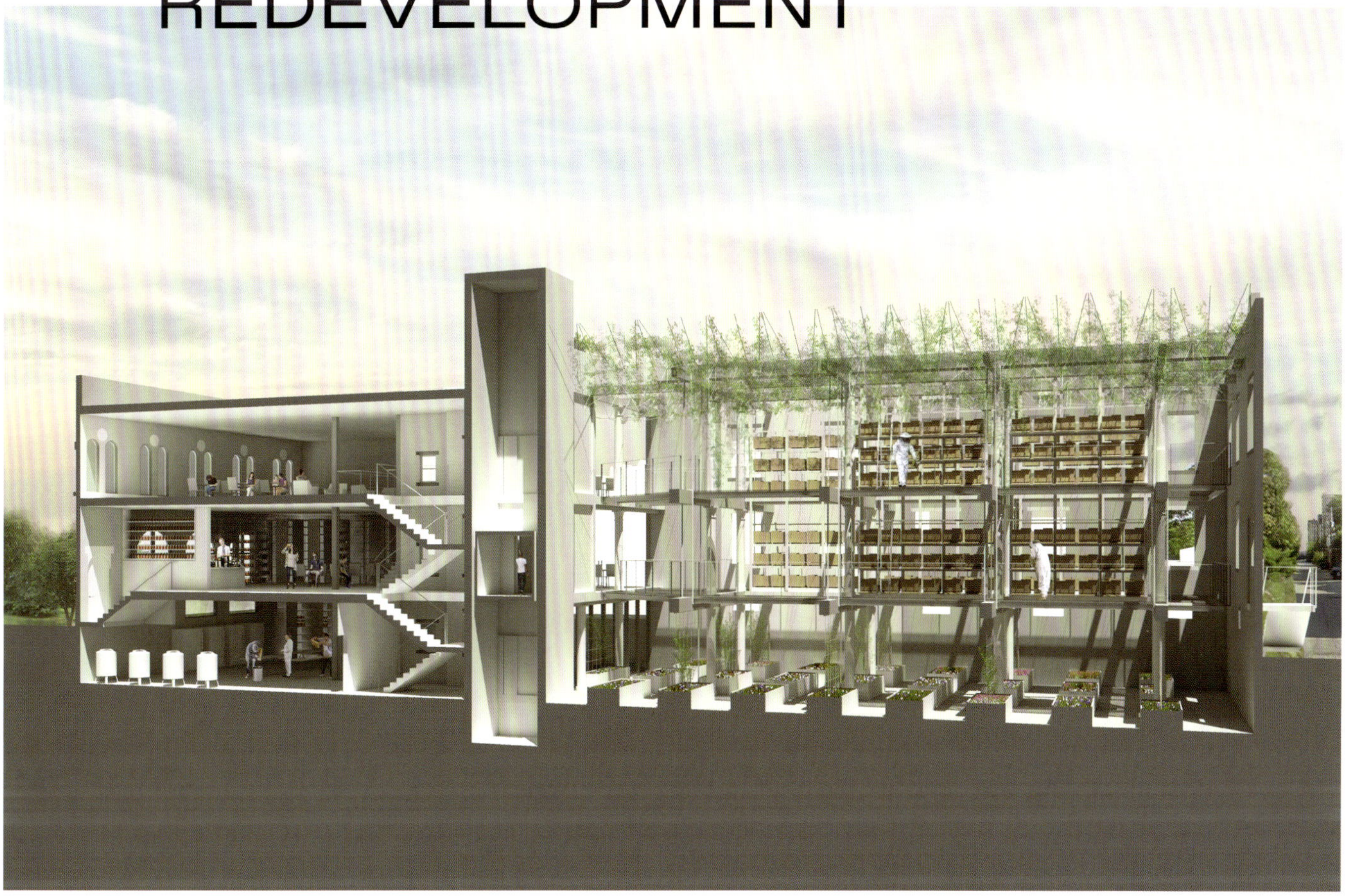

Our design for the Olive Street Redevelopment in Grand Center takes three existing buildings and reconfigures them into new programs that open the area up to the community. The new design transforms the urban context by interfacing the artificial with the natural to create a diverse ecology. This renewed urban landscape nurtures a robust environment that brings people, flora, and fauna together to experience nature within the city.

Grand Center has become an isolated urban desert, its diverse biological landscape and soil ecology neglected since its abandonment. The landscape of the site is comprised of concrete, brick, and asphalt surfaces, all homogeneous man-made materials that limit the migration of microbes into the soil. This isolation of soil on the cellular level has diminished its health and its capacity for function and performance within the urban landscape.

This project brings urban life back into an empty city by creating synergy between public programs (playgrounds, a TV studio, gardens, a beekeeping area, a bird observatory, a butterfly sanctuary, and a library) and privatized programs (housing, cafes, restaurants, galleries, and a food truck depot).

The Olive Street Redevelopment design encourages a variety of migratory birds and monarch butterflies into the landscape to facilitate the development of local bacteria diversity; it also maintains honey bees, which provide native microbes. The combination of these insects and animals results in a rich spectrum of bacteria in the soil, which in turn enhances environmental sustainability, increases water absorption, and improves the nutrient profile of the landscape. Because of their biological properties, soil microorganisms are essential to the healthy ecology of human, flora, and fauna in a contemporary city.

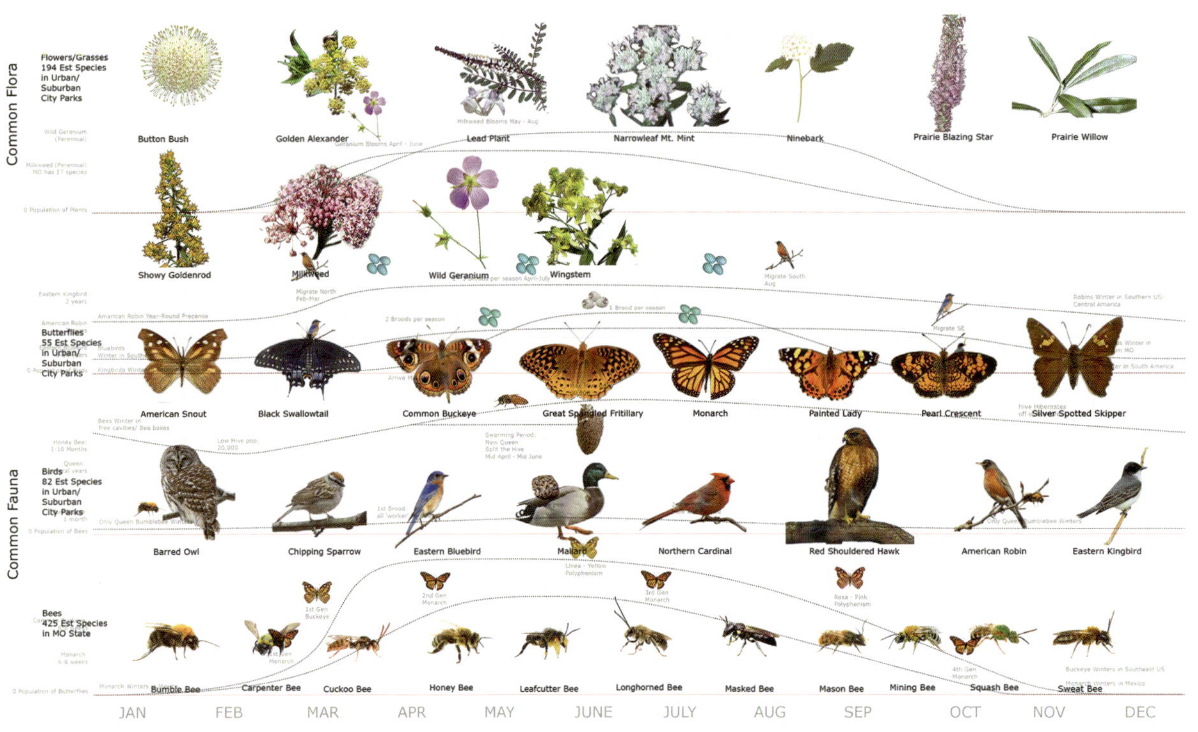

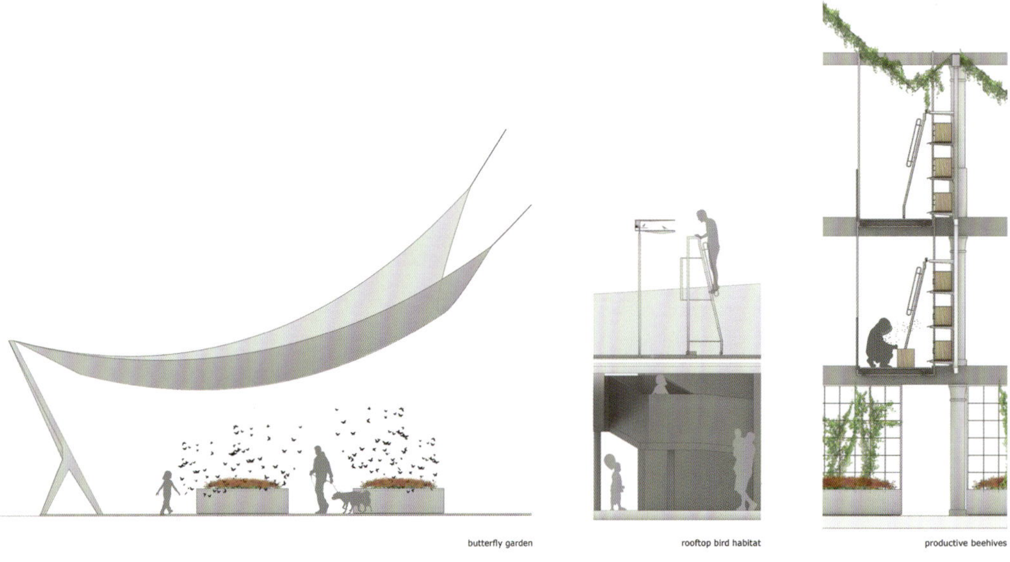

Flora and fauna season diagram (above), ecological component design diagrams (below)

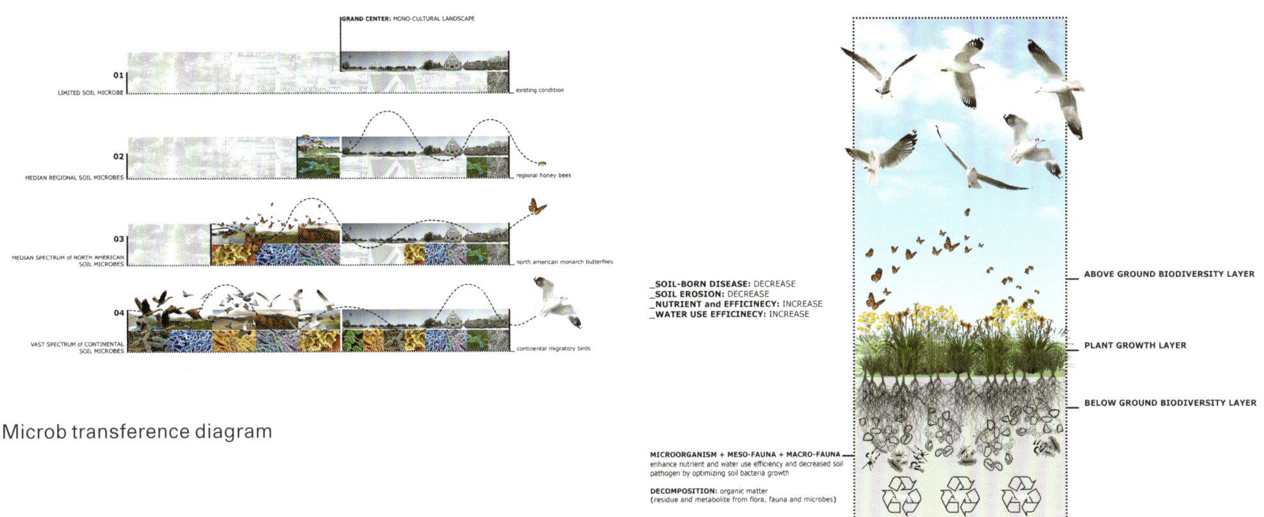

Microb transference diagram

Microb performance diagram

Landscape

GREEN SPACE

PLAYGROUND

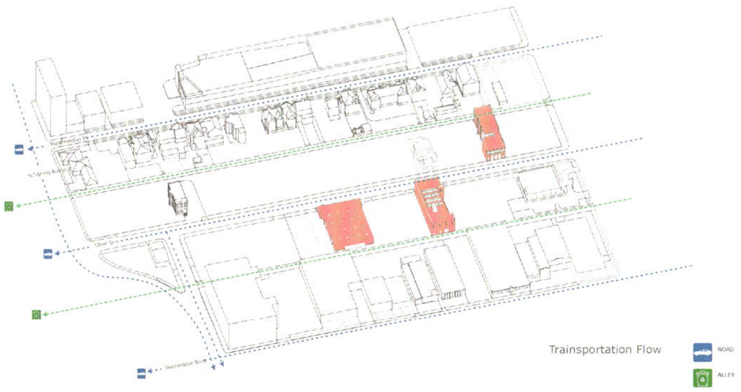

Trainsportation Flow

ROAD

ALLEY

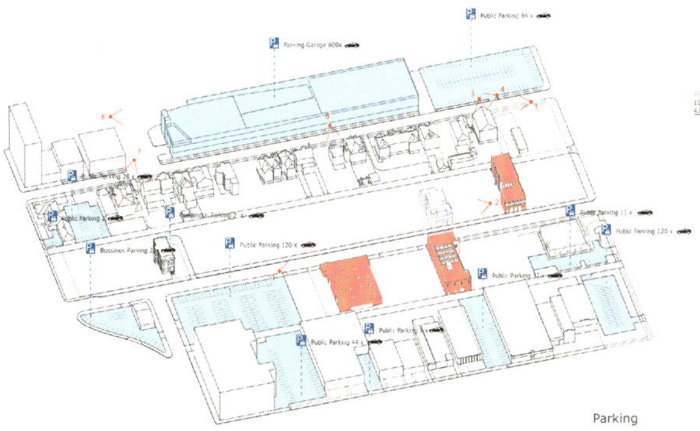

Parking

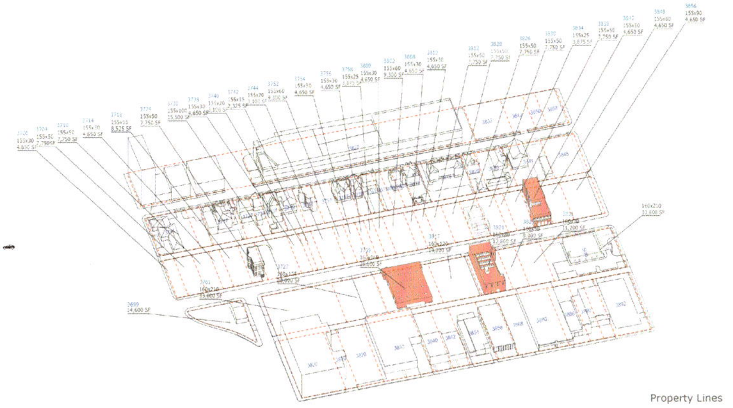

Property Lines

Site research diagrams

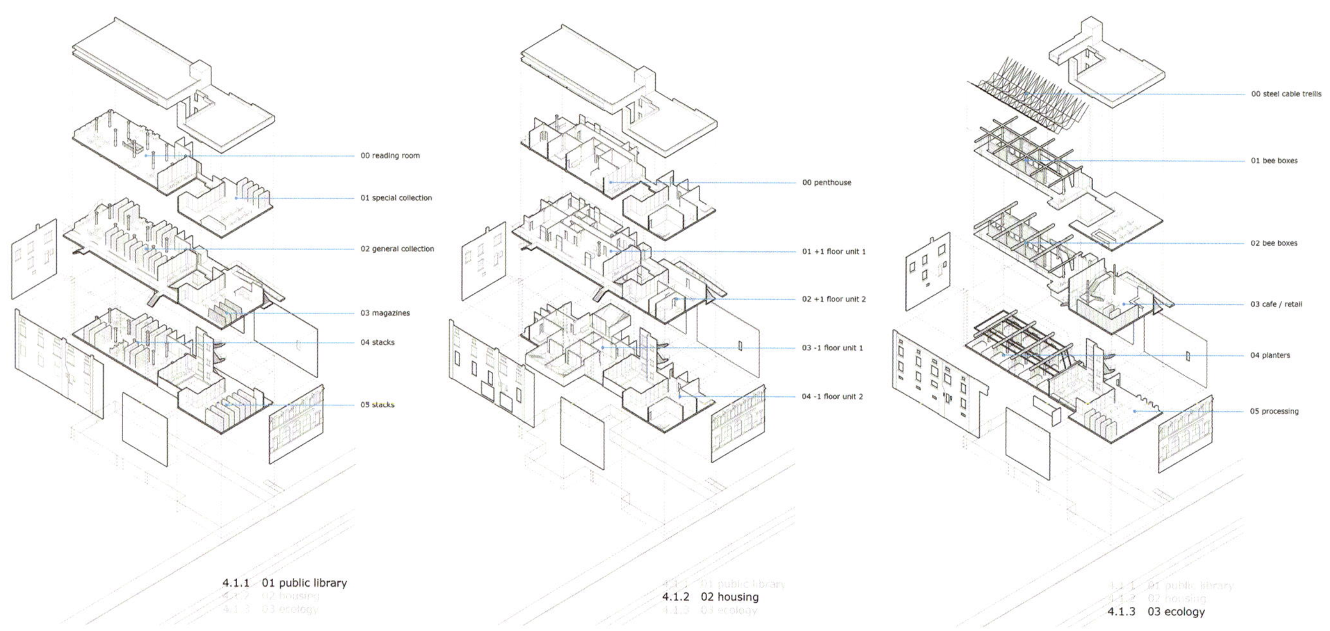

Public Library, Housing, and Ecology compoment diagrams

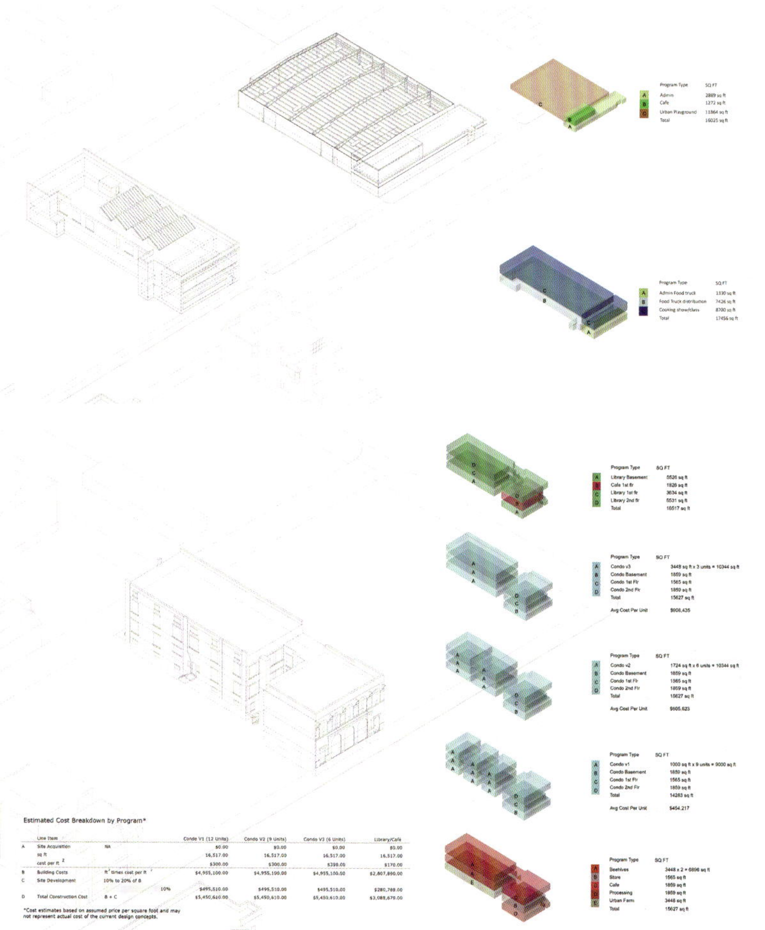

Estimated Cost Breakdown by Program*

	Line Item			Condo V1 (12 Units)	Condo V2 (9 Units)	Condo V3 (6 Units)	Library/Cafe
A	Site Acquisition	NA		$0.00	$0.00	$0.00	$0.00
	sq ft			16,517.00	16,517.00	16,517.00	16,517.00
	cost per ft 2			$300.00	$300.00	$300.00	$170.00
B	Building Costs	ft 2 times cost per ft 2		$4,955,100.00	$4,955,100.00	$4,955,100.00	$2,807,890.00
C	Site Development	10% to 20% of B					
			10%	$495,510.00	$495,510.00	$495,510.00	$280,789.00
D	Total Construction Cost	B + C		$5,450,610.00	$5,450,610.00	$5,450,610.00	$3,088,679.00

*Cost estimates based on assumed price per square foot and may not represent actual cost of the current design concepts.

Olive Street master plan programmatic diagrams

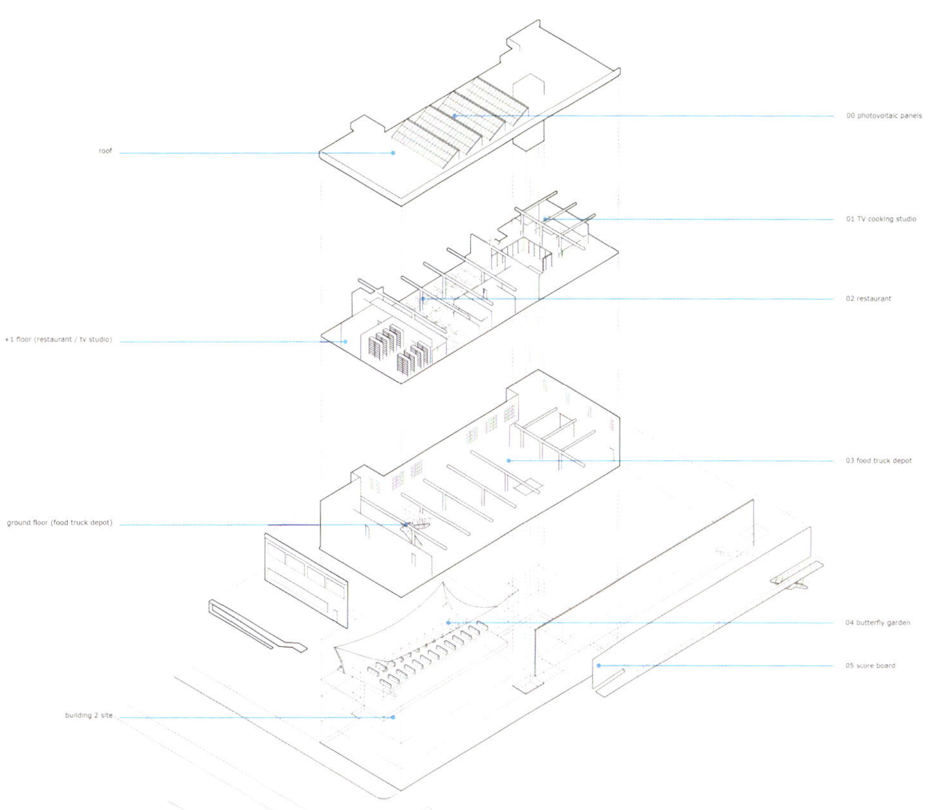

Butterflies and Food
component diagram

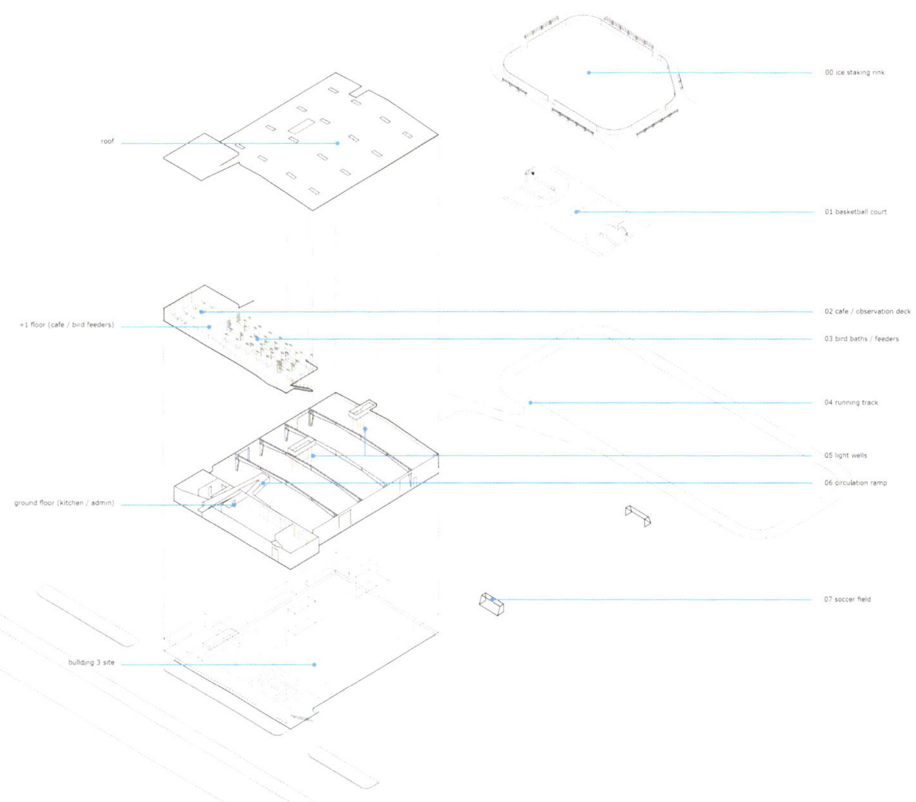

Birds and Play
component diagram

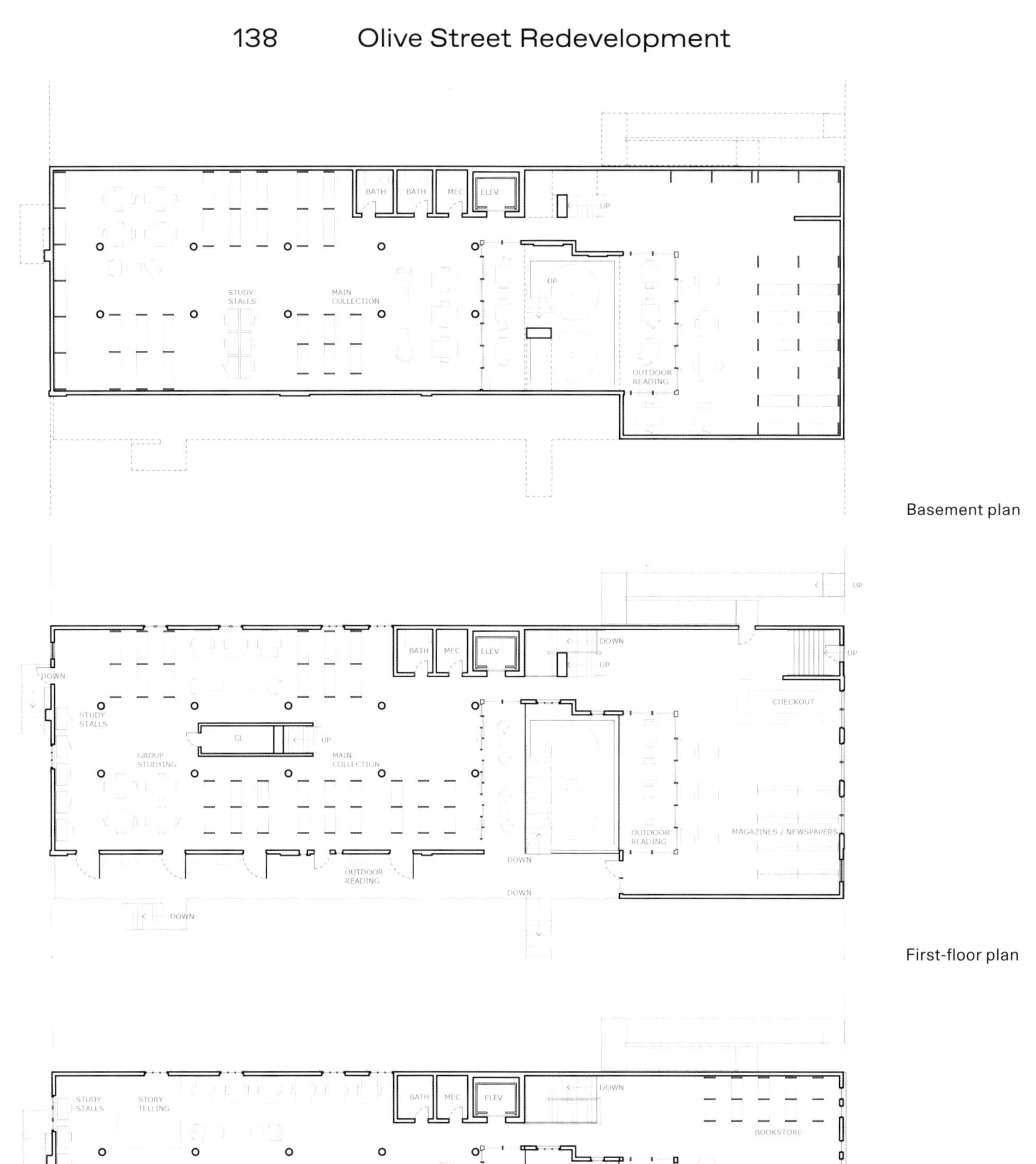

Basement plan

First-floor plan

Second-floor plan

PUBLIC LIBRARY

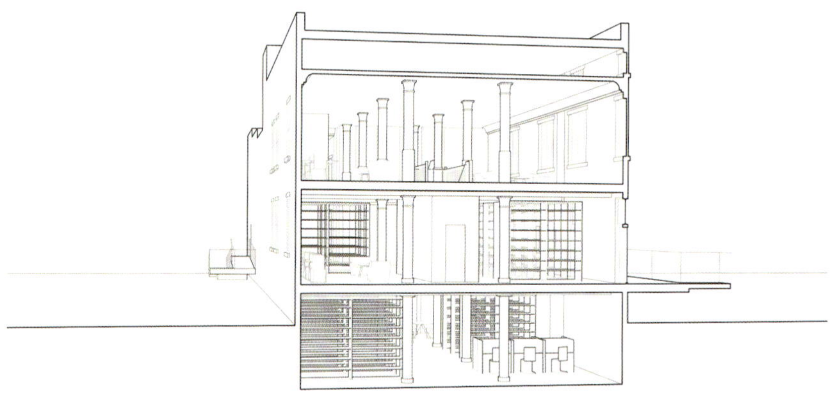

Transverse perspectival section

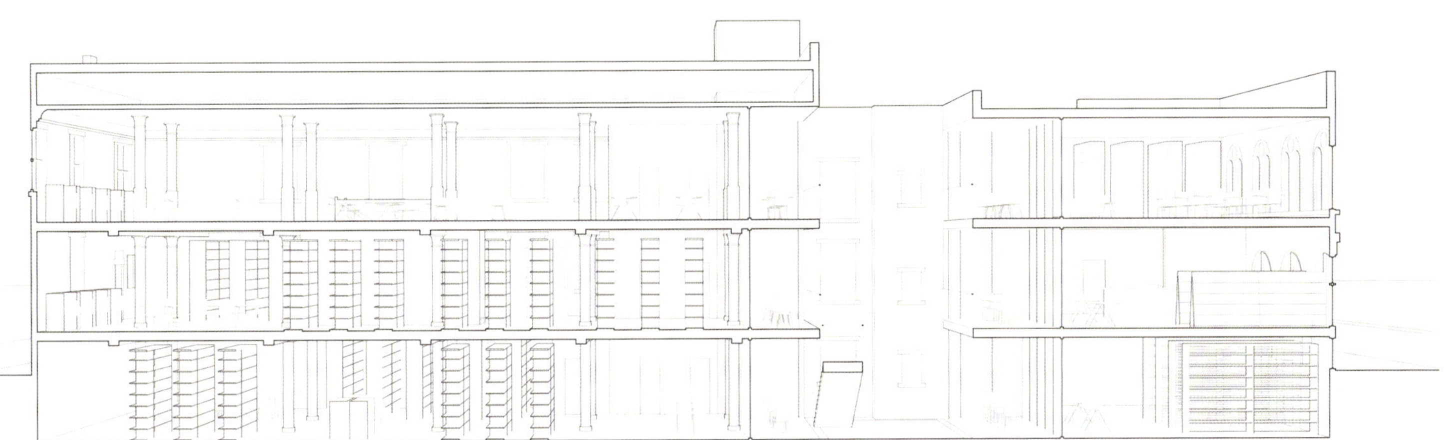

Longitudinal perspectival section

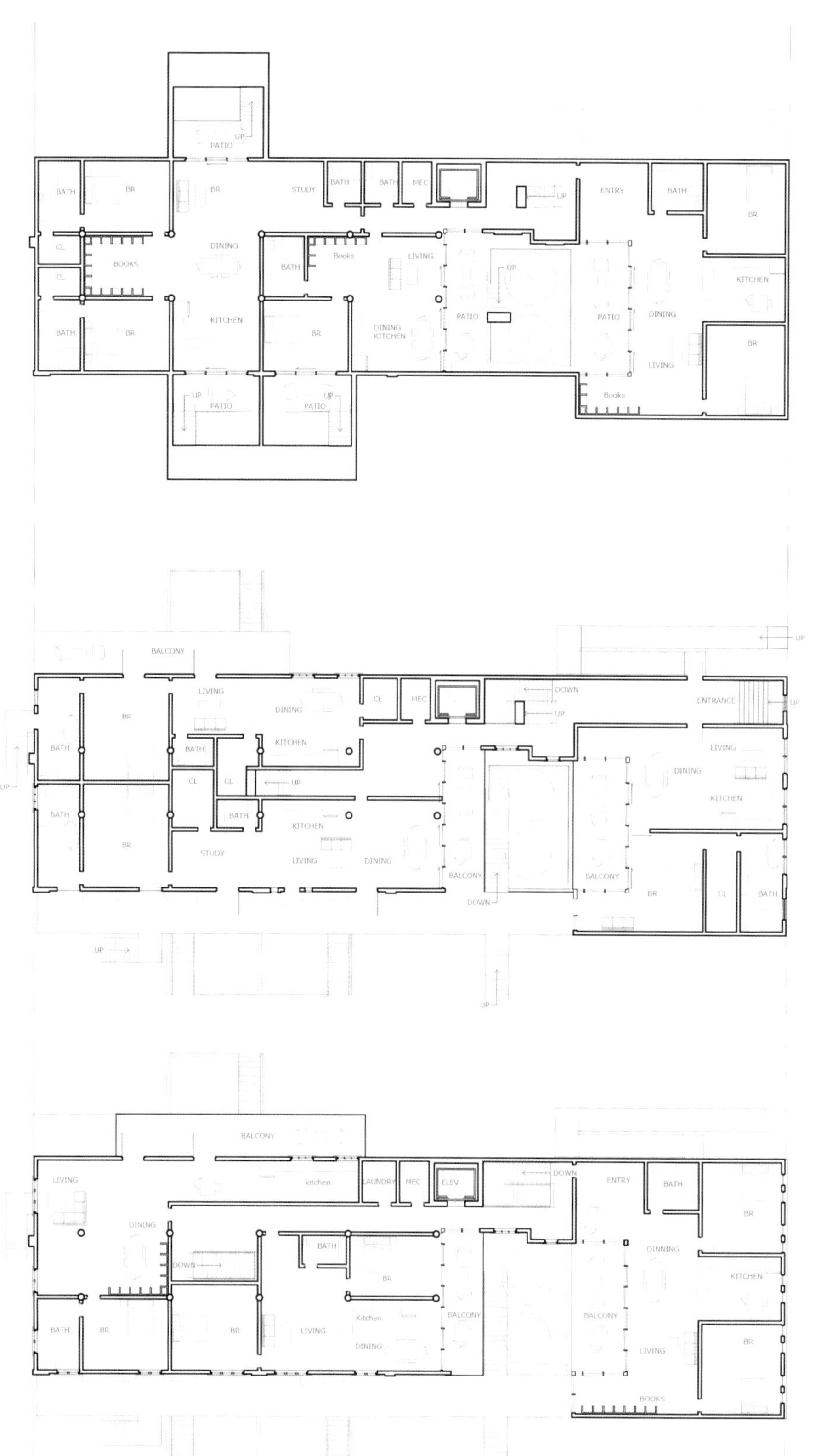

Basement plan

First-floor plan

Second-floor plan

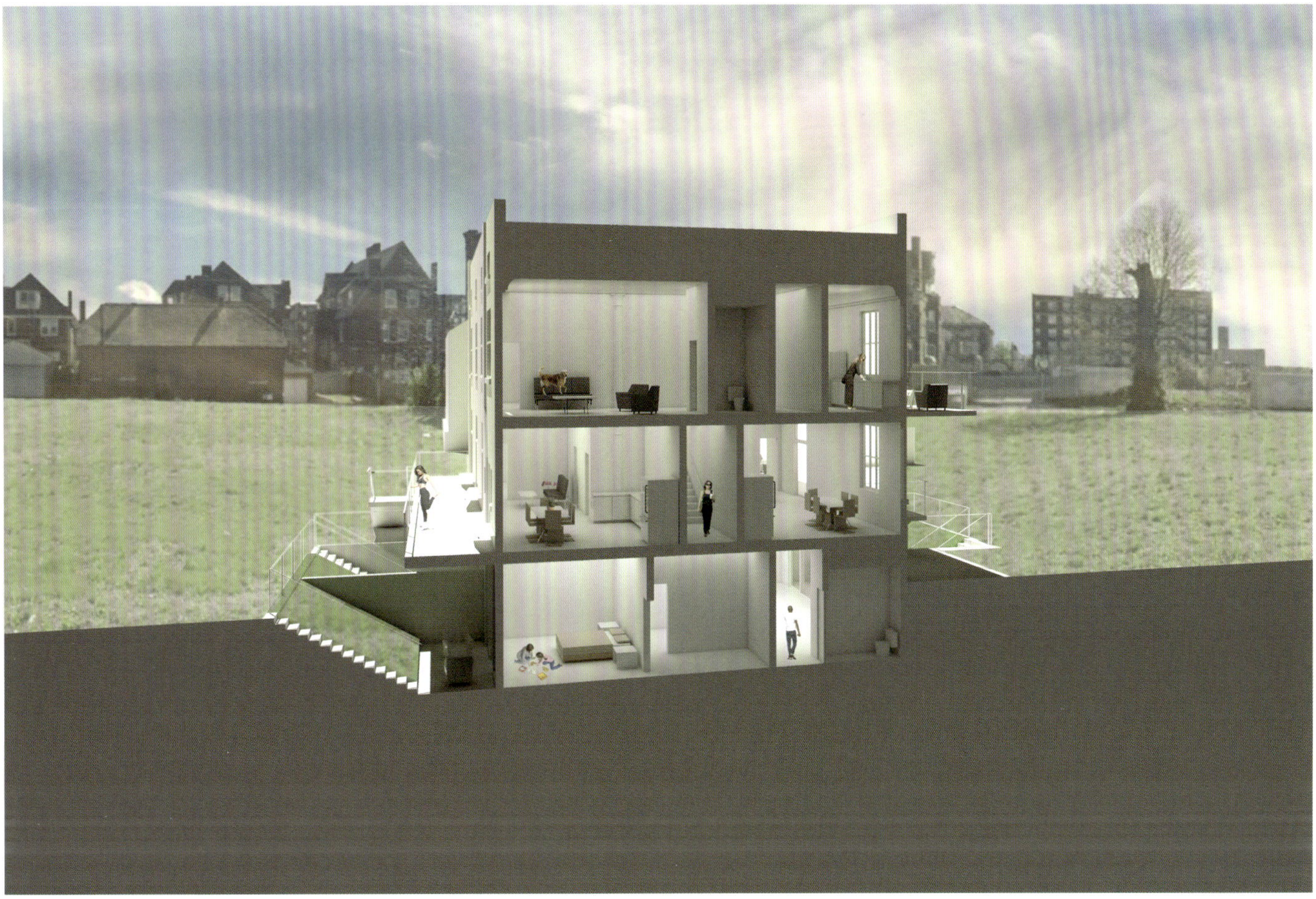

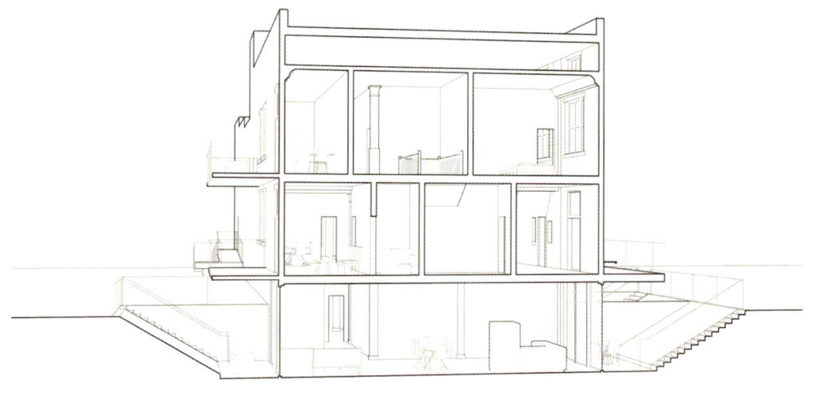

Transverse perspectival section

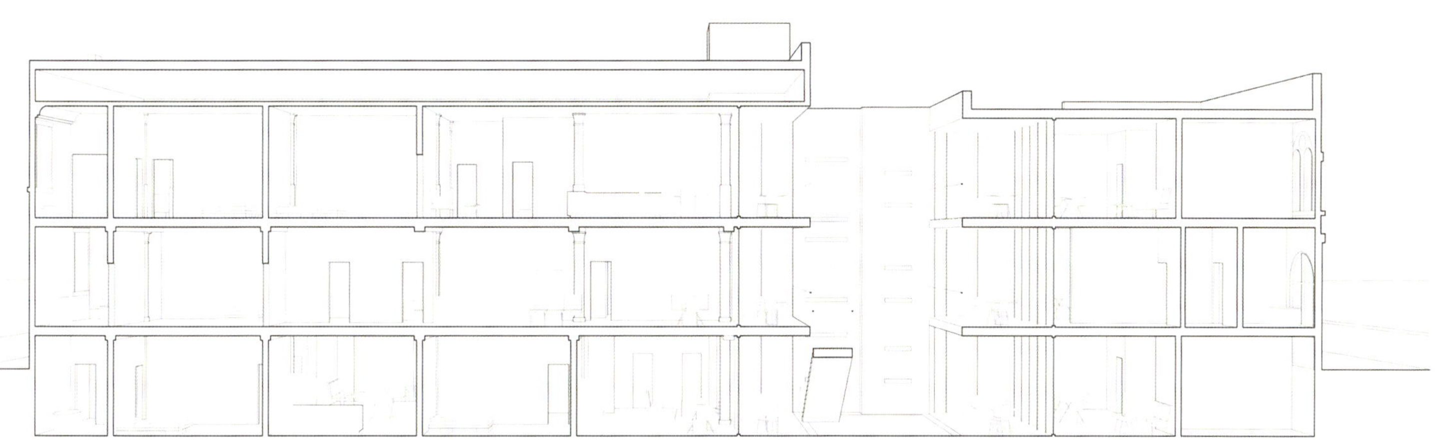

Longitudinal perspectival section

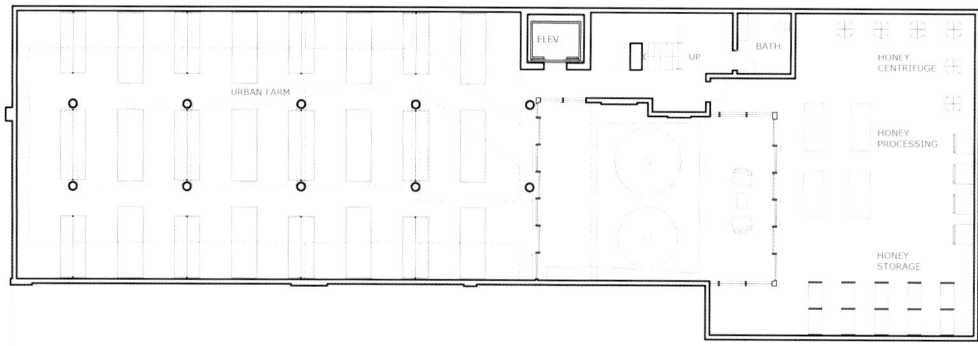

Basement plan

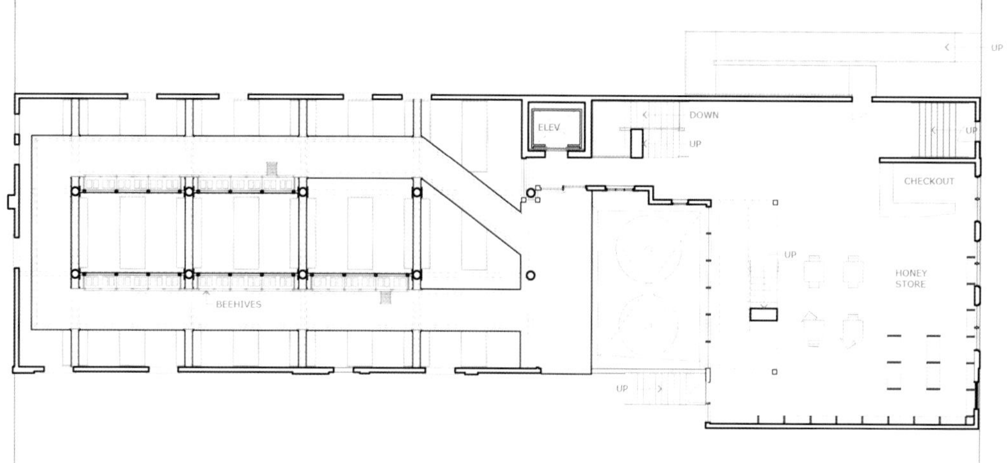

First-floor plan

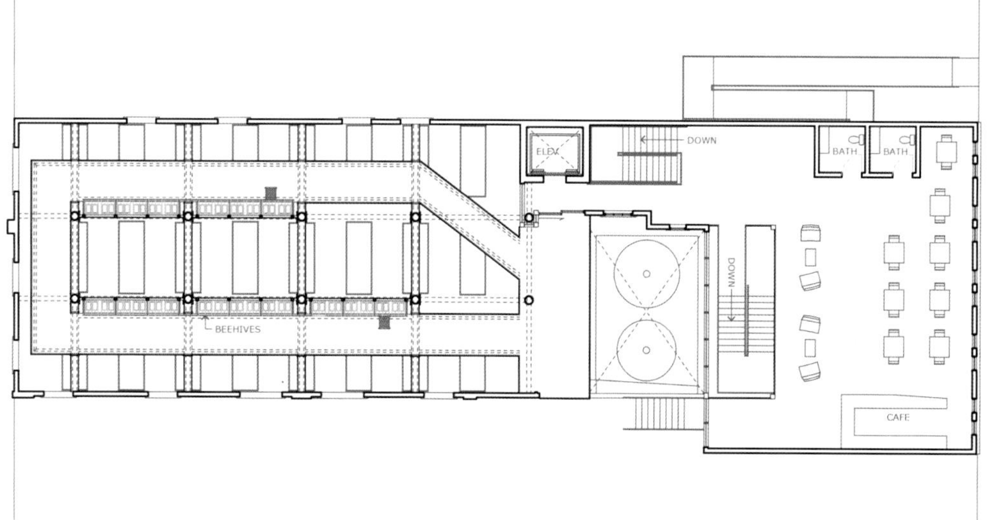

Second-floor plan

ECOLOGY

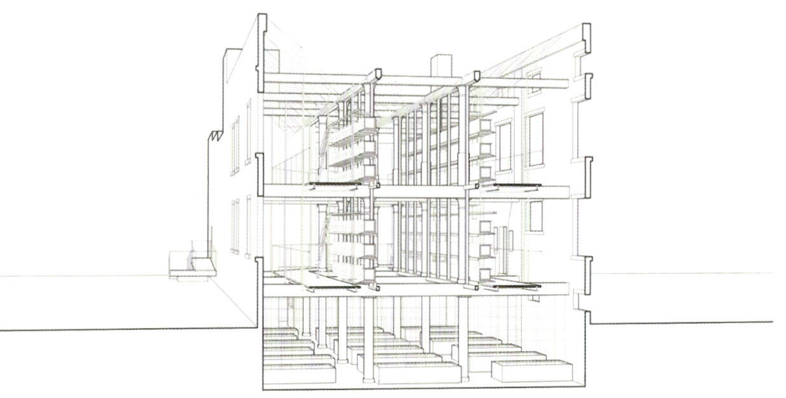

Transverse perspectival section

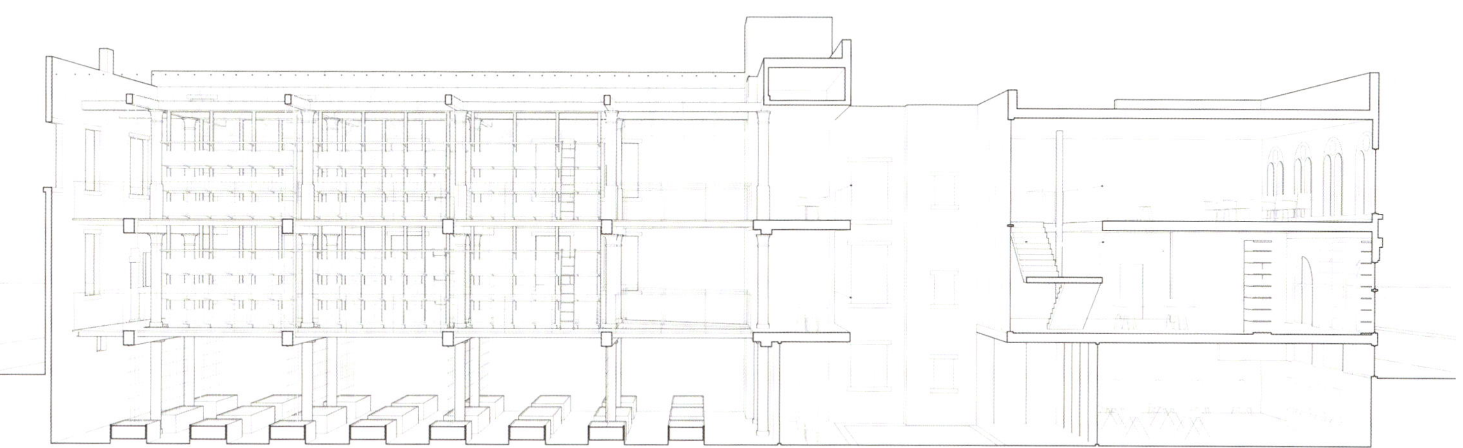

Longitudinal perspectival section

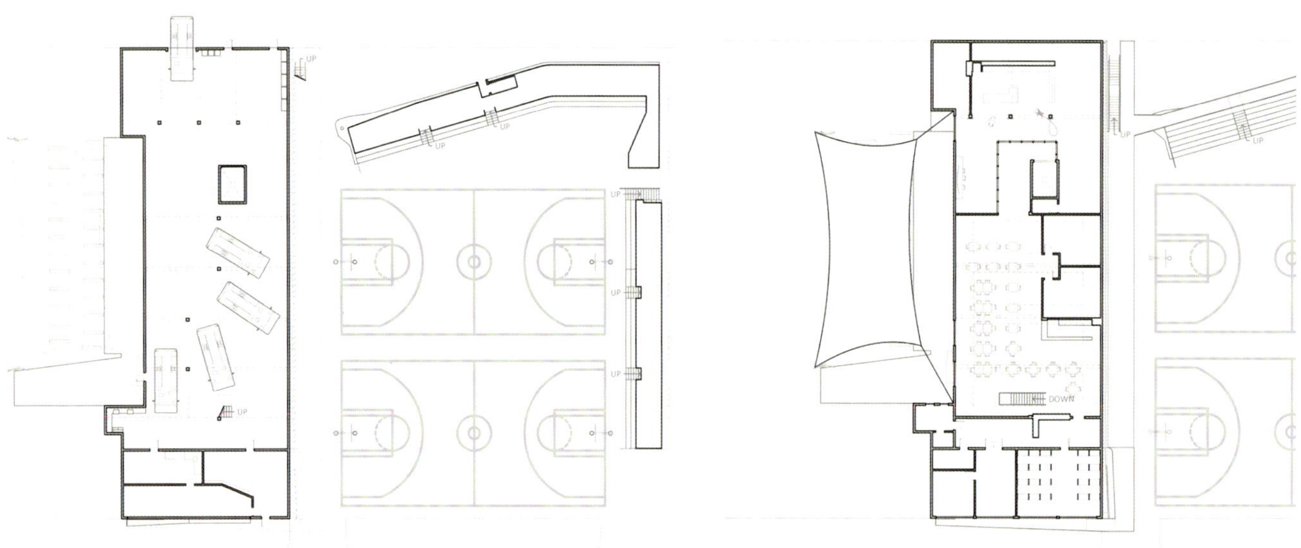

First-floor plan

Second-floor plan

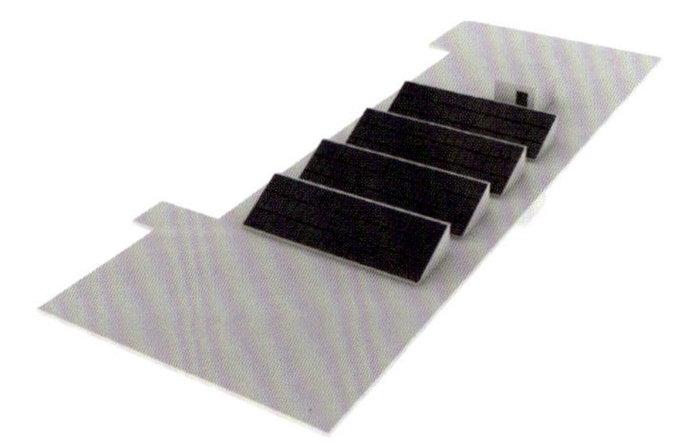

Photovoltaic panel detail

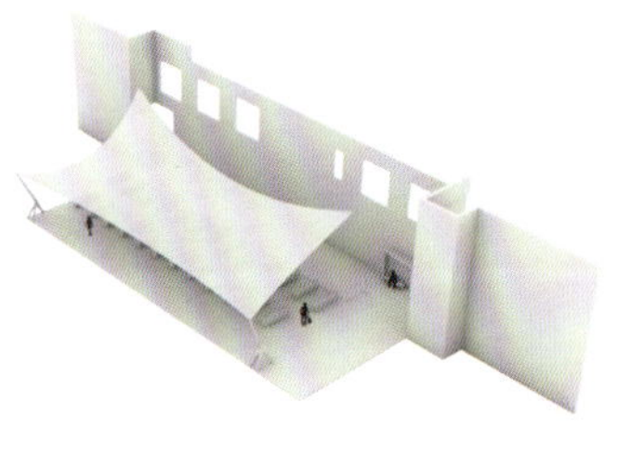

Butterfly garden canopy detail

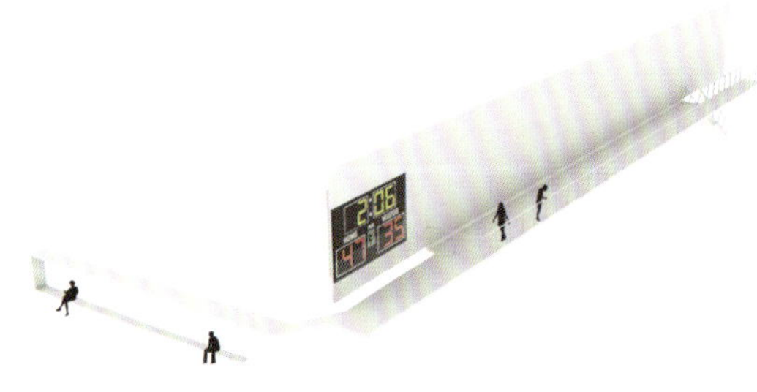

Scoreboard detail

BUTTERFLIES AND FOOD

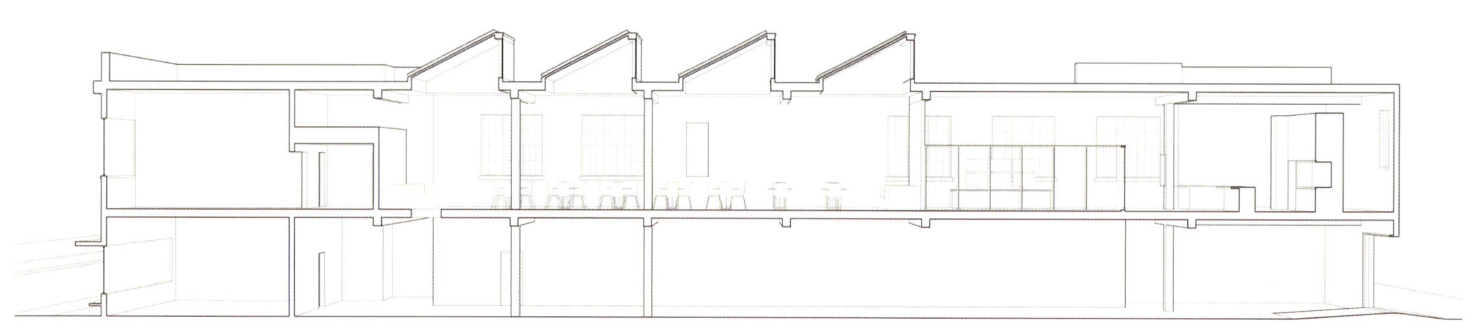

Longitudinal perspectival section

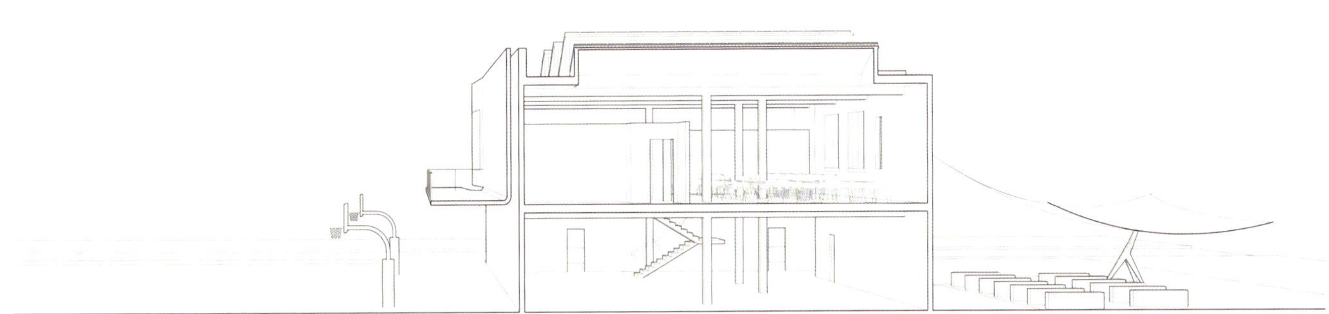

Transverse perspectival section

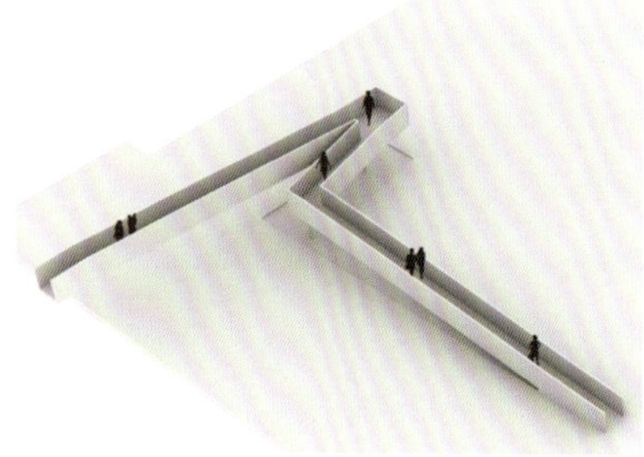

Lightwell courtyards, ramp and viewing platform, bird bath and feeders (left to right)

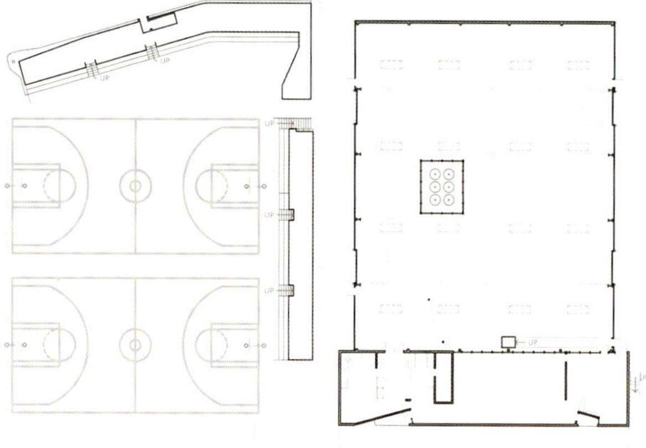

First-floor plan

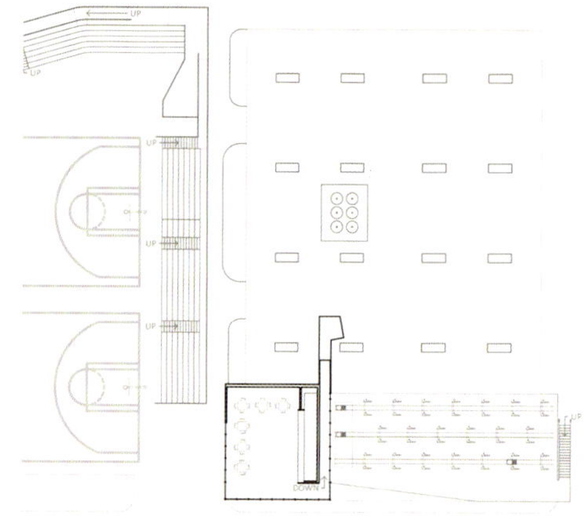

Second-floor plan

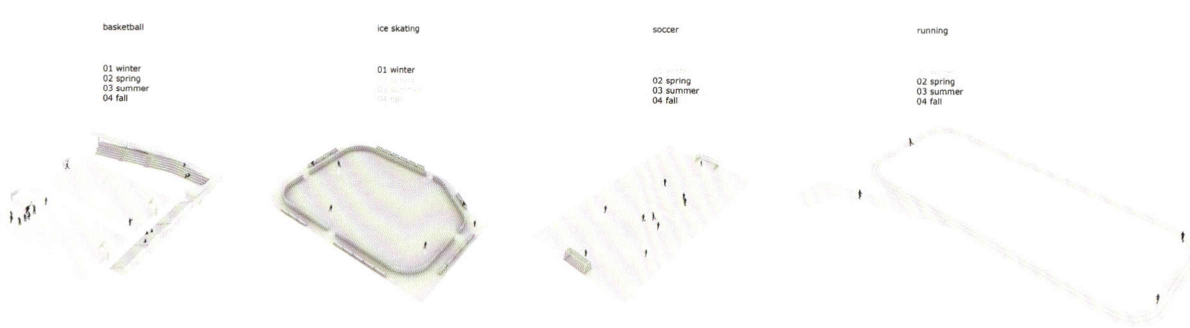

Play programmatic diagrams

BIRDS AND PLAY

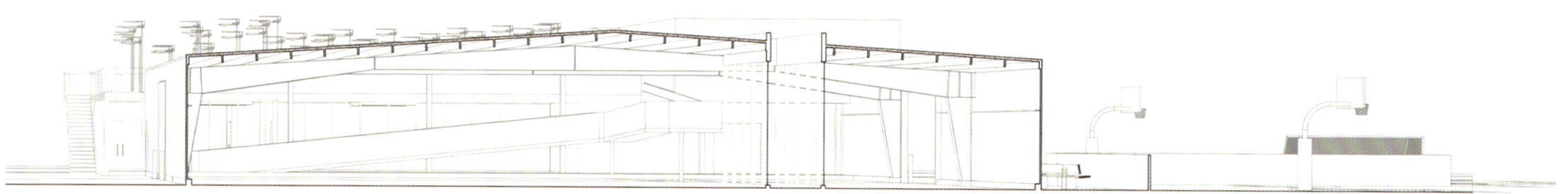

Transverse perspectival section

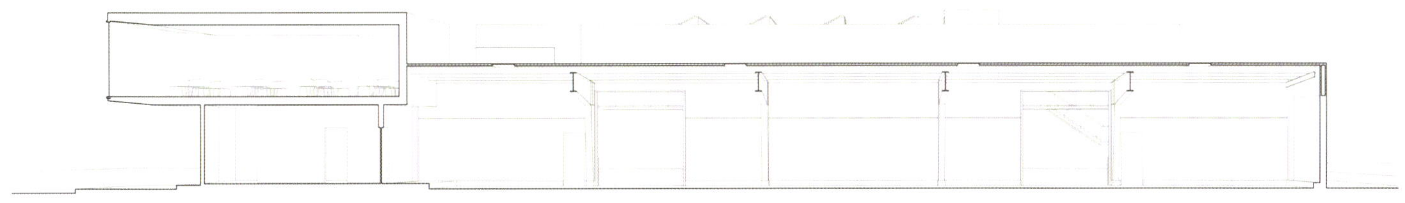

Longitudinal perspectival section

Site St. Louis, MO, United States

Status Schematic Design

Program Residential · Commercial

Client Olive West Development

WOLFNER LIBRARY REDEVELOPMENT

The first building to house what was once the Wolfner Memorial Library for the Blind was originally built in 1898 as the Lindell Exchange for the Bell Telephone Company and designed by Shepley, Rutan, and Coolidge. The second library building to the south was designed by Mauran, Russell, and Garden, and built in 1904. In 1938, the two buildings were repurposed and put into service as the first library for the blind, holding the largest braille book collection in the United States outside of the Library of Congress. The library served as a community gathering space for the blind from the 1950s to 1970s and eventually became a community space for all physically-disabled people. The surrounding landscape of the Wolfner Library will be integrated with a master plan developed by Tatiana Bilbao Studios.

A variety of small courtyard gardens, a large communal pool, and other amenities provide a public urban landscape for the residential community. The Wolfner Memorial Library buildings will be transformed into a new clubhouse for the Olive Street Development project in St. Louis' Grand Center neighborhood. The design aims to create a focal point within the community that enlivens the neighborhood and nurtures new and old relationships alike. The multi-level garden space along the south façade pays respect to the history of the original courtyard, which once served as a place of respite to the many occupants of the telephone company, library, and community center. The design considers various microclimatic conditions such as solar and terrestrial radiation, wind, air temperature, humidity, and precipitation to make the spaces thermally comfortable and encourage outdoor activities.

Multi-level garden sections and material diagrams

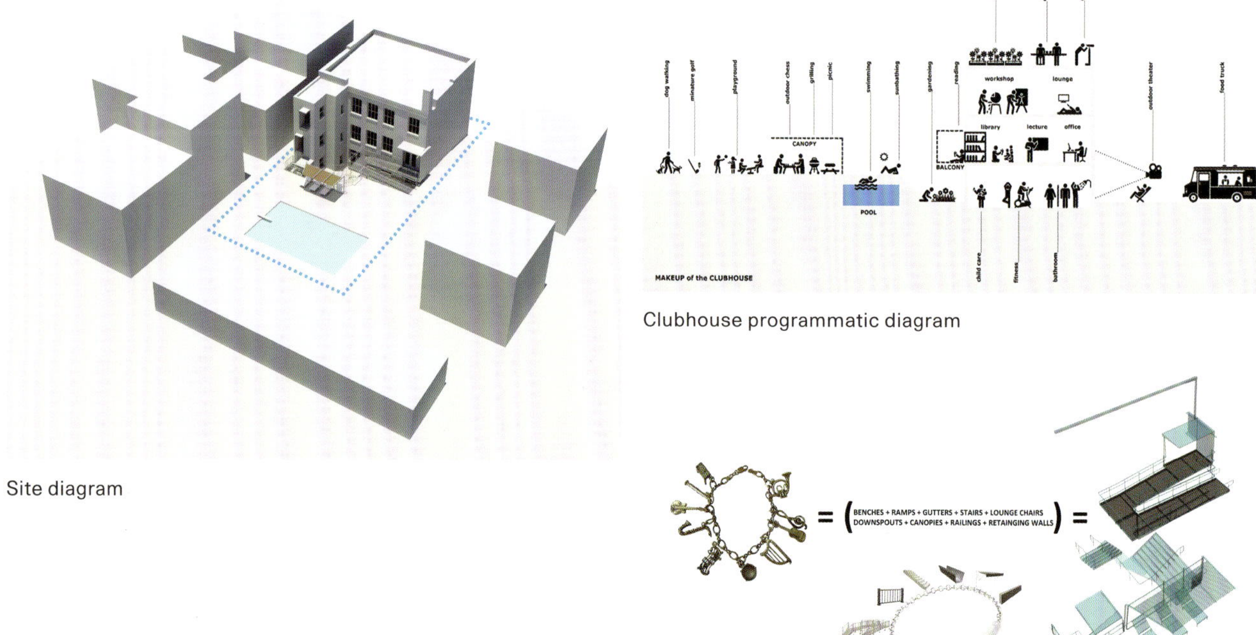

Site diagram

Clubhouse programmatic diagram

Jewel component diagram

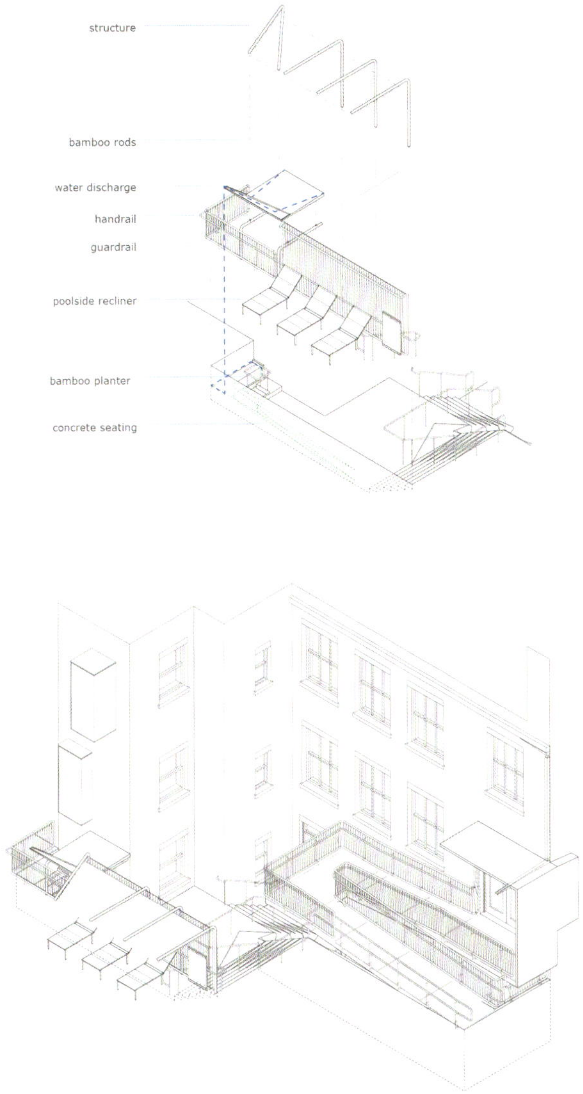

structure
bamboo rods
water discharge
handrail
guardrail
poolside recliner
bamboo planter
concrete seating

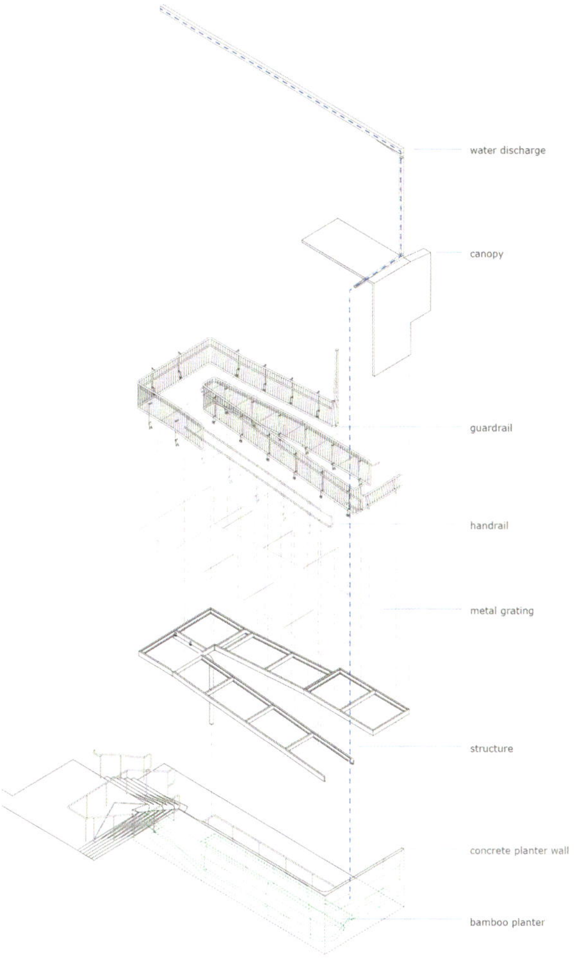

water discharge
canopy
guardrail
handrail
metal grating
structure
concrete planter wall
bamboo planter

Exploded water infrastructure axon of canopy and poolside recliners (above), overall axon of the integrated performance infrastructure (below)

Exploded water infrastructure axon of canopy and ramp

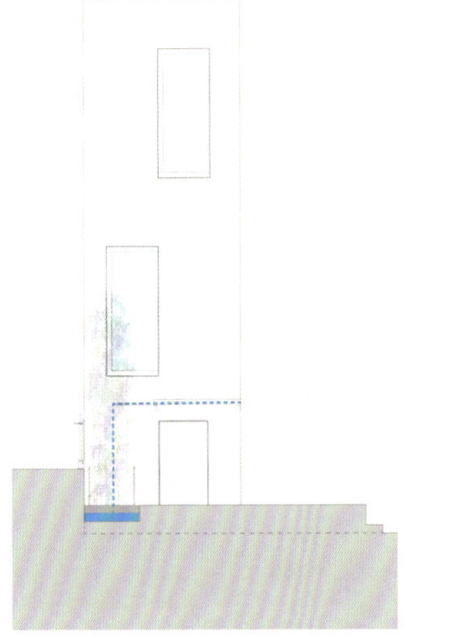

Multi-level garden sections

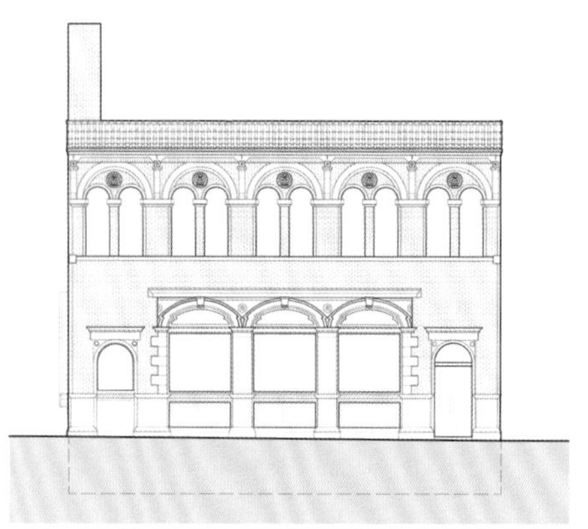

North elevation

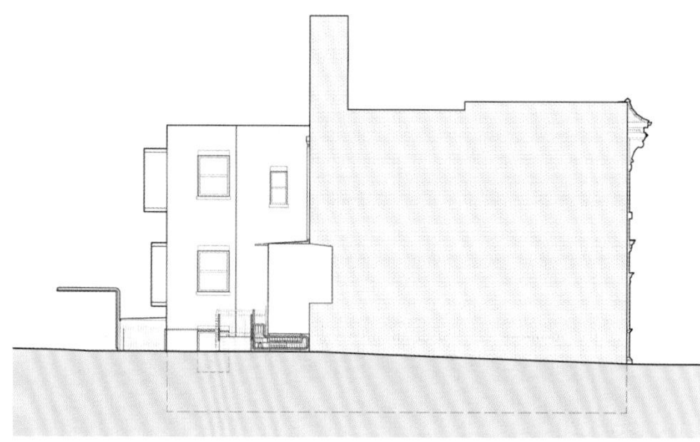

East elevation

South elevation

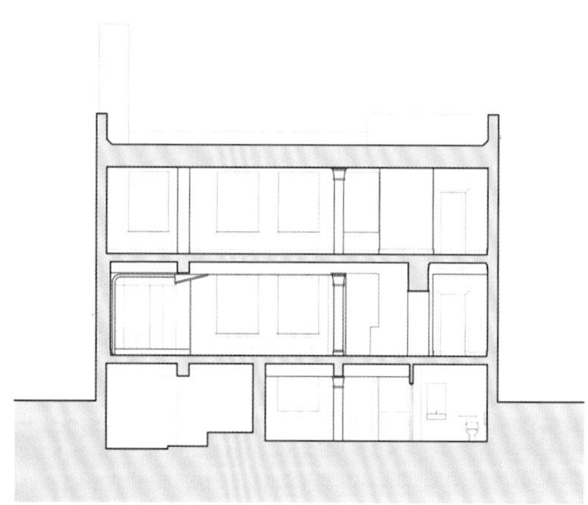

West elevation

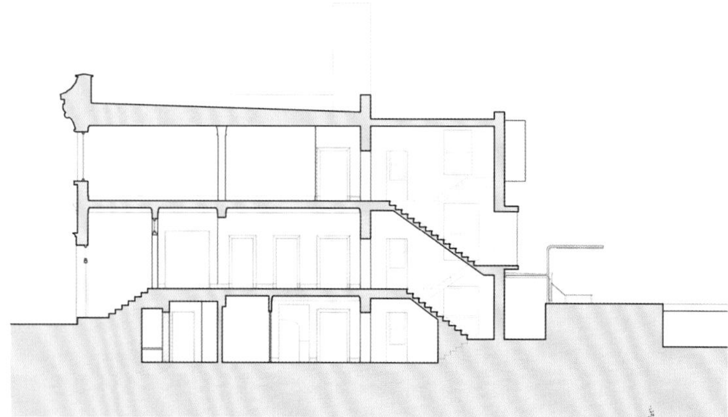

Longitudinal section 01

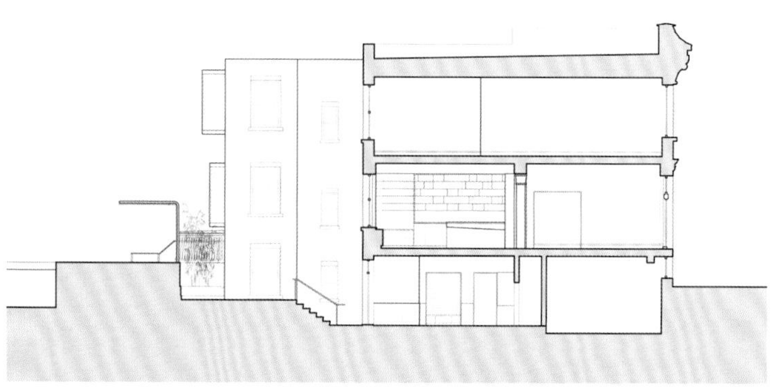

Longitudinal section 02

WOLFNER MEMORIAL LIBRARY MOVIE NIGHT

Site St. Louis, MO, United States

Status Conceptual Design

Program Landscape · Urbanism

Client Lawrence Group

LENS BRIDGE AND URBAN DECK

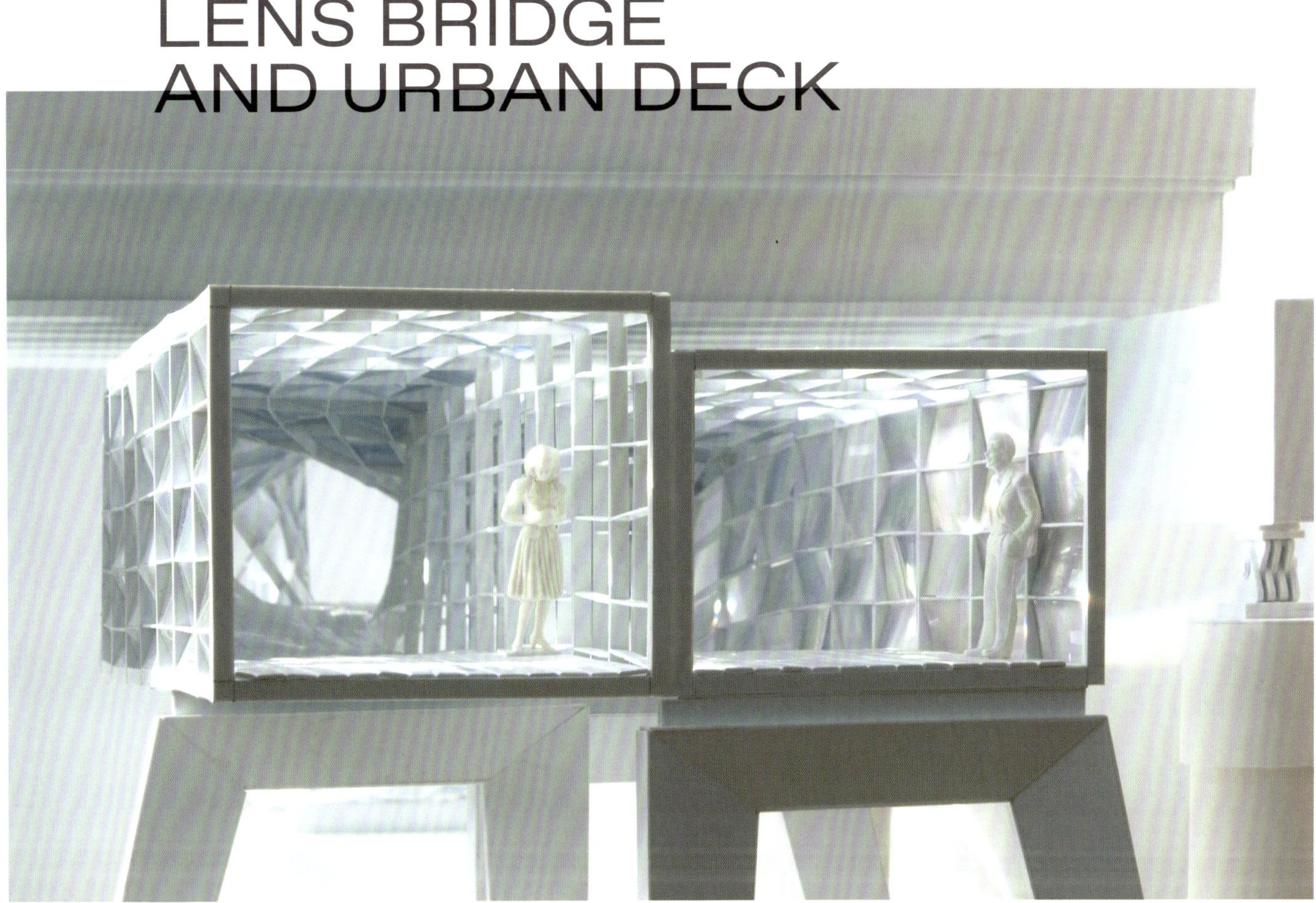

Lens Bridge and Urban Deck form the central artery to the City Foundry Redevelopment project, a mixed-use food court and shopping complex that links the entertainment district to the St. Louis Armory. The redevelopment project functions as a network of nodes along the Brickline Greenway pedestrian project, which transformed St. Louis into a walkable and bikeable city. Lens Bridge spans two elevated interstate highways. It is clad with dichromatic and Fresnel lenses to produce split colors and light collimations. These lenses generate optical perceptions of magnification that heighten the visual phenomena of the site. Urban Deck, in contrast, is part of the landscape and is conceived as an extension of the ground surface that transforms the topographic landscape into a recreational complex. Together, Lens Bridge and Urban Deck comprise an infrastructural project that engages the public in dialogue with the engineering, architecture, landscape, and environmental science that influence their design. This project is generated as a new destination within a fragmented urban condition, one that brings a larger inquiry into civic discourse.

Lens Bridge is an urban gateway visible from I-64 to east- and westbound motorists. An engineered and filtered gutter system directs polluted runoff from the highway while rainwater flows into retention ponds surrounded by remediating gardens populated with regional plant species. The pedestrian bridge twists between the highways to allow vertical space for semi-truck clearance heading east and expands into LED screens visible to westbound motorists. In the City Foundry district, the bridge transforms into a stage for an amphitheater, while its canopy merges into a suspended vegetative grove that generates microclimatic conditions and offers shade. The amphitheater seating area is designed to function as both a farmers' market and a performance space.

Urban Deck is a community recreation center with a pool and basketball and racquetball courts interwoven with running tracks and public amenities including bathrooms, showers, playgrounds, gardens, and food stalls. In the evening, the upper deck becomes a dance hall and an outdoor cinema, stimulating nightlife and promoting density for new development projects along the pedestrian paths.

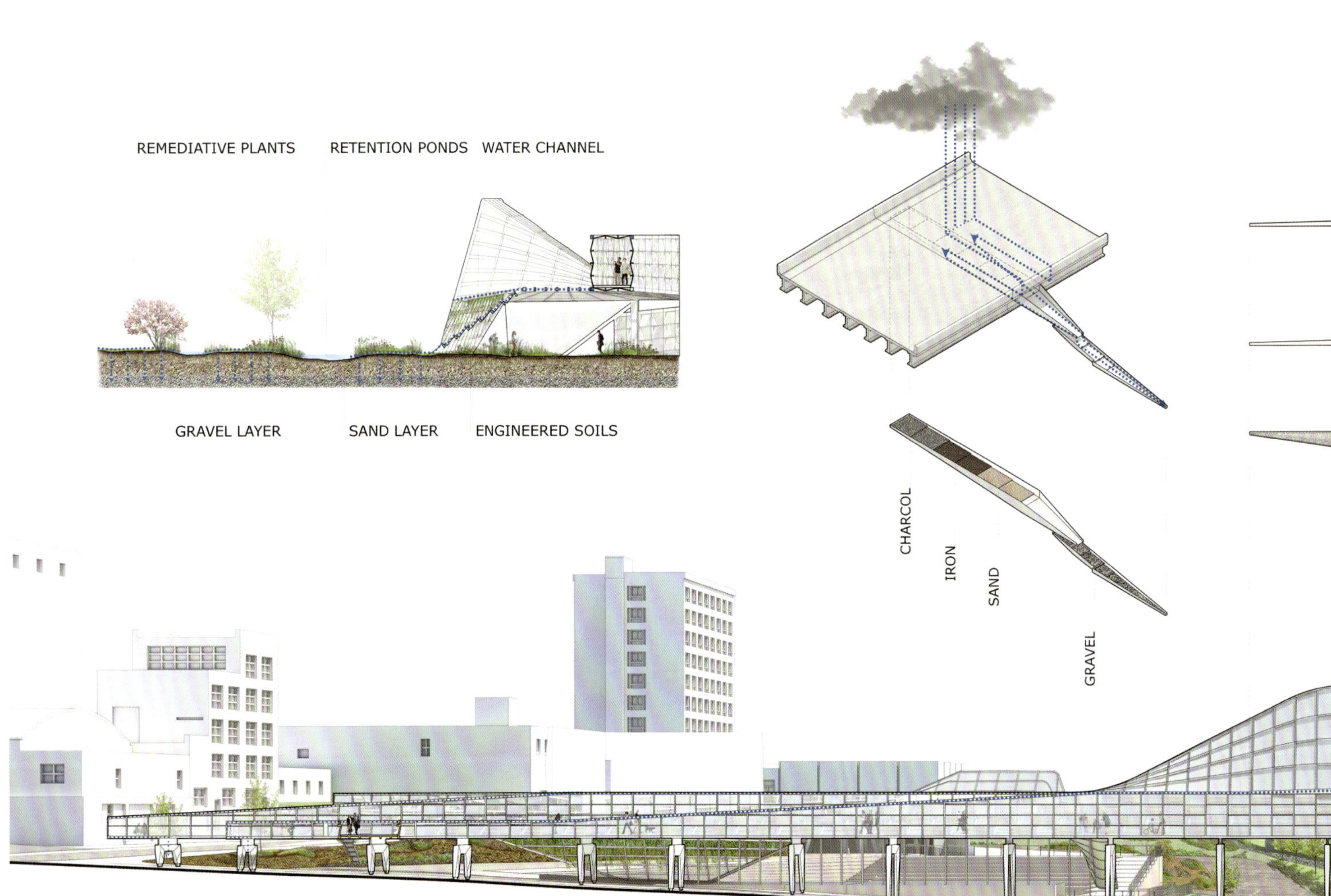

Lens Bridge water infrastructure systems diagrams

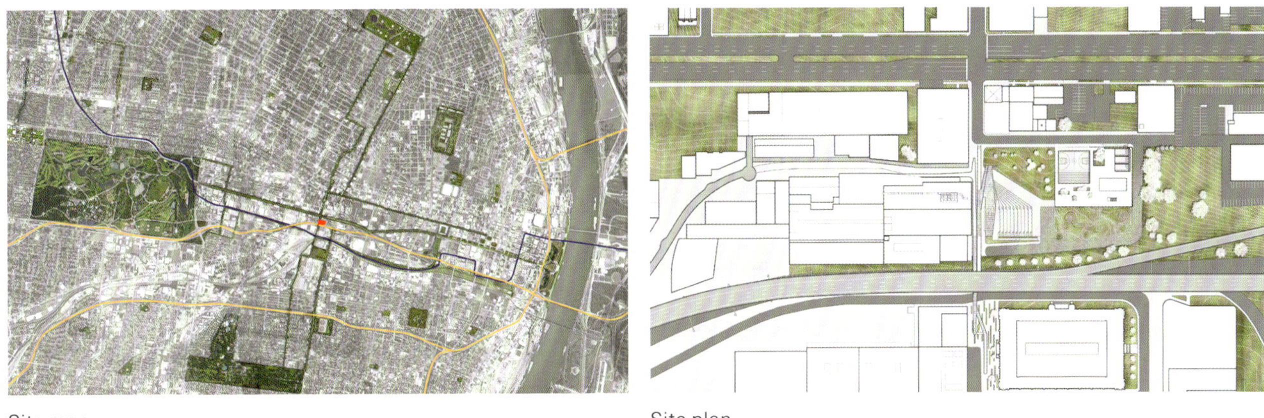

Site map

Site plan

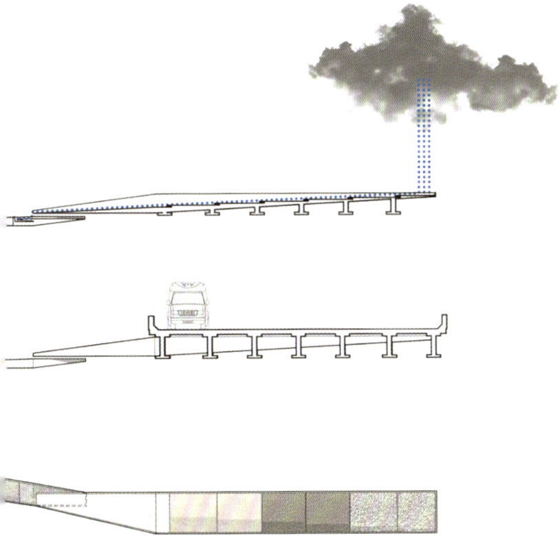

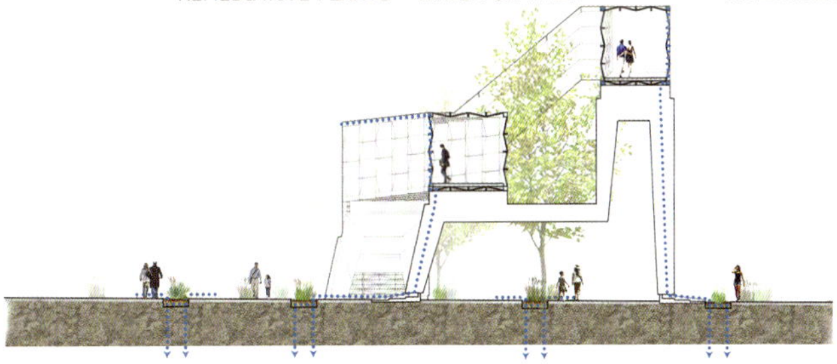

REMEDIATIVE PLANTS WATER CHANNEL

RETENTION GARDEN

CONCRETE PAVEMENT

GROUND

FOOTING

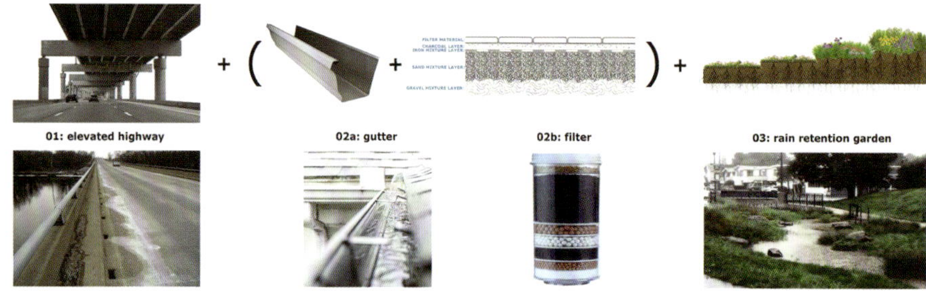

Lens Bridge gutter diagram

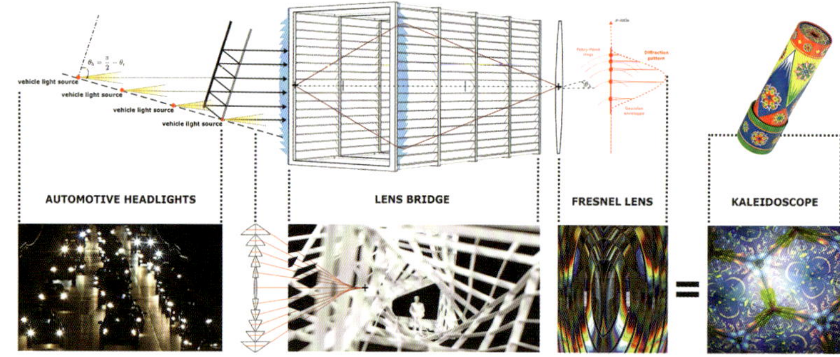

Lens Bridge performance diagram

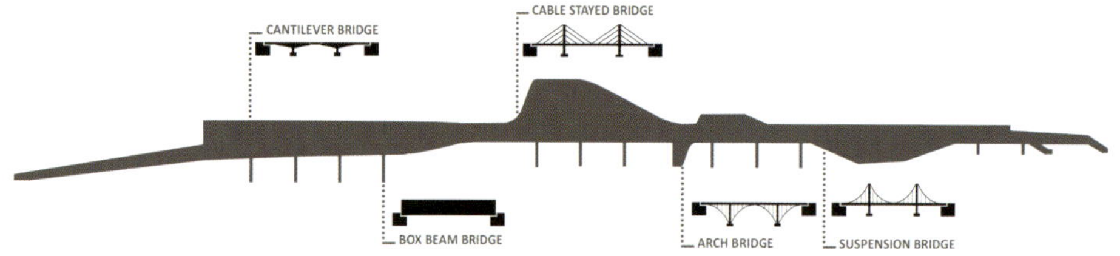

Lens Bridge structural iconogram

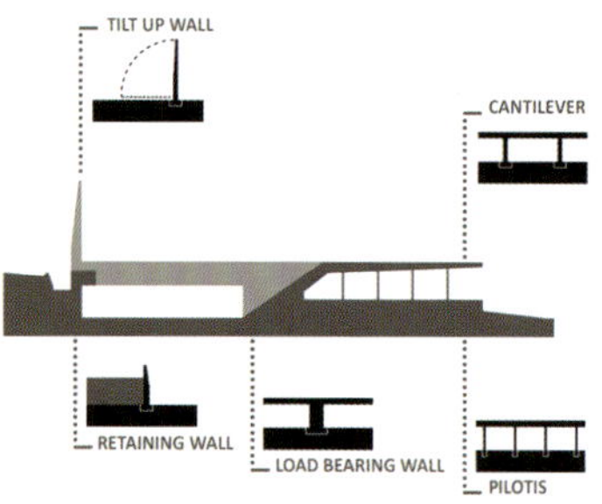

Urban Deck structural iconogram

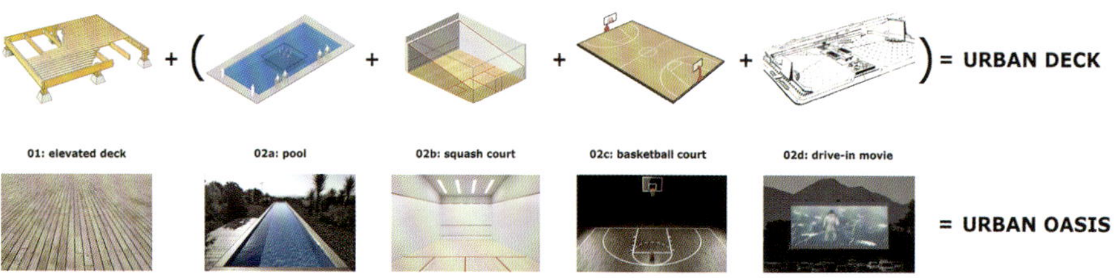

Urban Deck function diagram

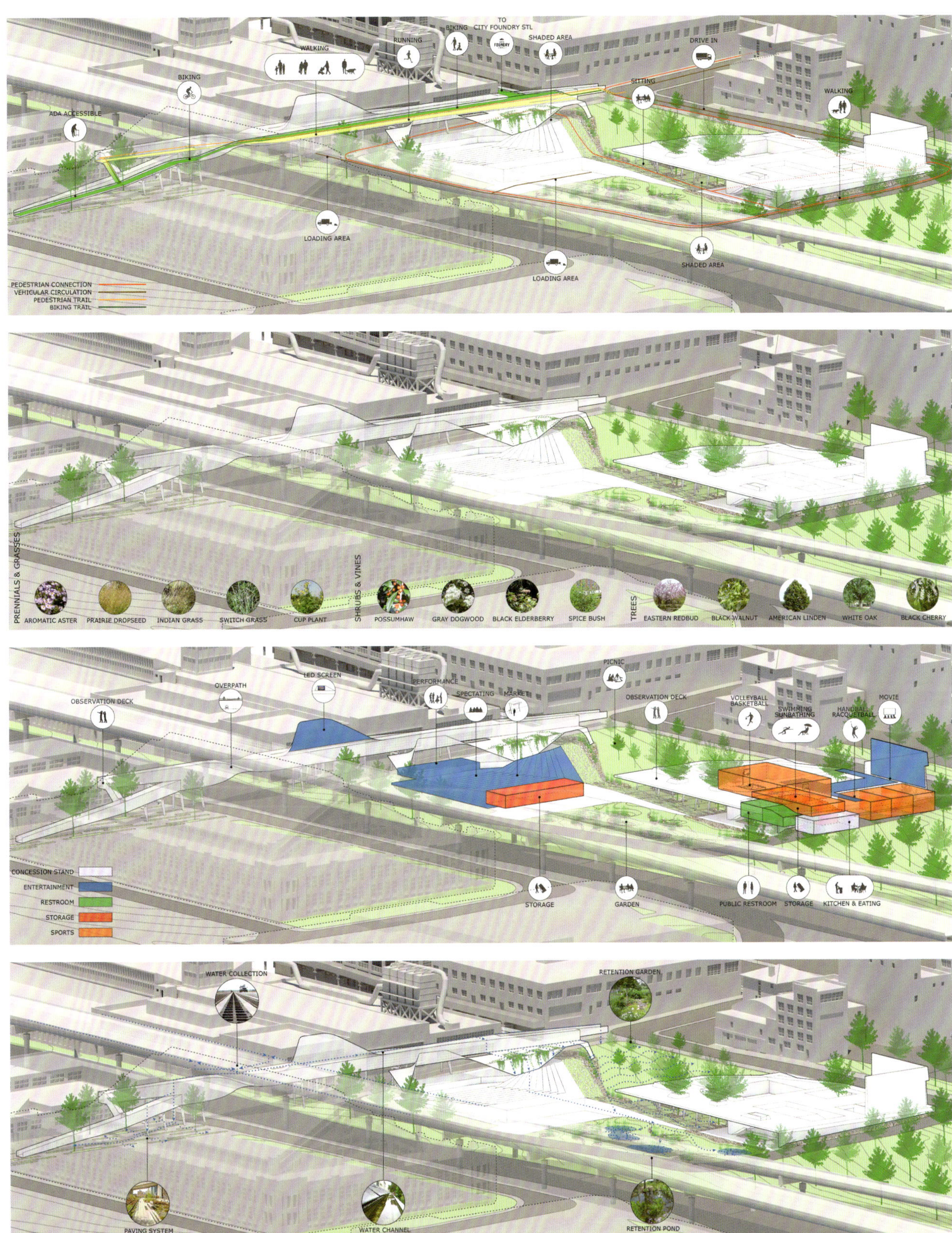

Pedestrian and vehicular flow, planting strategy, programmatic function, water retention strategy (top to bottom)

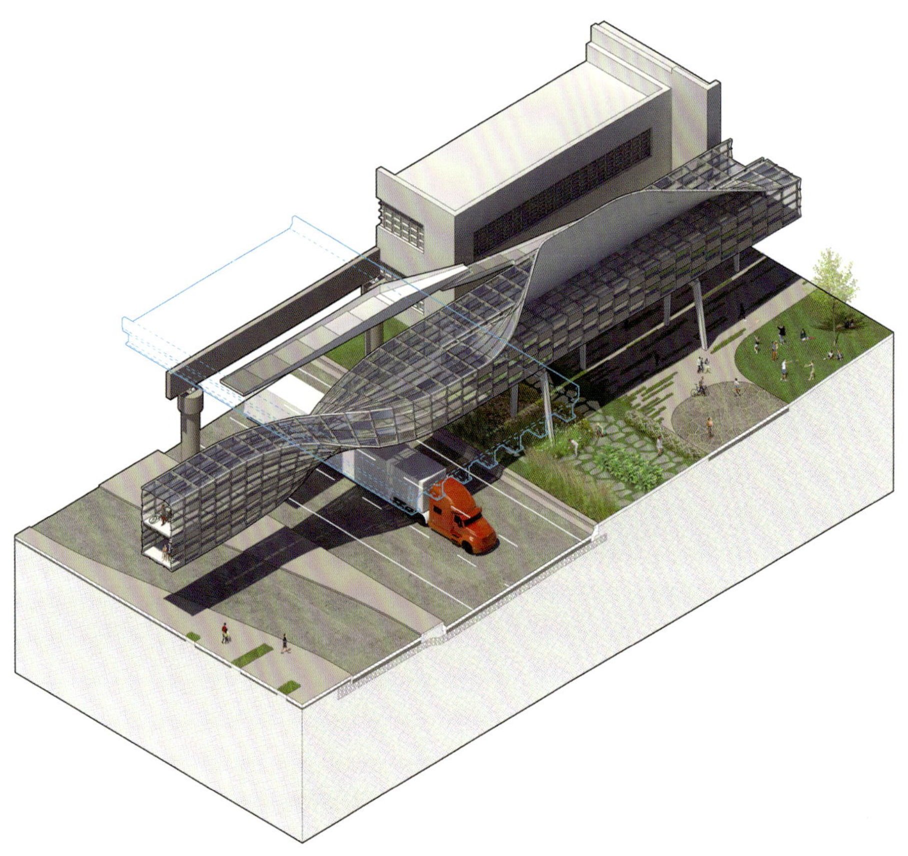

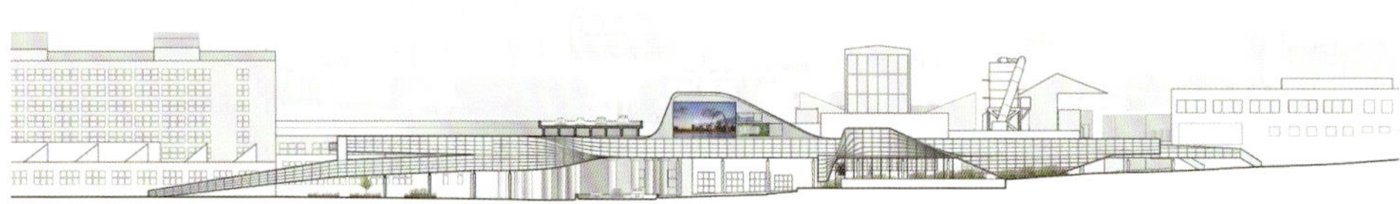

Lens Bridge eastbound elevation

Lens Bridge westbound elevation

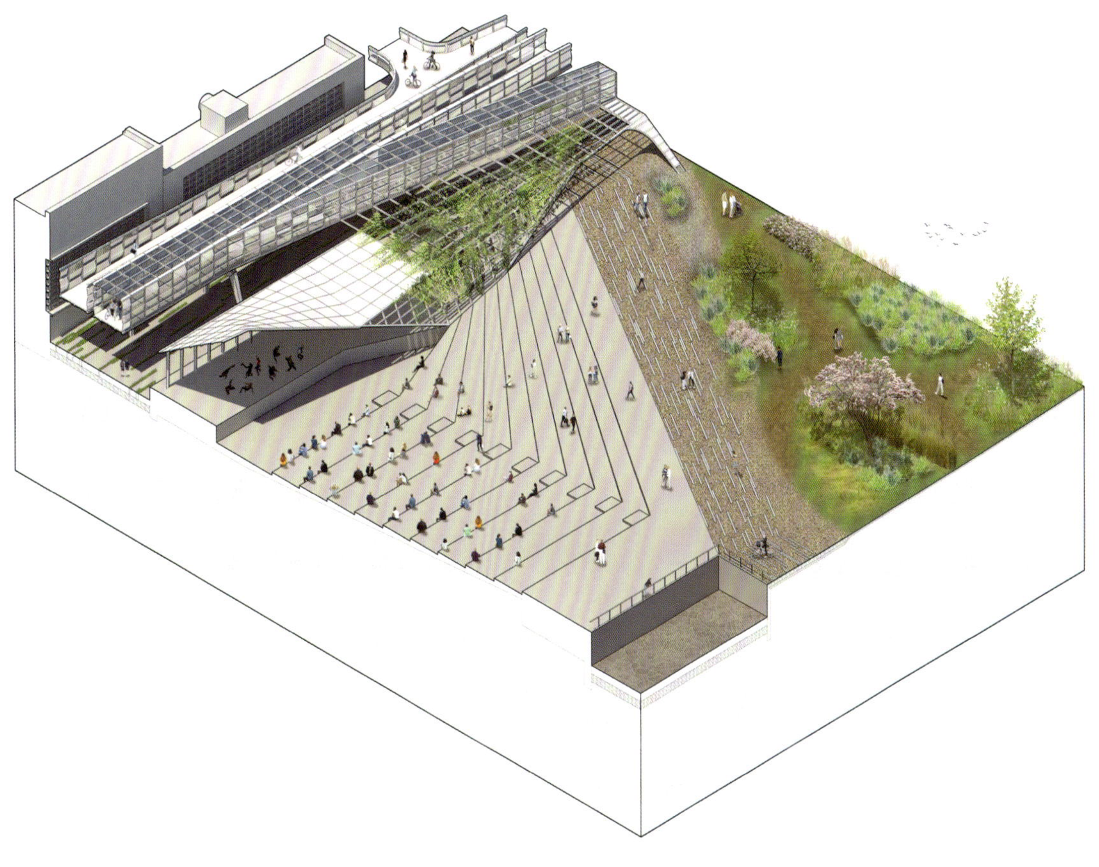

Lens Bridge eastbound section

Lens Bridge westbound section

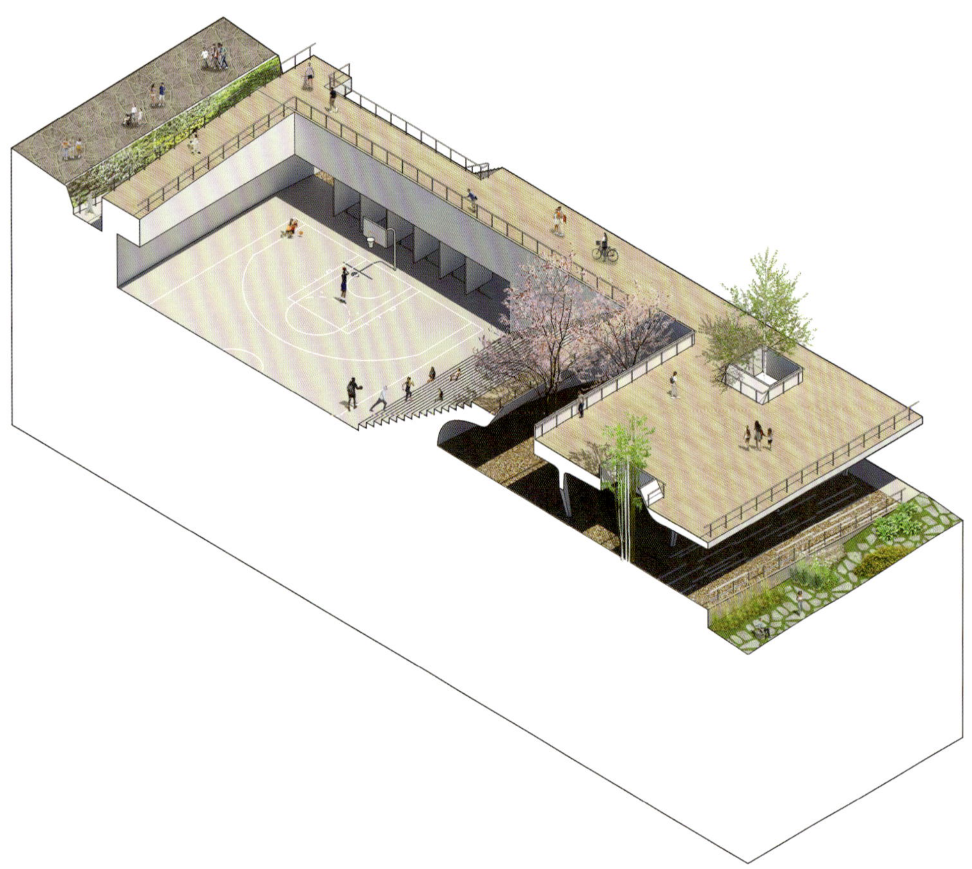

01

02

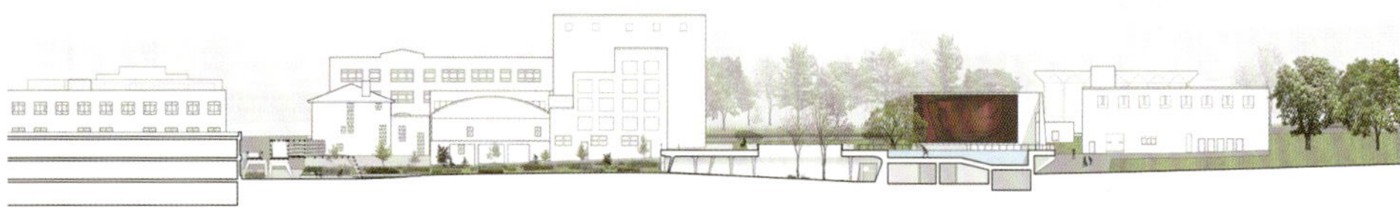

03

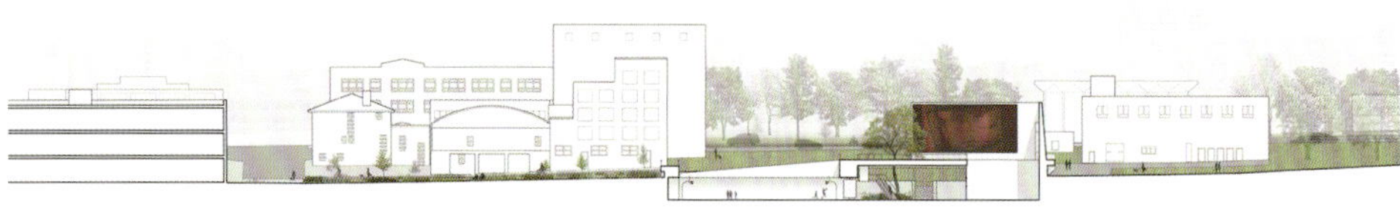

Lens Bridge and Urban Deck northbound sections 01 – 03

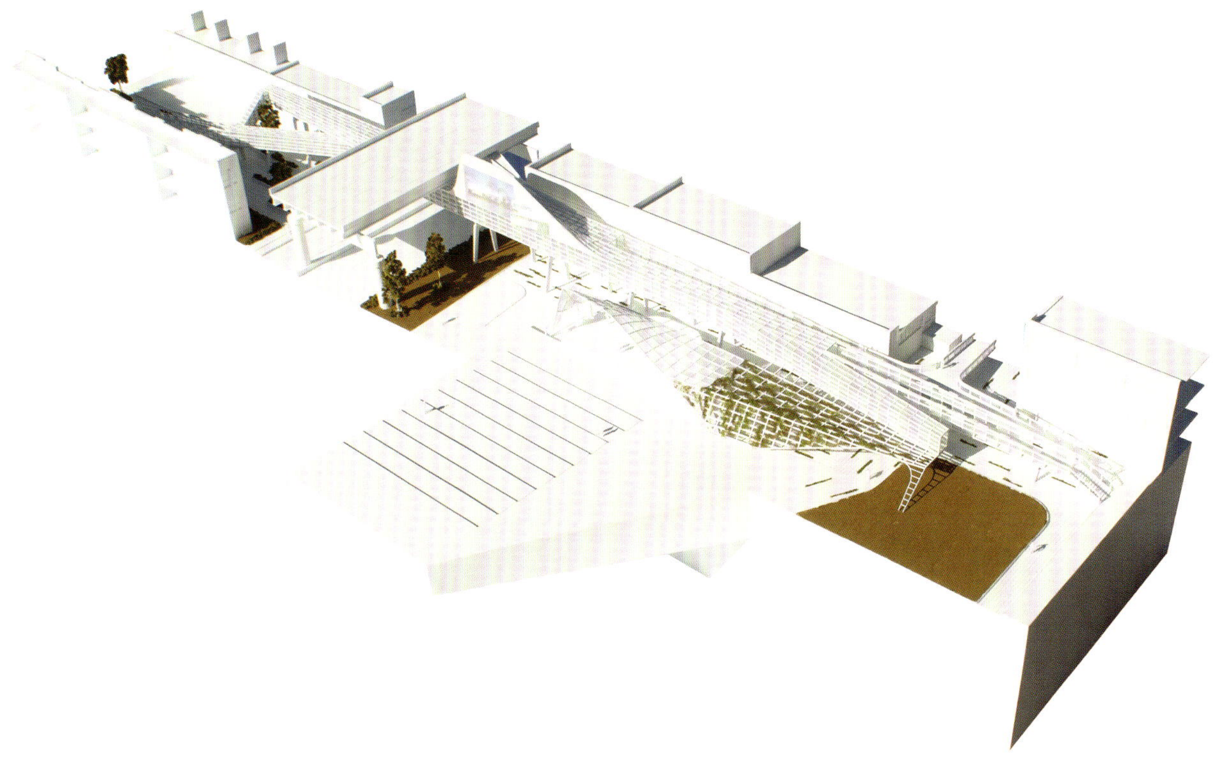

01

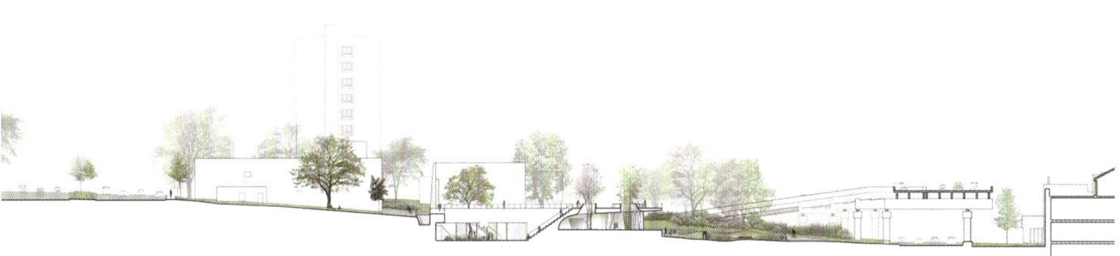

02

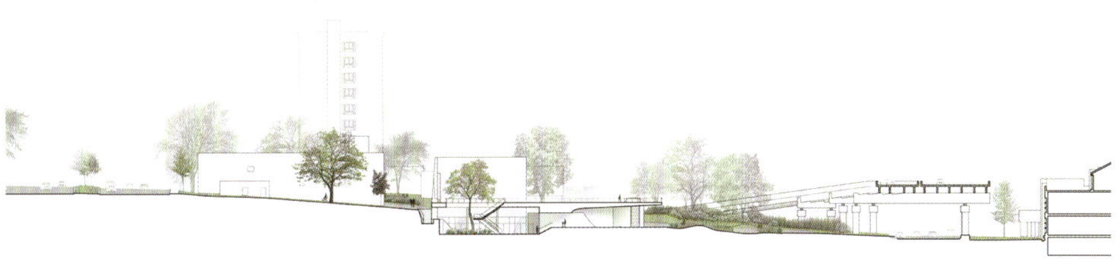

03

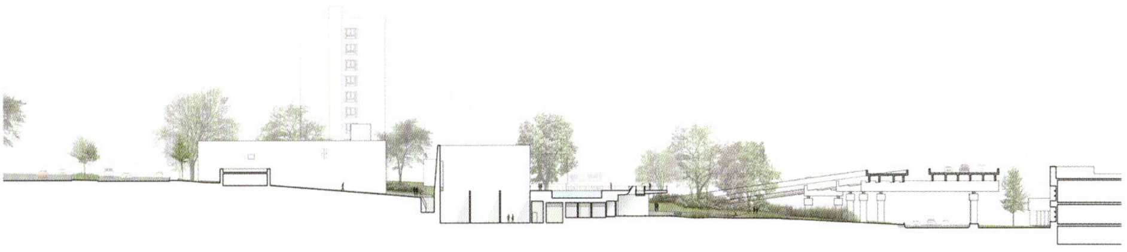

Lens Bridge and Urban Deck eastbound sections 01 – 03

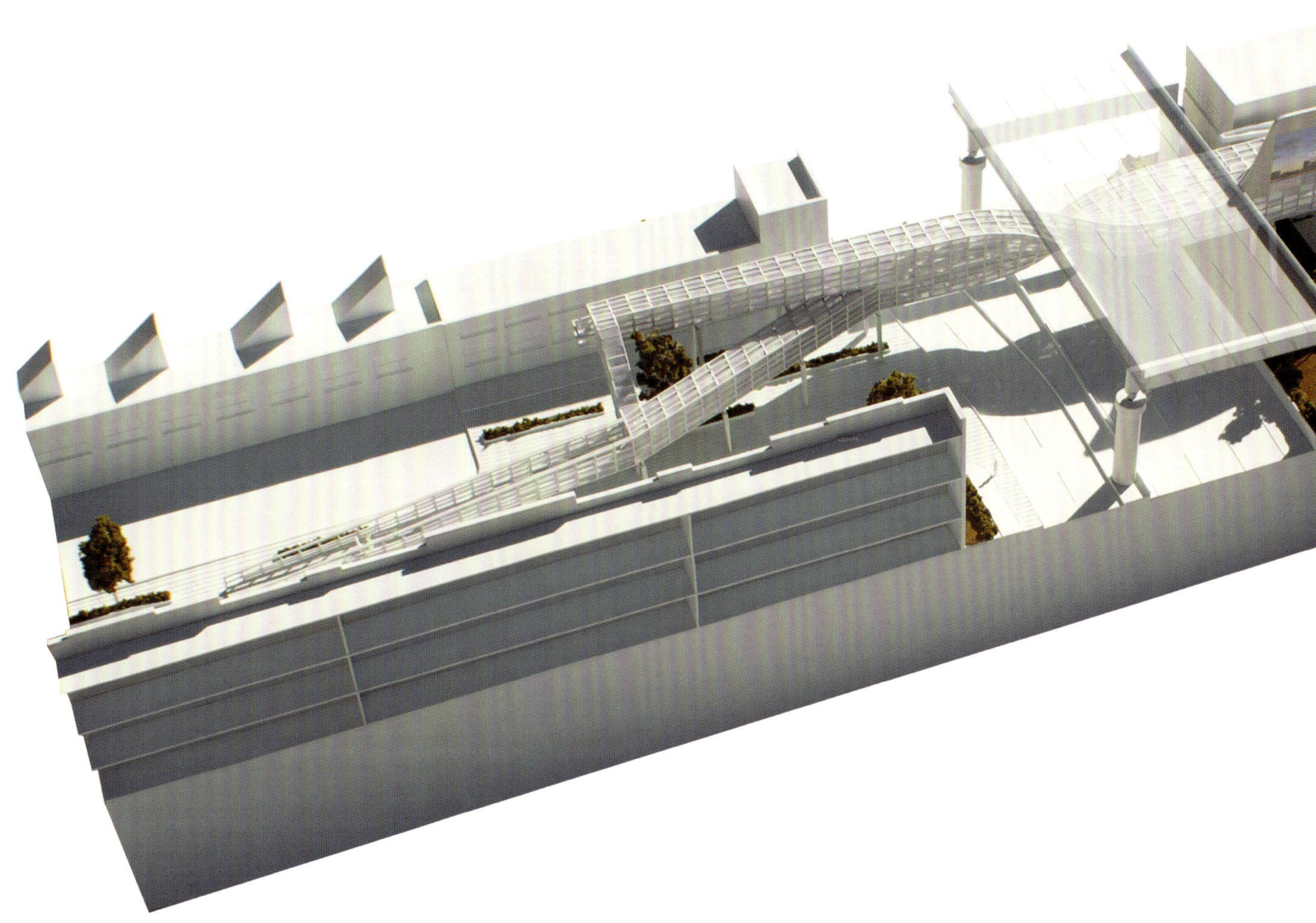

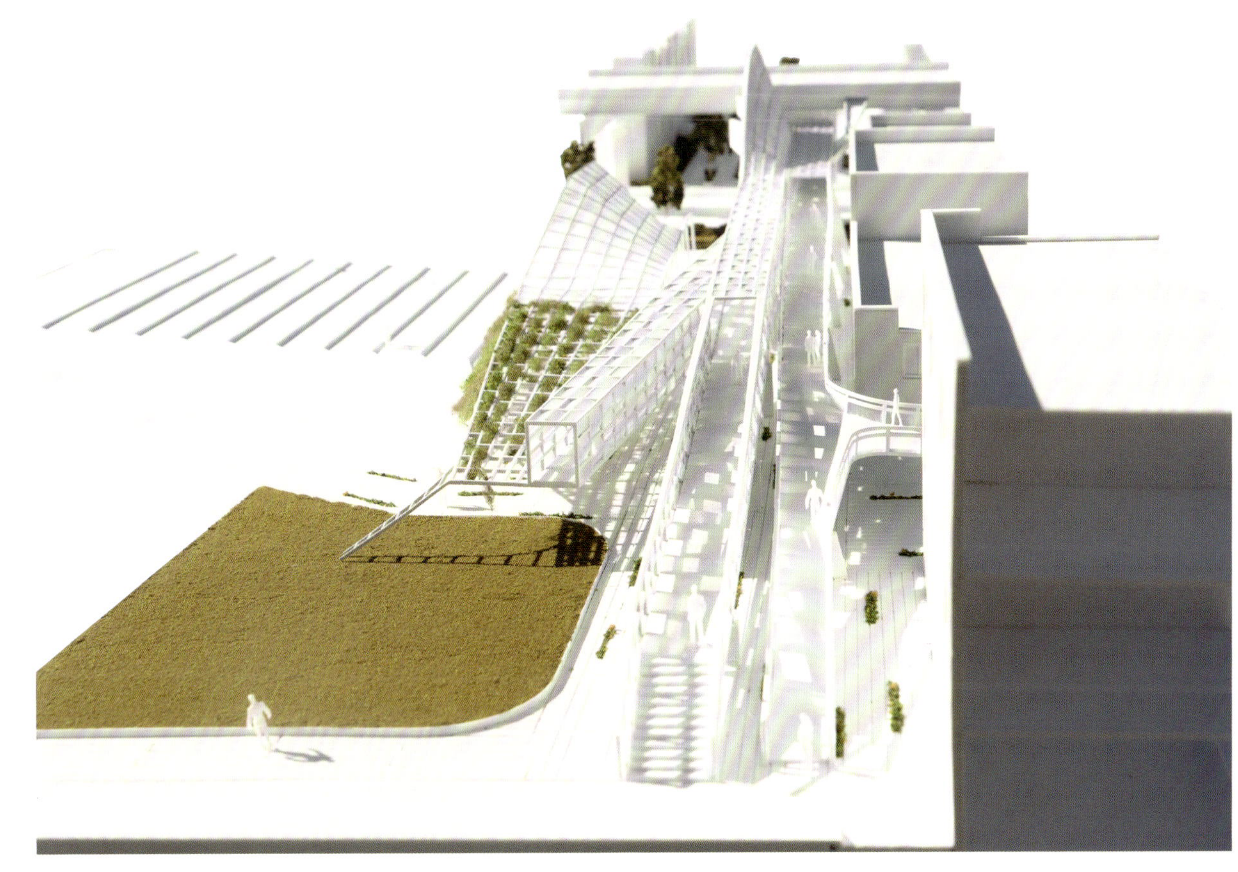

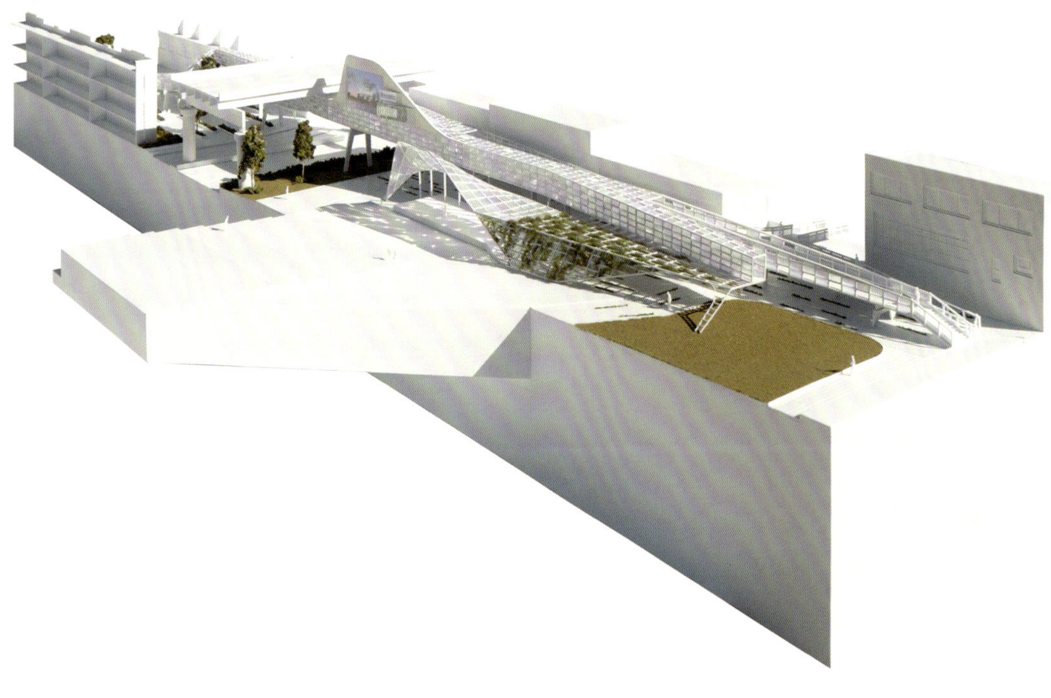

ST. LOUIS
STL
FARMERS
MARKET
ALLIANCE

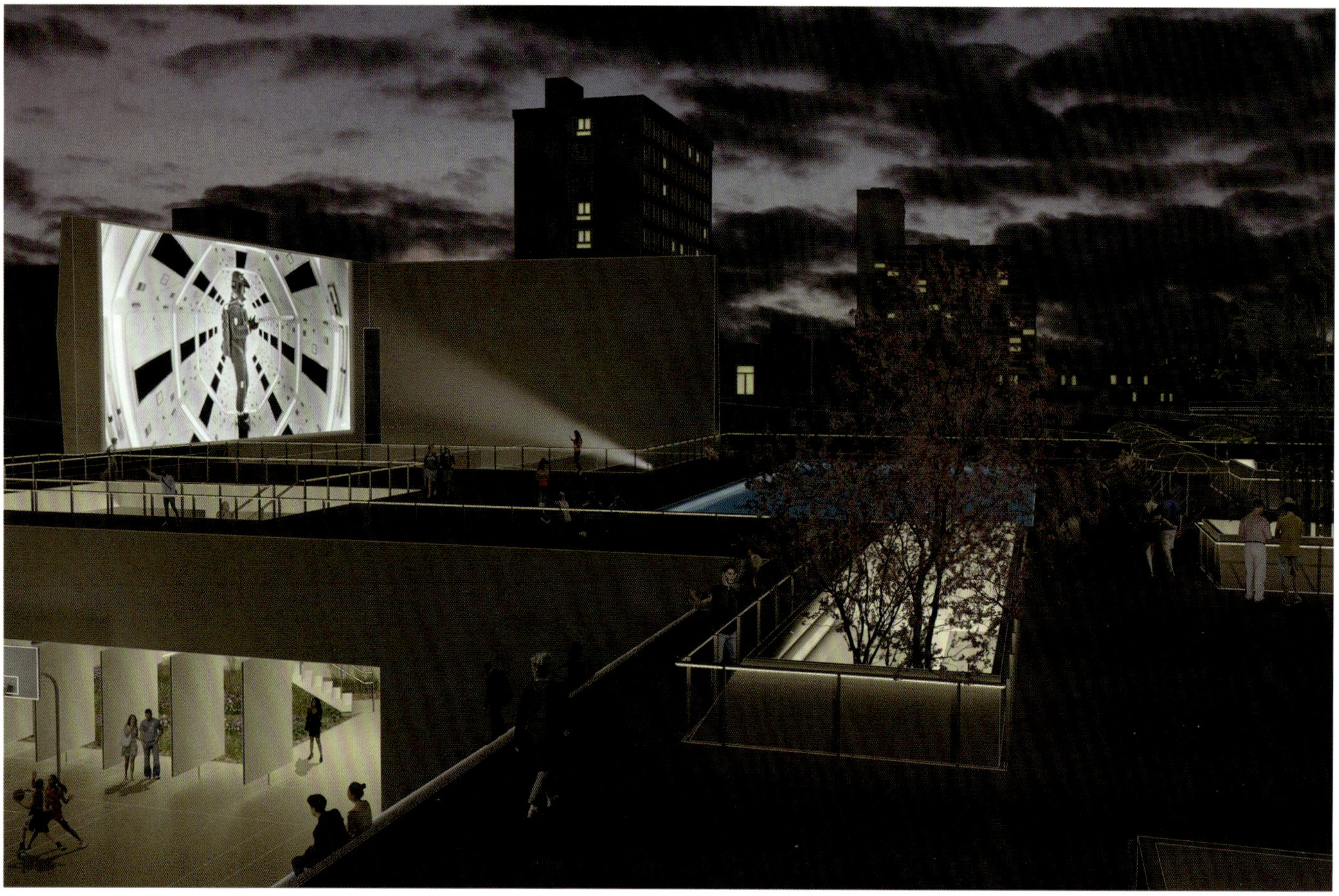

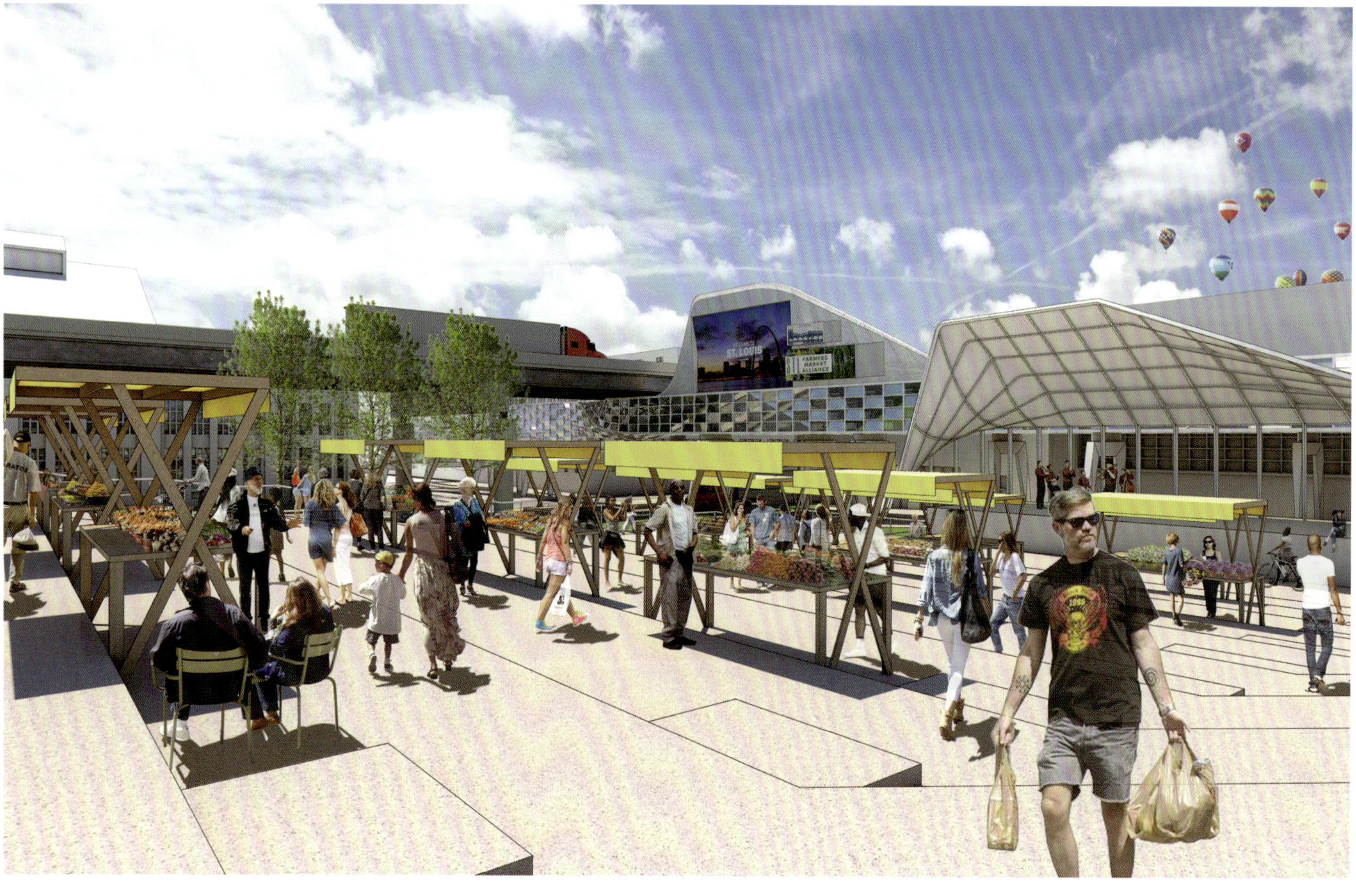

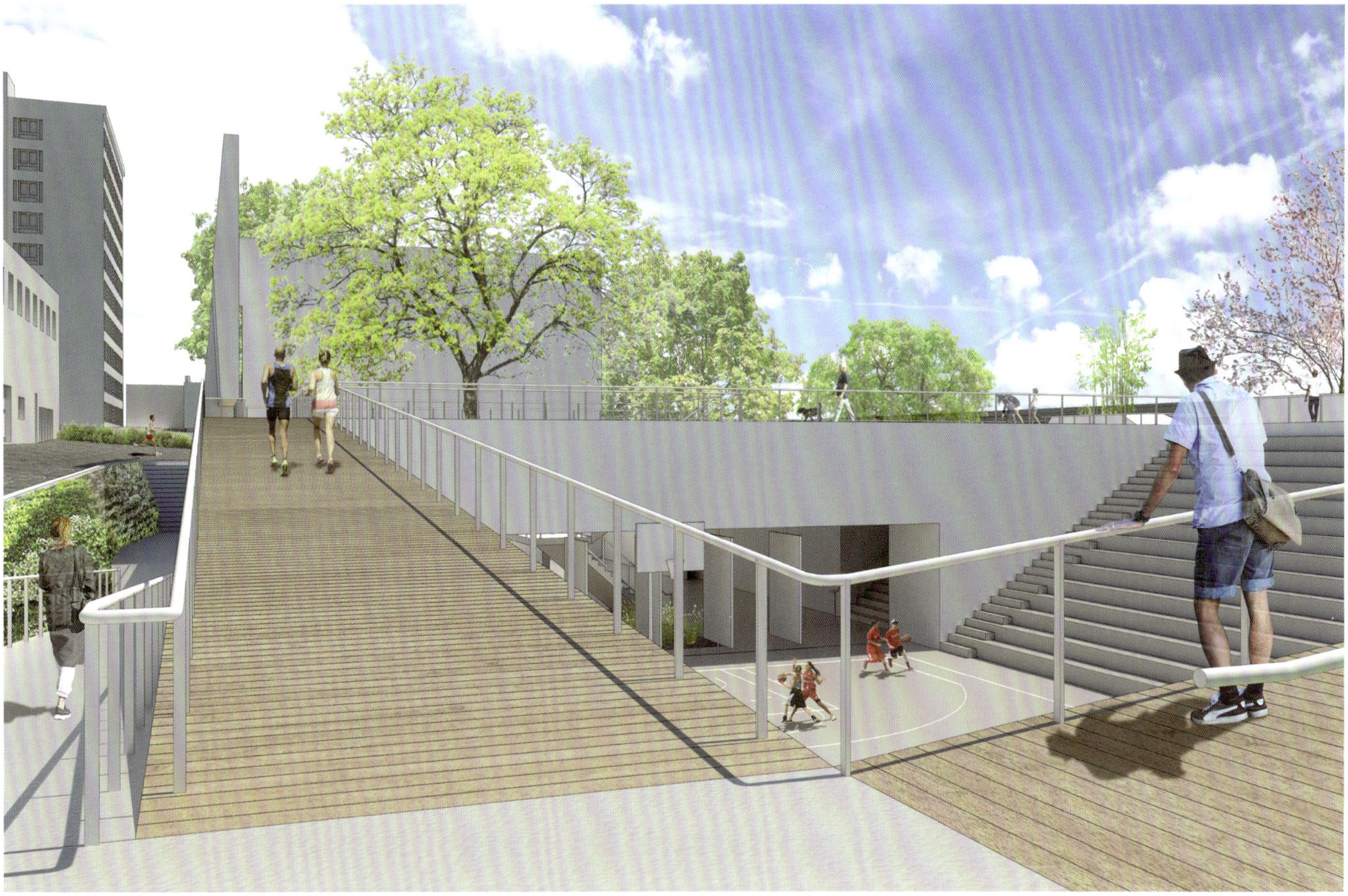

Site Clayton, MO, United States

Status Under Construction

Program Residential

Client Hager and Ford Family

NORTHWOOD RENOVATION

Northwood Residence is a renovation of a three-story brick condominium building built in 1925. Each floor is an individual residential unit. The client, a young family of three, owns the first and second floors and wished to combine the two units into a two-story apartment better suited to their daily lives. The project embraces a contemporary lifestyle where family activities are no longer restricted to individual rooms; instead, an open-plan design strategy enables fluid circulation. However, this also means that the load-bearing walls segregating the spaces of the original plan no longer support the family's daily functions.

The existing apartment floor is divided into three zones by load-bearing walls that run parallel to the length of the building. Maneuvering through these zones requires moving through the doorways and thresholds that punctuate the walls. The renovation design introduces a new foyer corridor on the first floor that connects the front and back entrances. It also opens up common spaces, which are integrated with the kitchen to create space to entertain guests, and introduces a new staircase at the center of the open floor plan to modulate light. On the second floor are the private spaces: a master bedroom suite, a second bedroom, and a family room. In response to the closet spaces lost in the demolition process, the new walls of the renovation are thickened to serve as both partitions and storage apparatuses. As built-in furniture, the walls also function as an armature for new plumbing, electrical, and ventilation systems. As partitions, they articulate daylight and views across the space, creating layers of transparency.

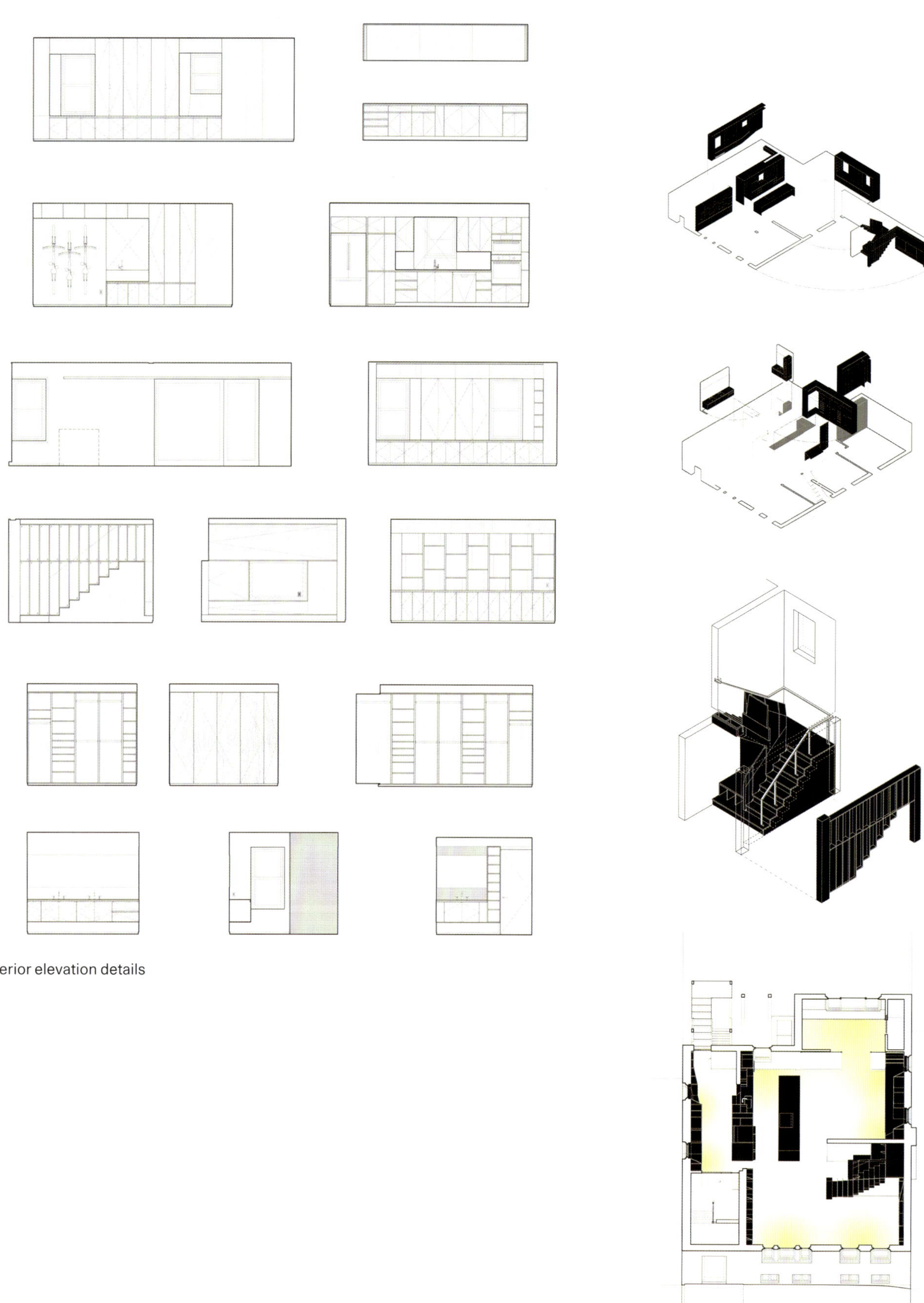

Interior elevation details

First-floor built-in armature diagram, stair diagram, second-floor built-in armature diagram, first-floor light diagram (top to bottom)

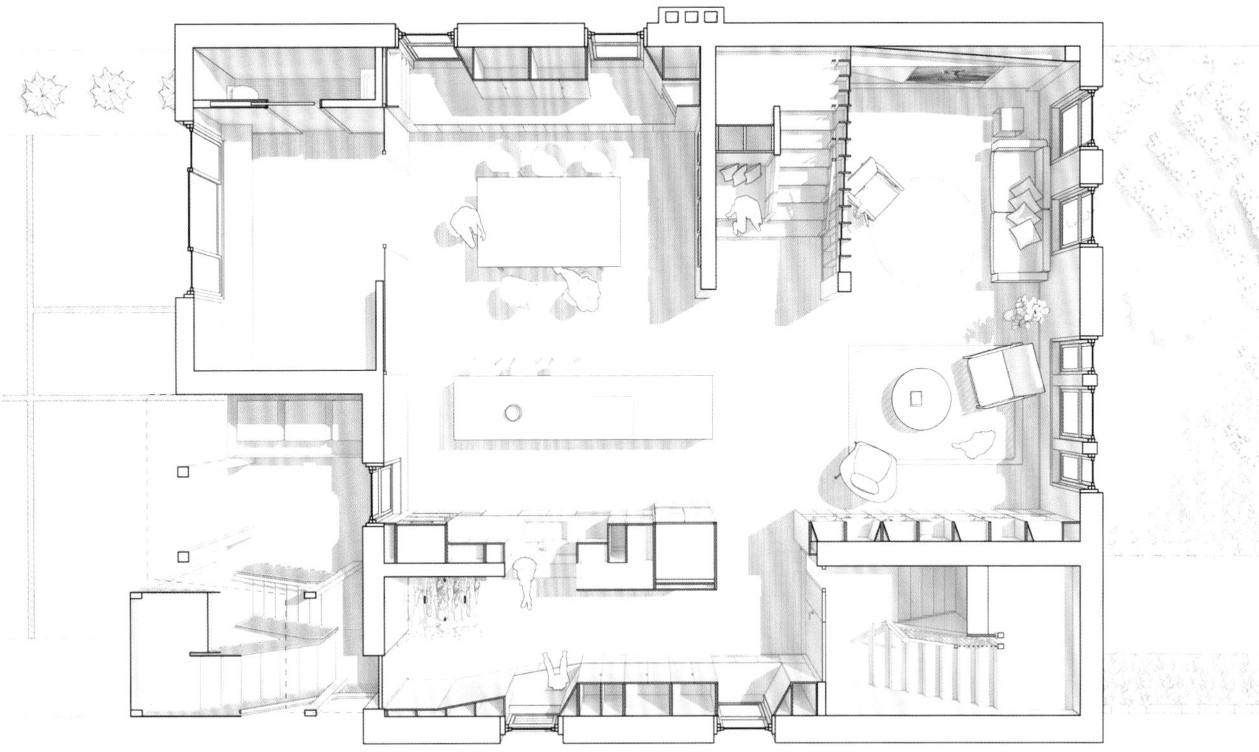

First-floor perspectival plan

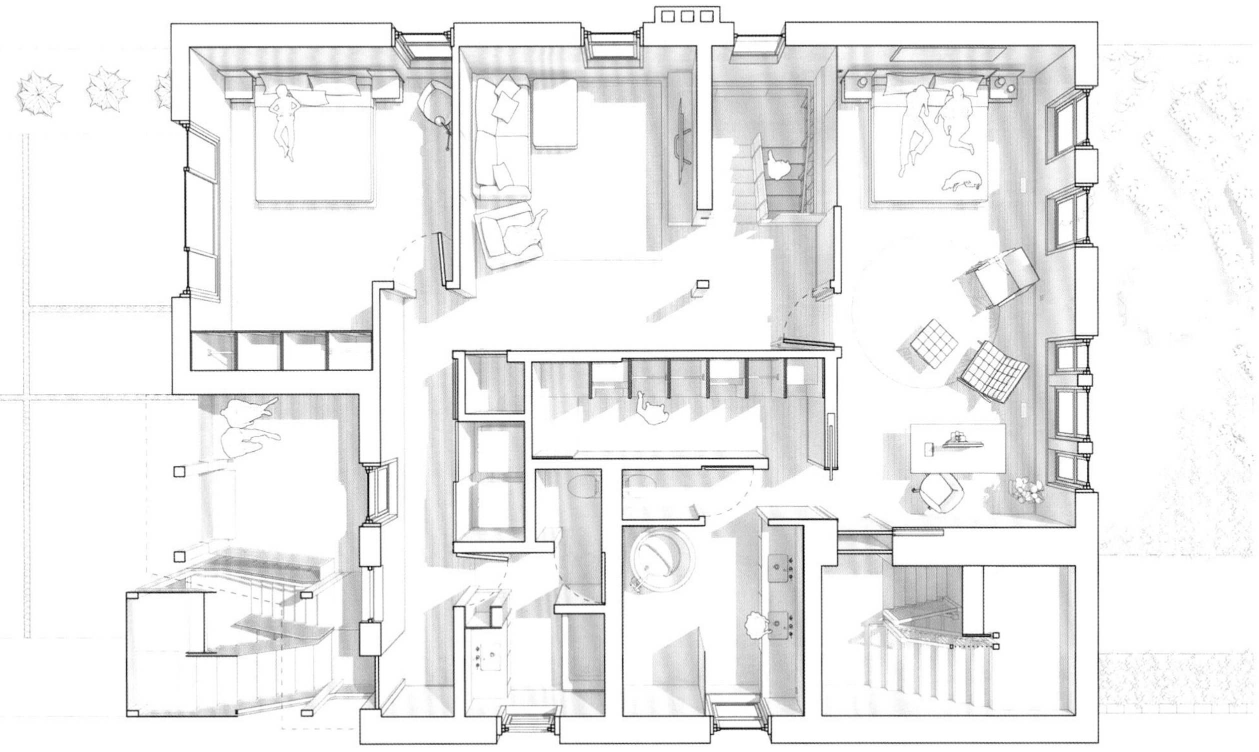

Second-floor perspectival plan

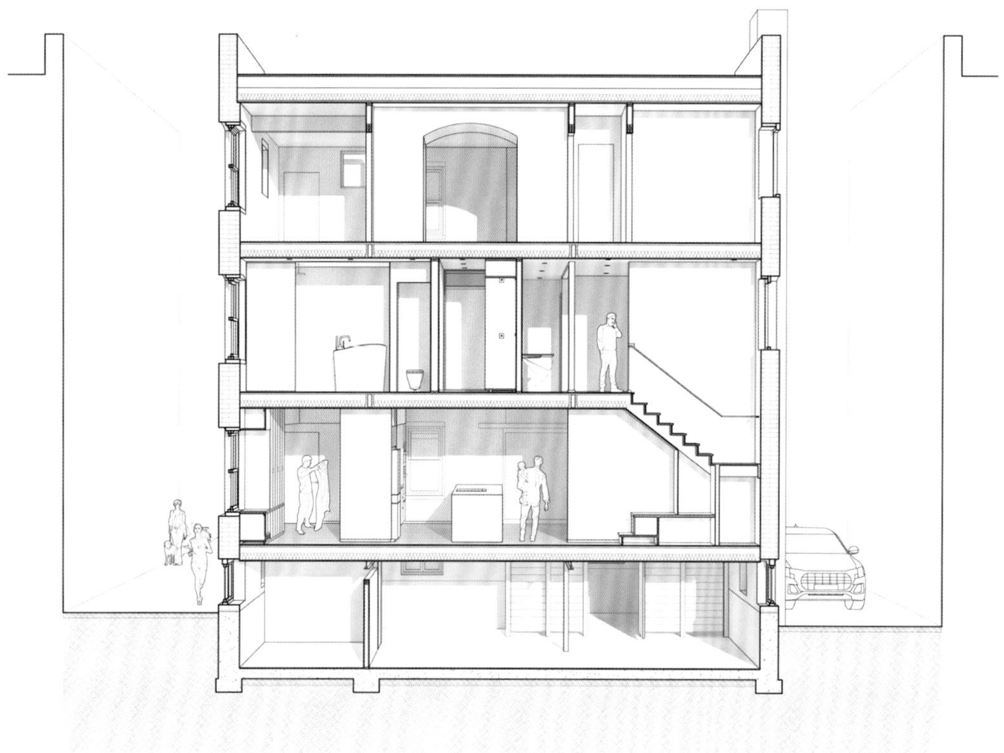

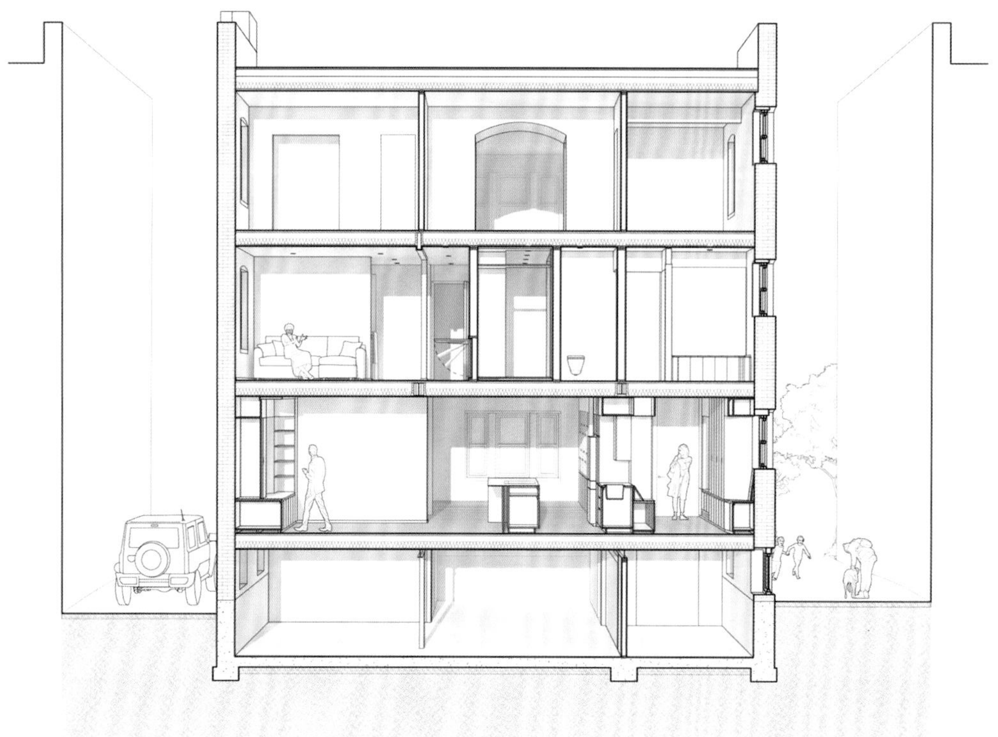

Transverse perspectival sections 01 – 02

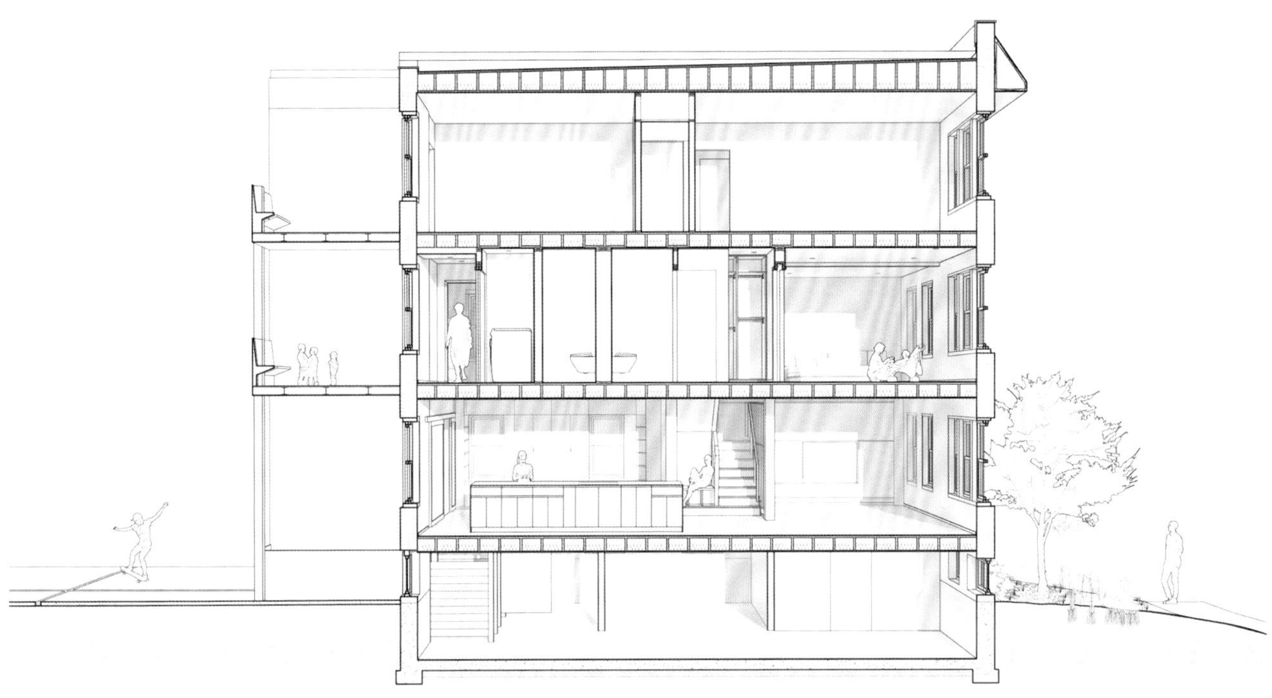

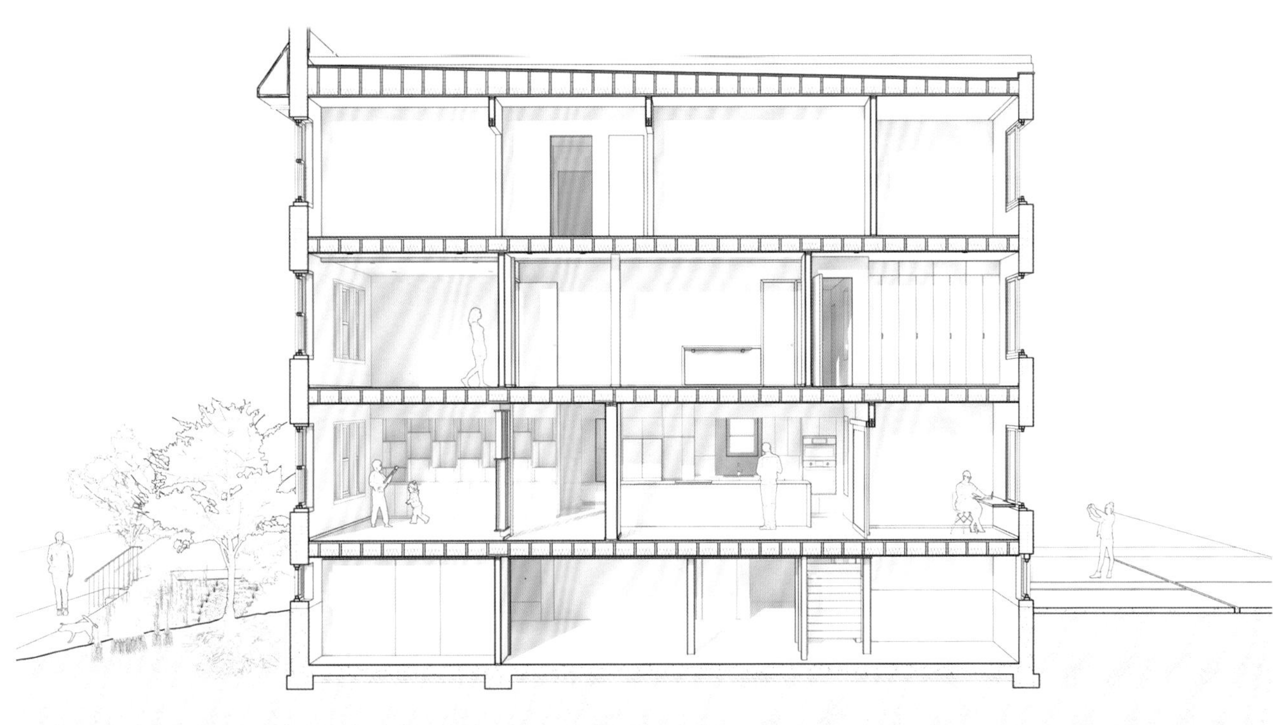

Longitudinal perspectival sections 01 – 02

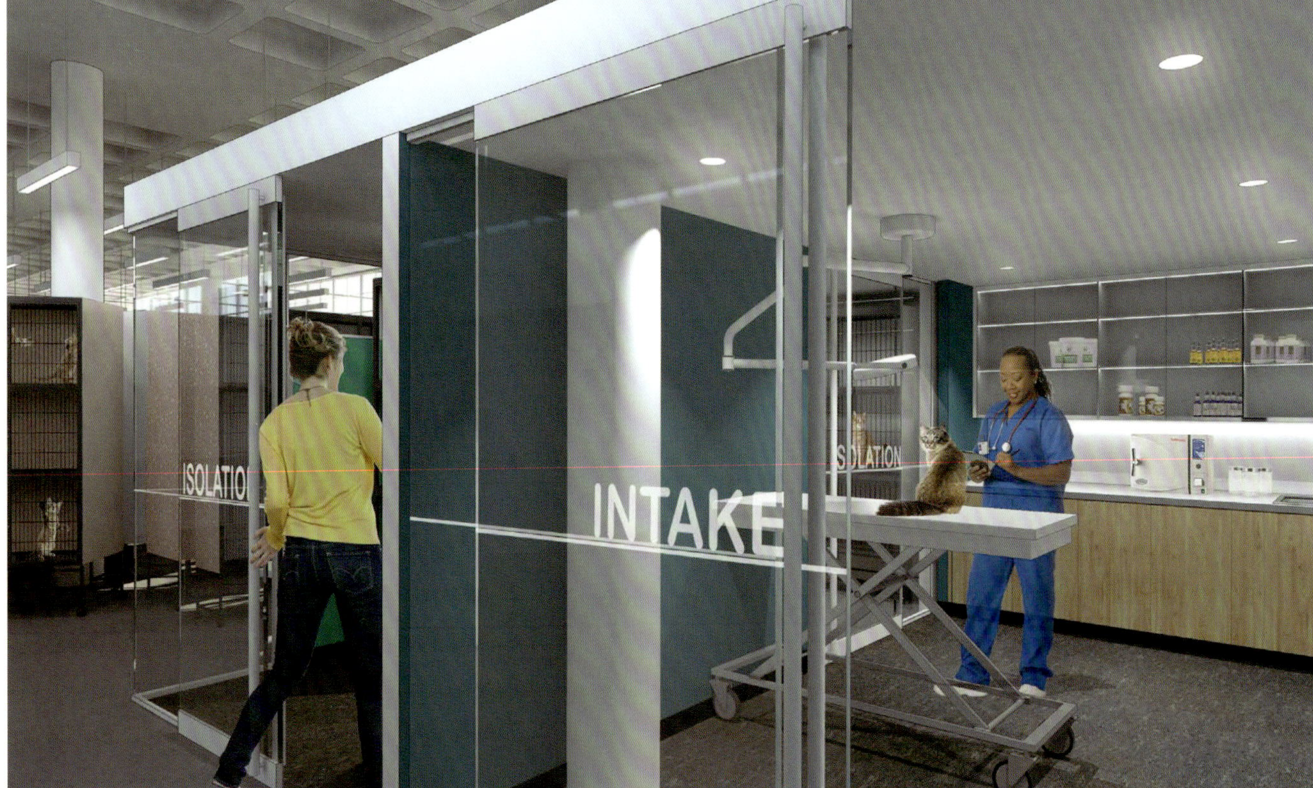

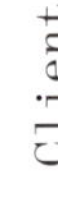

Site St. Louis, MO, United States

Status Conceptual Design

Program Residentia · Commercial

Client Animal House

MAISON FELINE

Maison Feline is a 6,640-square-foot renovation of Animal House: Cat Rescue and Adoption Center in St. Louis. The design strategy reconfigures the flow of thresholds throughout the building to reflect the animals' transition toward adoption. The design for the renovation facilitates smoother human and animal experiences by promoting the idea of a flow-through process. It does this by opening up the floor plan and articulating space through material palettes and built-in casework.

The front façade, landscape, and entry were developed to respond to ADA requirements, as well as to open the facility to community participation, inviting people in the door in order to get cats out. Maison Feline creates a welcoming destination where people want to spend time regularly, rather than a place where people only go every ten to fifteen years when they want a new cat. The design creates a volunteer-friendly environment that thrives on community involvement and nurtures people's desire to visit every month to purchase cat products, take advantage of veterinarian visits, and attend birthday parties for pets or special events.

Maison Feline's design reorganizes the building's existing plan to welcome the public and create new places for people and cats to mingle. These spaces boost adoptions, fosters, and transfers while also creating new revenue streams. Maison Feline maximizes the individualization of rooms dedicated to cat socialization, separating each unit with acoustic panels while also providing vibrant spaces for the animals to interact. At the same time, openness and flexibility encourage the staff and volunteers to enjoy being in the facilities as they aid in caring for the animals.

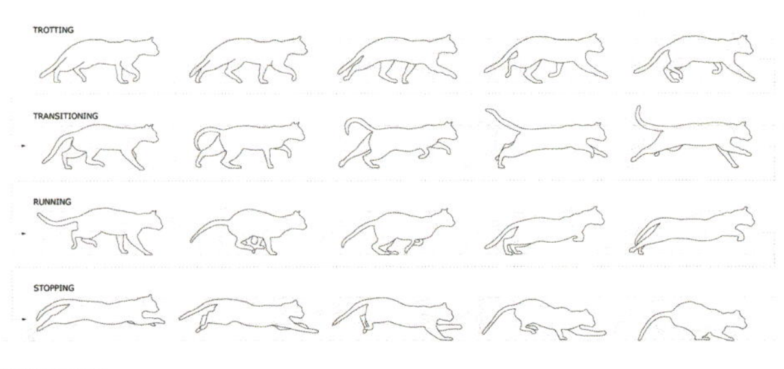

TYPICAL RESTING POSITIONS

TYPICAL SIZE & LEAP

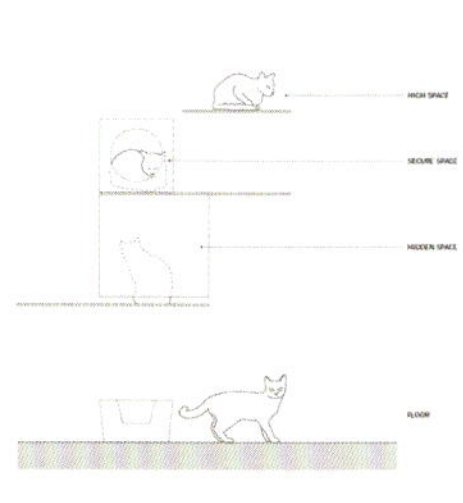

Cat movement analysis diagrams

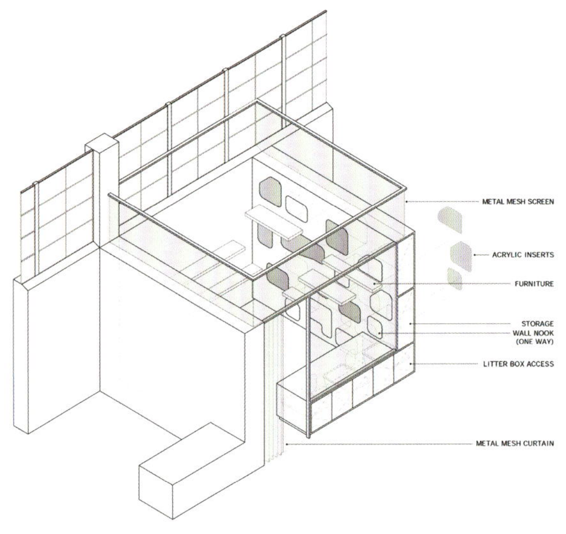

Cat room axon

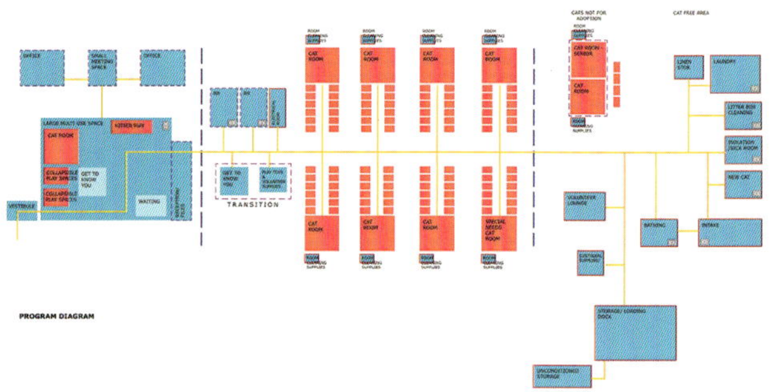

Programmatic diagram

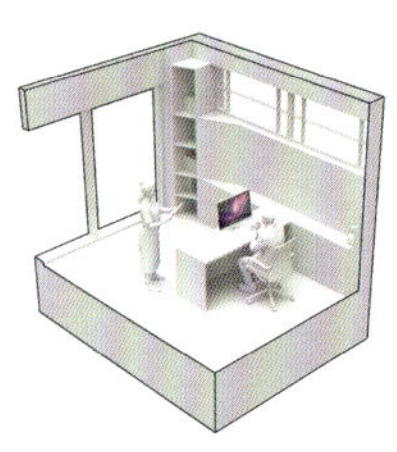

Office

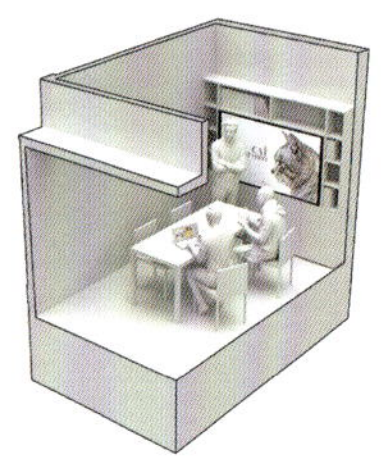

Conference room

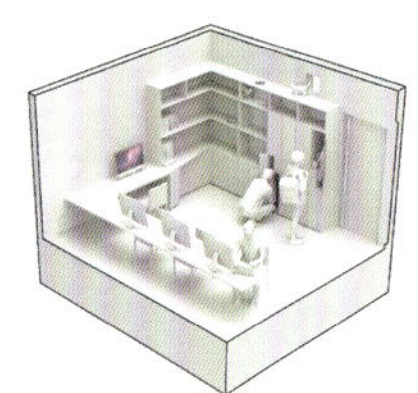

Staff room

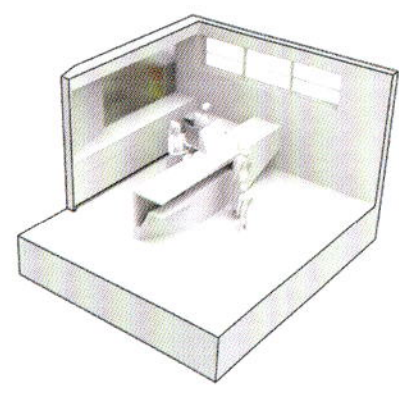

Lobby

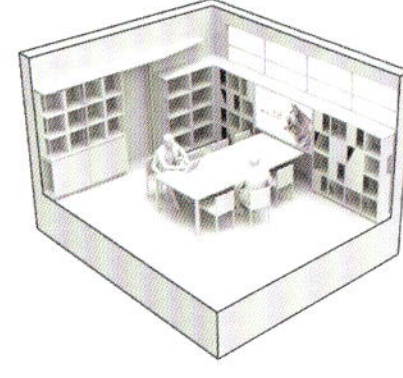

Work room

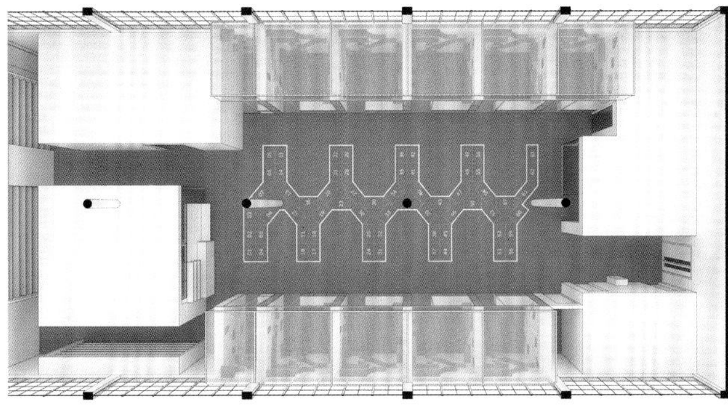

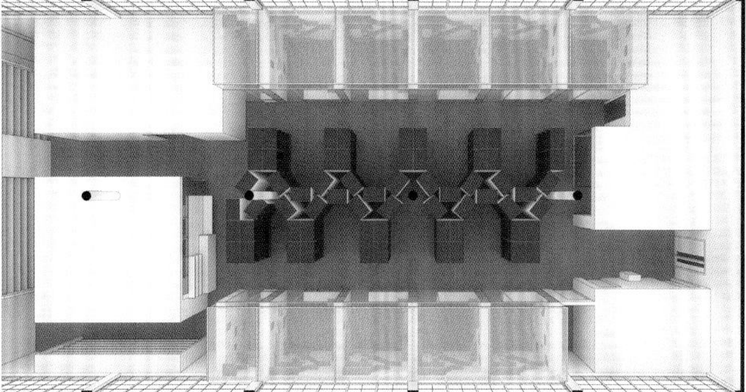

Back of house diagrams

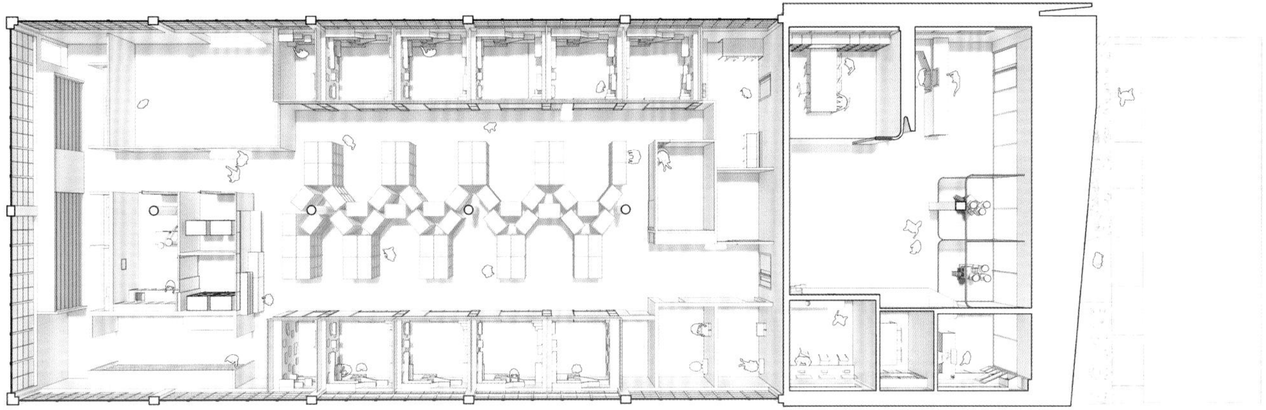

Overall first-floor perspectival plan

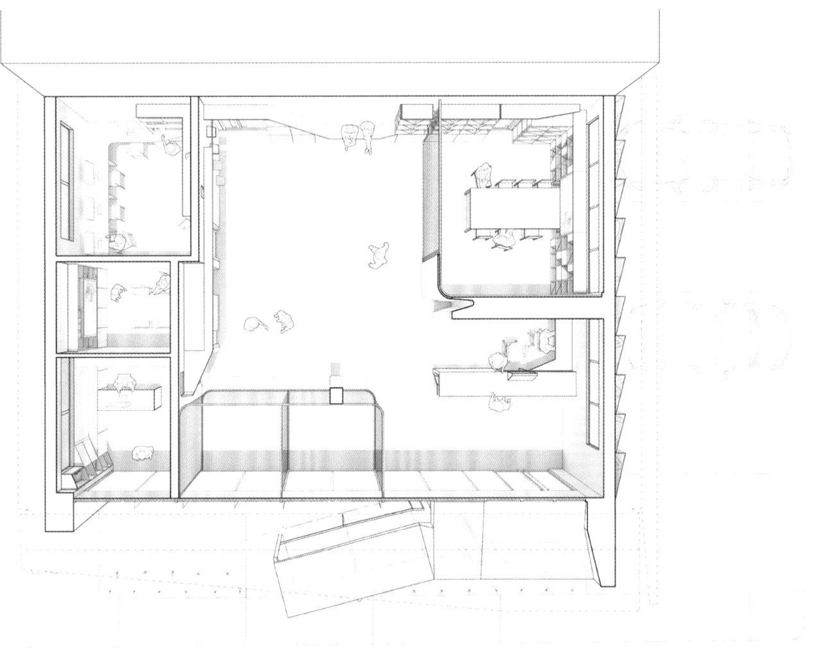

Front of house perspectival plan detail

Transverse perspectival section 01

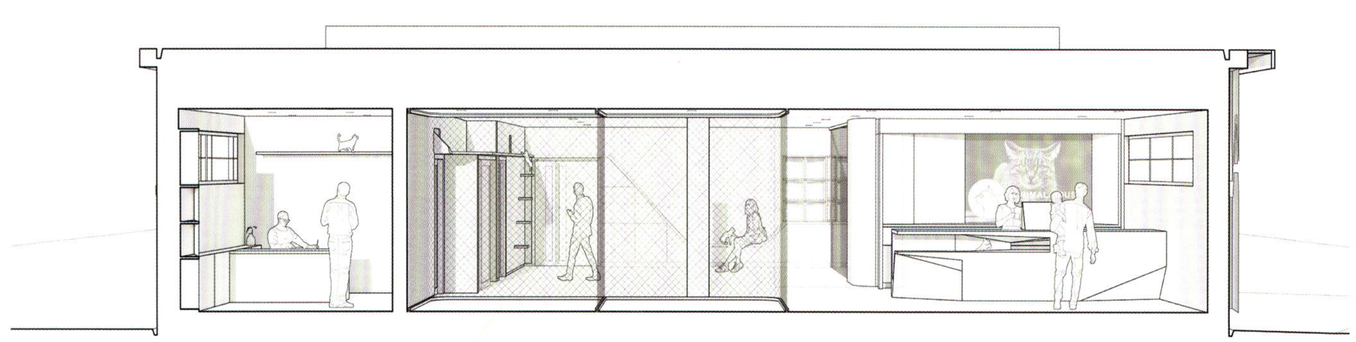

Longitudinal perspectival section 01

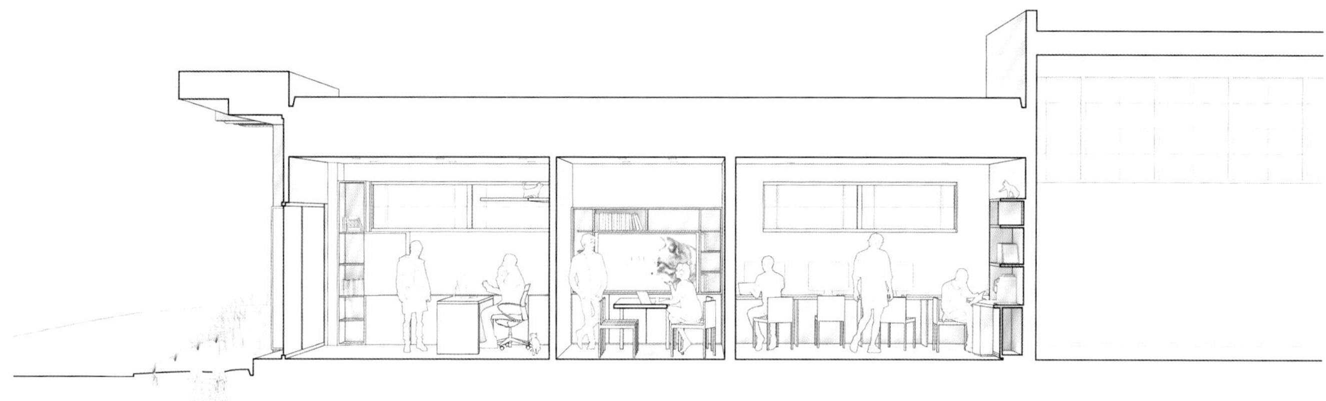

Transverse perspectival section 02

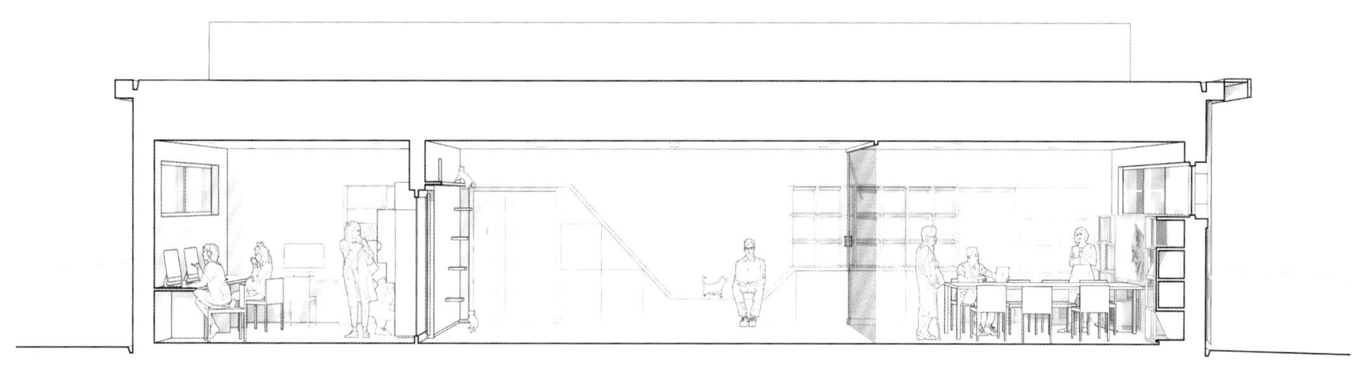

Longitudinal perspectival section 02

ANIMAL HOUSE

ANIMAL HOUSE
Cat Rescue and Adoption Center
ROOM 01
ROOM 02

218

210

INVISIBLE WITHIN PRACTICE AND RESEARCH

274

252

234

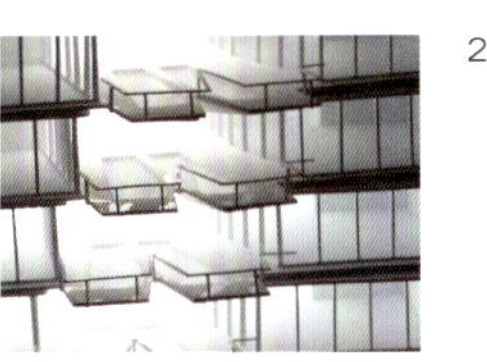

244

288

314

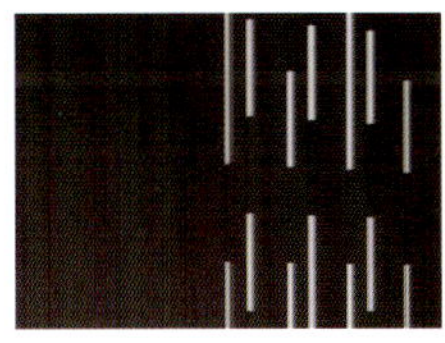

302

280

336

WITHIN PRACTICE AND RESEARCH

Jennifer Yoos

When not located on a coast—and particularly when located in the Midwest—an architectural practice is frequently defined and delimited by its regional identity, described by formal characteristics that unify local practices. While their work is an argument against this type-casting, Axi:Ome's practice and methodology developed out of a close focus on the specificity and unique challenges of their St. Louis context, producing sensitivities and a point-of-view less recognizable as distinctly regional but still applicable to a place-specific method of practice that can be operated globally.

The city of St. Louis and the lessons of building an experimental practice there can also be seen as informing Axi:Ome's approach to international projects. This includes their interest in a material economy that connects architectural experimentation and labor, their conception of buildings as equally urban and architectural, and their prioritization of climate and social context in shaping daily life and culture. The challenges found in their local context and in their roles in academia are essential for developing a form of inquisitive practice that can generate complex questions from architecture. The series of projects that follow demonstrate these methodologies, along with their relevance to projects in other places and cultures, which are informed by both a unique set of conditions as well as common questions to be pursued across diverse locations and types. Axi:Ome's academic and local grounding leads to a very different approach to international work than most globally-oriented practices because it interweaves a wide range of concerns and questions about our contemporary discipline—concerns that are at once broadly social, cultural, and ethical while also highly specific and local. Their more agile model of practice is inherently multi-disciplinary and thus better able to work within economical constraints, respond more sensitively to local labor practices and interests, and create connections with nature that promote sustainability in architecture and build healthier social environments. In contrast with this definition of regional practice, the familiar critique of practices that work internationally is that they often impose their own identity on a place, erasing existing histories and cultures.

The projects toward which Axi:Ome gravitates are not the high-profile building typologies often identified with high design, instead they are projects that are grounded in community such as housing, schools, and factories, which deserve equally ambitious design aspirations. These are places where communities gather to live and work, and where architecture elevates everyday experience. In school projects in Senegal and China and housing and transportation projects in Korea, to name a few, Axi:Ome extends the everyday rituals of use into the processes of making a building, processes that, in turn, shape and are shaped by local life. Labor is not seen as abstract but as visible and articulated; their buildings are designed to express and teach new methods and to honor material technologies and the intelligence of their assembly. Axi:Ome explores the importance of form and economy through both familiar and emerging technologies to facilitate their transformation of place.

This grouping of projects is organized by location and functional type, not as a way of narrowing but rather articulating the importance of these identifiers to their body of work. Axi:Ome's use of type as a generator occurs through a dialectical process of type relative to history, and through an awareness of and respect for historic structures rather than erasure. Heather Woofter and Sung Ho Kim reference a 1978 essay where Raphael Moneo described working within typology as "belonging to a class of repeated objects, characterized, like a class of tools or instruments, by some general attributes," (Moneo 1978, 23) where type could be conceptualized as "a frame within which change operates" (27). This use of type demands not formal repetition but an acknowledgment that we can and must learn from what came before while designing for our own time and circumstances. This approach also highlights the role of buildings in forming context and place, furthering the use of type over time in forming a larger cohesive urban context.

Projects that emphasize and strengthen our connections to nature, landscape, and cultural ritual are found throughout this body of work. Axi:Ome's projects frequently employ biophilic methods of design; for example, their design for the Albany Housing in the Bahamas references nearby coral reef structures, known for their ability to reflect and move light, and applies knowledge inspired by bioluminescent organic forms to larger-scale functional, aesthetic, and performance ideas. In work such as the Silver Tower proposal for Chicago and Factory + Fence in Korea, material realization is an important part of its formation and ecological response. Emerging from the project's context, these methods become instigators of architectural invention.

We are at a point where one of our biggest problems is our estrangement from nature. The idea of sustainability is flawed because it lacks serious interest or investment in new and radical forms of design that could have long-term benefits. Instead of proposing a new way forward, the field emphasizes short-term maintenance of current states or practices that slow down—but do not stop—inevitable problems. Moving beyond the mere clinical management of best practices centered on operation energy or embodied carbon in materials, Axi:Ome's work makes an argument for rediscovering that which is our intrinsic relationship to nature. By reconnecting us to nature and its processes, they show that we can build in a manner that uses material and energy to reform our ways of living—for daylight, for thermal comfort, and by articulating new, expressive methods and materials of building. In their two Micro-Housing projects in Jecheon, Korea, Axi:Ome relates these essential connections with nature back to the rituals of ancestors that grew out of the mountain landscape. They use programmatic patterns to reconstitute past rituals that connect built form and landscape.

In projects such as Silverlake International High School, Axi:Ome looks for cues to restore our intellectual and spiritual connections to nature. Drawing from a more scholarly study of traditional Chinese landscape paintings and referencing nature-based traditions such as *Feng Shui*, they produce building forms that respond to the contexts of landscape with inflections of their architectural forms and use layers, veiling, and translucency to experientially link the interior to the more complex reading of the exterior. This can also be seen in architectural projects that are not bound by the idea of building but instead expand the definition of architecture into site and across many scales to where building form begins to lose its legibility within a larger topographically-defined reading of space and form.

Woofter and Kim would argue that their buildings are not "stand-alone" objects but rather connect to larger systems, contexts, cultures, and histories, and as such are also a part of suggesting and creating new futures. The important issues of our time may be discovered and approached through this method of finding ideas in conditions—and then using this as a frame in which to work and from which to propose change. This method is introduced not as a new individually-driven alien proposition but as a continuation and advancement of the history of a place.

Axi:Ome's projects are neither generic nor stylistic. Their design process emerges from a close reading of place and its less visible defining features—social, political, cultural, and philosophical. We read place not simply through form but through layers of history and its traces of community and culture. Through what the pair calls a "relativist historicist" process of design, we perceive layers of experience and reform representations of material phenomena. The architectural language of Axi:Ome's work consists of these layers, textures, and veiled surfaces that they design, which emerge from the material specificity required for a project to move beyond academic contexts and be constructed in the real world. The discovery of these methods of assembly derived from context are used to articulate surfaces and create specific sites and cultural connections that integrate traces of our past into our current place and time.

Their work is a validation of a model for local practices expanding internationally—where the work is designed as if it were local, based on context, specificity, and knowledge of regional social practices and rituals. These are significant interests for an experimental practice that distinguishes their approach as one defined by a form of research that highlights these topics through their academic ambitions, which, in turn, both inspire students and influence more normative practices.

Woofter and Kim's positions in academia parallel their professional practice, enabling them to develop interests outside the region to aid in understanding their role locally. Their academic research and interests in subjects such as the Japanese Metabolists, biology, and cellular structures help them to frame issues of permeability, urban life, and architectural ideas in their work. This is part of a long lineage at Washington University in St. Louis, dating back to Fumihiko Maki; global practices and practitioners are imported into the school's academic culture, impacting local building culture while also provoking conversations about technology, ecology, and society amongst an audience that is both local and global.

As both academics and architects, Axi:Ome and their work is best understood through the intersection of these dual roles. Their questioning and challenging of the discipline of architecture plays out through their own continual interrogation of the practices through which they design and make buildings. As academics and as architects, Woofter and Kim are deeply concerned with the ethical expectations of practice while also giving equal importance to aesthetic and formal expression. Their inherent pragmatism is unlike other practices in that their generosity and deep care for people and place is coupled with complexity, with poetry and play, and with inventiveness and formal experimentation. I would argue that their body of work is both a critical response and contribution to the challenges of our time—to the technical, ecological, social, and economic realities of current and future practice.

References

Moneo, Rafael. (1978). "On Typology." *Oppositions* no. 13 (Summer): 22–45.

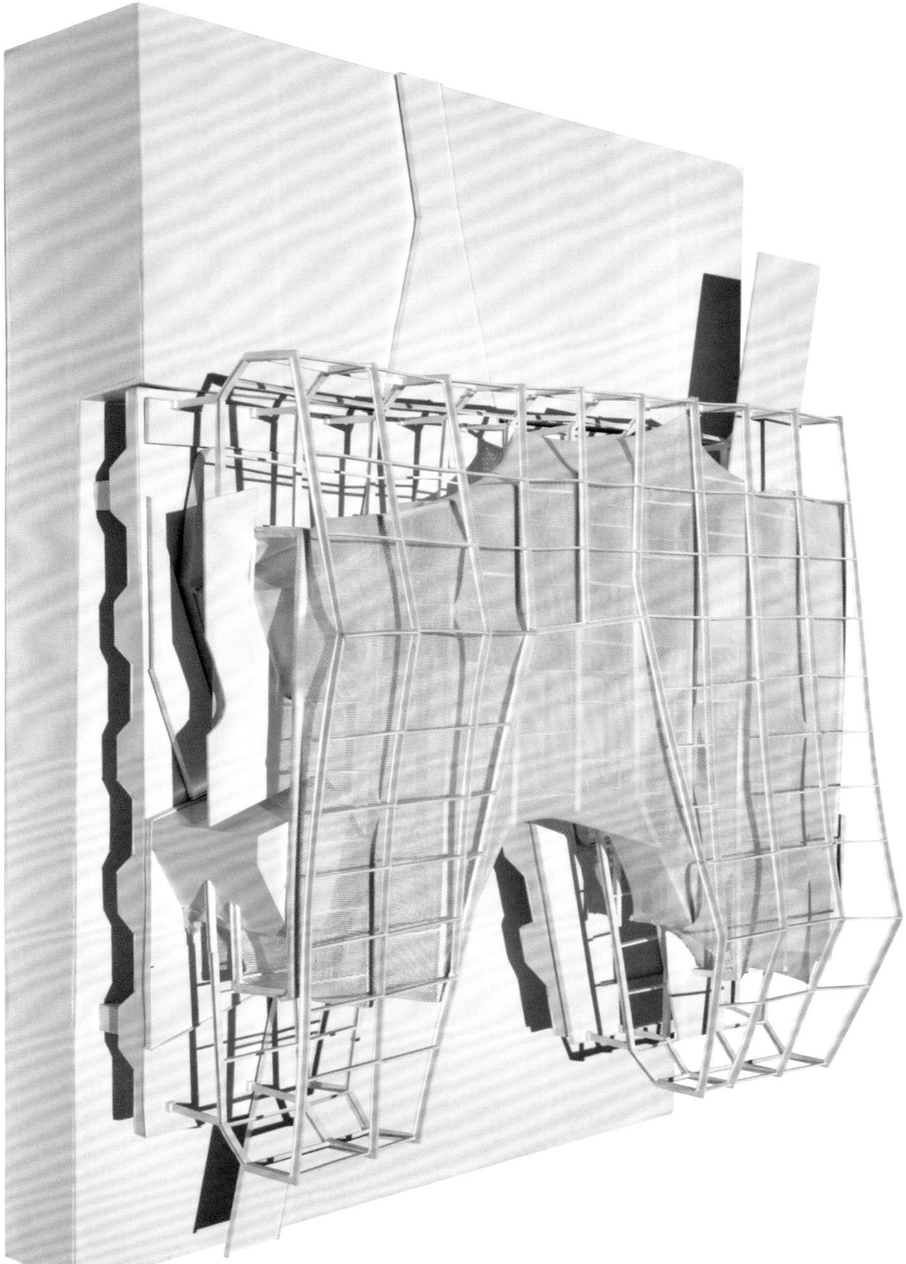

Site	Seoul, South Korea	Status	Conceptual Design	Program	Cultural	Client	Seoul Metropolitan Government

FERRY TERMINAL THE CLOUD

The Cloud at the Yeoui-Naru Ferry Terminal serves as a multi-level observation deck that overlooks the Han River and its marina landscapes. An undulating roofscape produces varied light patterns and imbues the space with a sense of lightness that mimics the flow of the river. Continuous light and an amorphous roofscape are distinguishing features of the terminal. The Cloud's floating roof skin is fabricated with tensile metal mesh and constructed using a lightweight steel-frame structure that frames views of the river and the city. This distinctive urban gesture aims to mirror the landscape's character and encourage social, cultural, and infrastructural improvements within an aesthetic and environmental context. In doing so, it sets an example for Seoul's sustainable and cultural future development.

In this landscape, visitors can enjoy picnicking, walking dogs, flying kites, playing sports, singing, dancing, and painting. Markets, food stalls, cafes, and restaurants for festivals and events also punctuate the program. The many ramps running through the terminal and landscape bridge programmatic conditions and connect the ever-changing views over the energetic city. Serving as architecture for infrastructural and social engagement on a site that fluctuates between water and land, The Cloud brings life to a marginalized territory.

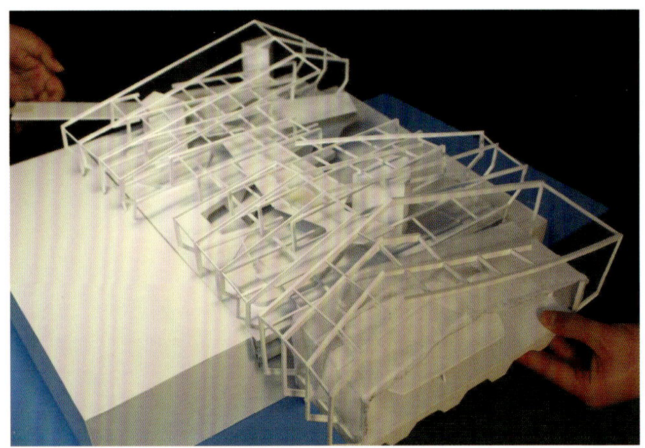

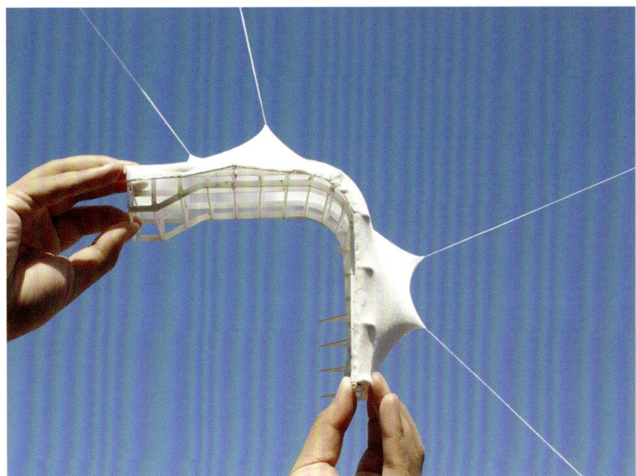

Structural process model (above), process cloud model (below)

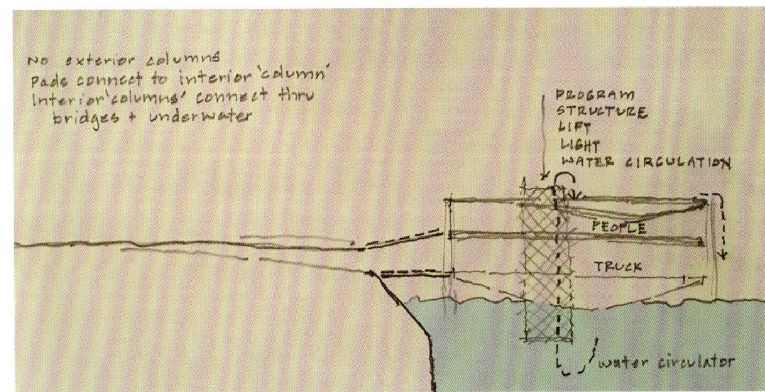

Section sketch diagram (above),
perspective view sketch diagram (below)

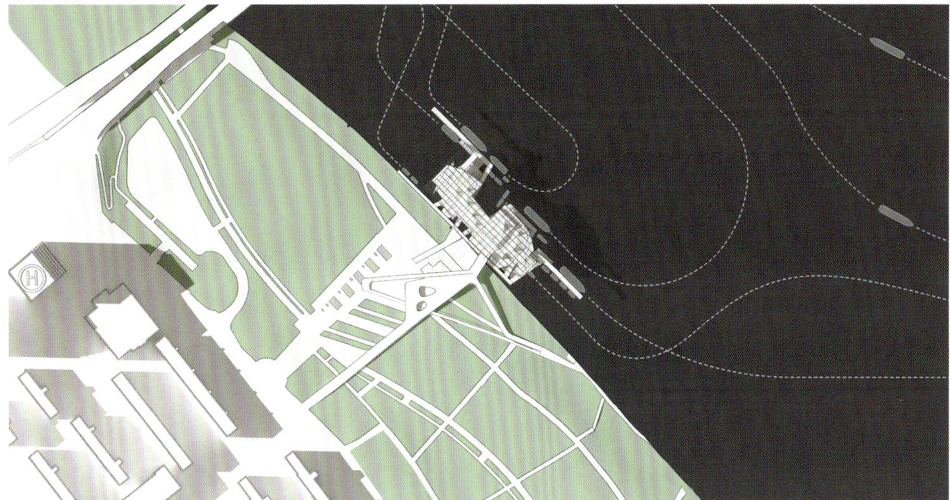
Site plan

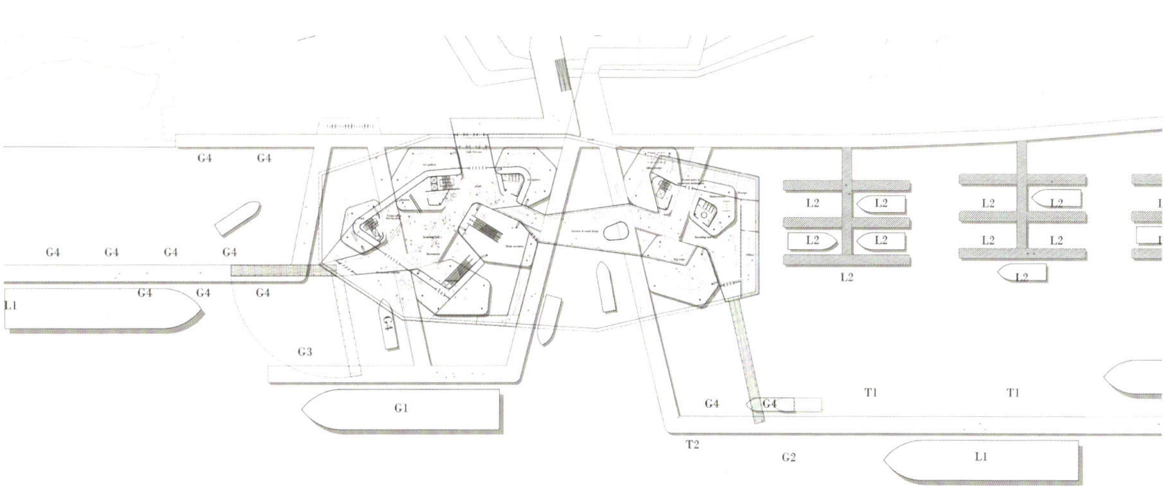

Plan diagram

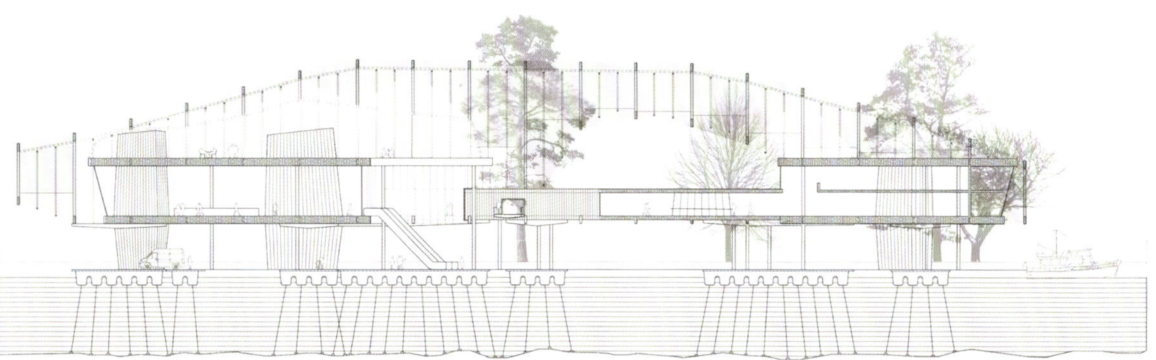
Longitudinal section diagram

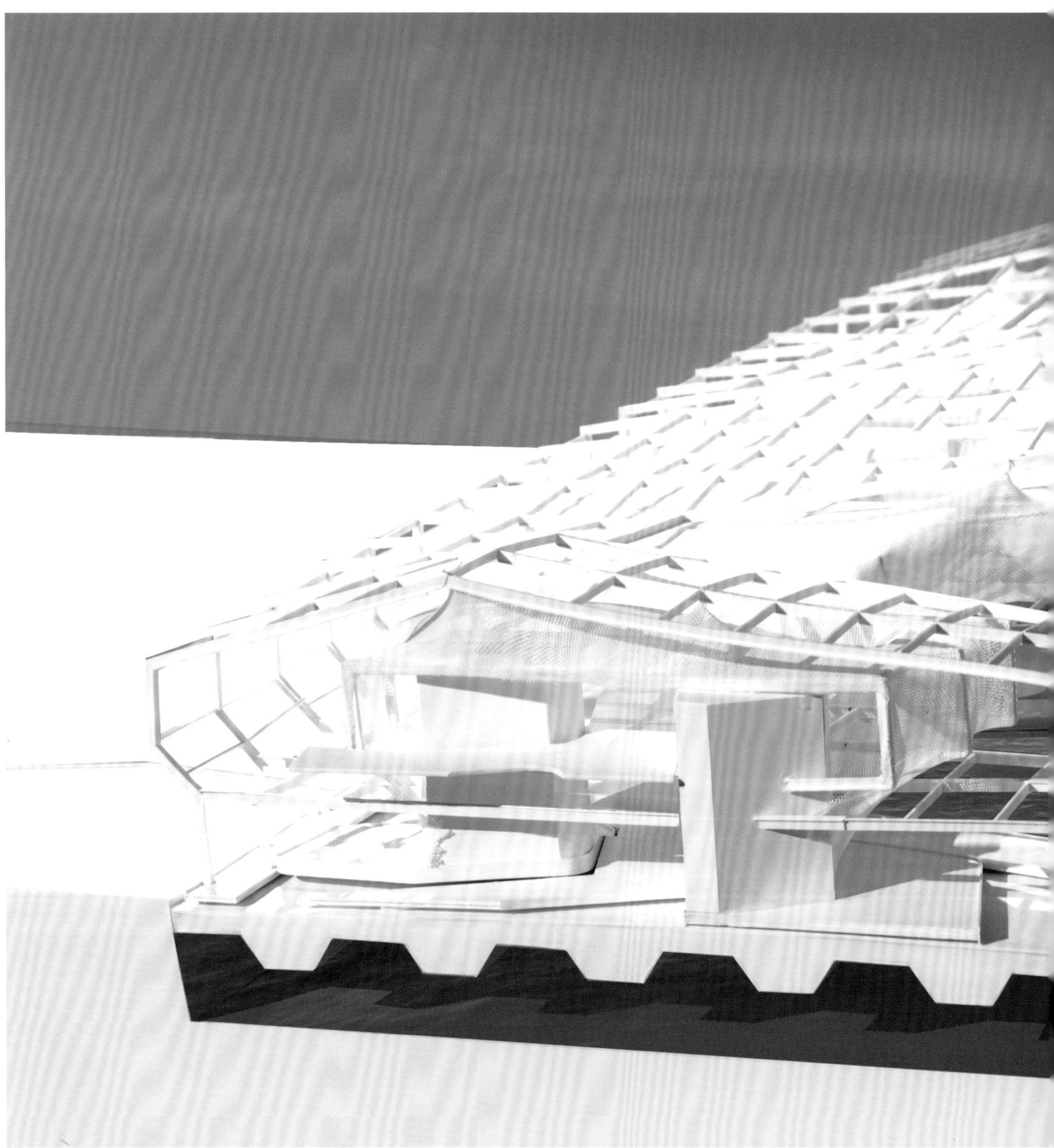

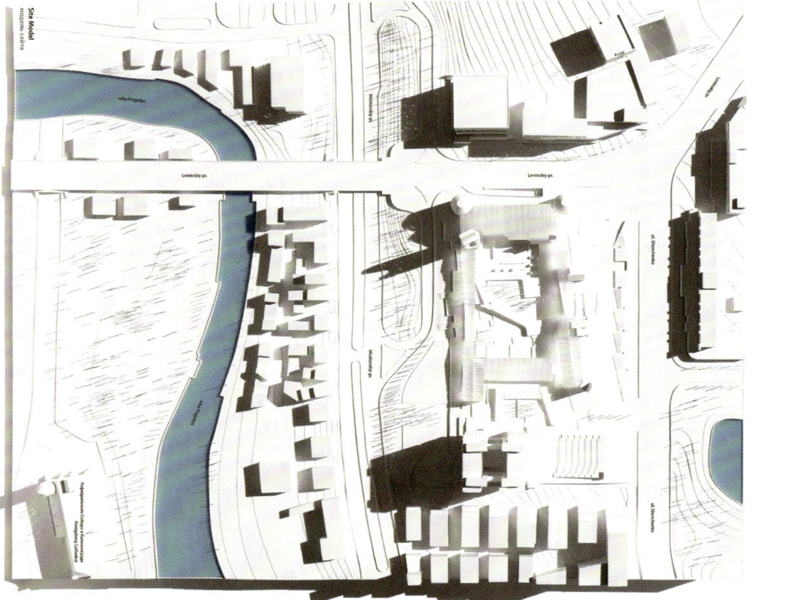

Site Kaliningrad, Russia

Status Conceptual Design

Program Cultural

Client Kaliningrad Oblast City Region Government

CRYSTAL ARMATURE

Kaliningrad City is representative of the complex historical divisions and connections characteristic of Eastern and Western Europe. A Russian exclave, the city is situated between Poland and Lithuania in a region marked by Prussian history that dates back to the Northern Crusades. Much of the city, formerly known as Königsberg under German rule, was reconstructed following WWII and, in 1946, was renamed Kaliningrad. Our site is located in the historic core of Korolevskaya Gora (King's Mountain), a location chosen for its proximity to two rivers and its heightened ground contours, which provide a natural vantage point from which to view the surrounding territories.

Crystal Armature pays homage to historic structures on the site while reinventing their composition as an icon of memory. We embrace the idea of fluid histories as a part of a systemic order, understood in relation to the generations of cultural influence that shape the spatial reading of the historic center of Kaliningrad. References to historic structures reveal an understanding of unfolding typologies rather than a commodification of history so that contemporary dialogues rooted in postmodern theory contrast with the principles of erasure dominant in the postwar era. Further, we evoke meaning in the manner of Rafael Moneo's 1978 essay "On Typology" for *Oppositions*, where he writes, "[type] does not necessarily imply mechanical reproduction" (Moneo 1978, 27). He goes on to argue, "The type can thus be thought of as the *frame within which change operates*, a necessary term to the continuing dialectic required by history. From this point of view, the type, rather than being a 'frozen mechanism' to produce architecture, becomes a way of denying the past, as well as a way of looking at the future" (27).

More specific to the proposed design, the project creates an armature derived from the original, non-extant castle, one clad in clear and translucent materials around core geometries. There is an interplay between solidity and lightness in the architecture as components of the castle frame relationships with the House of the Soviets and the surrounding city. By juxtaposing the distortion of dense towers with crystalline connecting structures, the architecture also engages with a history of contrasts on site, including with the House of Soviets, a symbolic Brutalist concrete exterior originally intended to be constructed of enameled glass. Crystal Armature's colored-jewel spaces housed within a translucent enclosure conjure references to the castle's famous Amber Room and represent alliances between cultures and the precious archives held within. The Kaliningrad region is known for its large supply of amber, a hardened, yellowish-colored material derived from the resin of trees. The original Amber Room was a gift from the eighteenth-century Prussian King Frederick William I to his ally Peter the Great, the tsar of the Russian Empire. In recent times, the city of Kaliningrad donated amber material for the reconstruction of the room, which had notoriously been stolen by German troops during WWII.

Programmatically, the design concept for Crystal Armature places the Office of Ministry in view of castle ruins, a library, and museum heritage sites. The building also sits opposite to the House of the Soviets, which this proposal engages as a staging ground for experimental outdoor events. In this manner, the House of the Soviets is transformed into a backdrop for this crystal bastion of culture, which encourages pedestrian flow through its forest courtyard and town squares in order to engage everyday citizens, tourists, and patrons of the arts alike.

References Moneo Rafael. 1978. "On Typology. *Oppositions* no. 13 (Summer): 23 – 45.

Transverse section

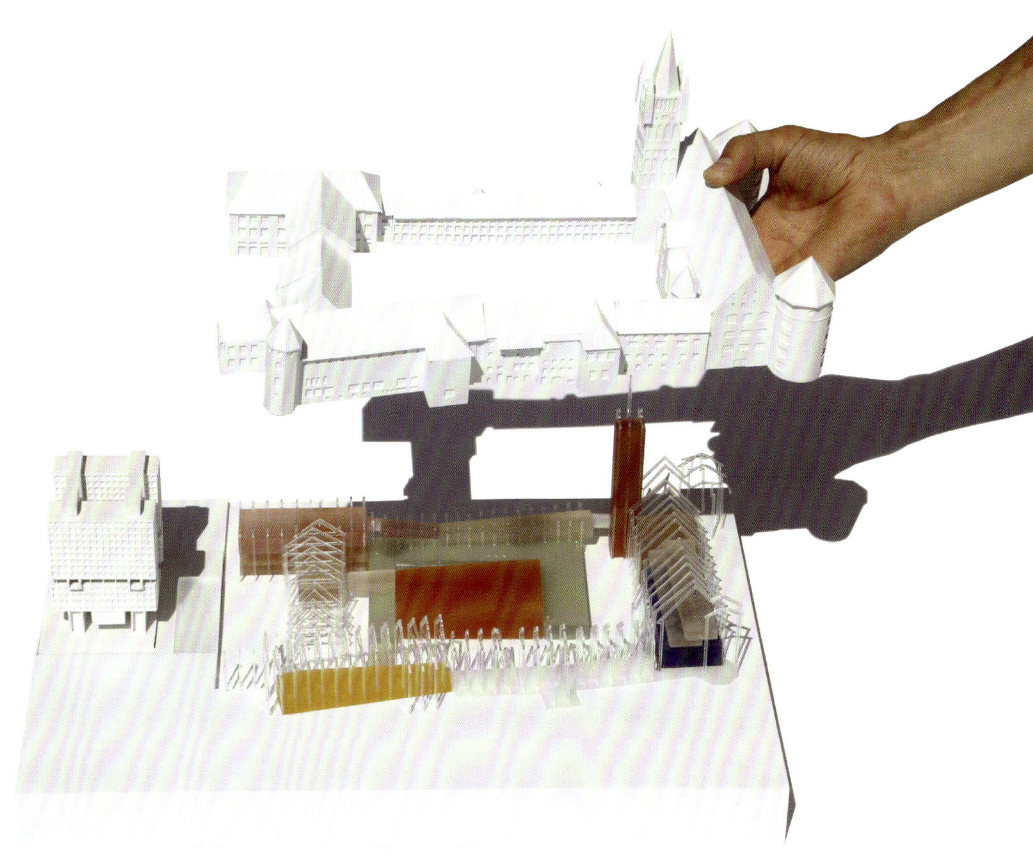

Historical castle concept model

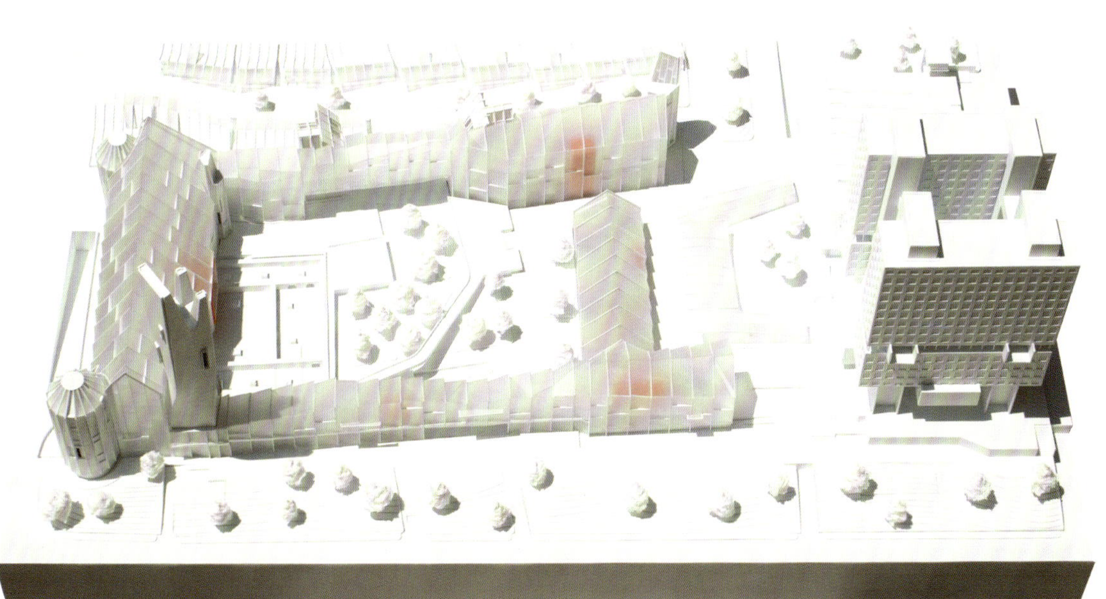

Detail model

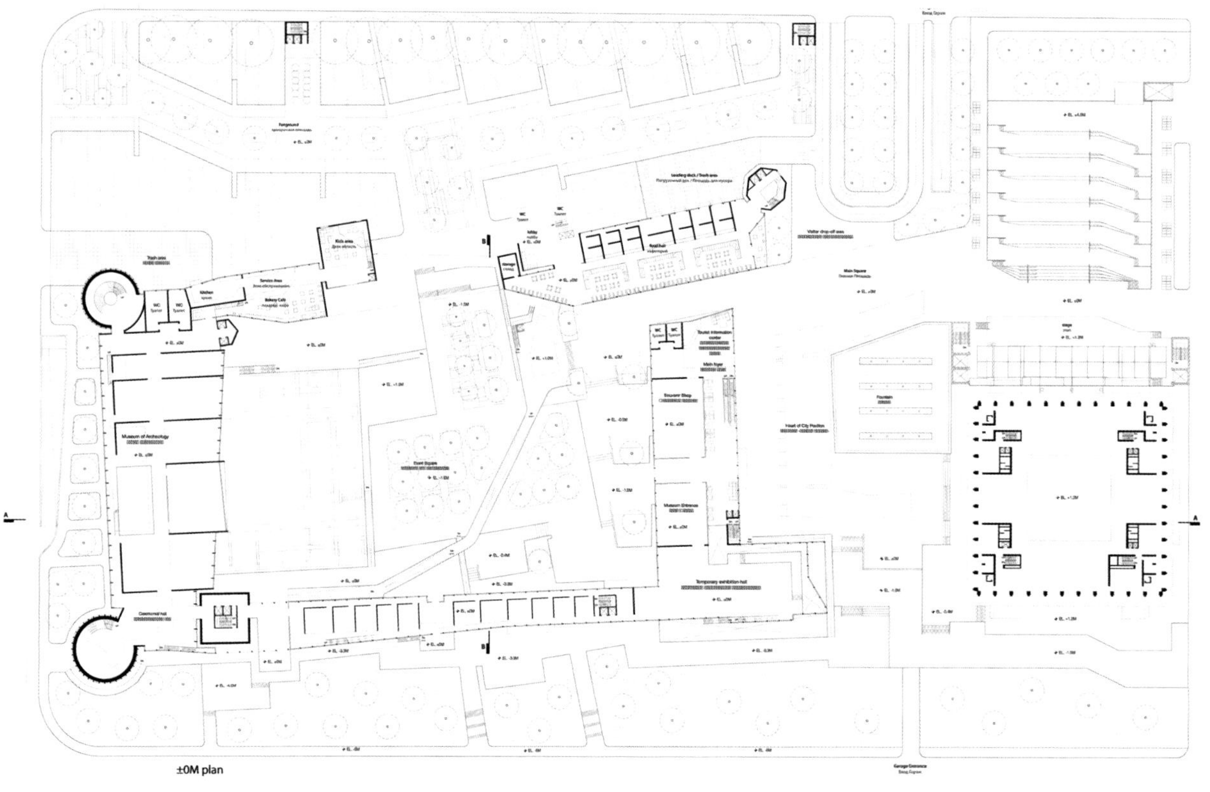

Basement floor plan (above), first-floor plan (below)

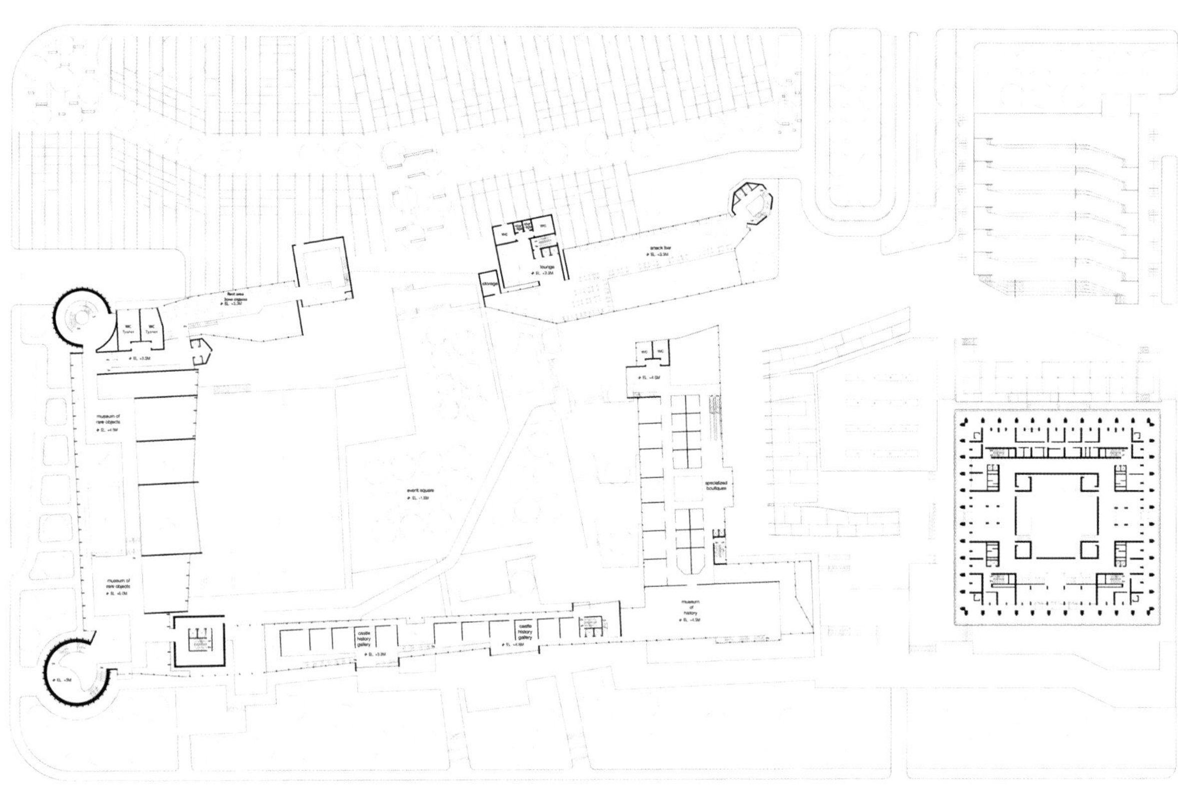

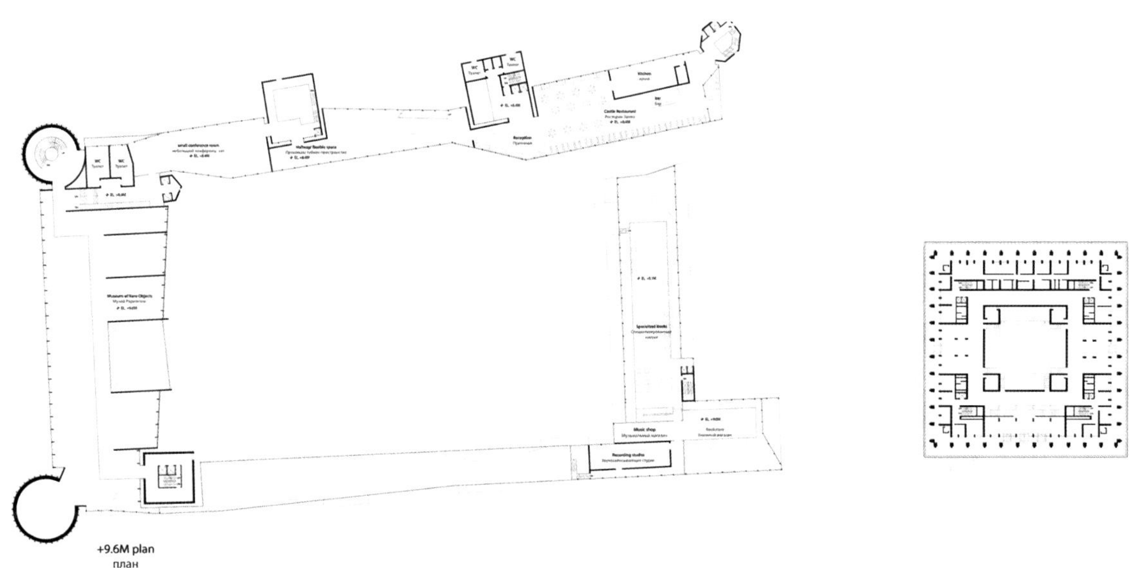

Second-floor plan (above), third-floor plan (below)

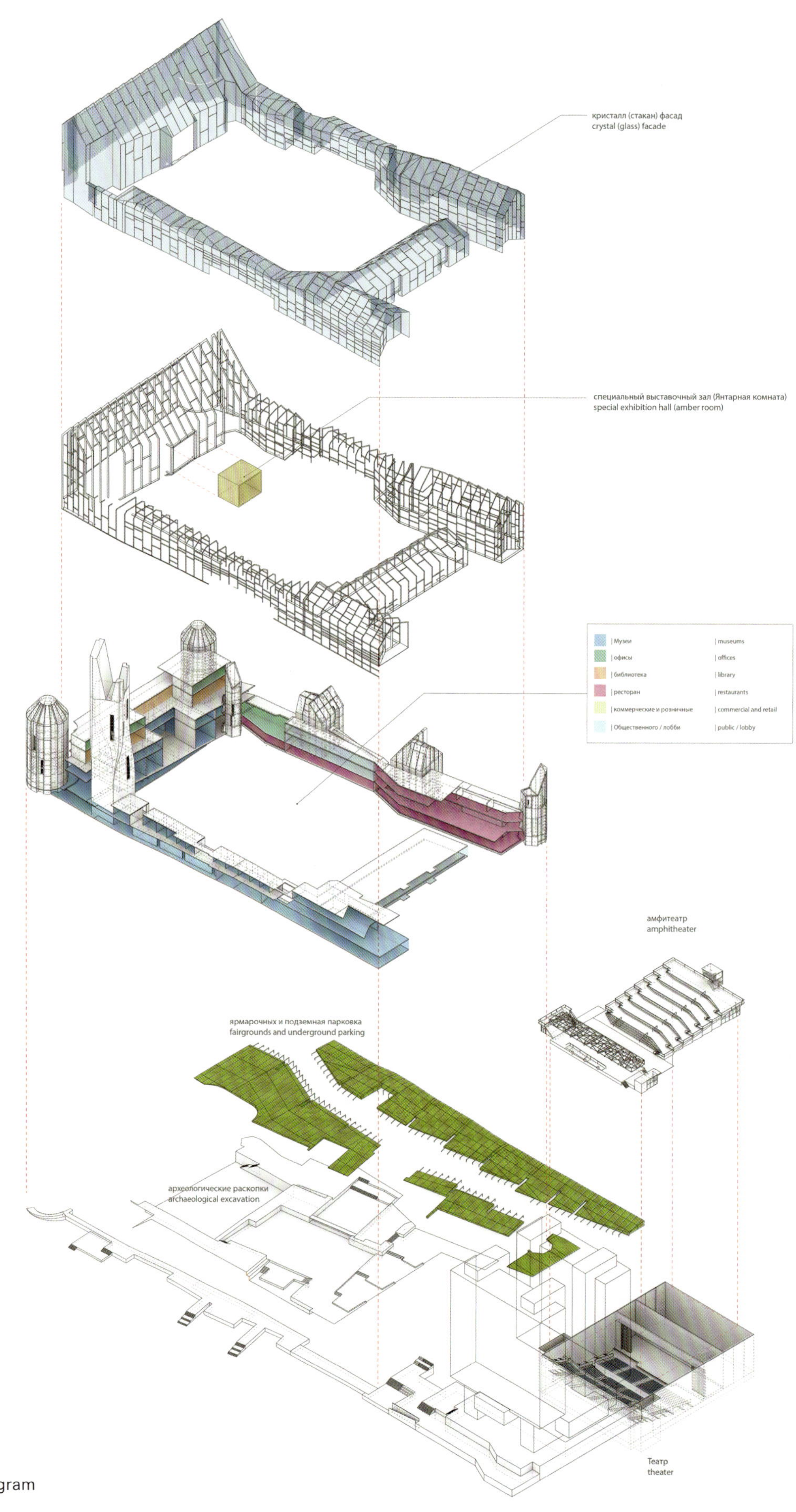

Exploded assembly diagram

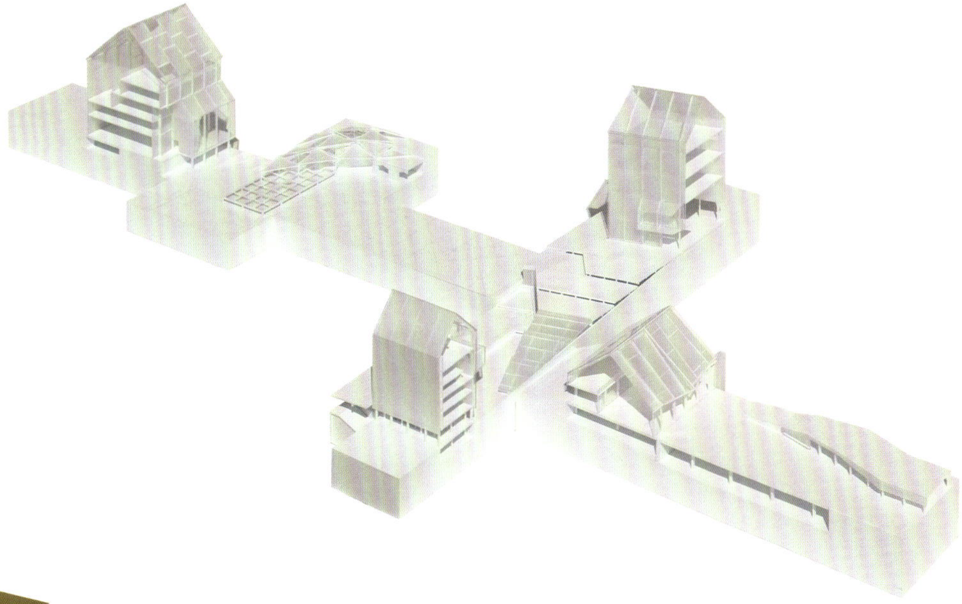

Sectional study model

Amber crystal conceptual model

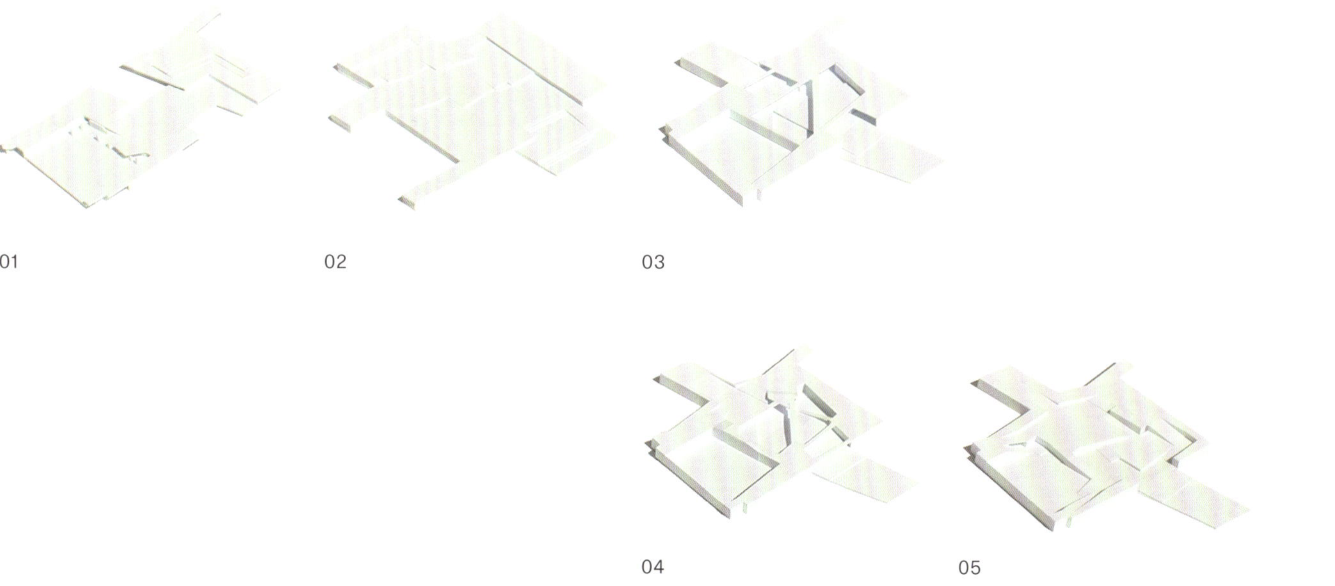

01

02

03

04

05

Courtyard study models

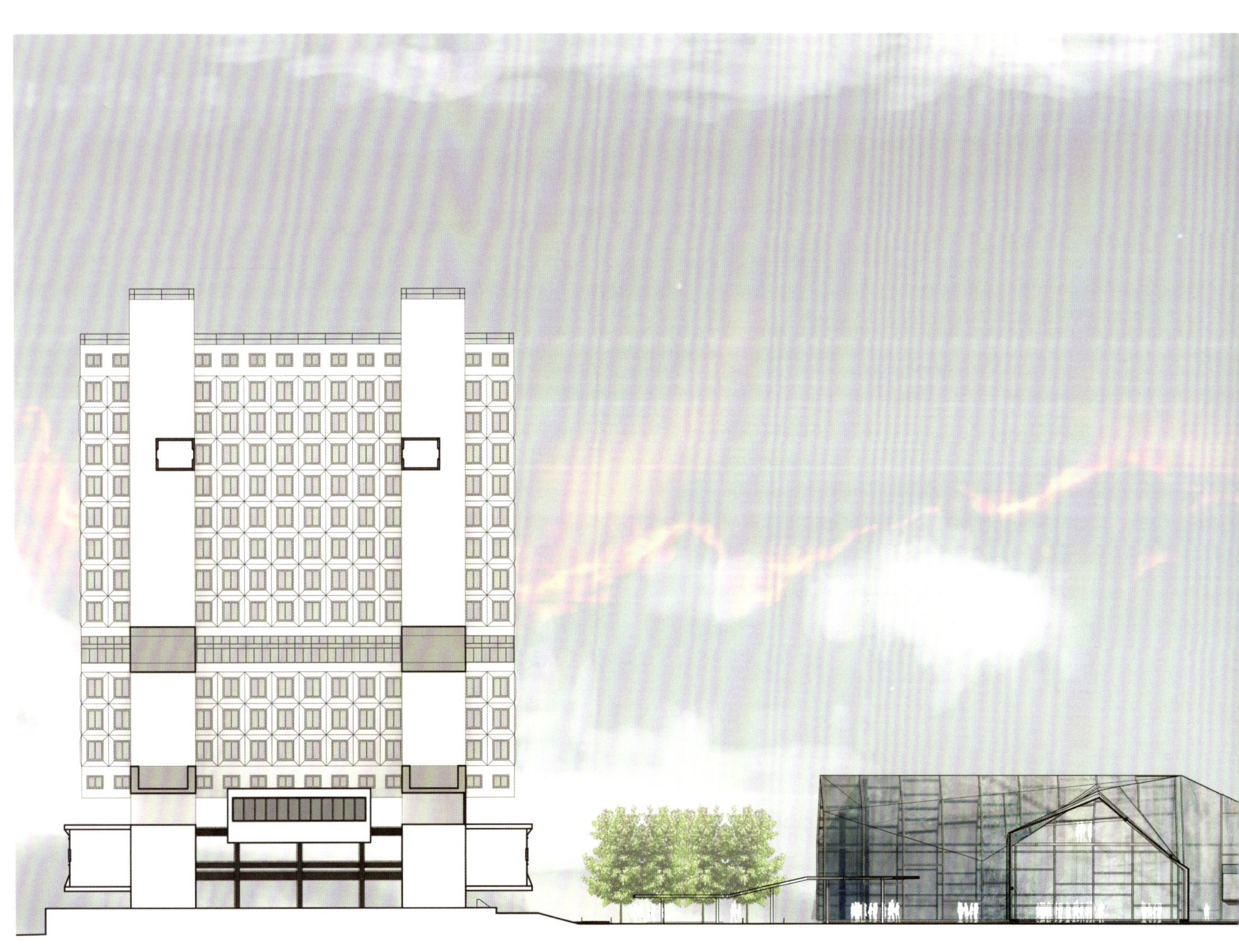

Longitudinal section

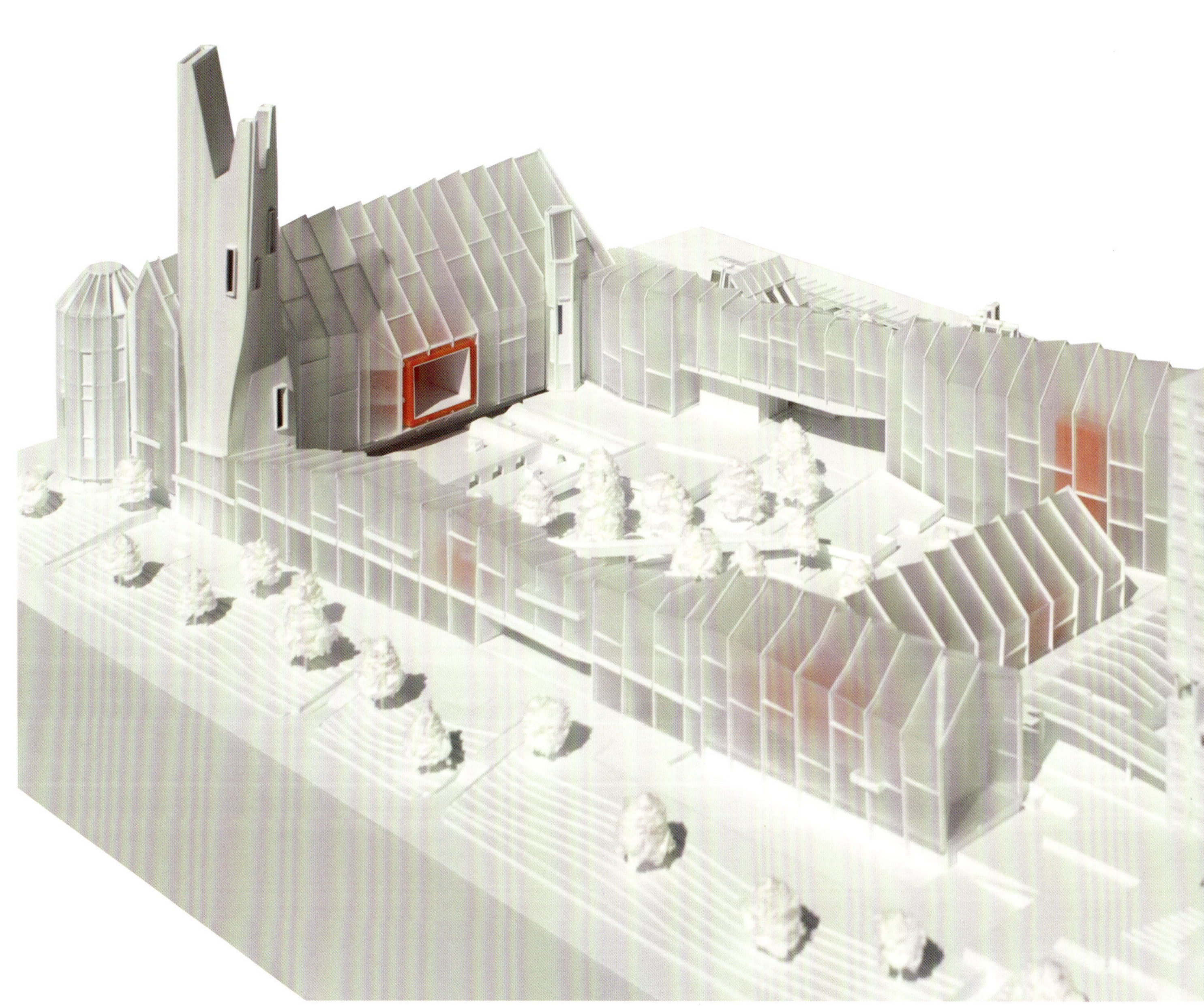

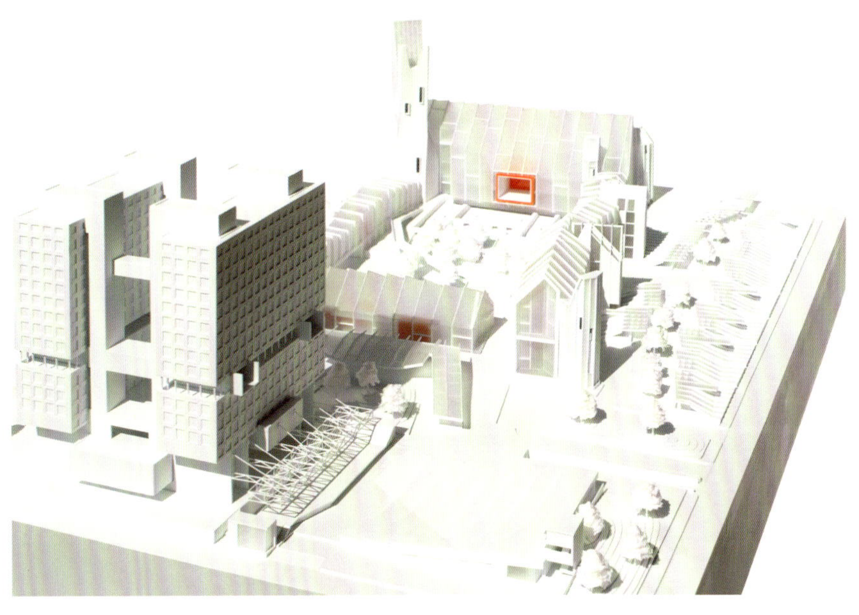

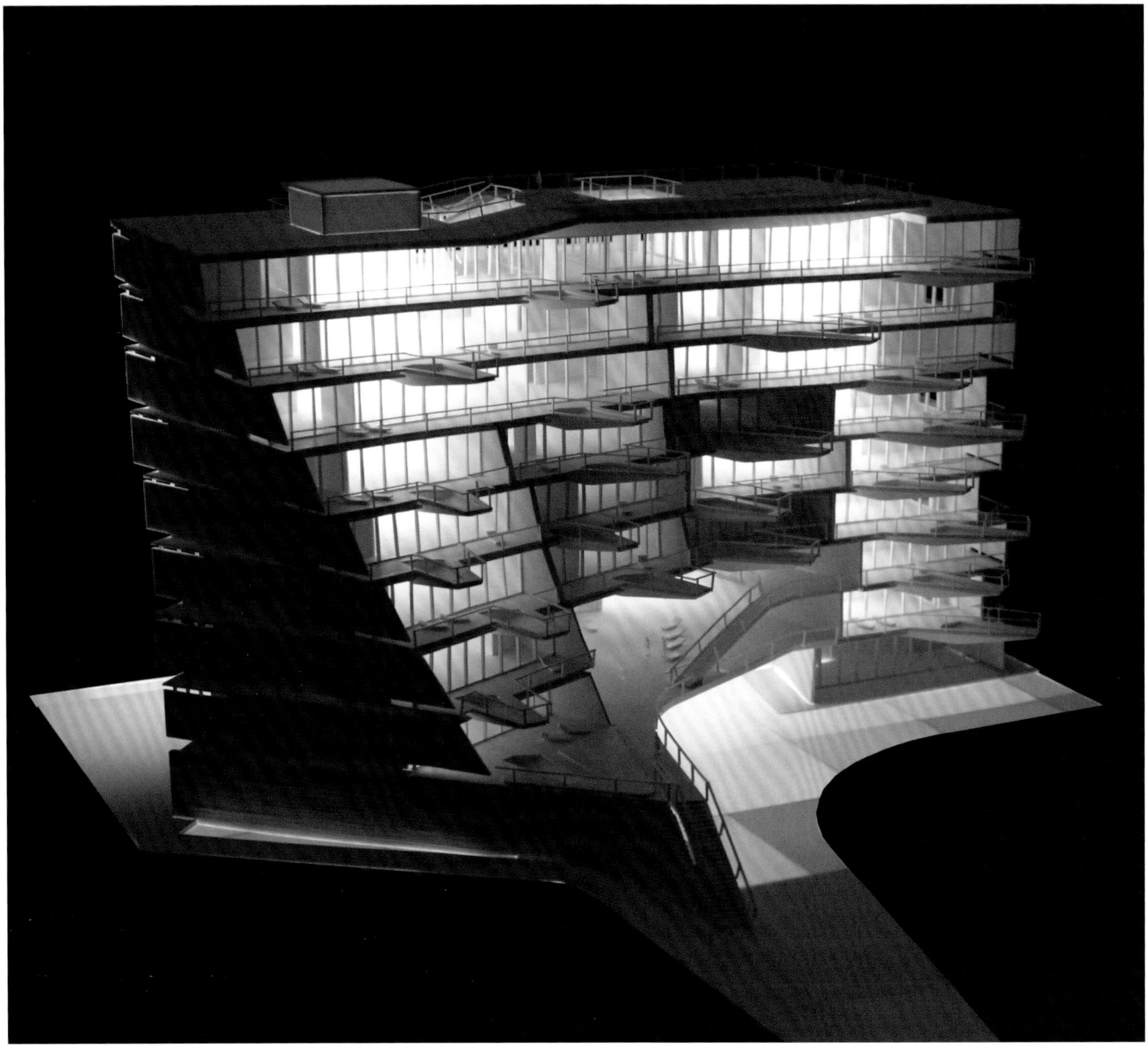

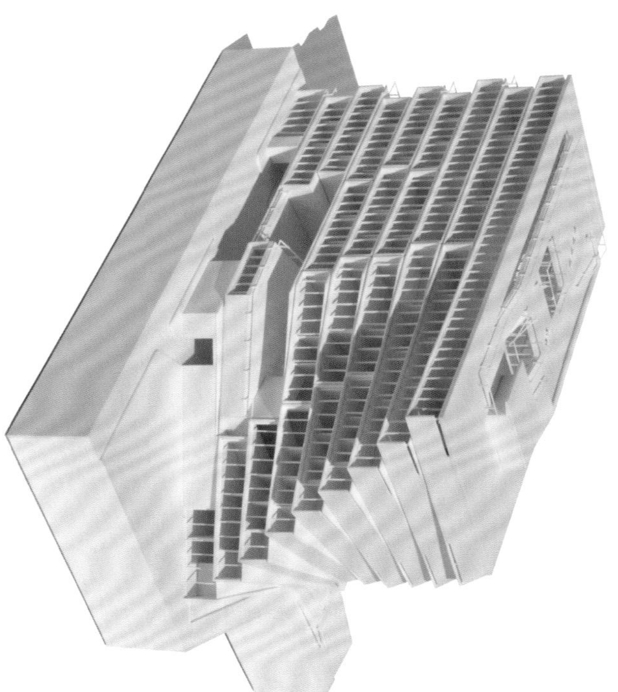

Site New Providence, Bahamas

Status Conceptual Design

Program Residential

Client Albany Resort

ALBANY HOUSING I FLOATING POOL

The Floating Pool Condominium at Albany Resort transforms a Bahamas site into a community for residents with active lifestyles. The atmosphere in Albany is sophisticated, friendly, and in constant dialogue with the outside environment. As recreation and outdoor living are paramount to the experience of the resort, our design prioritizes views of the marina, ocean, and golf course, access to air and light, and the creation of a community platform "beach," which is raised from the ground to meet easement requirements while also accentuating views of the marina.

The Floating Pool Condominium is inspired by the natural ecology of the Bahamas. Albany Resort's built landscape modifies the natural environment by layering onto native ecological systems of landscapes and waterways. One of the hidden resources of the area is the coral reef, a living organism with its own ecology that acts as a light catcher deep in the sea.

Bioluminescent organisms in the ocean inspire a design that includes façades clad with thin white layers of stone that are opaque and reflective during the day but become translucent at night thanks to color-changing LEDs. Here the building becomes not just an object but a beacon that marks the boundary between water and land. At the same time, in marking a geometric turn on the site, the building signals the place as an event and a juncture, one where friends and family can gather together.

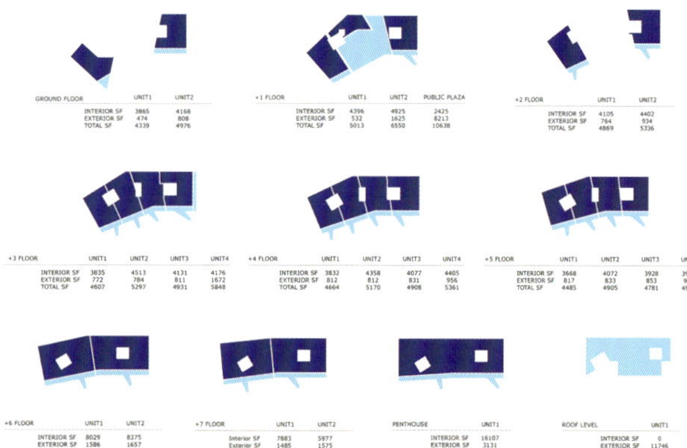

Housing unit diagrams

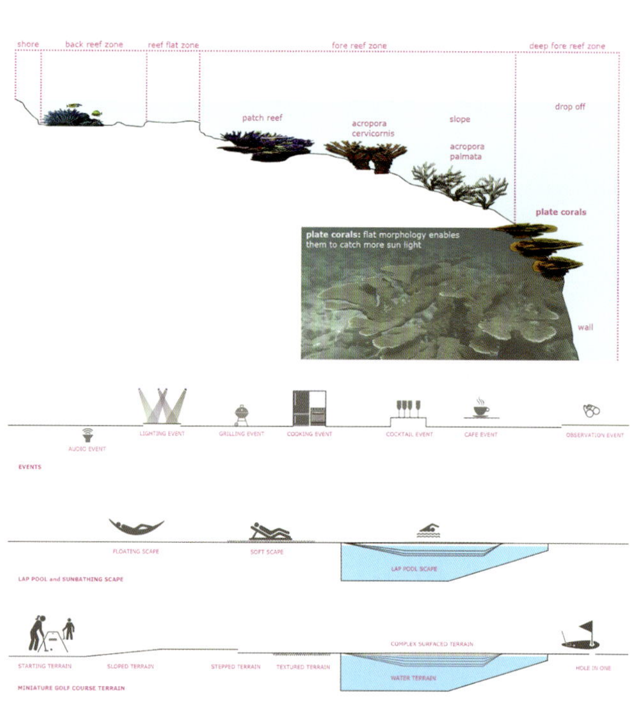

Ecological diagram (above), programmatic diagram (below)

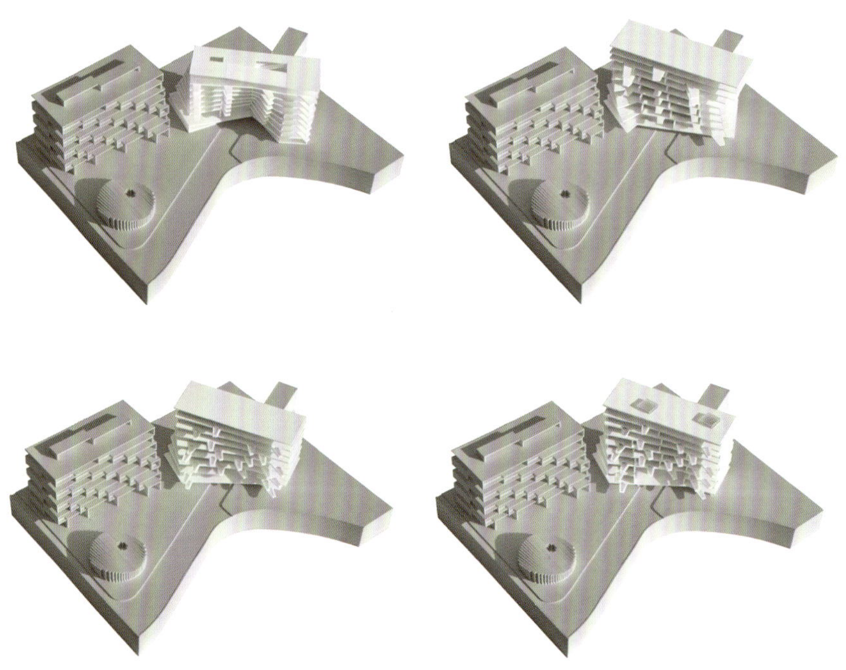

Massing models

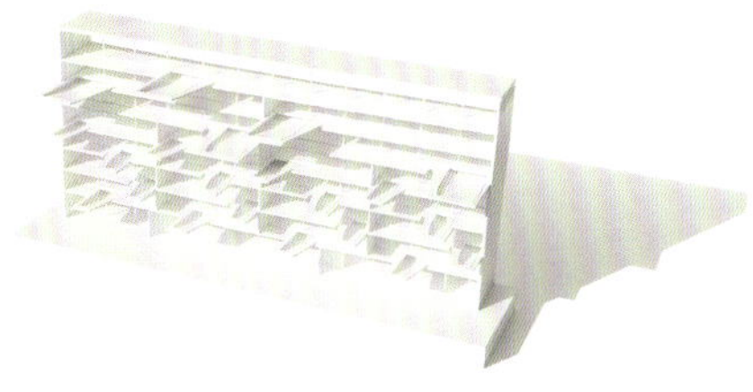
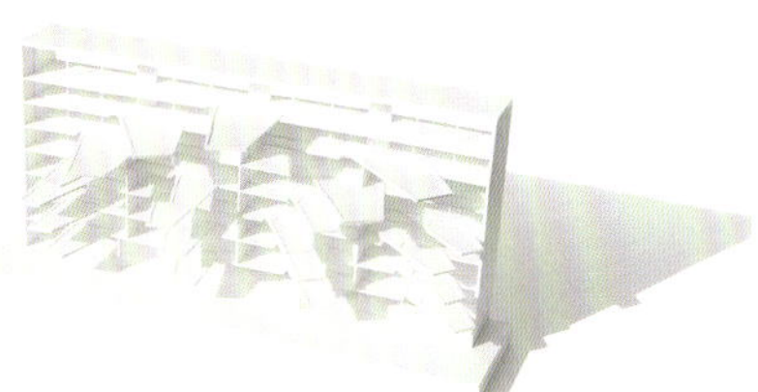
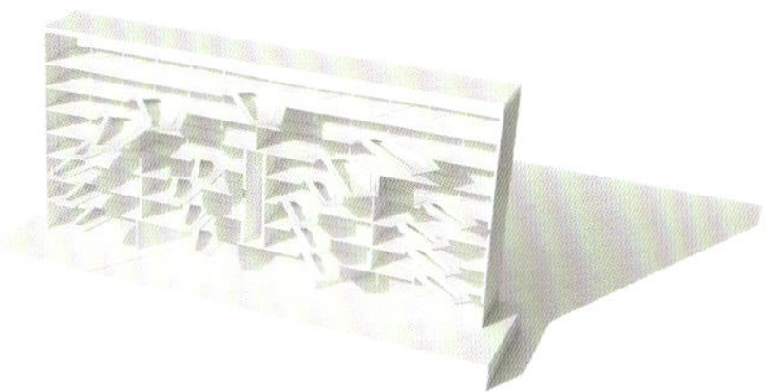

Cantilever pool study models

Skin system diagram

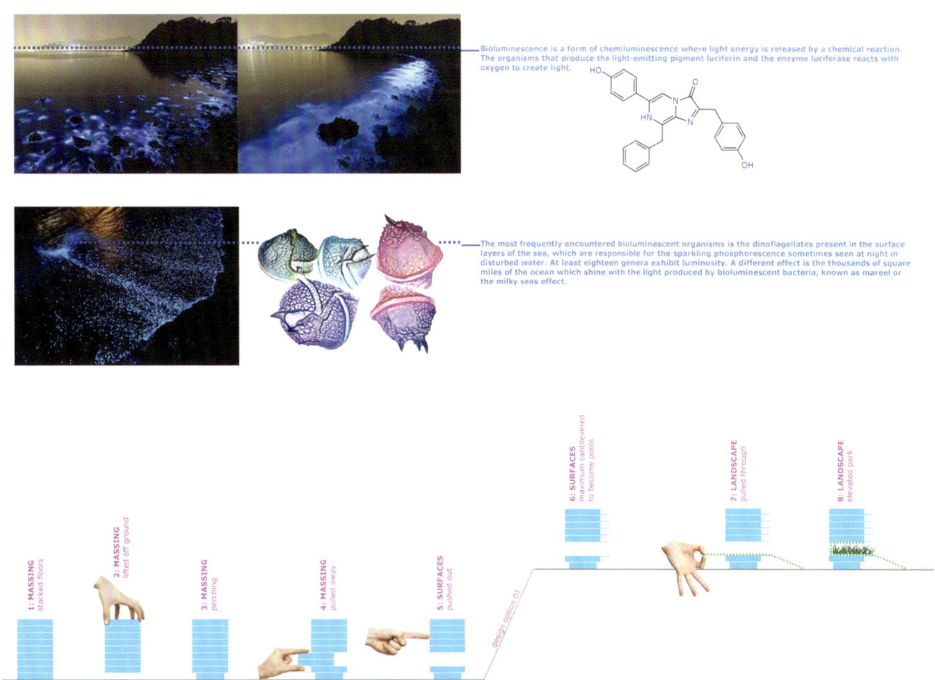

Design process diagram

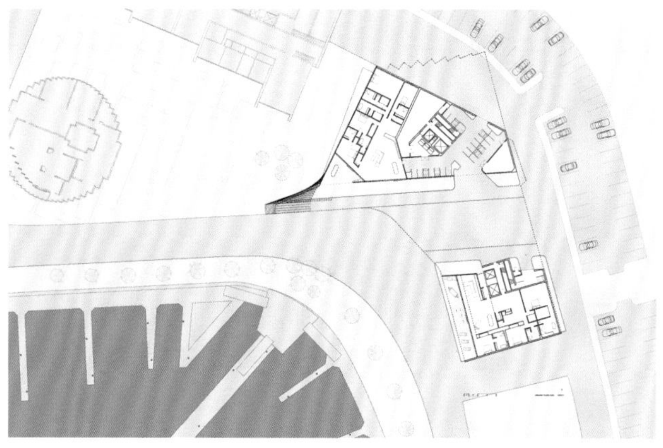

First-floor plan

Second-floor plan

Site plan

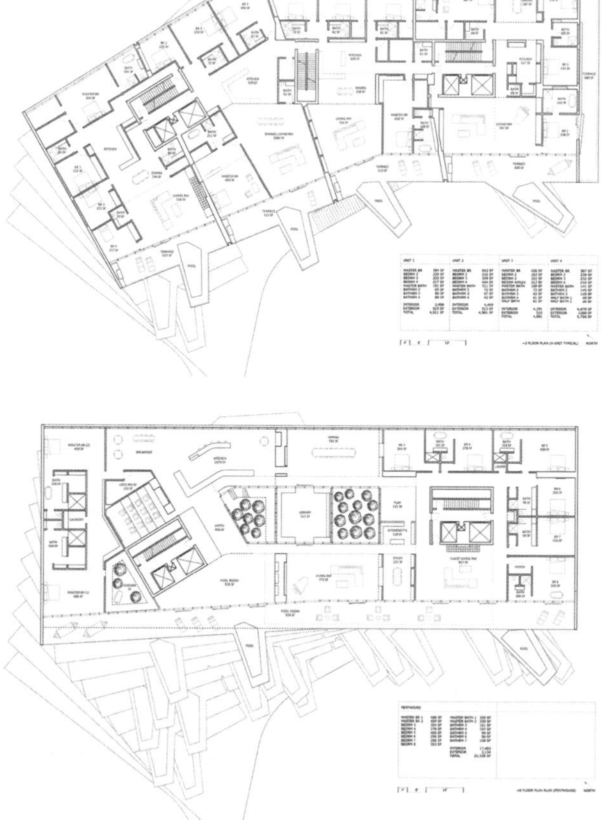

Fifth-floor plan (above), ninth-floor plan (below)

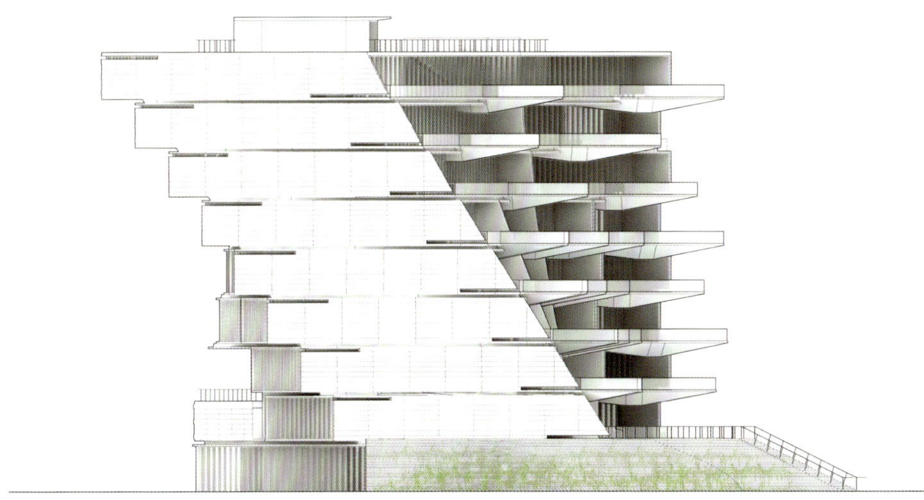

East elevation (above), north elevation (below)

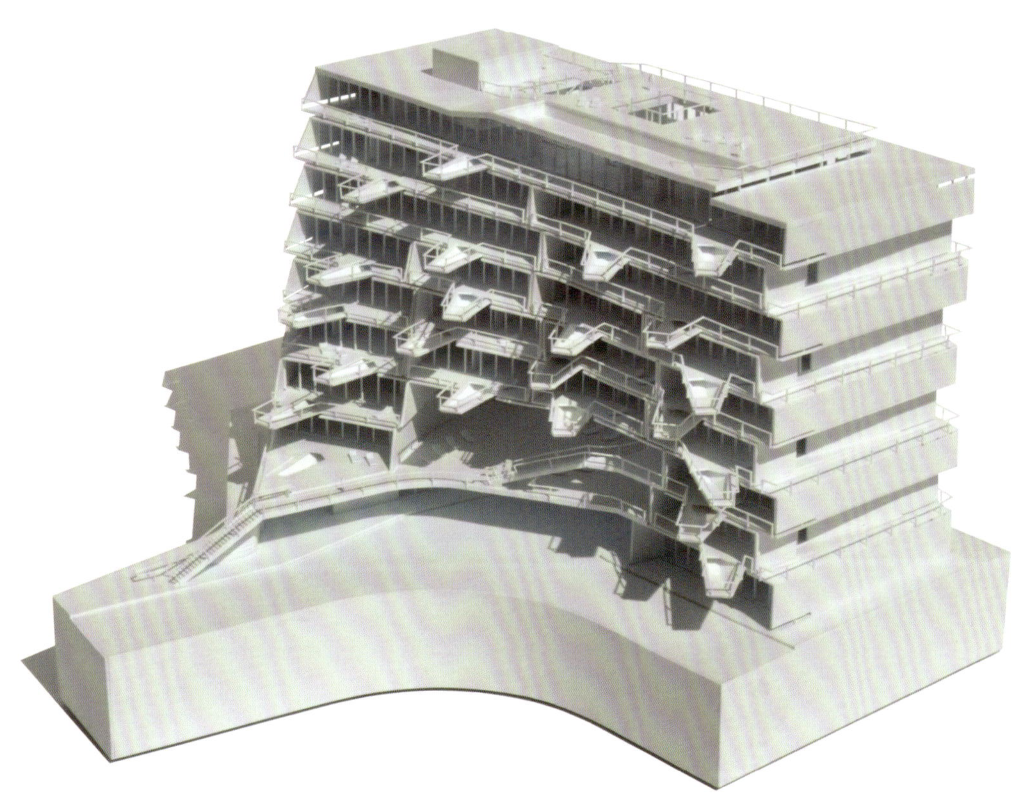

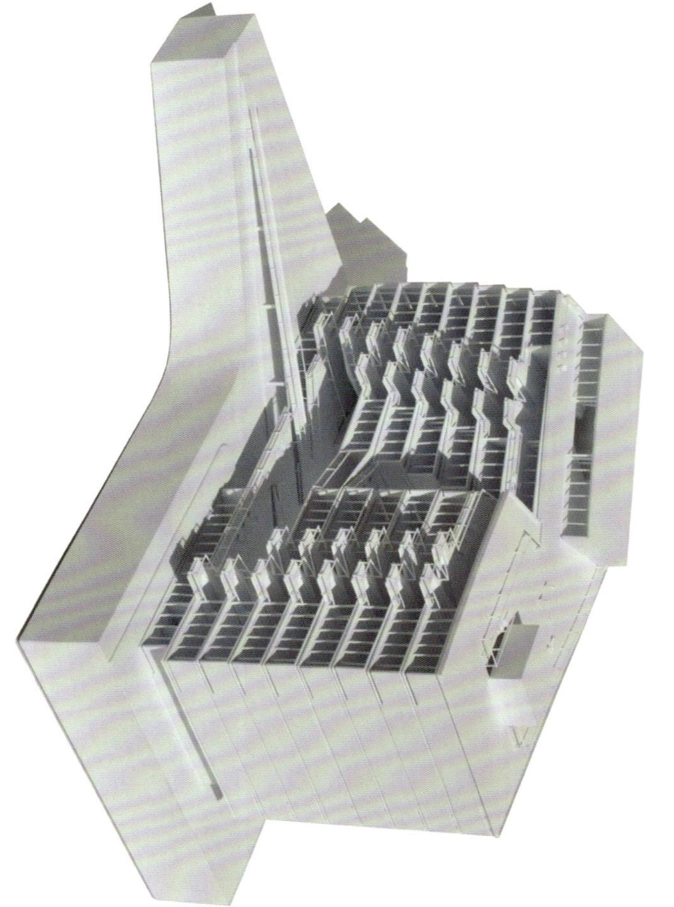

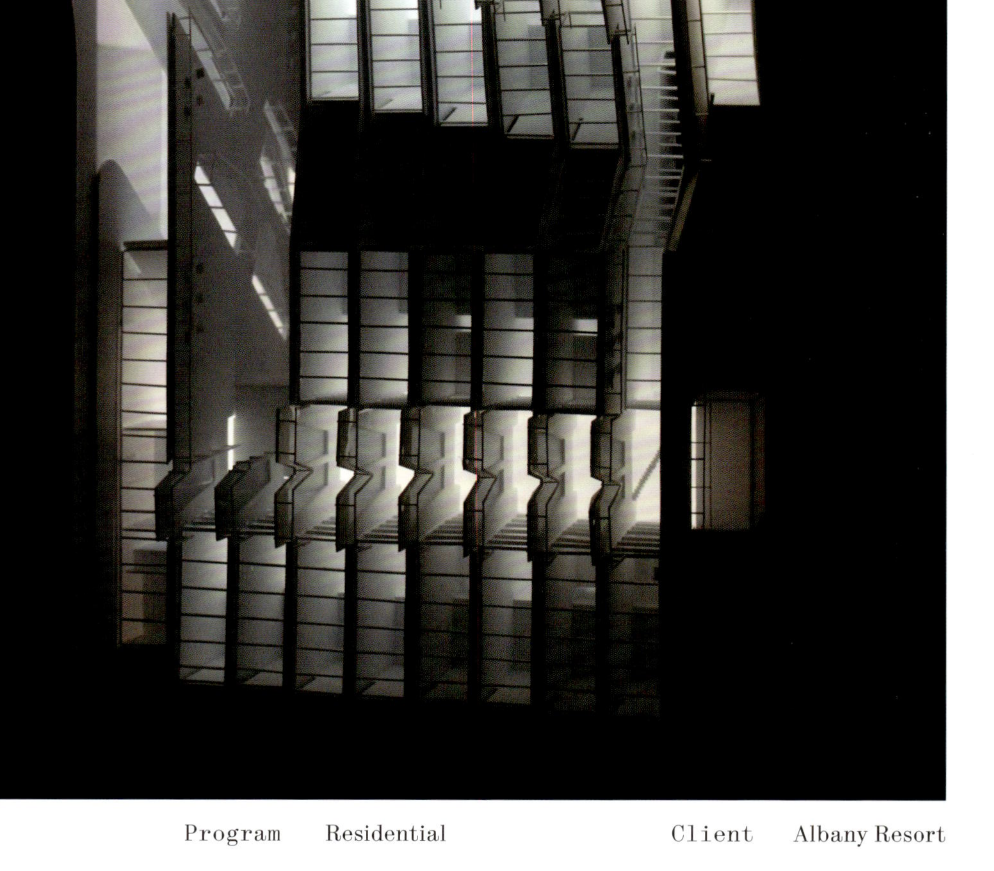

Site New Providence, Bahamas

Status Conceptual Design

Program Residential

Client Albany Resort

ALBANY HOUSING II ELEVATED GROUND

The Elevated Ground Condominium creates new pedestrian experiences by rerouting people through elevated streets defined by ramps. The building's position at a bend in the road alongside a marina separates the housing into two towers, which makes it possible for each condo unit to have at least three exterior edges, increasing access to light and opening up deck space. The design of the units themselves is more akin to individual houses than condos. Pools protrude from the building, making space for overlapping configurations of pools and covered decks. They are partially located within the building volume for structural purposes, as well as to create adjacencies with adjoining living spaces.

The Elevated Ground Condominium demonstrates that architecture cannot stand alone as a barren isolated object on the landscape. Rather, it should be considered as a part of a network of infrastructure that connects events and people together. Buildings require sensitive approaches toward creating cultural pairings with their surroundings and ecologies.

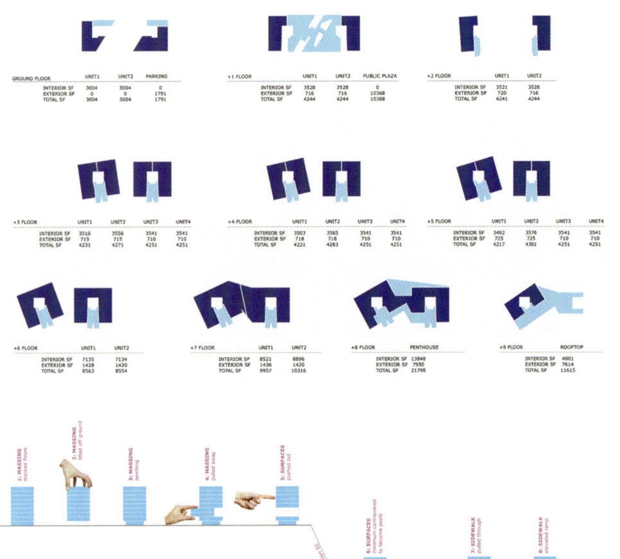

Housing unit diagrams

Design process diagram

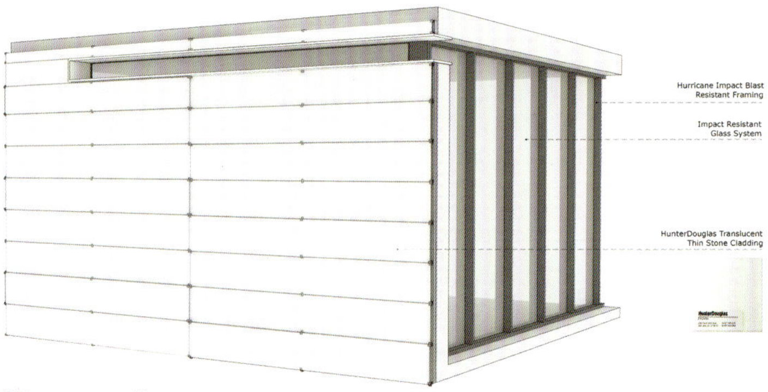

Skin system diagram

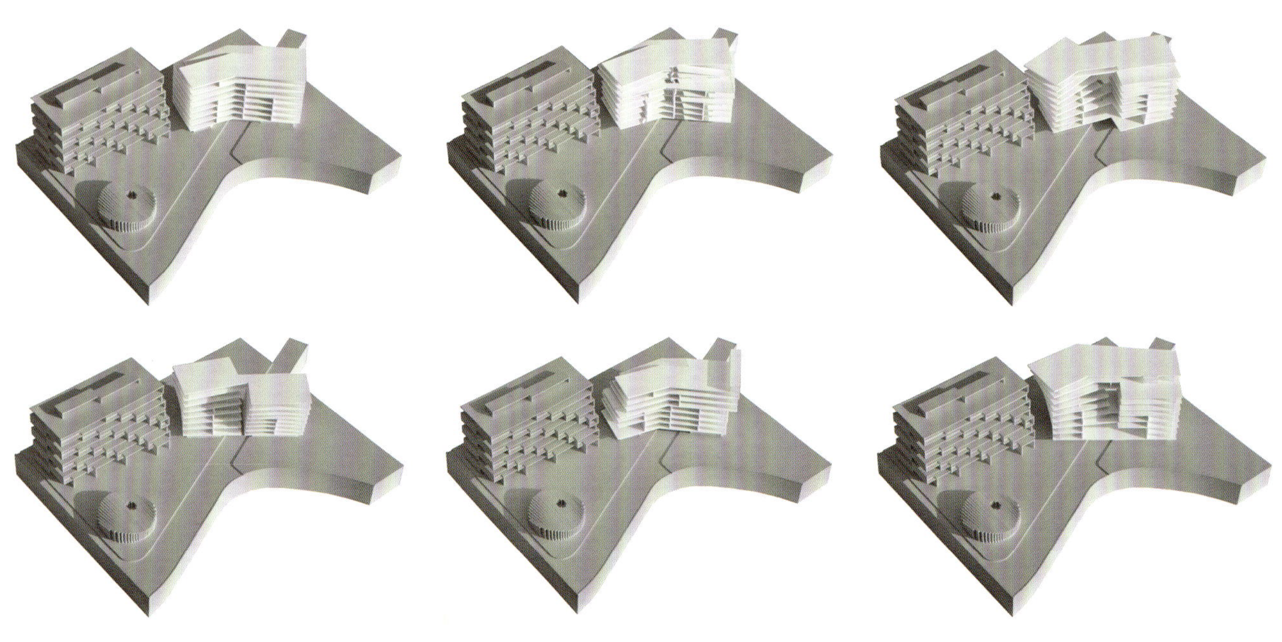

Fifth-floor plan (above), ninth-floor plan (below)

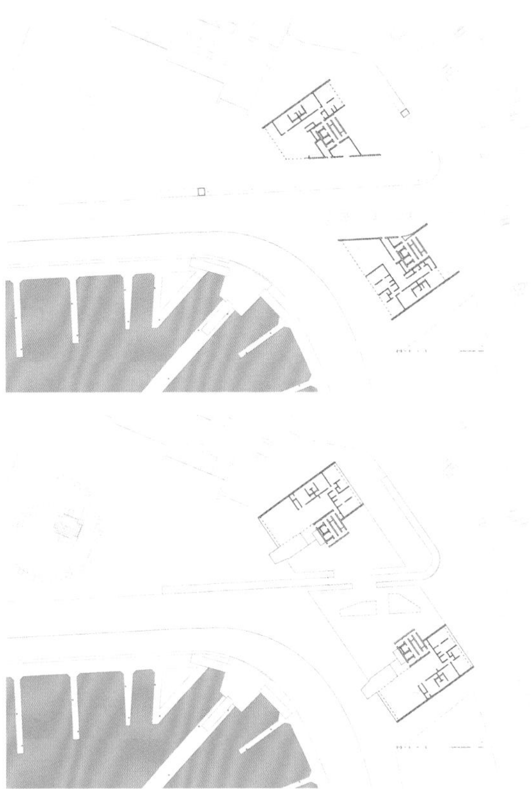

First-floor plan (above), second-floor plan (below)

Site plan

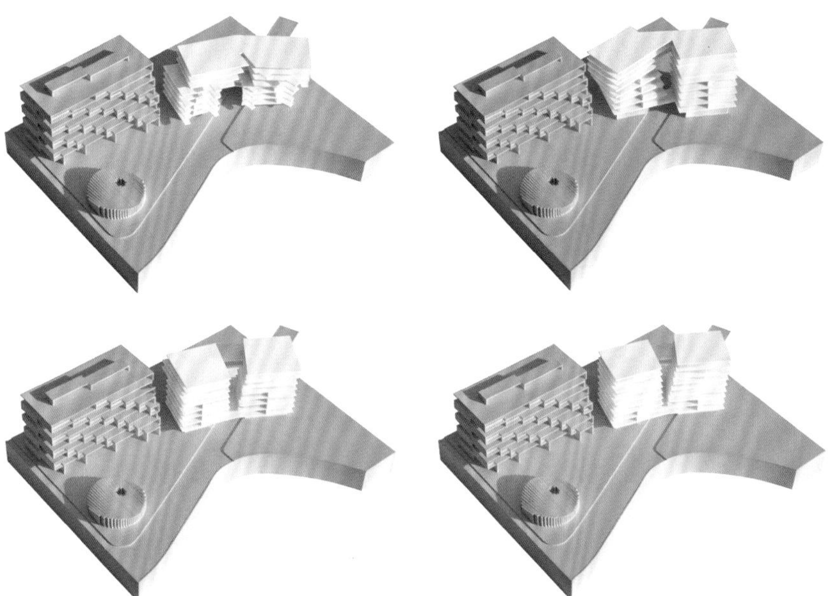

Massing models

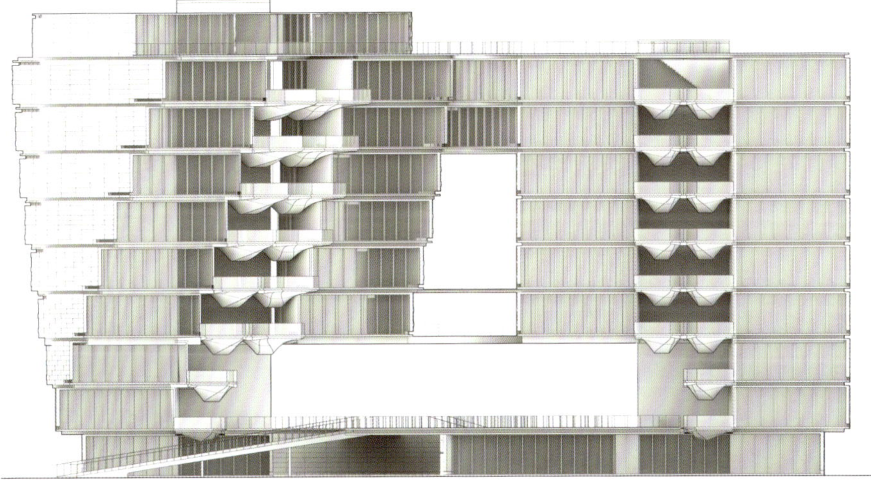

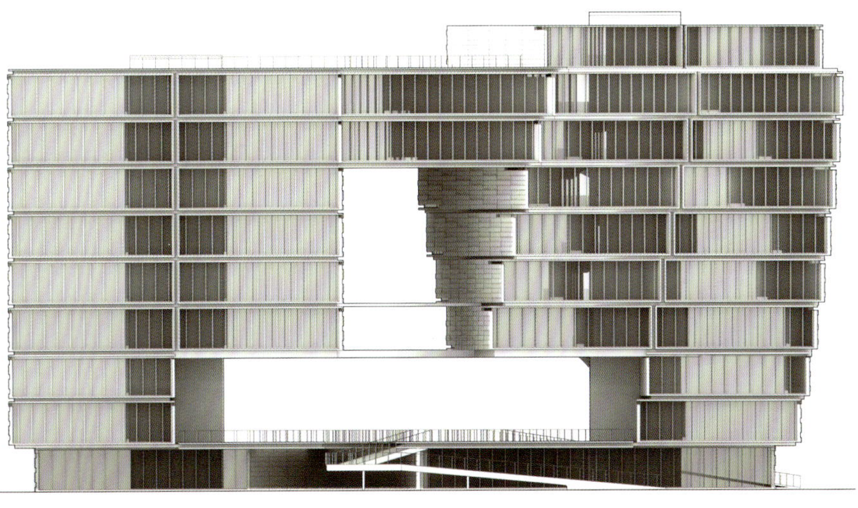

East elevation (above), west elevation (below)

Site Fuyang District Hangzhou, Zhejiang Province China

Status Built

Program Educational

Client Yongxing Education Group

SILVERLAKE INTERNATIONAL HIGH SCHOOL

Silverlake International High School is a premier educational institution located in Hangzhou, a cultural hub and nature resort destination in Zhejiang Province, China. The site is located at the foot of the mountains in the Fuyang district in a newly-constructed campus for a privately-run elementary, middle, and high school developed by the Yongxing Education Group.

The high school is designed to integrate Western and Chinese educational curricula. The Yongxing Education Group has extensive experience working with Western staff and administrators to develop a unique teaching, learning, and cultural environment for educators and students alike. Silverlake International High School acts as a bridge between traditional Chinese education and the globalized community, aiming to educate international citizens and the leaders of tomorrow.

The project's design is inspired by traditional Chinese landscape painting, the art form's deep relationship to the natural world serving as a conceptual foundation. Chinese depictions of nature in traditional landscape paintings are rarely mere representations of the external world; rather, they are articulations of the mind and heart of individual artists, enlightened landscapes that embody the cultural and social vision of a society. Such painted landscapes express the freedom of inhabiting a space with philosophical and political conviction. They challenge visual perceptions and atmospheric phenomena, opening up the possibility of a scholarly reading of the landscape, one embedded with poetry and calligraphic expressions.

The form of the building was inspired in part by *siheyuan* (traditional Chinese courtyard homes), in part by the practice of *feng shui*, and in part by the characteristics of the surrounding site. For example, the front angle of the southern façade references the mountains that serve as a beautiful backdrop to the campus.

A variety of materials are used for the building, some more neutral while others highlight areas of significance. The main exterior façades use a glazed white tile for the exterior, each with a consistent pattern. The north façade is notable for its more dynamic approach; some bricks angle outward to create texture and movement along the façade. The shadows created by these small deviations add another layer of complexity by recalling the shadows created along the mountainside by trees and foliage.

The interior of the building echoes the transparency and layering used in Chinese landscape paintings by overlapping areas of program, circulation, and common space to produce transparent dimensions throughout the spaces.

The exterior landscape is designed to give the user a unique journey through layers of different experiences: the rain garden, courtyard, building entry procession, and bridges that connect the buildings each have their own distinct character. Incorporated into the landscape is a misting technology used to create a surreal environment that is inspired by the atmospheric perspective found in traditional Chinese landscape paintings. The mist also serves the functional purpose of watering native plants and creating a cooler microclimate at the base of the building. The landscape is integrated not only into the area around the building but also into the building itself. Hanging plants ornament the connecting bridges, green roofs cover most exposed roof planes, and the courtyard becomes a lush area of indigenous foliage.

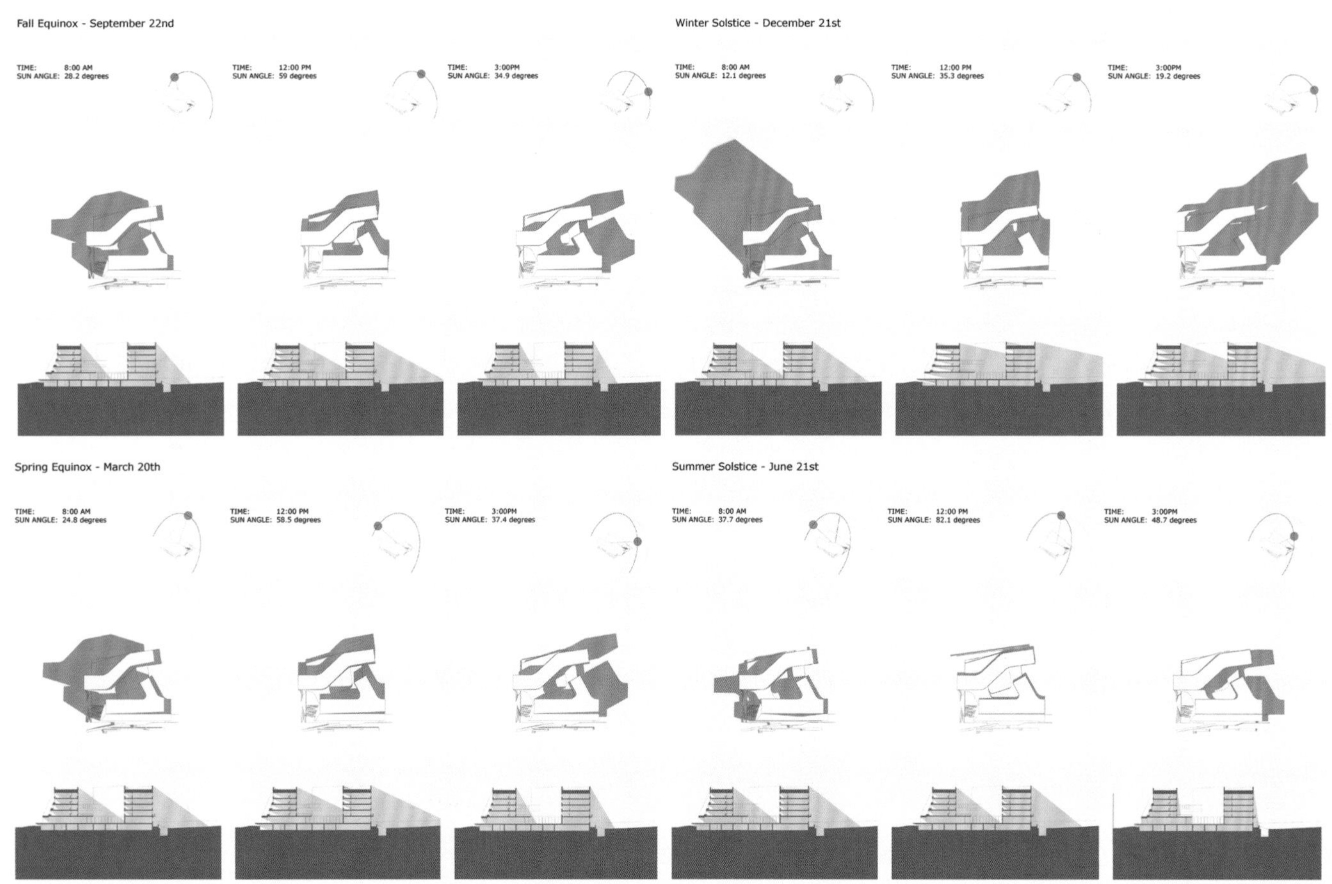

Shadow study diagrams

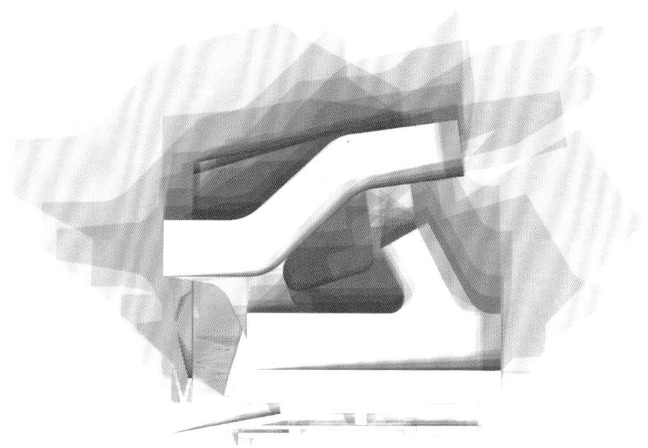

Overlapping shadow studies

Due to the sloping nature of the site, the building's entrances are split between the lower level (on the east side) and the first level (on the west and south sides). The lowest level accommodates a parking garage, a restaurant with a full Western-style kitchen, a workout room, and a music department. The latter has a large classroom, storage, two small practice rooms, and a small amphitheater at the base of an open stair which can also be used for small-scale performances audible in the lobby above. Some of the other programs also serve multiple purposes, such as a restaurant that can be enjoyed by off-campus visitors as well as a retreat for faculty to dine in.

Almost every area of the building has a dedicated view of natural elements, which helps to reestablish the connection between human beings and the environment. The main entrance is on the first level, facing the campus and its large open lobby serves as a hub for people visiting from off campus. A reception room for parents is comfortably situated next to trophy cases, a small cafe, and a reading and gallery space where students can exhibit artwork. The generously-sized student dining area also opens directly up to the adjacent courtyard, allowing students to eat outside.

In keeping with the Chinese tradition of hierarchy, the main administrative offices are located on the top floor, while some additional administrative services are provided on the first floor including counseling, advising, admissions, and the nurse's station. In response to code requirements, the chemistry labs are located on the first floor next to a flexible space reserved for a future library or other function when the school expands. The bulk of the classrooms and faculty offices are located on the upper four floors. The south wing primarily hosts the Chinese homerooms and the north wing is mainly occupied by AP and specialty classrooms such as art, calligraphy, and a maker space. Both wings have spaces for either faculty or department offices.

On each floor, small areas referred to as "soft spaces" are set aside to allow students to gather informally, to socialize, rest, and study between classes. These spaces foster the collaborative environment and events that truly define an advanced educational system. The Silverlake International High School is designed to respond to the transformations of traditional Chinese culture and education brought about by social engagement with the West.

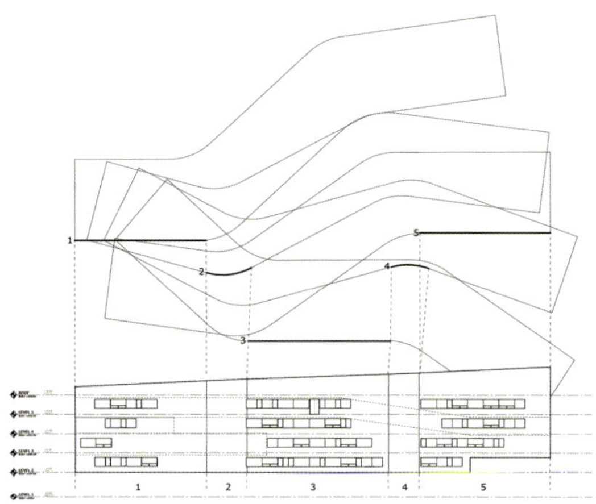

Unrolled south courtyard elevation

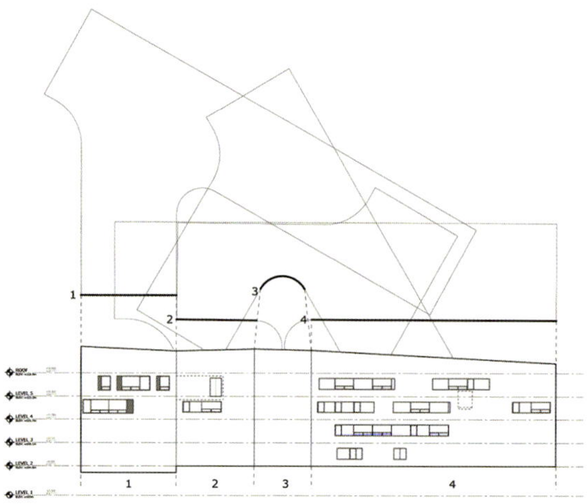

Unrolled north courtyard elevation

Chinese landscape painting sectional diagram

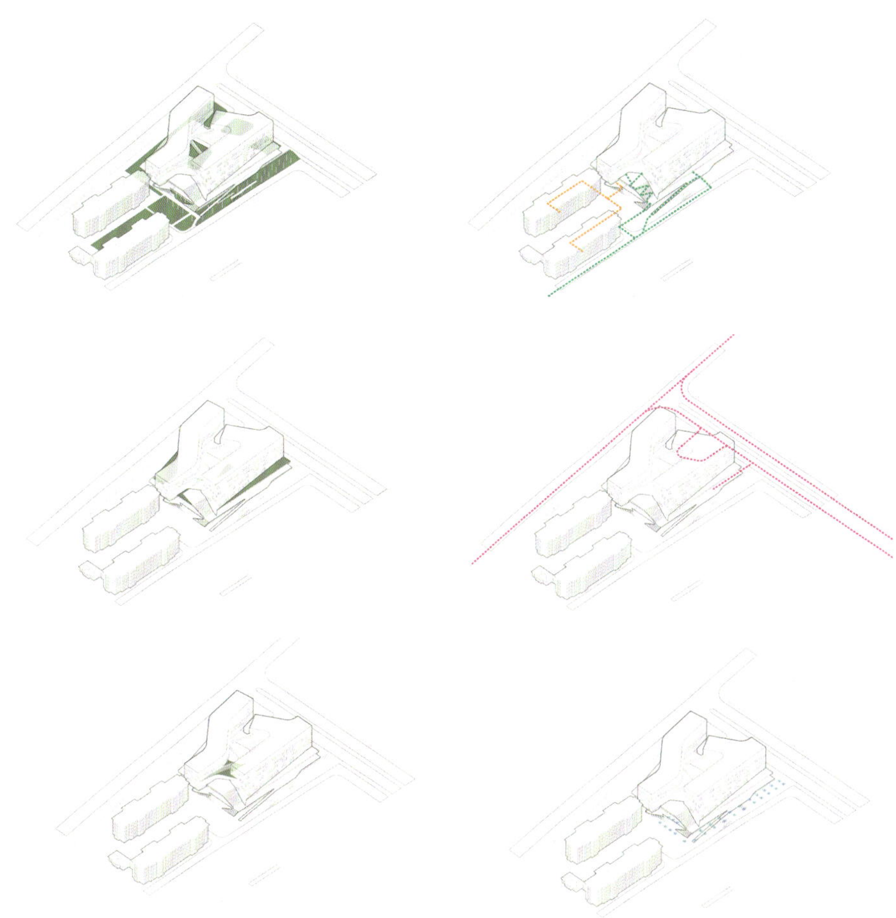

Green space: first level, second level, third level (top to bottom)

Pedestrian campus connection, vehicle circulation, micro-climate mister locations (top to bottom)

Aerial master plan

Site context diagram

Context

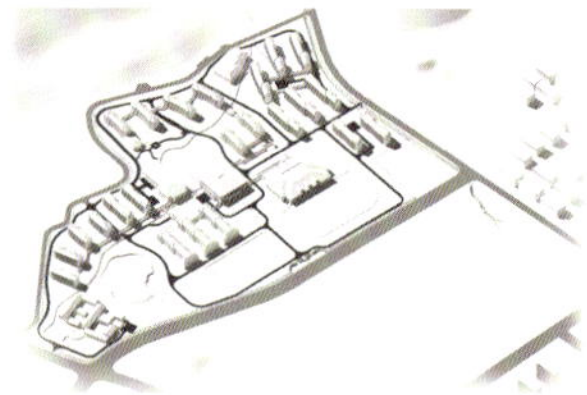

Roads

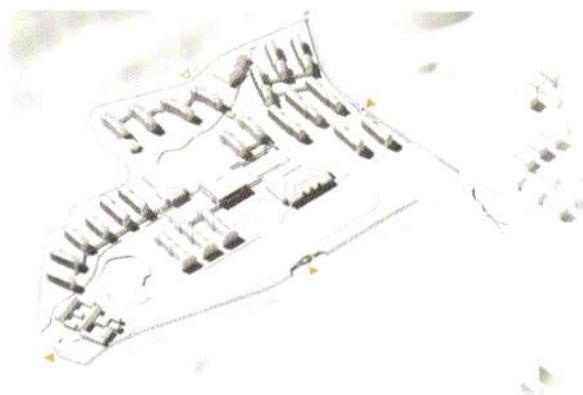

Entrances

Campus extent

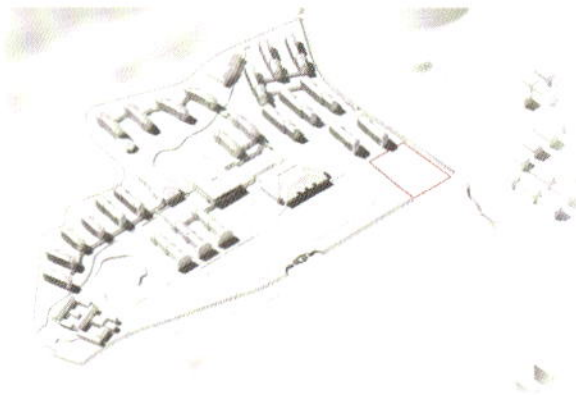

Site location

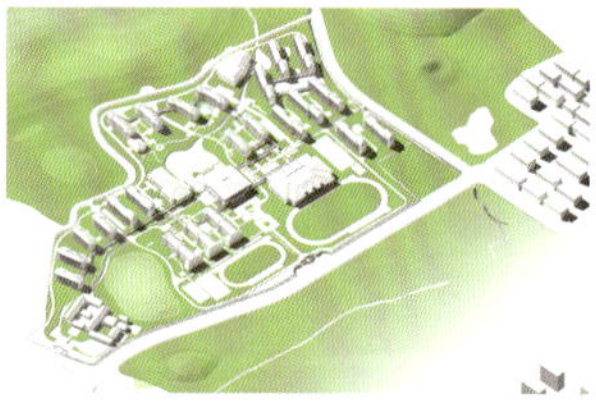

Green space

Water

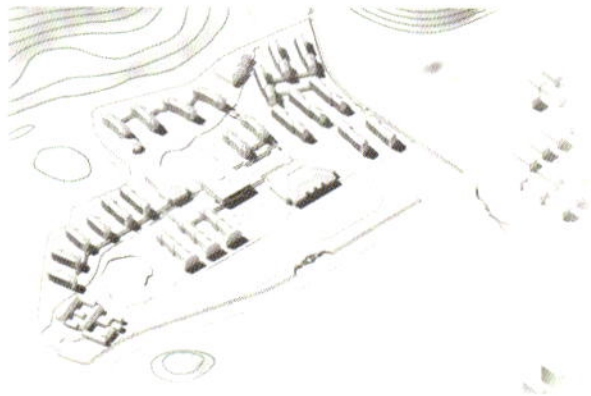

Topography

Program

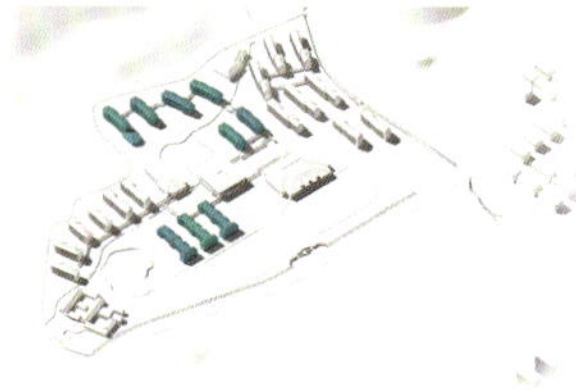

Classrooms

Dining halls

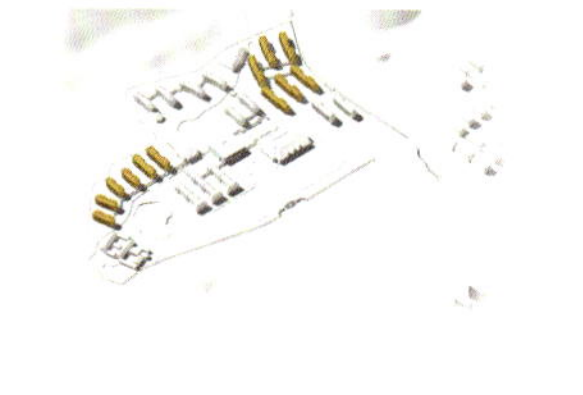

Student dorms

Faculty dorms

Administration

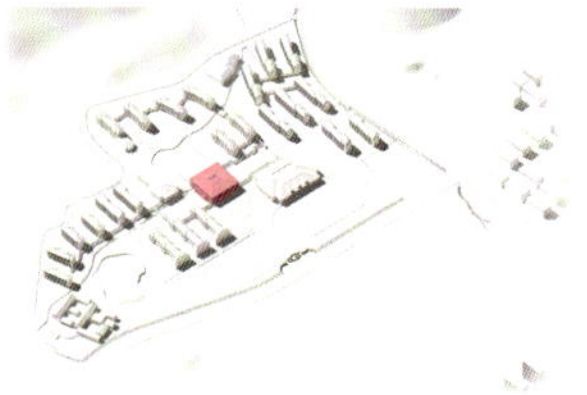

Library

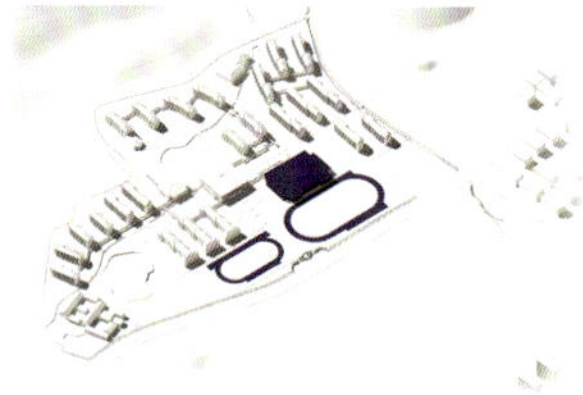

Athletic facilities

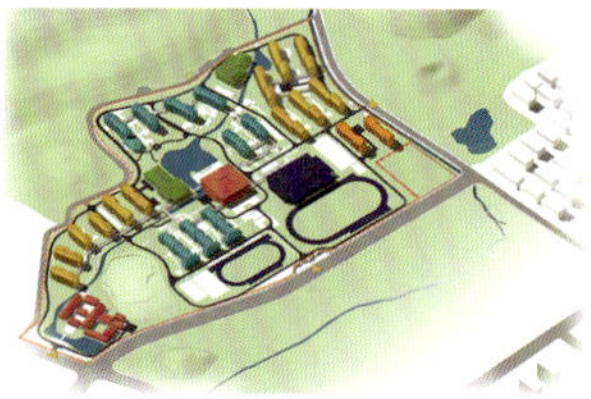

Combined

Chinese landscape analytical diagrams

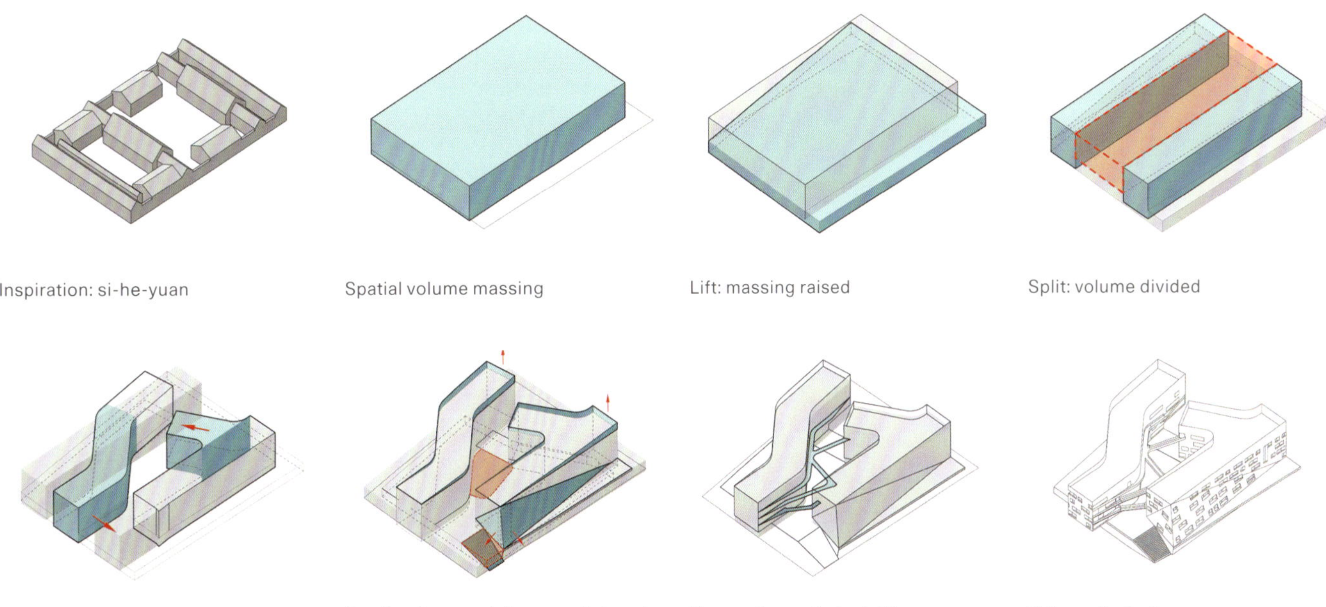

Inspiration: si-he-yuan

Spatial volume massing

Lift: massing raised

Split: volume divided

Form: pull massing

Detail: raise east / slope south facade

Connection: exterior bridges

Schematic design

Lower-floor plan

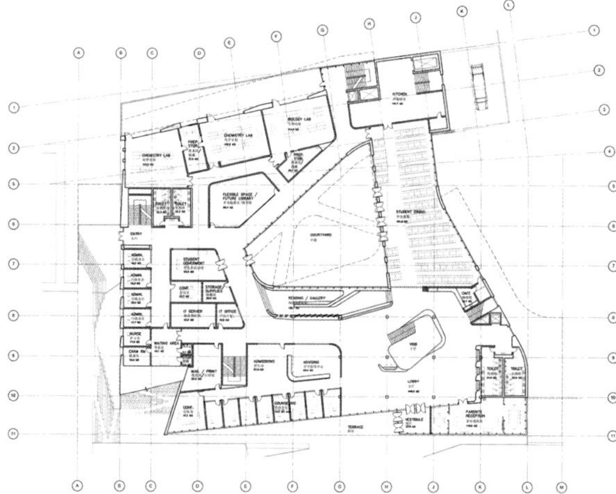

First-floor plan

Second-floor plan

Third-floor plan

Fourth-floor plan

Fifth-floor plan

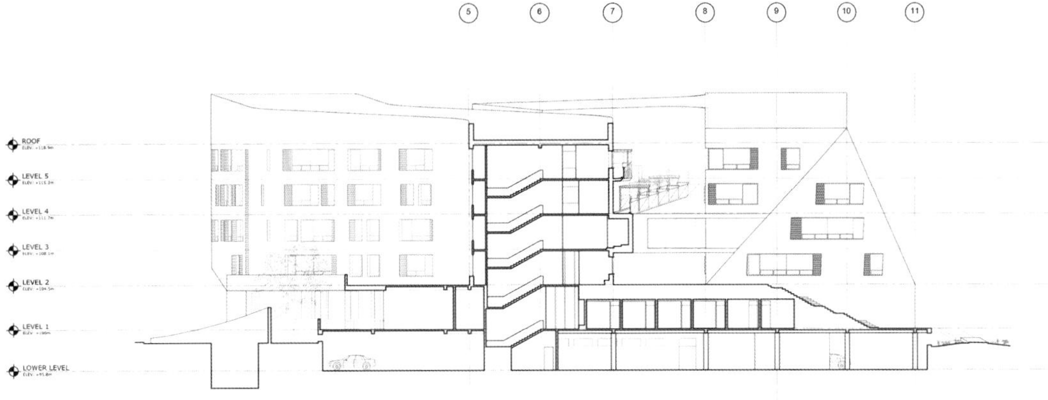

Transverse section 01

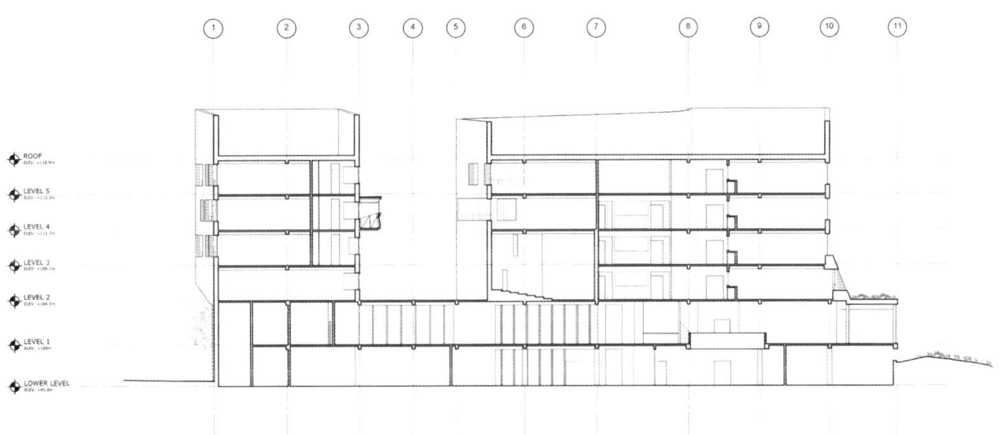

Transverse section 02

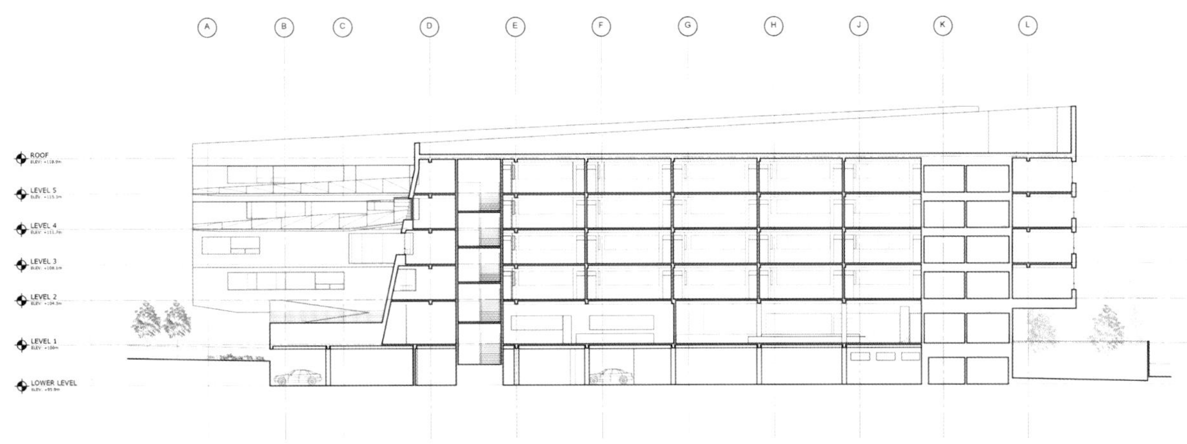

Longitudinal section

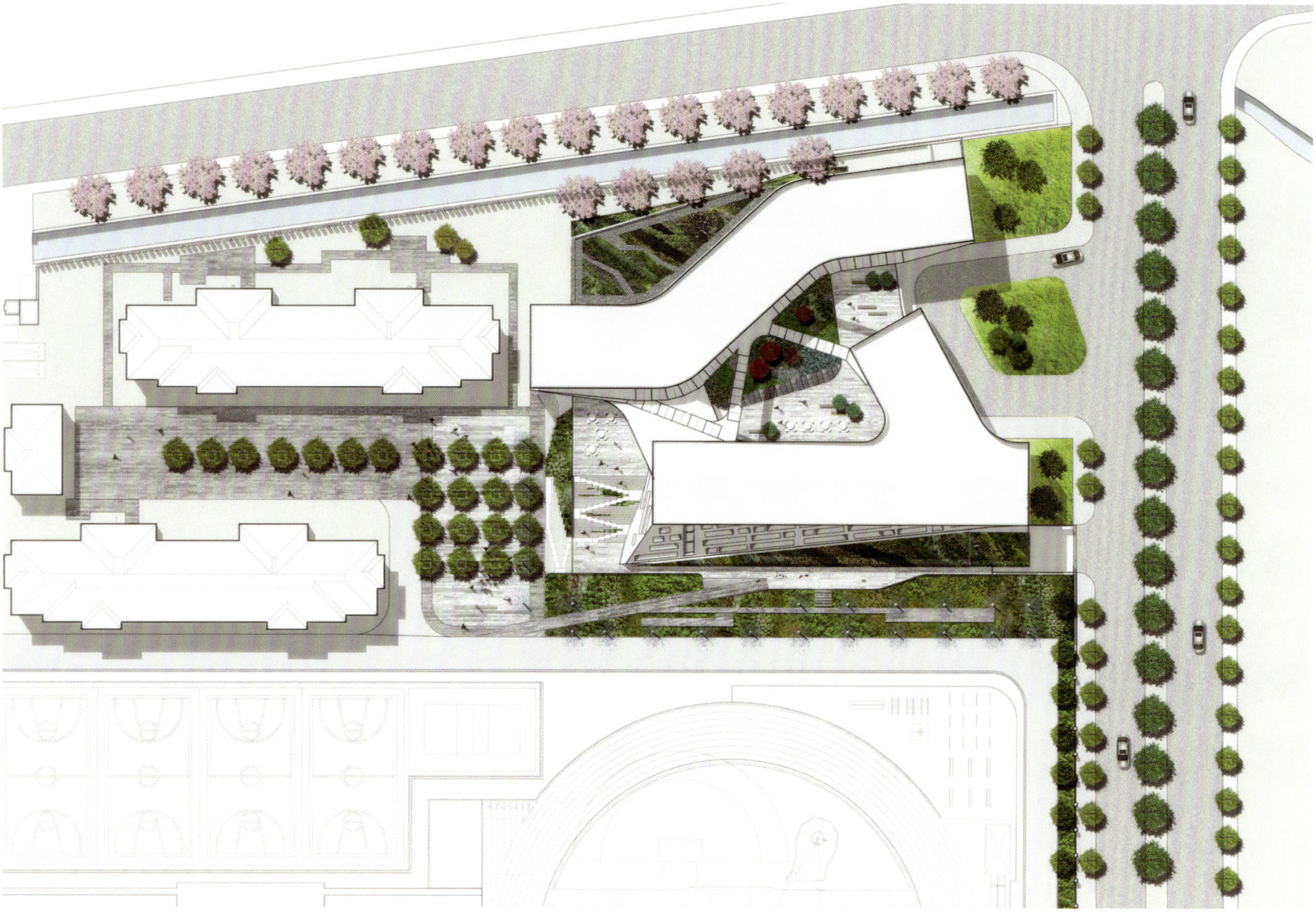

Site plan

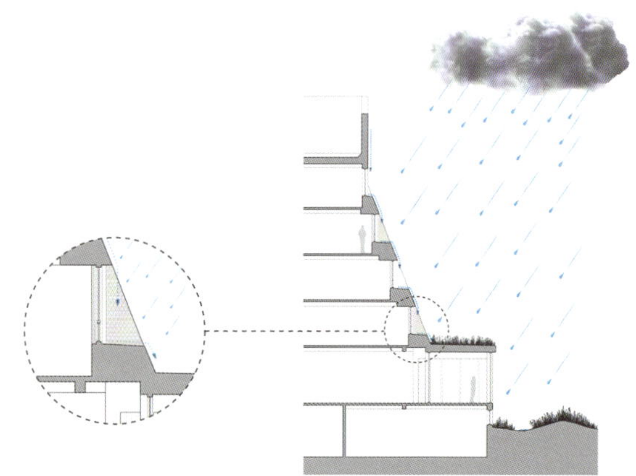

Water infrastructure diagram

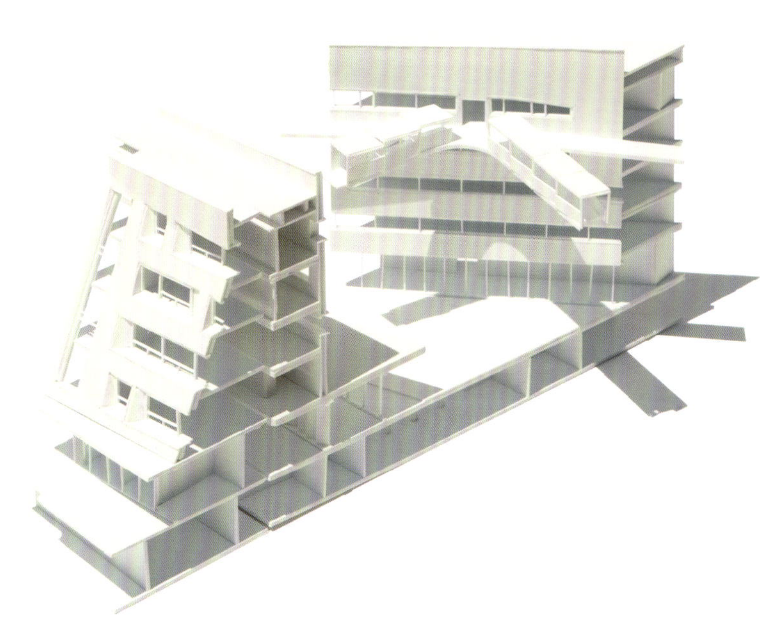

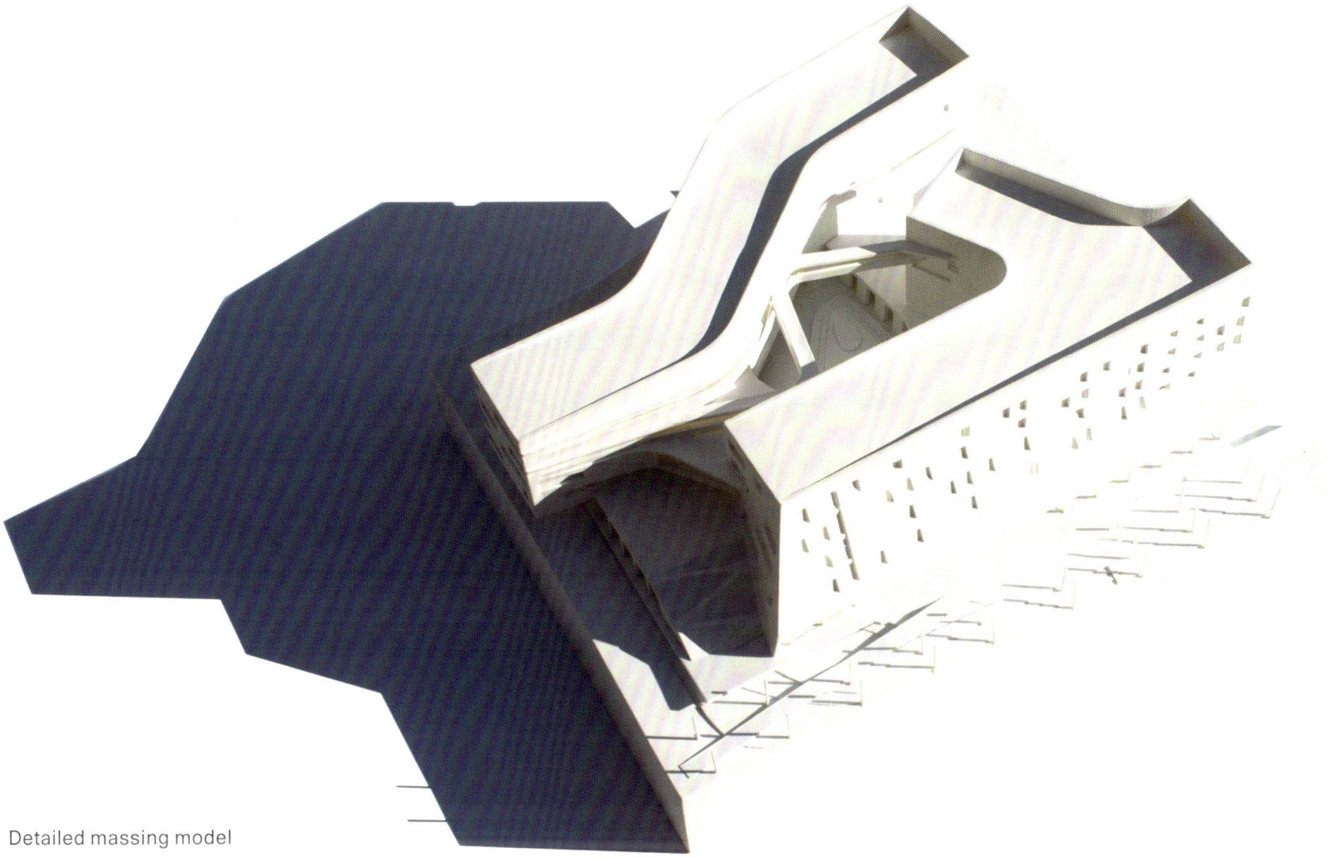

Detailed massing model

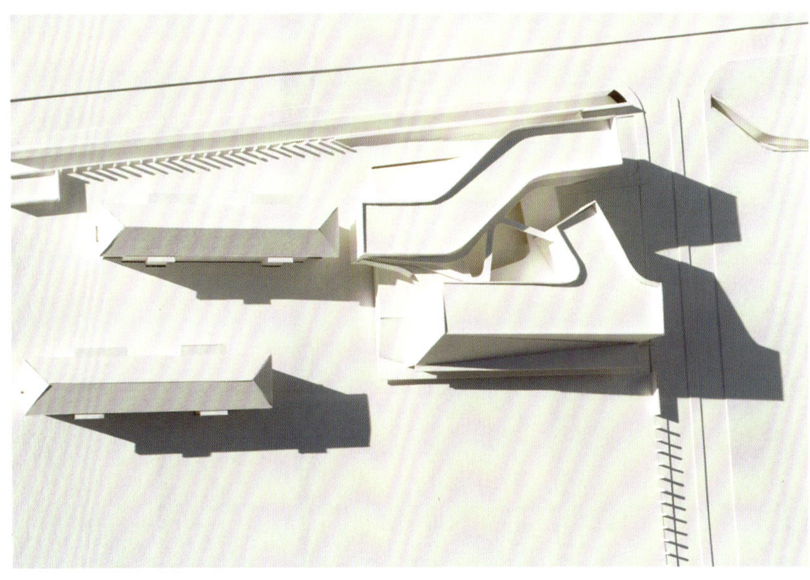

Site model

South elevation

East elevation

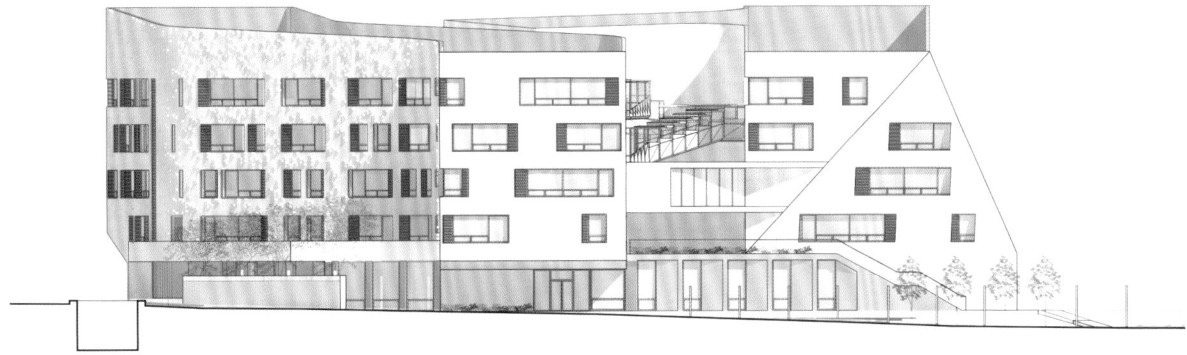

West elevation

North elevation

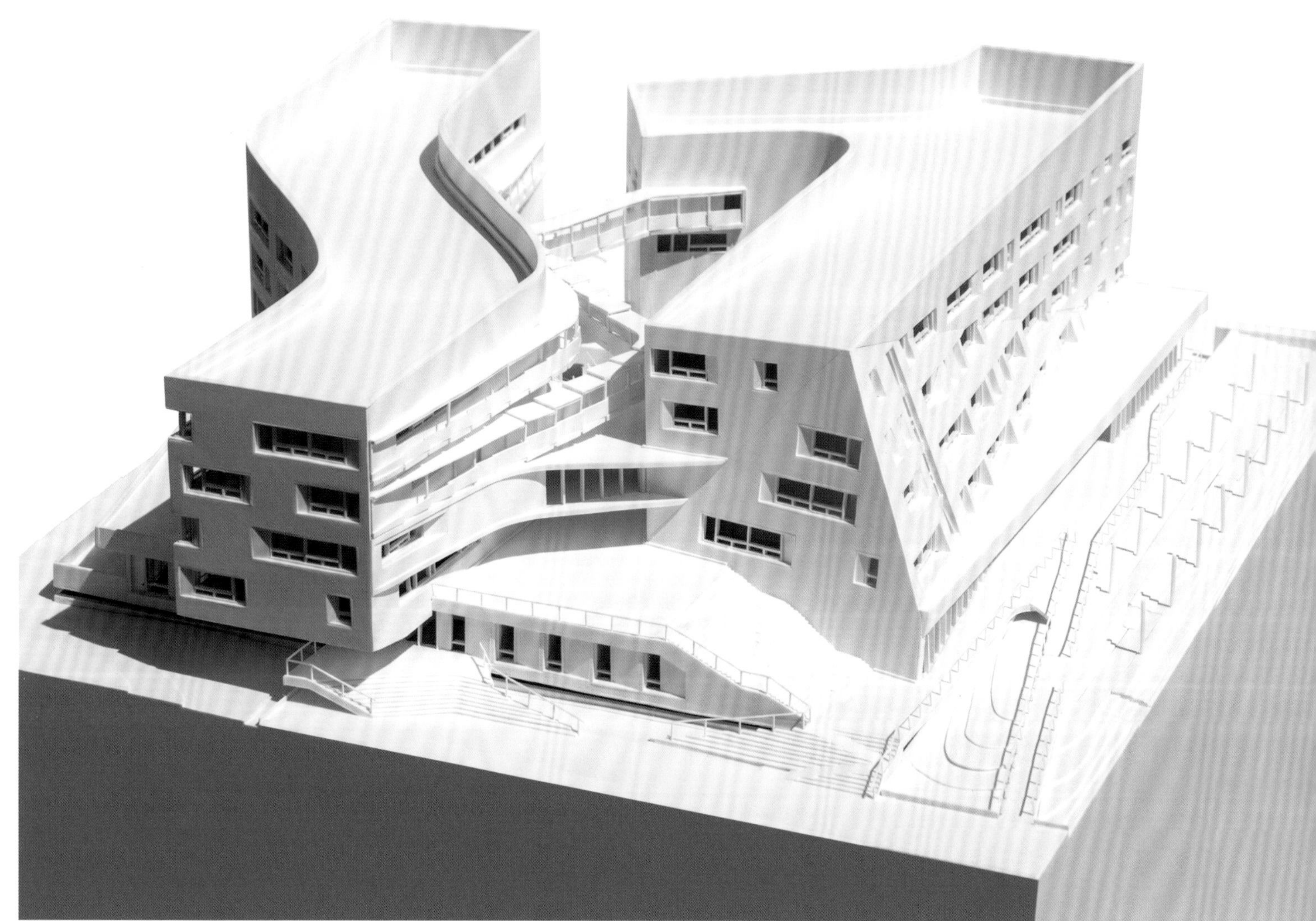

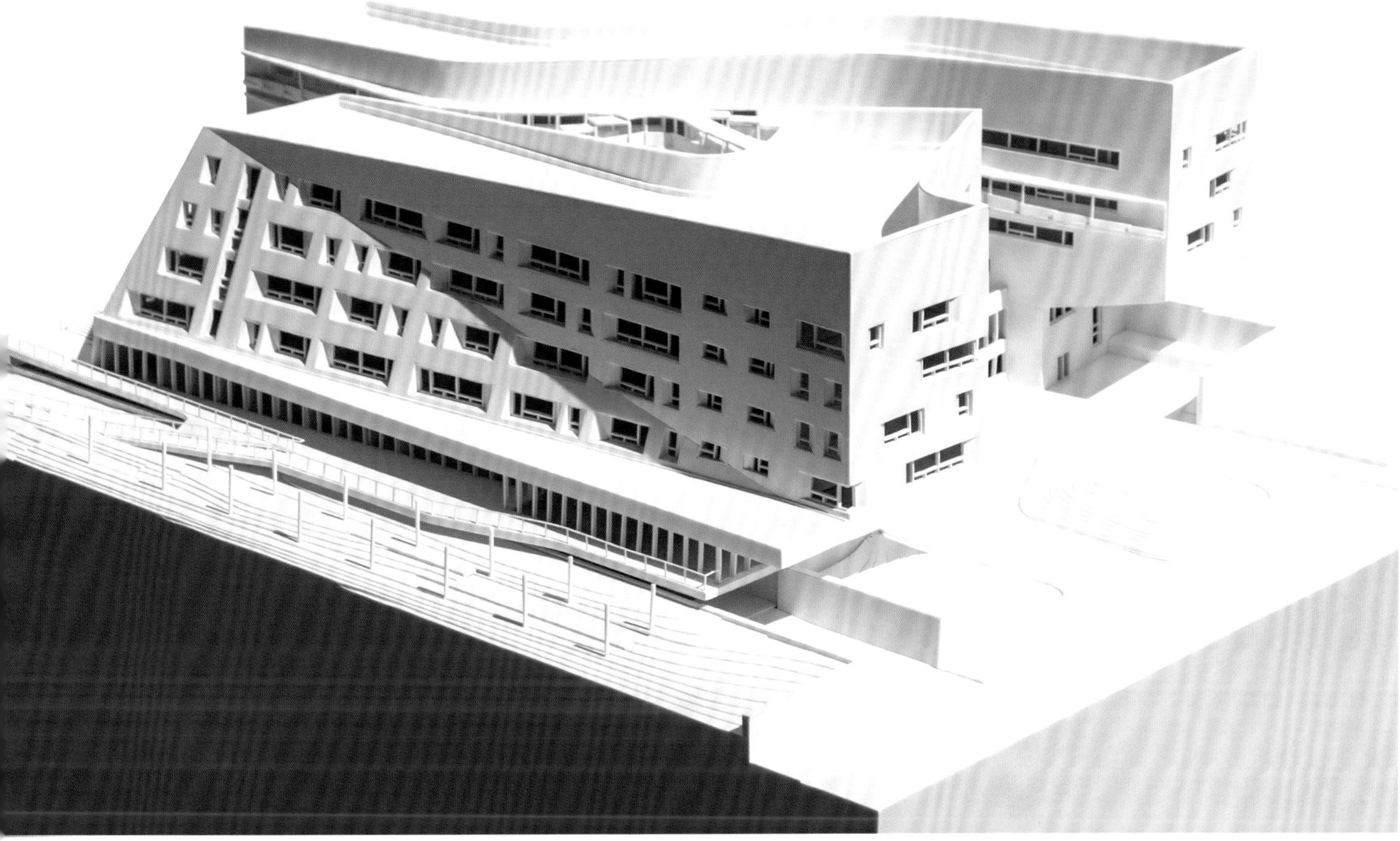

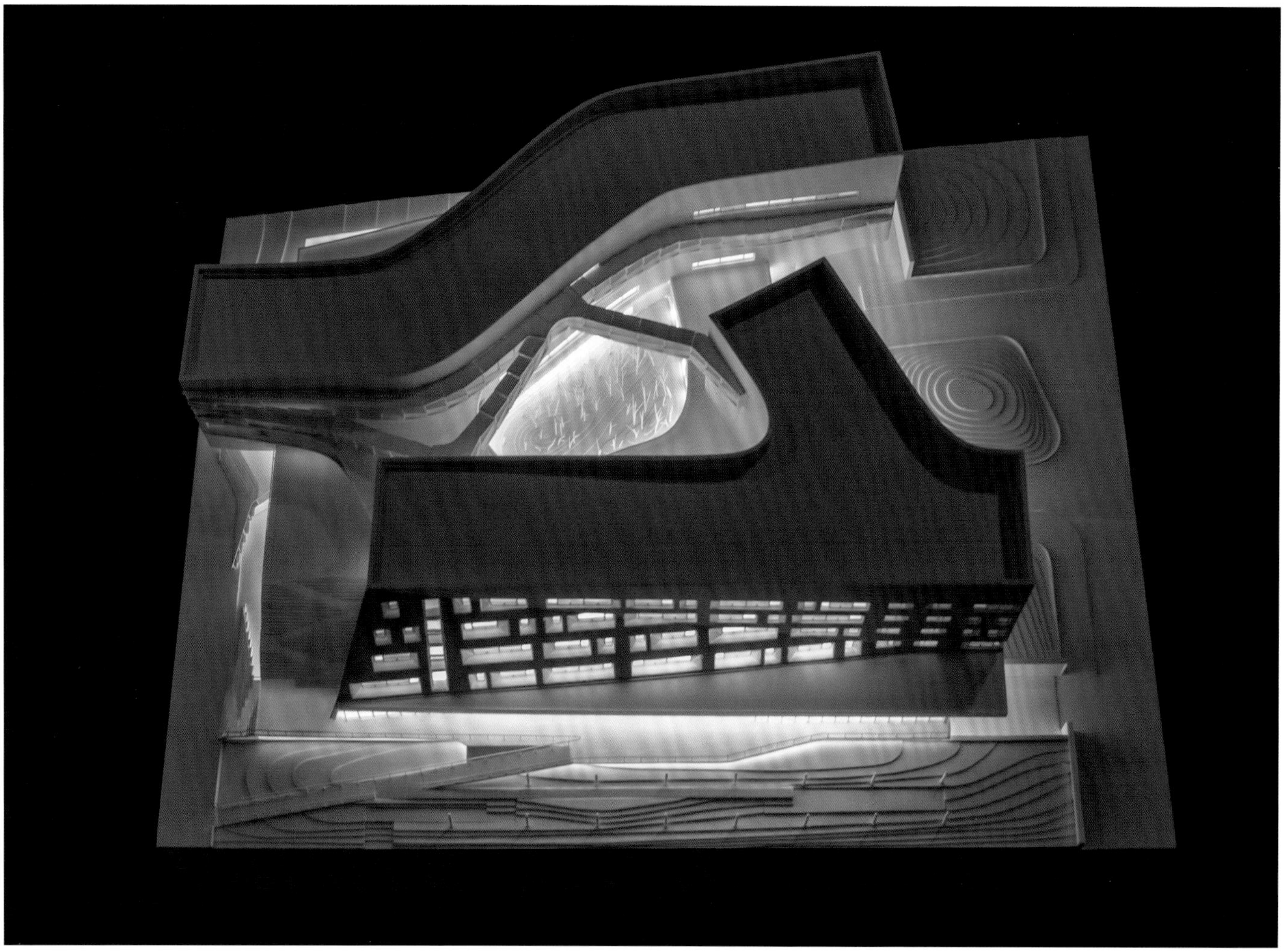

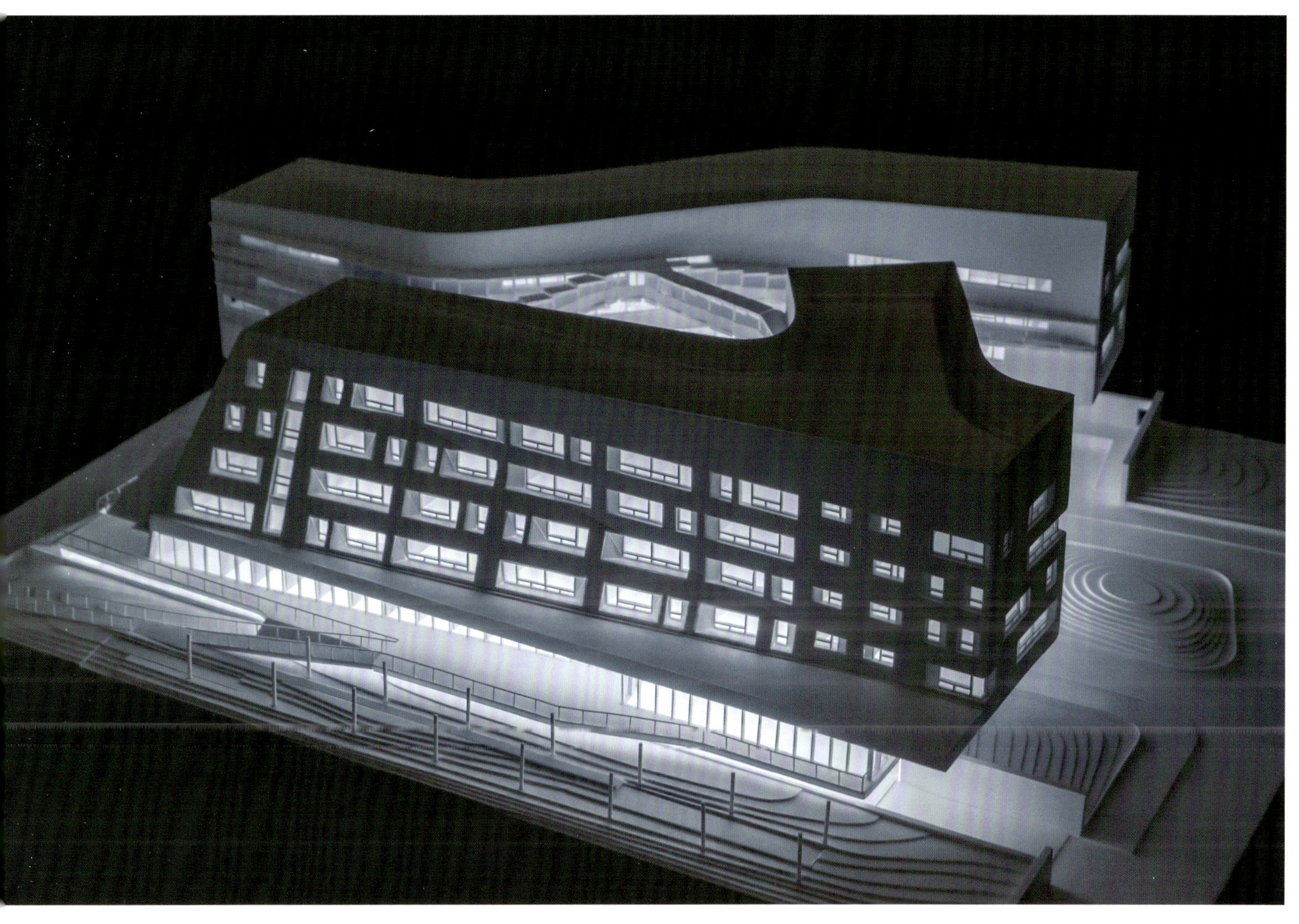

silverlake international
high school

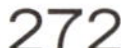

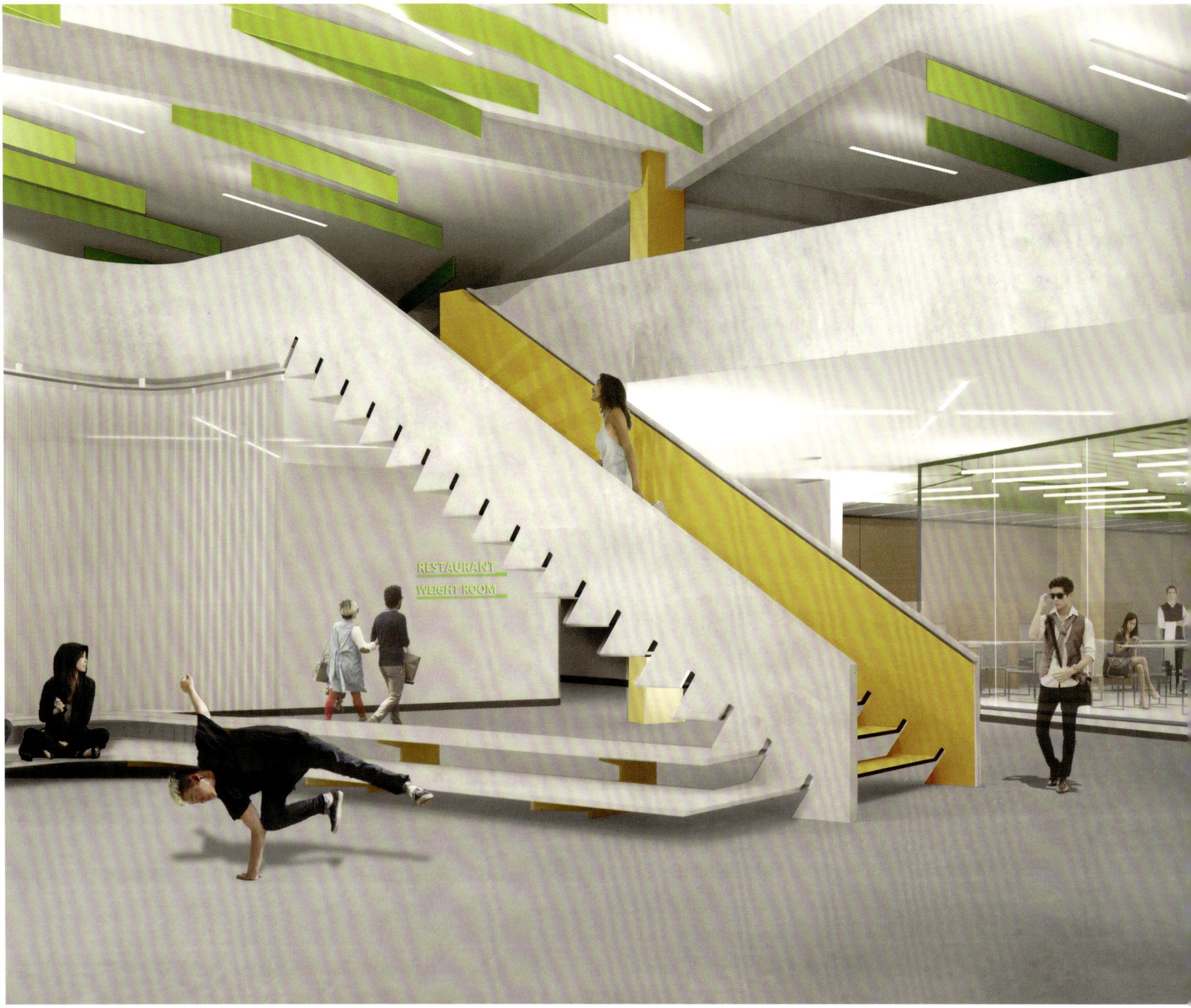
RESTAURANT
WEIGHT ROOM

Site Jecheon, South Korea

Status Design Development

Program Residential

Client YC Saw Mill

MICRO HOUSING I

Micro Housing I—inspired by the Korean tradition of connecting the mountains with one's ancestral rituals—provides basic shelter from both the open wilderness on weekends and dense urban life on weekdays. This single-family prefabricated dwelling unit integrates the comforts of the modern home with a profound freedom that unites the spirit of life with the landscape. This off-grid, compact home is designed as a simple small cabin sheathed in zinc and wood with plywood interiors.

Micro Housing I contains a kitchenette, upper-level sleeping quarters, a bathroom, storage, hot water heaters, waste management units, and power generators. The building is designed as an energy-efficient home fabricated with high and low thermal mass wall assemblies. To maintain a stable temperature within the house, the roof folds seamlessly into the walls, which house the insulation, glazing, shading, and ventilation systems that perform together to absorb any excessive heat energy. Exterior decks encourage outdoor family activities and help to blend the architecture into the landscape.

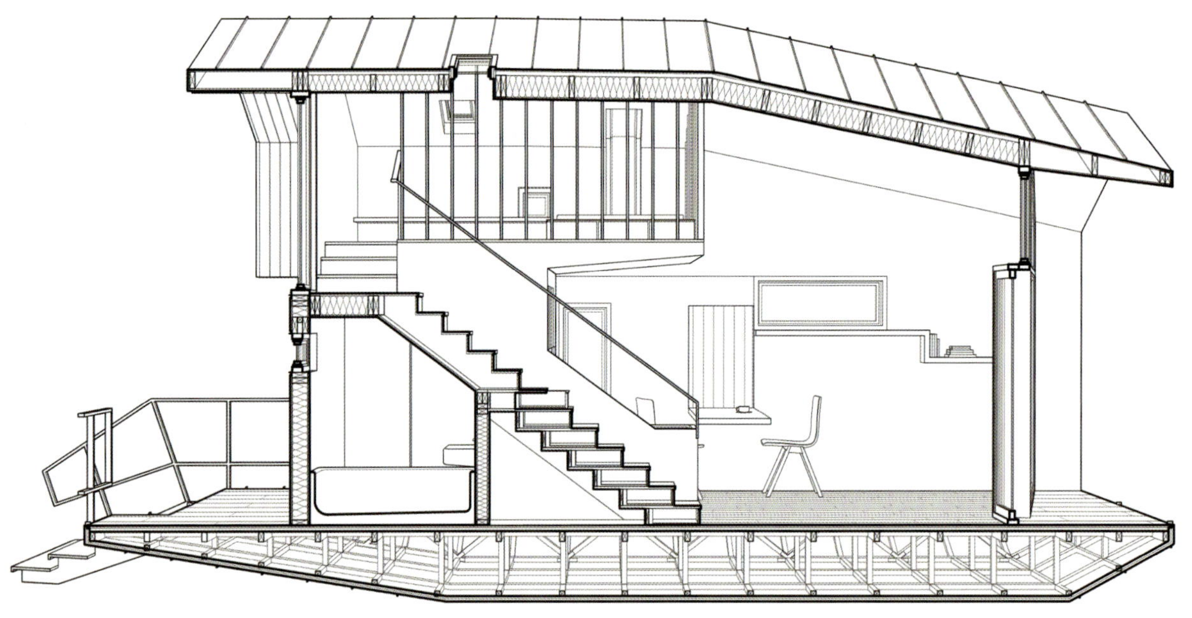

Longitudinal perspectival section

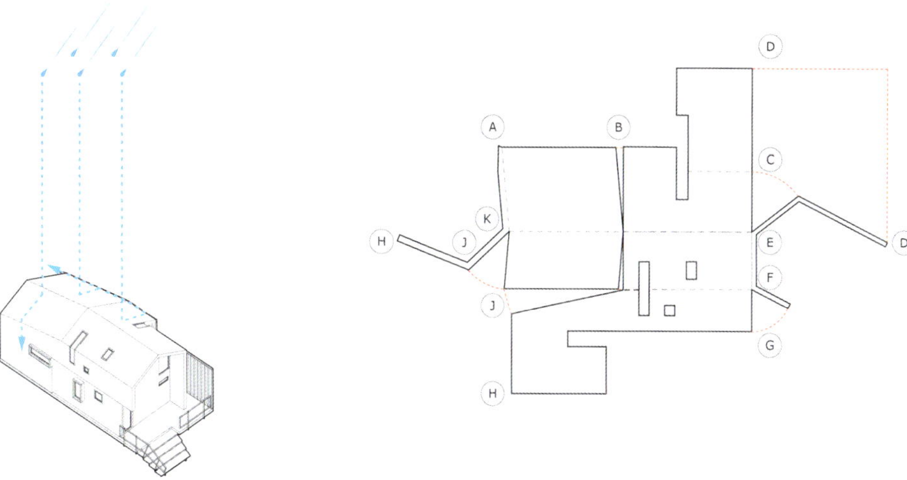

Water flow diagram

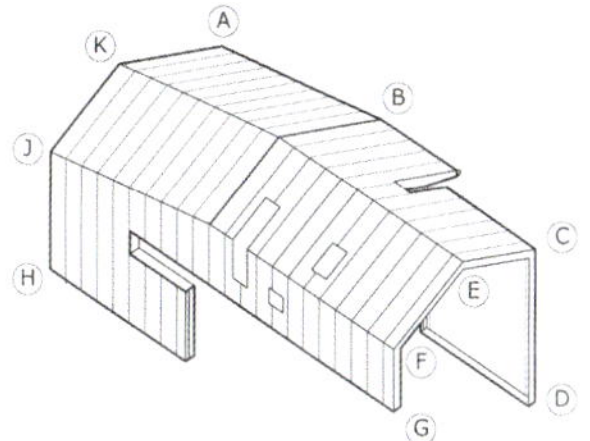

Unfolded roof diagram (above), roof panelization diagram (below)

Unfolded study model

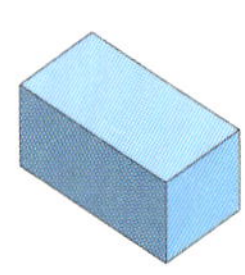

Massing

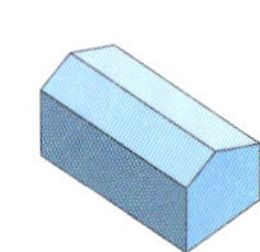

Roof angles

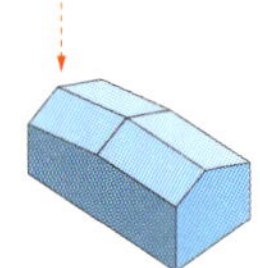

Push roof

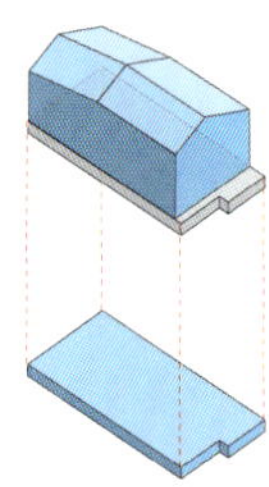

Plinth

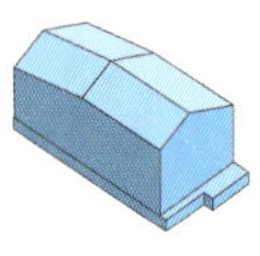

Detail massing

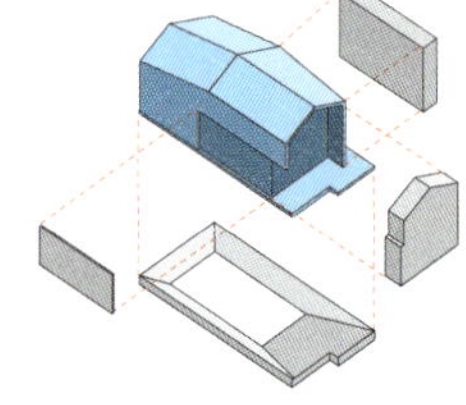

Articulating mass

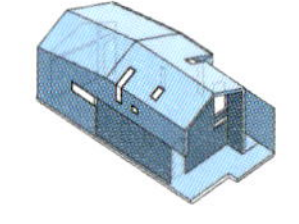

Fenestration

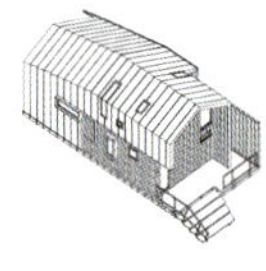

Material details

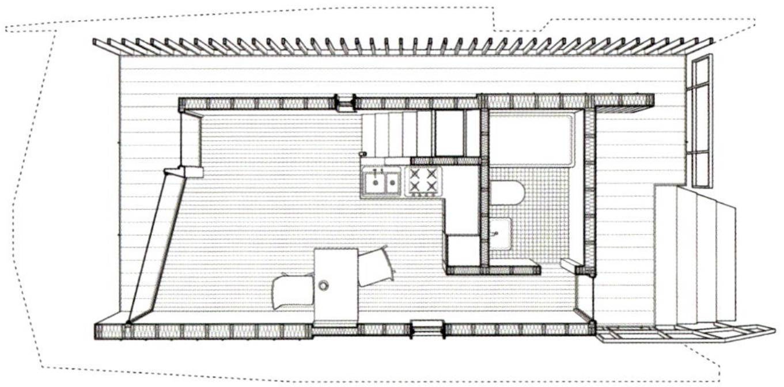

First-floor perspectival plan

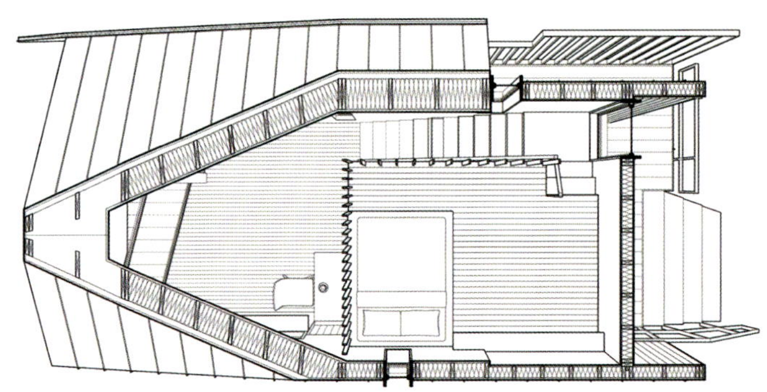

Second-floor perspectival plan

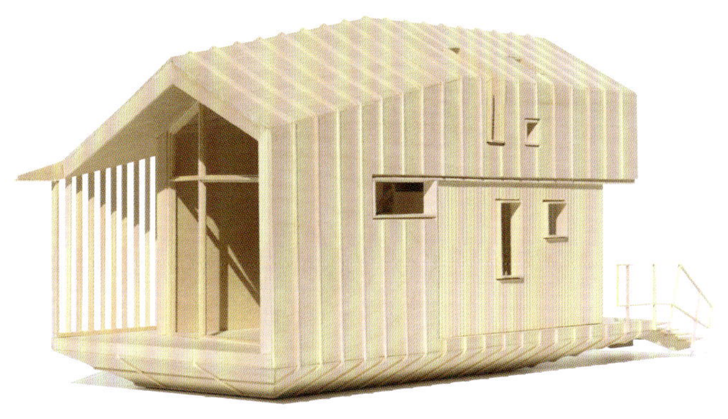

Site Jecheon, South Korea

Status Design Development

Program Residential

Client YC Saw Mill

MICRO HOUSING II

While Micro Housing I comprises one unit designed for a nuclear family, Micro Housing II combines two units within one structure to accommodate a multi-generational family. Korean lifestyles require domestic spaces characterized by fluid rather than fixed separations because historically Korean homes resisted designating rooms by a single function and instead often had multiple programmatic overlaps. In order to maximize flexibility, the design for Micro Housing II focuses on the creation of sufficient privacy while still prioritizing space that fosters a sense of collectivity.

The kitchenette and dining room are designed to be shared by all family members while the communal areas used by elders are increased in volume; the children's unit, on the other hand, occupies the more private zones of the house. This approach places the elder generation at the center of the family system. Room sharing among generations also improves interior space efficiency and encourages multiple uses of each space. In addition, the project embraces the landscape through its use of outdoor patios and decks that blend exterior and interior functions.

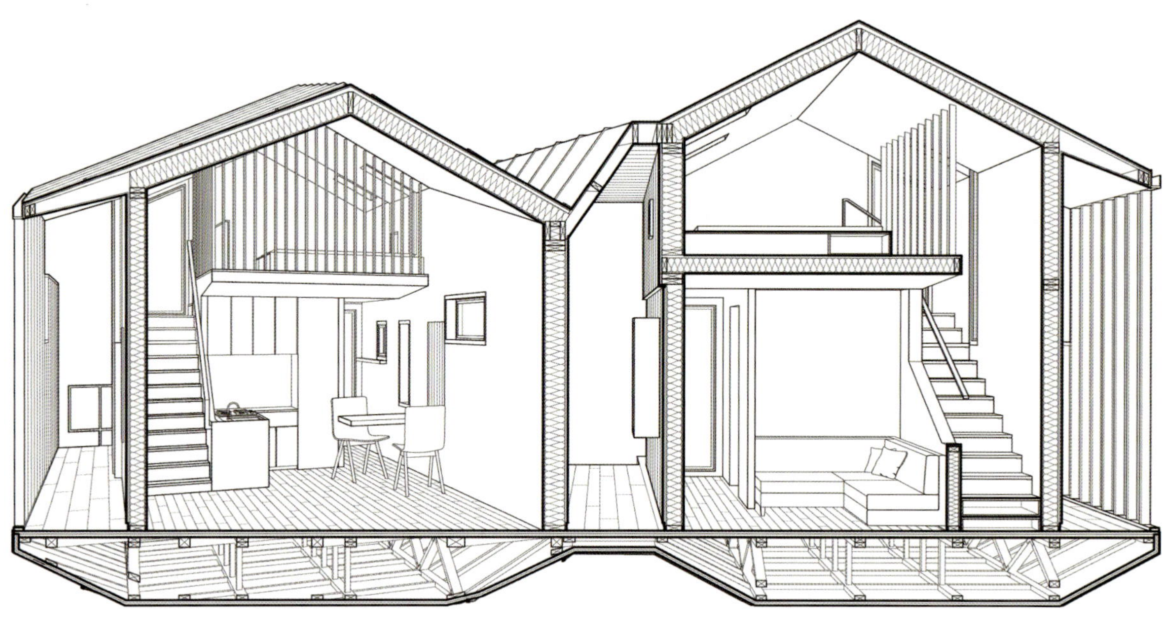

Transverse perspectival section

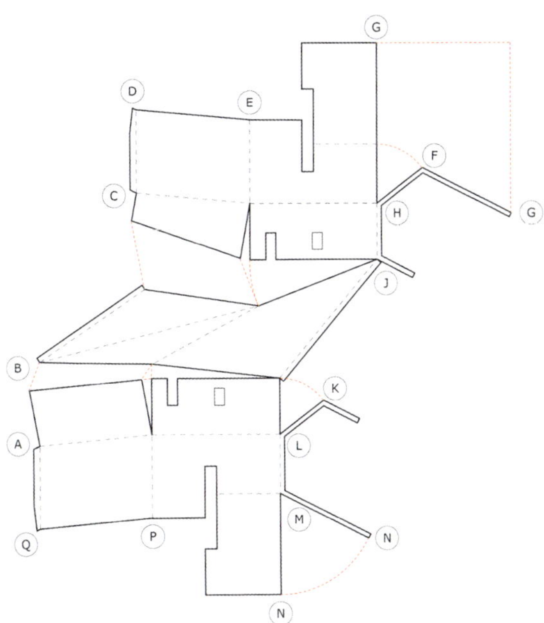

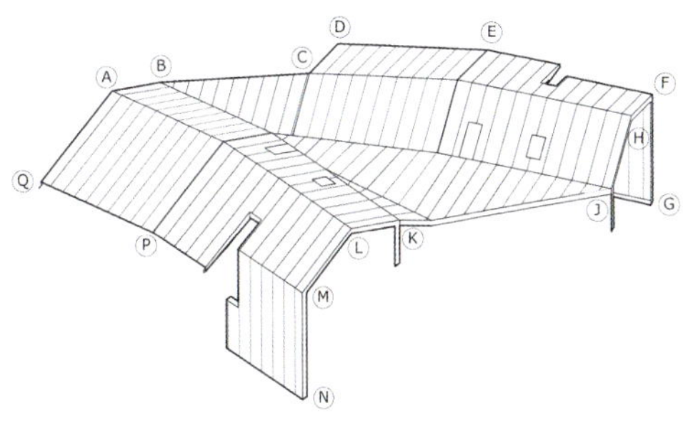

Roof panelization diagram

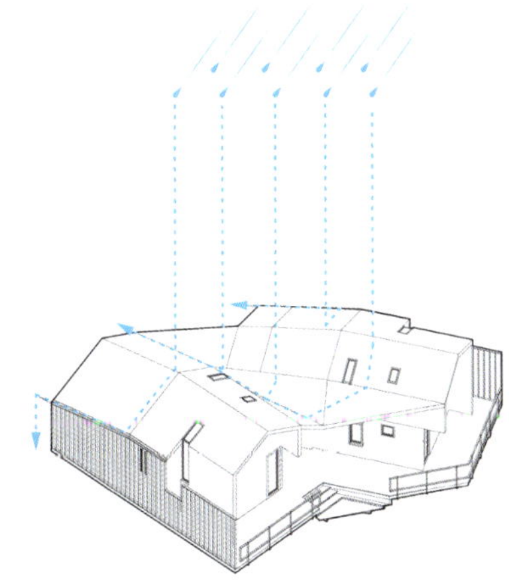

Unfolded roof diagram (above), water flow diagram (below)

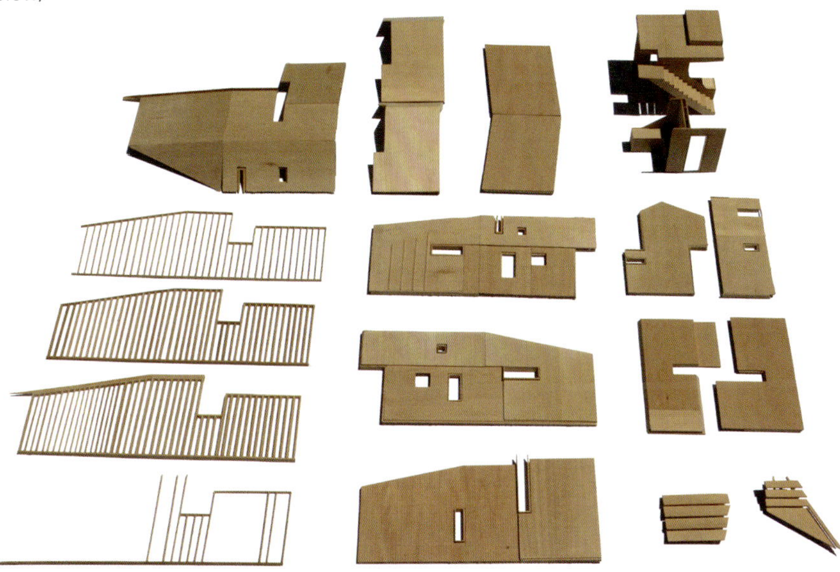

Component study models

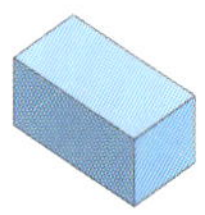

Massing

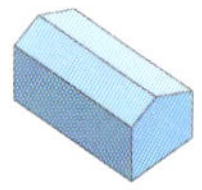

Roof angles

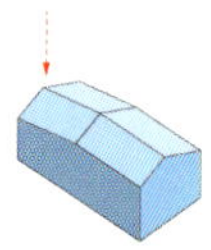

Push roof

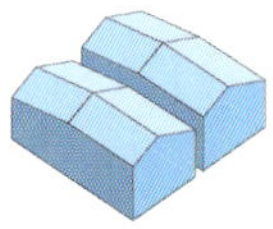

Double

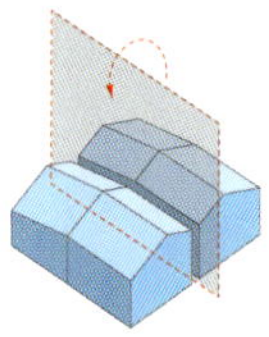

Mirror

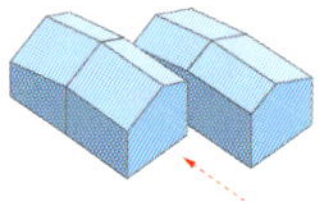

Push

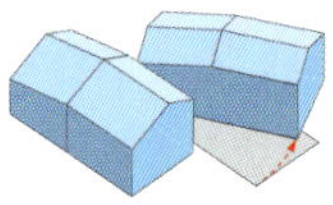

Rotate

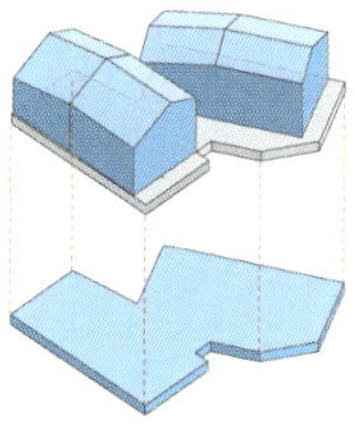

Pinch

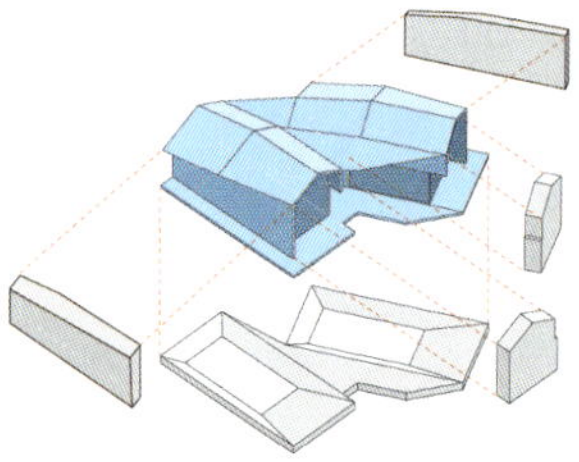

Articulating mass

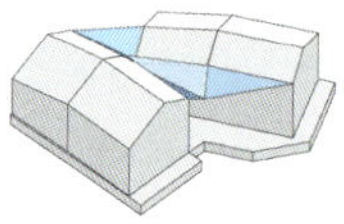

Roof connection

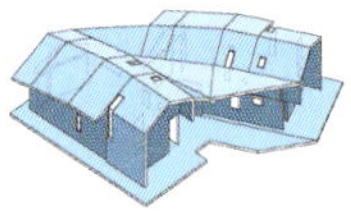

Fenestration

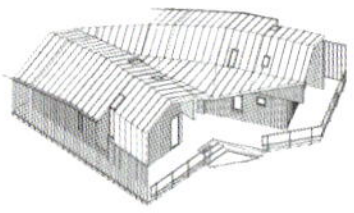

Material details

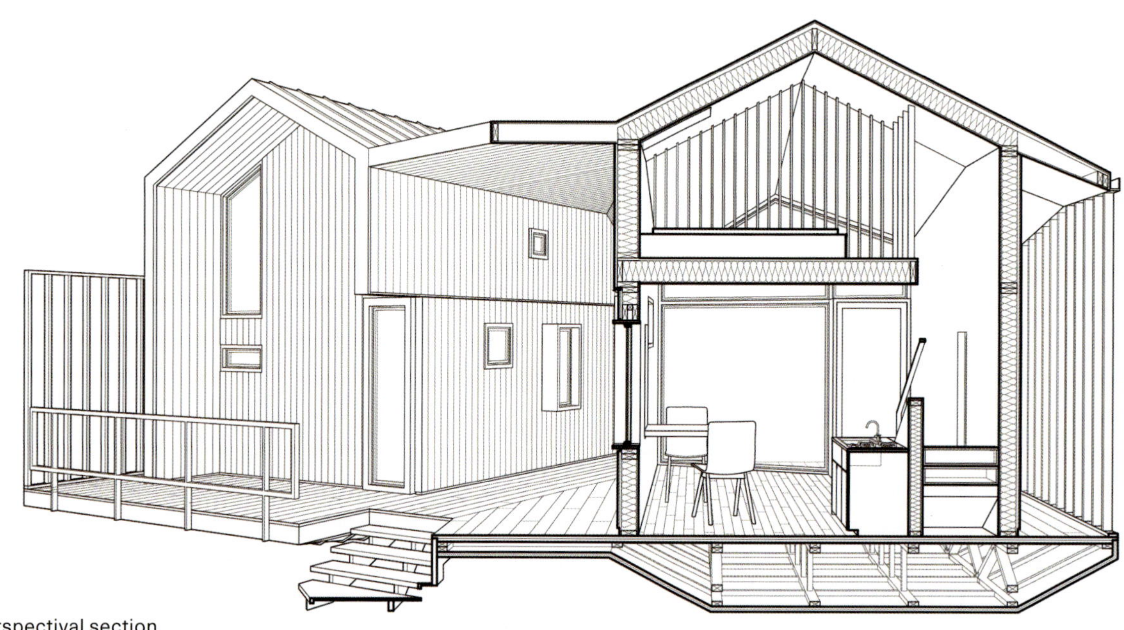

Transverse perspectival section

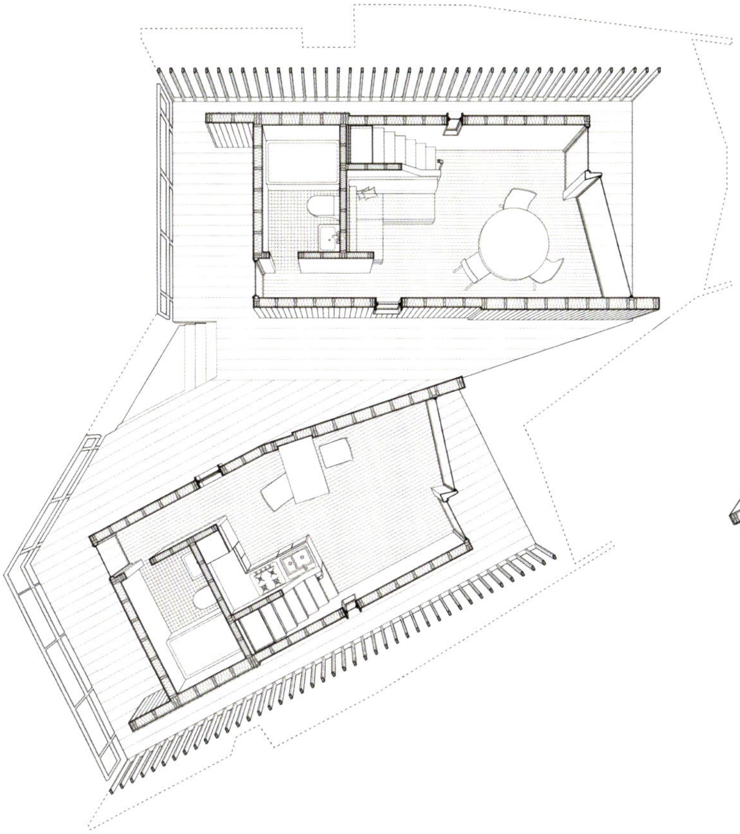

First-floor perspectival plan

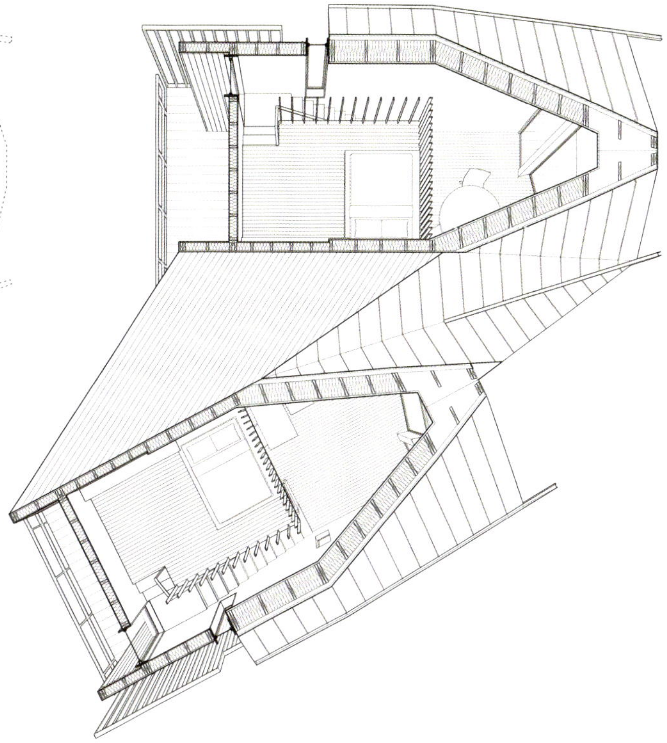

Second-floor perspectival plan

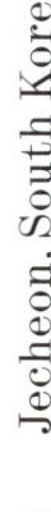

Site Jecheon, South Korea

Status Schematic Design

Program Commercial

Client YC Saw Mill

ROOFSCAPE HAUS

Roofscape Haus takes its inspiration from the rainy, mountainous landscape of Jecheon, Korea. The geometry of the roof is vectorized to encourage the shedding of liquids that might otherwise accumulate on the surface of the roof. Its architecture reflects the sectional conditions of traditional Korean Hanok roofscapes by utilizing a deep, overhanging roof that blocks high summer sunlight and allows low winter sunlight to penetrate deep into the space.

Roofscape Haus is a three-story commercial building that houses a design studio on its upper floors. Its lower floors, meanwhile, provide space for storage and a showroom for a timber manufacturing company. The structural framing system is constructed of glue-laminated timber (glulam), a material that can span larger distances than traditional timber and which permits greater design flexibility without sacrificing structural integrity.

The design optimizes the material values of wood as both a renewable resource and ecological system. The carbonized wood cladding, for example, retains the cellular structure of the wood and prevents the formation of cracks and weathering. Current debates surrounding sustainability in architecture focus largely on energy issues. However, the construction techniques and material selection of Roofscape Haus aspire to reflect longstanding sustainable practices in Korean vernacular architecture. The project explores a wide spectrum of design resolutions, merging engineering and environmental design with regional and traditional architectural practices to provoke new forms of contextualism.

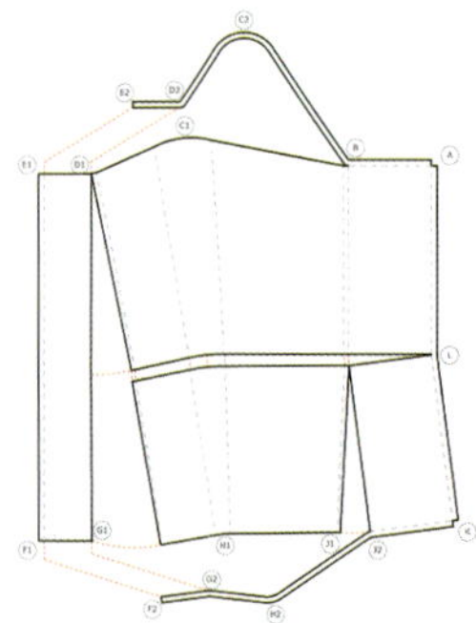

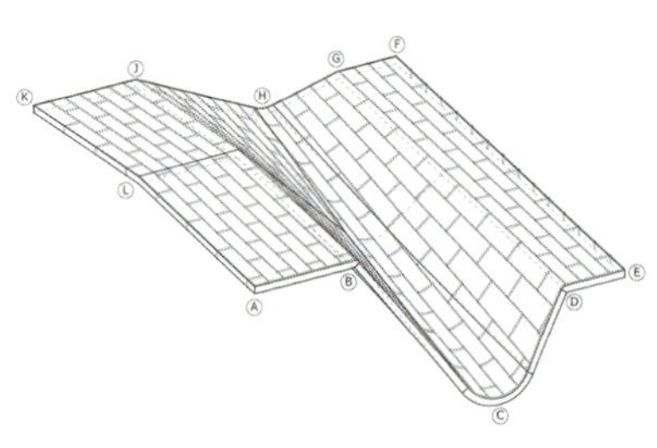

Unfolded roof diagram

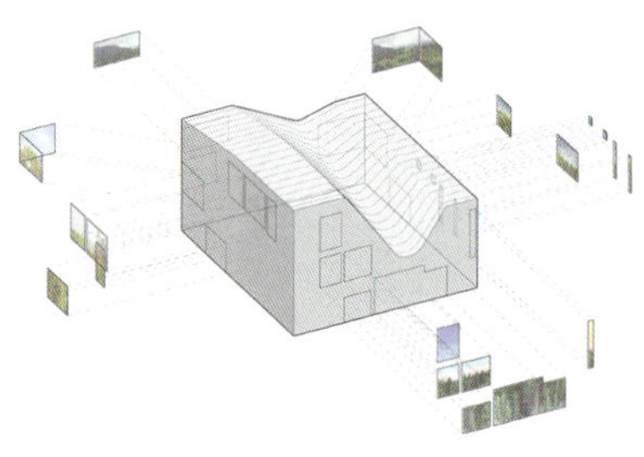

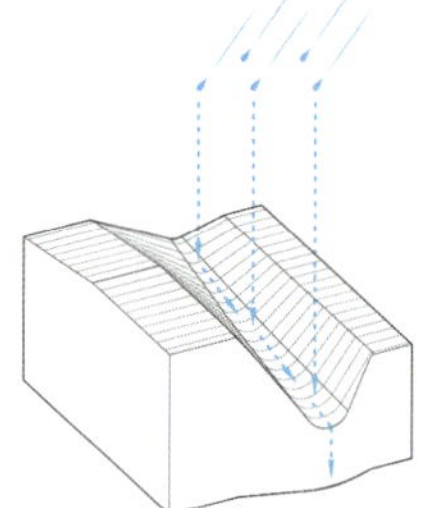

Roof panelization diagram (above), viewport diagram (below)

Water flow diagram

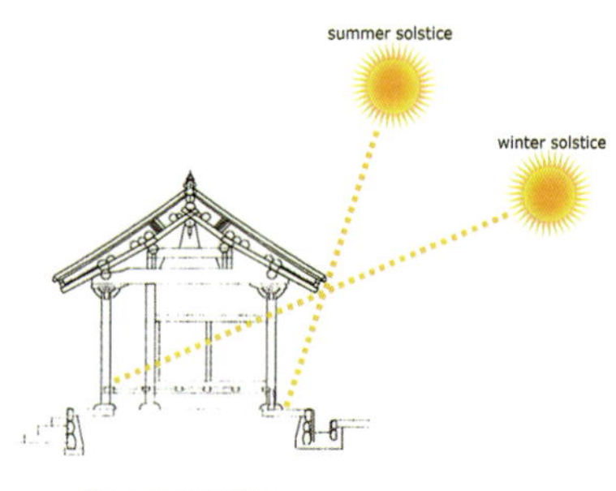

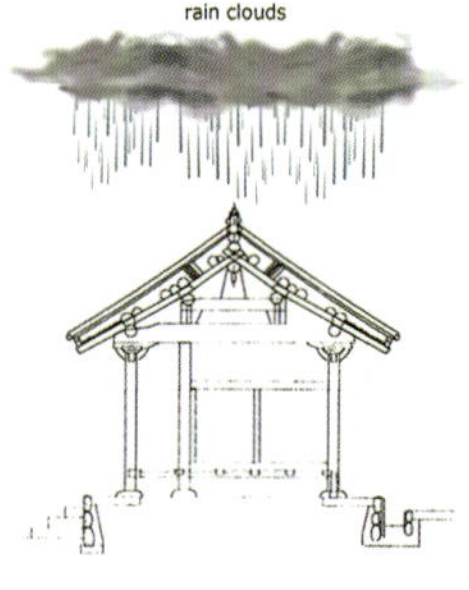

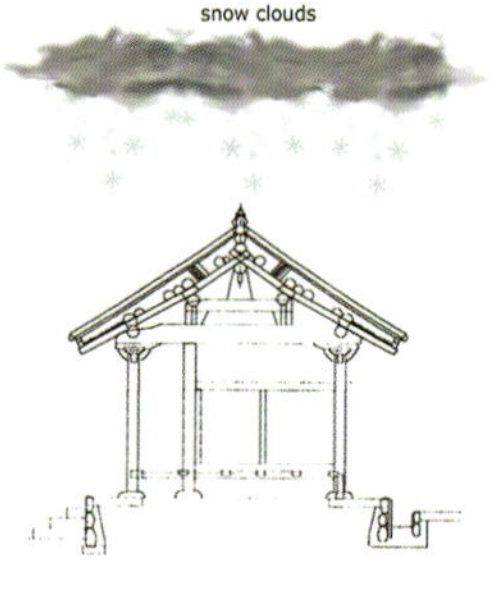

Roofscape ideograms

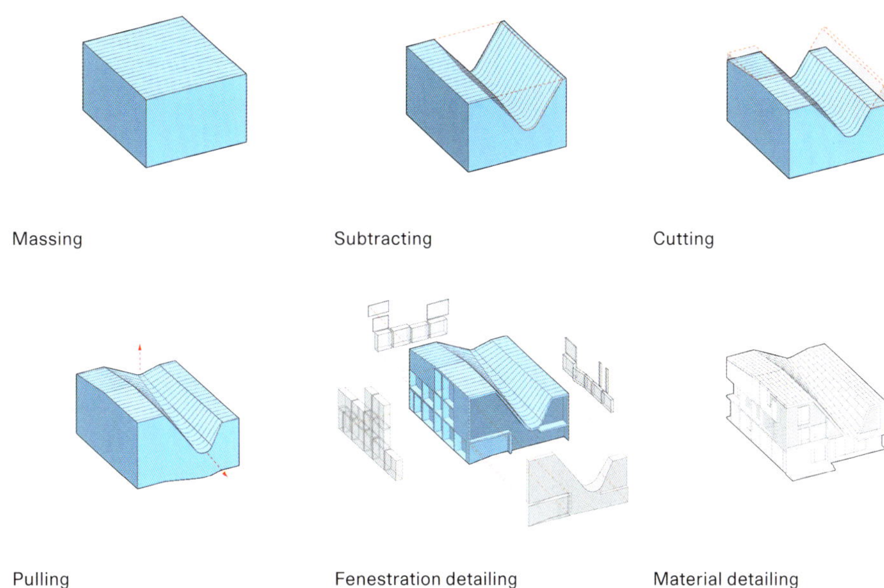

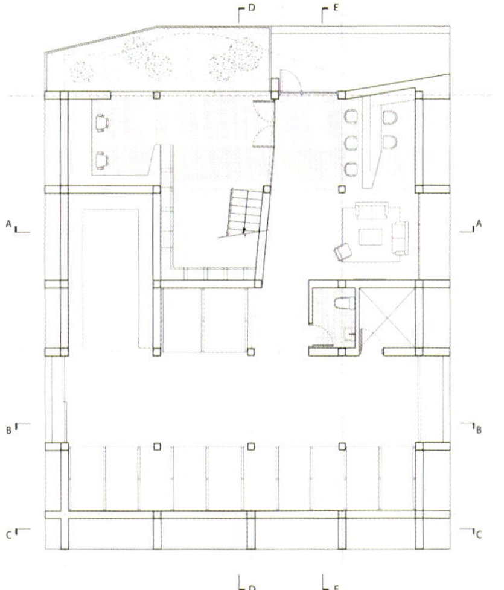

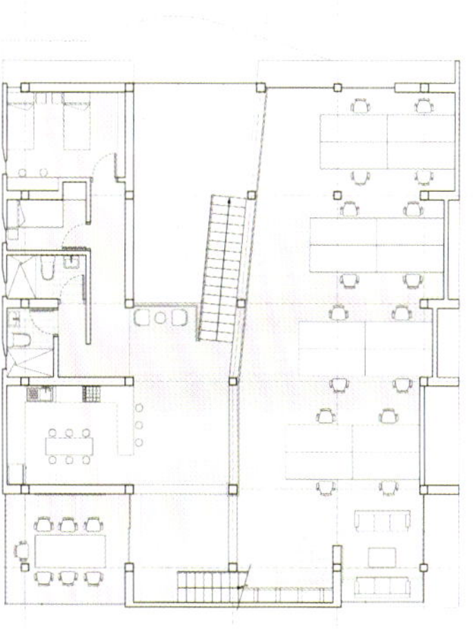

First-foor plan (left),
second-floor plan (right)

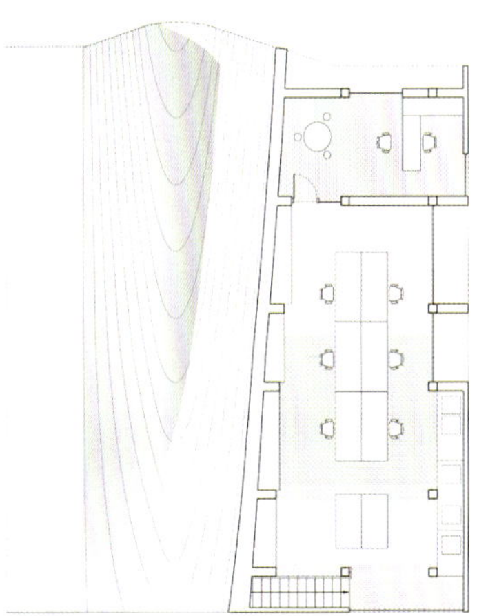

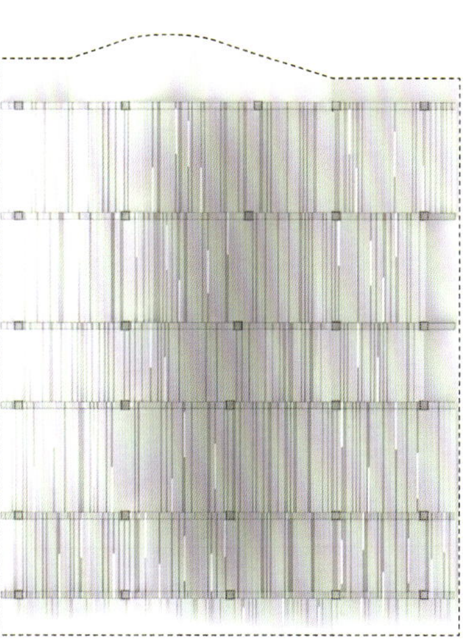

Third-floor plan (left),
reflective coiling plan (right)

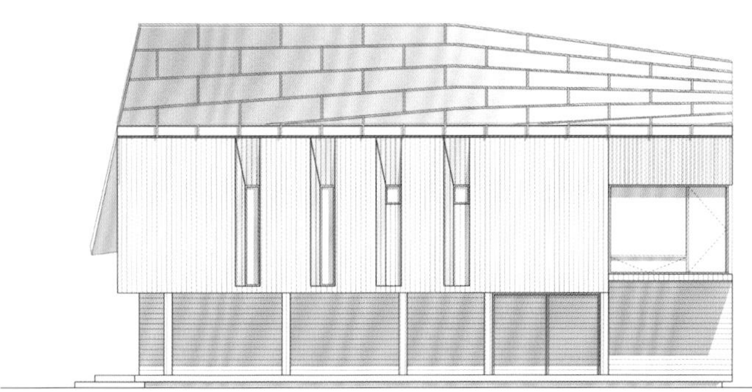

East elevation

West elevation

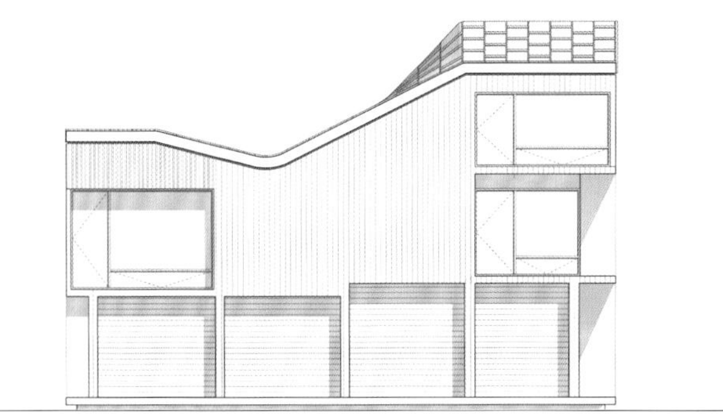

North elevation

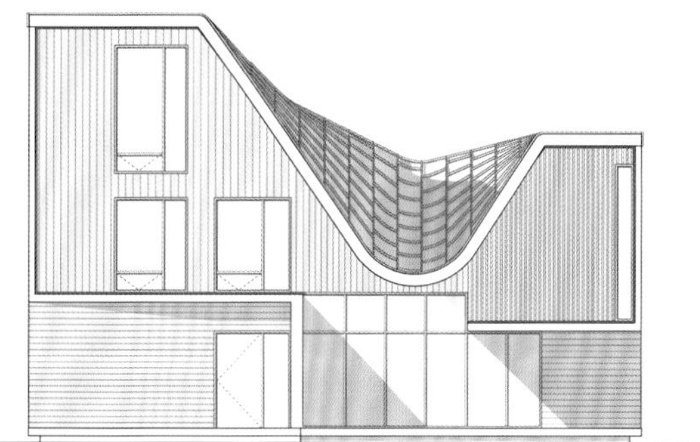

South elevation

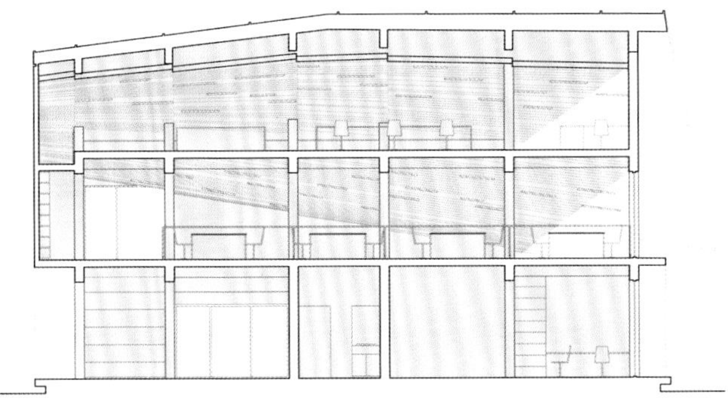

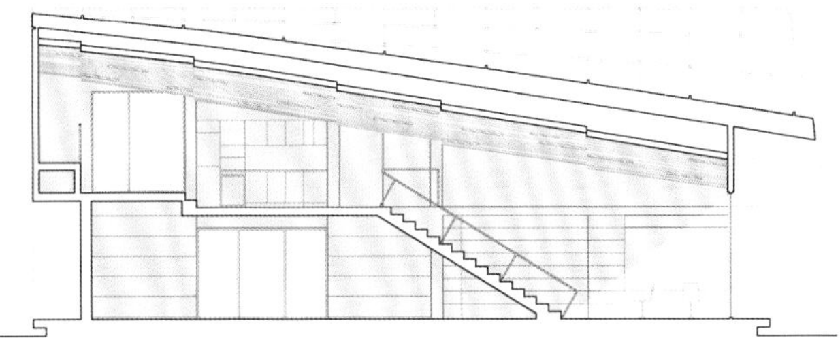

Longitudinal sections 01 – 02

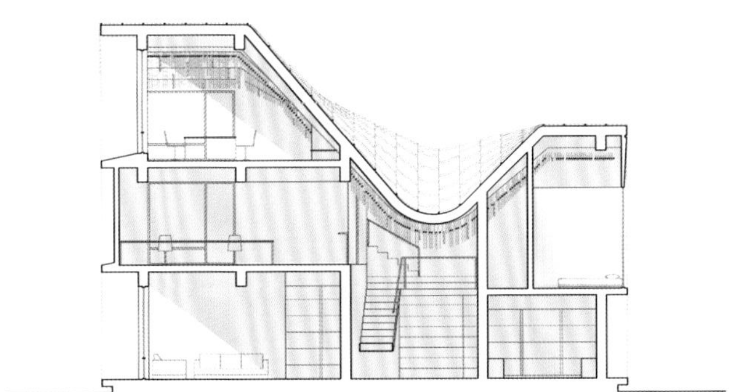

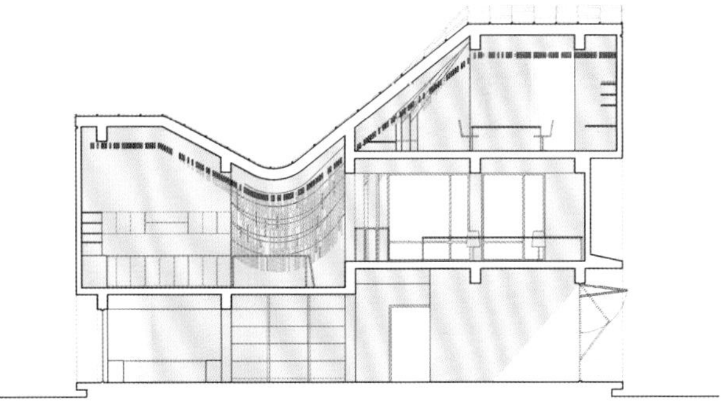

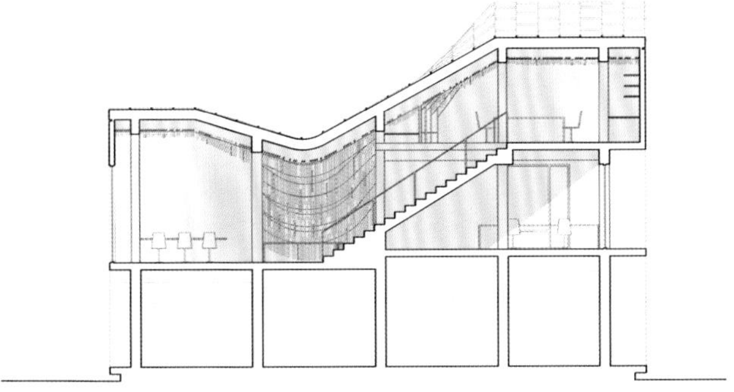

Transverse sections 01 – 03

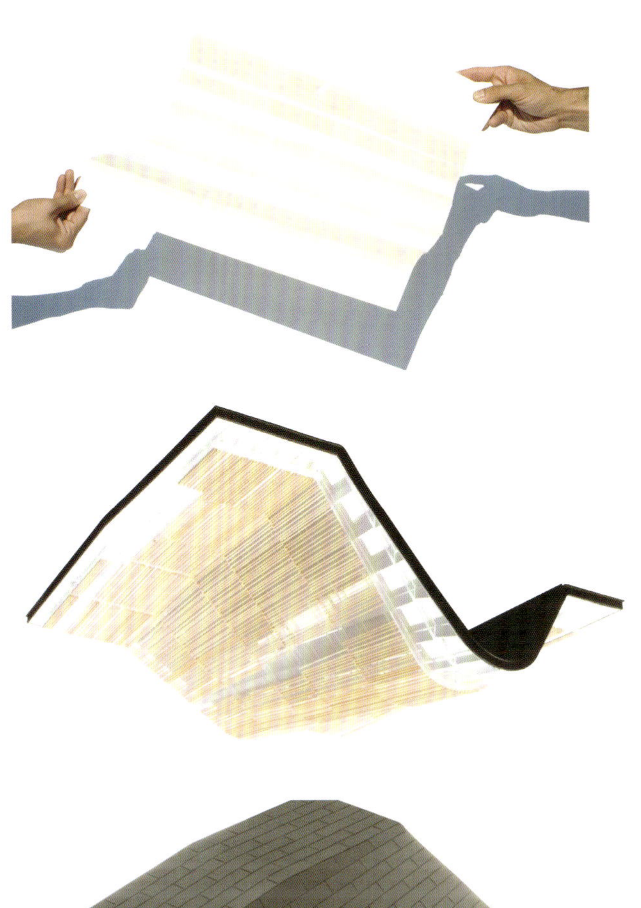

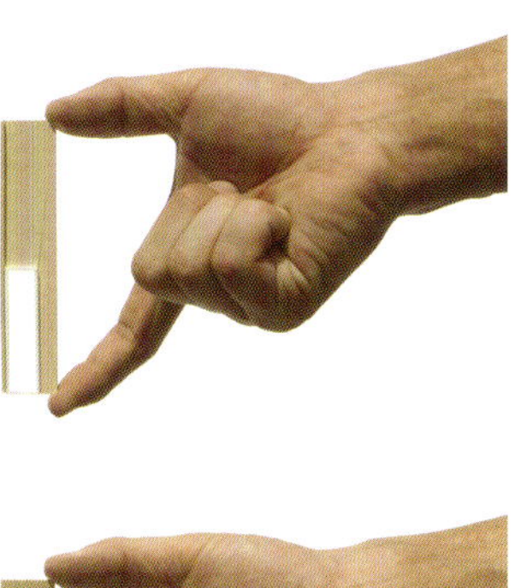

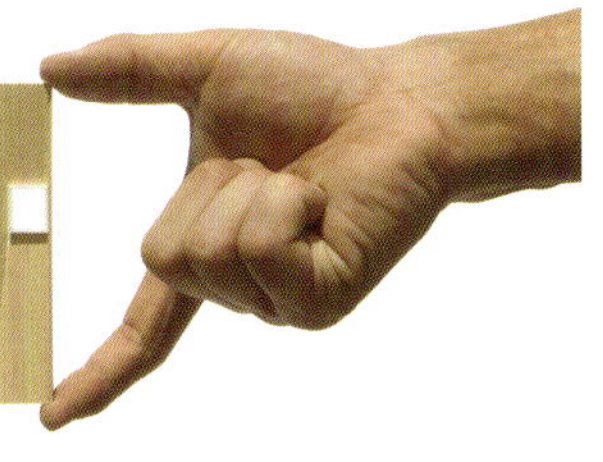

Window detail models

Roofscape paper model (above), ceiling slope detail model (center), roofscape detail model (below)

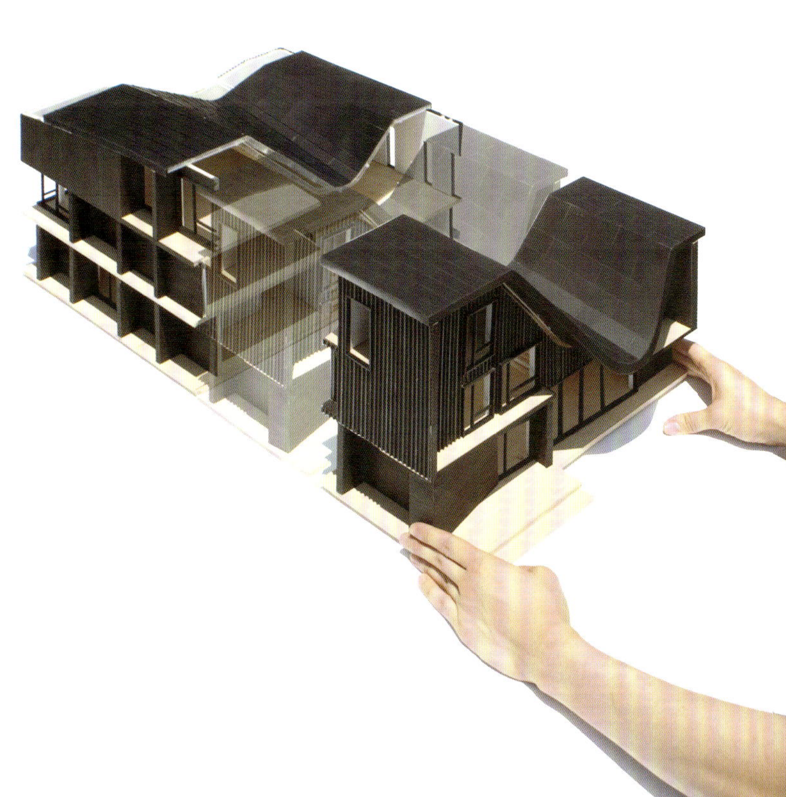

ANYCUBIC I3 MEGA

Site Jecheon, South Korea Status Schematic Design Program Commercial Client YC Saw Mill

FACTORY + FENCE

The YC Saw Mill Factory is a fabrication facility where timber is cut to standard or custom sizes (dimensional lumber) with a CNC automated saw. The building conforms to a primitive shed typology and uses a light steel prefabricated structure and angled metal roof. The composite panels used for the façade and enclosure are custom fabricated at the sawmill using recycled lumber from the manufacturing off-throw processes.

The YC Saw Mill has historically been a prominent lumber supplier, as well as construction provider, of traditional Korean Buddhist temples in the Jecheon region. Although the factory has minimal decorative elements, it takes its cues from nineteenth-century Korean chests, particularly in its hinge designs and various openings. A cantilevered roof takes inspiration from the Korean Buddha Temple Lantern Festivals and acts as an armature for lighting effects, signage, and a canopy.

The YC Saw Mill Factory also responds to a major highway to the northeast of the site and to the valley conditions created by the mountainous region. Its architecture poses a subtle intervention between a manmade environment and the natural landscape.

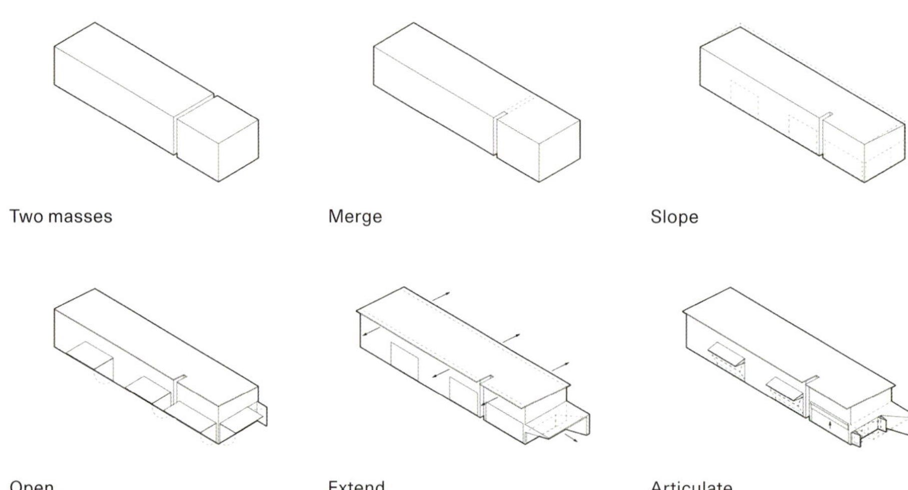

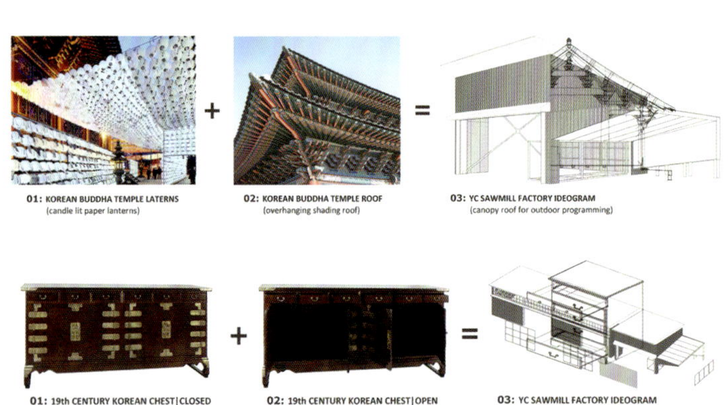

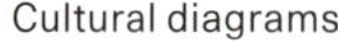
Cultural diagrams

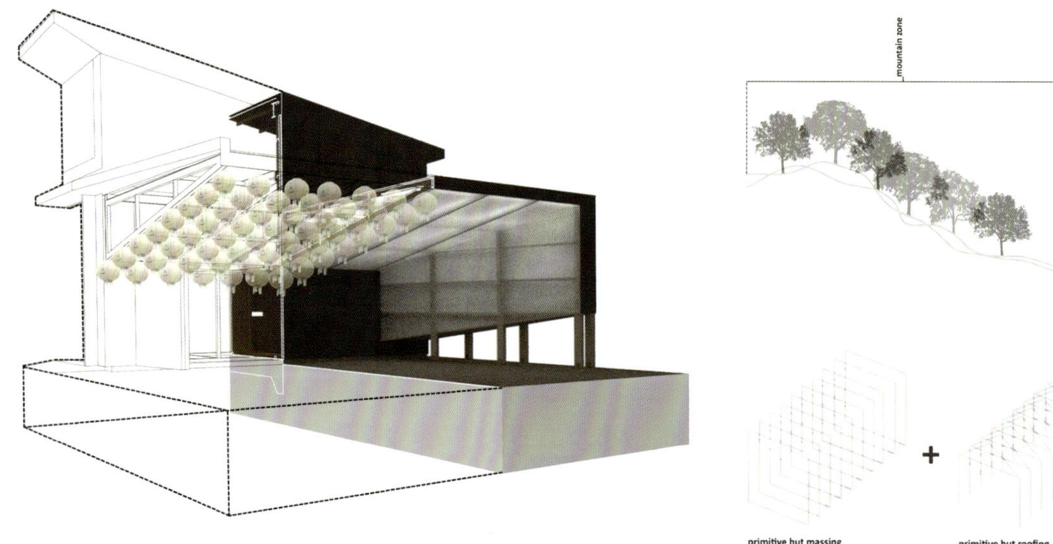

Korean Buddhist temple lantern light inspiration diagram

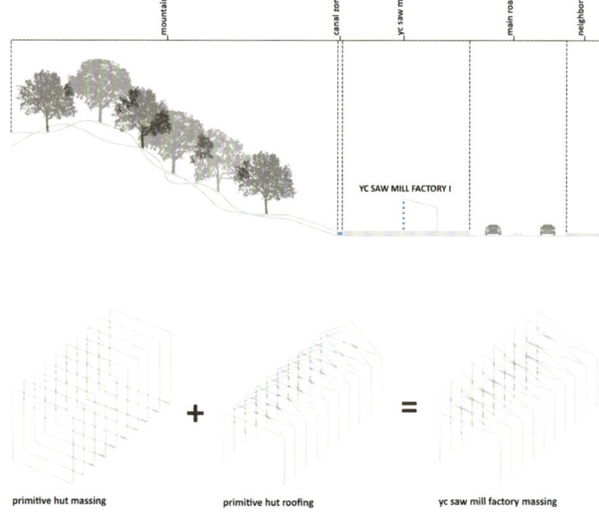

Sectional site diagram (above), massing diagram (below)

Site plan

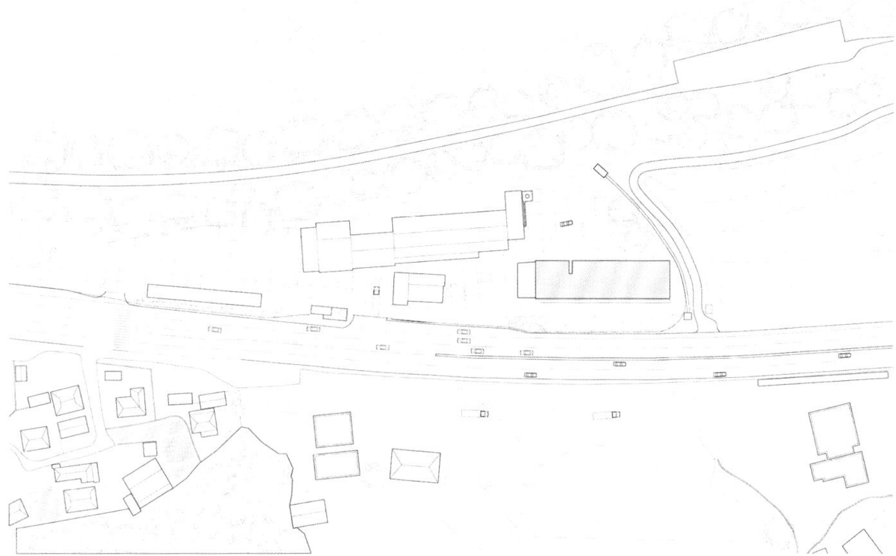

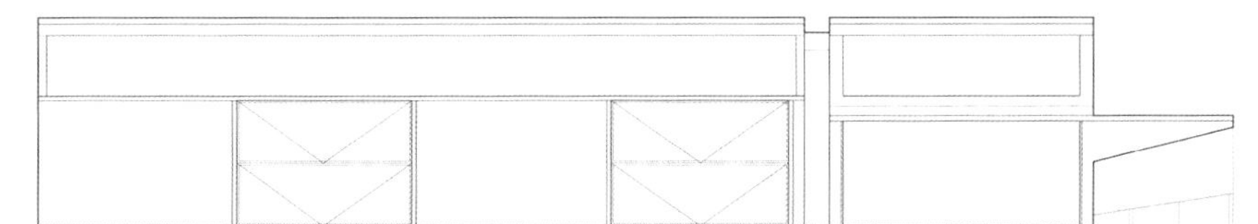

North elevation

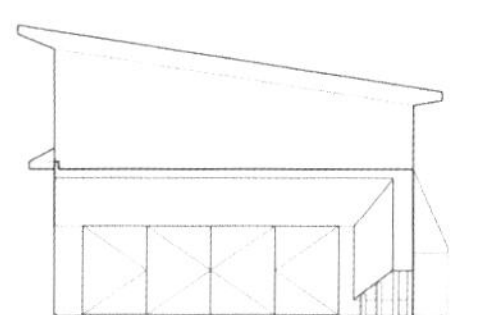

West elevation

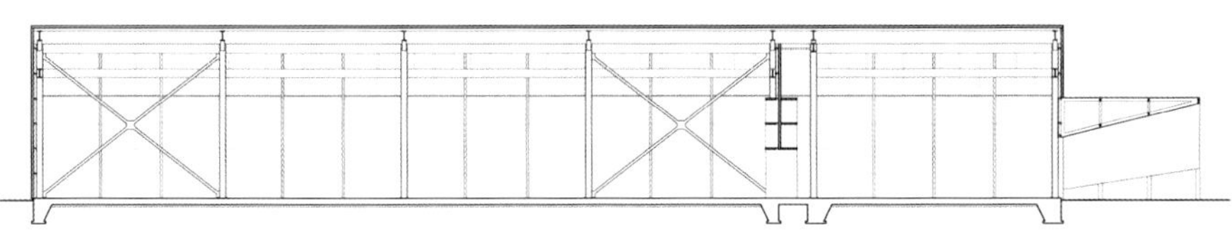

Longitudinal section

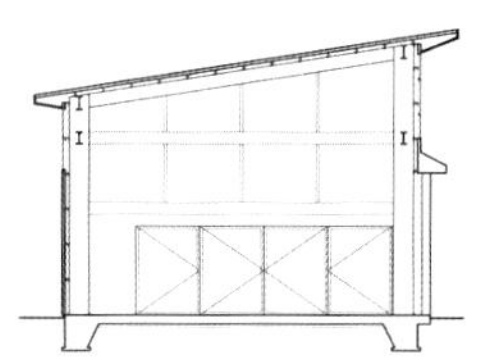

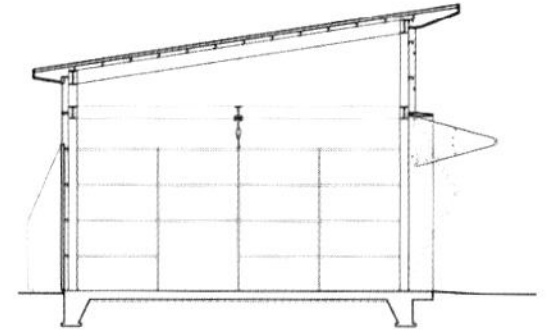

Transverse sections

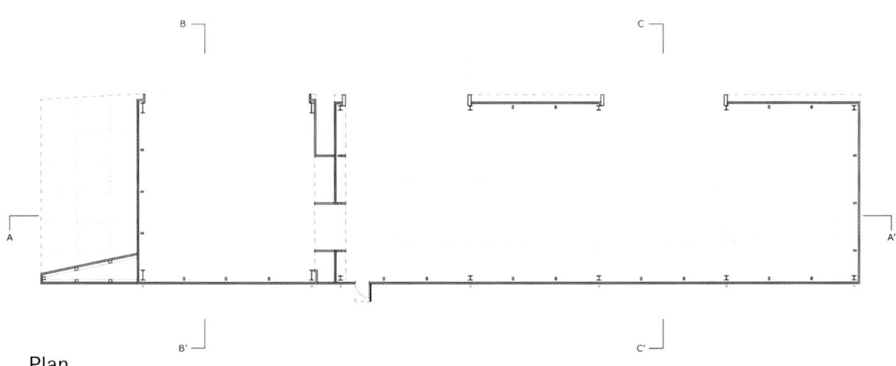

Plan

YC SAWMILL

The YC Saw Mill Fence project conceptualizes the fence not as a barrier but as a veil that narrates the history of a place. The traditional Korean Chaekgeori screen is the design's point of departure. The Chaekgeori screen represents its owner's social status through its visual imagery. The YC Saw Mill Fence references the dynamic flows of the geographic nature of the mountains and rivers of the site. The fence's wall density changes as it opens parallel to the road, allowing the edge of the YC Saw Mill campus to transform into a smooth, interactive façade that defines an entry sequence.

The fence is constructed out of timber blades and concrete channel footings with steel connections. The vertical timber blades fan out to provide veils for the buildings and property beyond the fence. The landscape, meanwhile, uses vegetation as a secondary layer against the fence in order to soften the space between the timber blades. This contrast of hard and soft edges blurs the boundary between the infrastructure of the city and the mountains in the background.

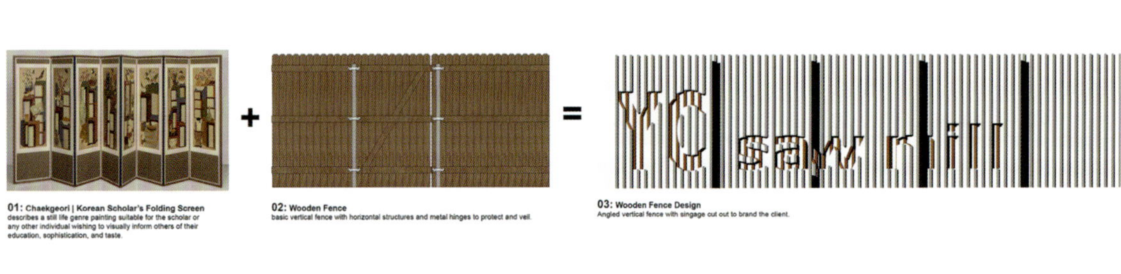

Cultural diagrams

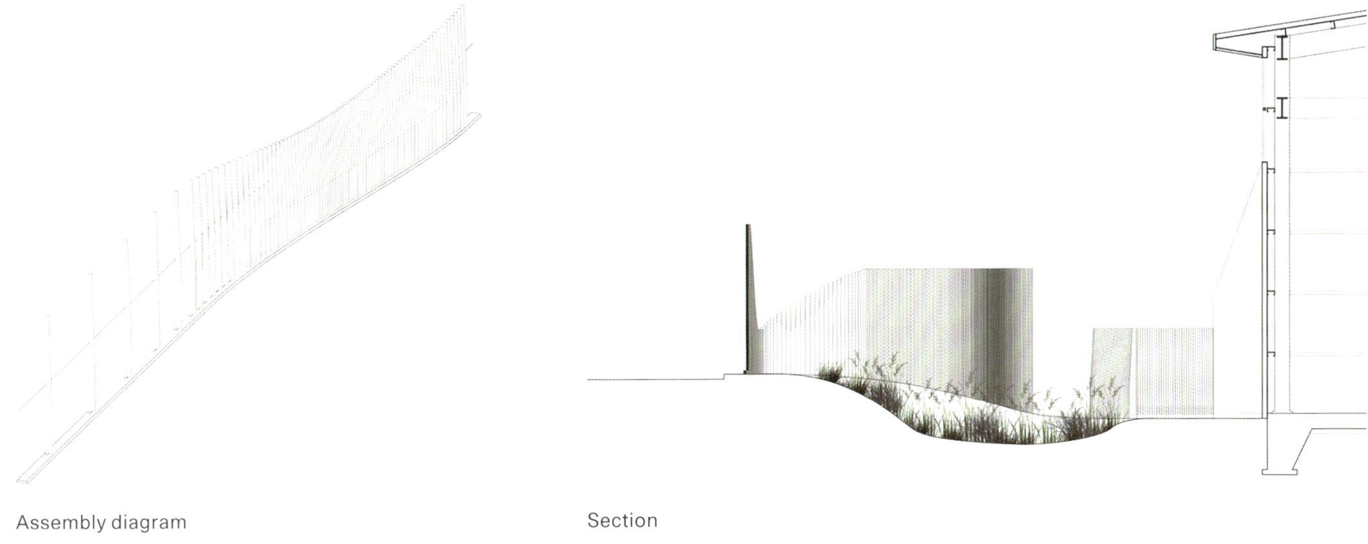

Assembly diagram

Section

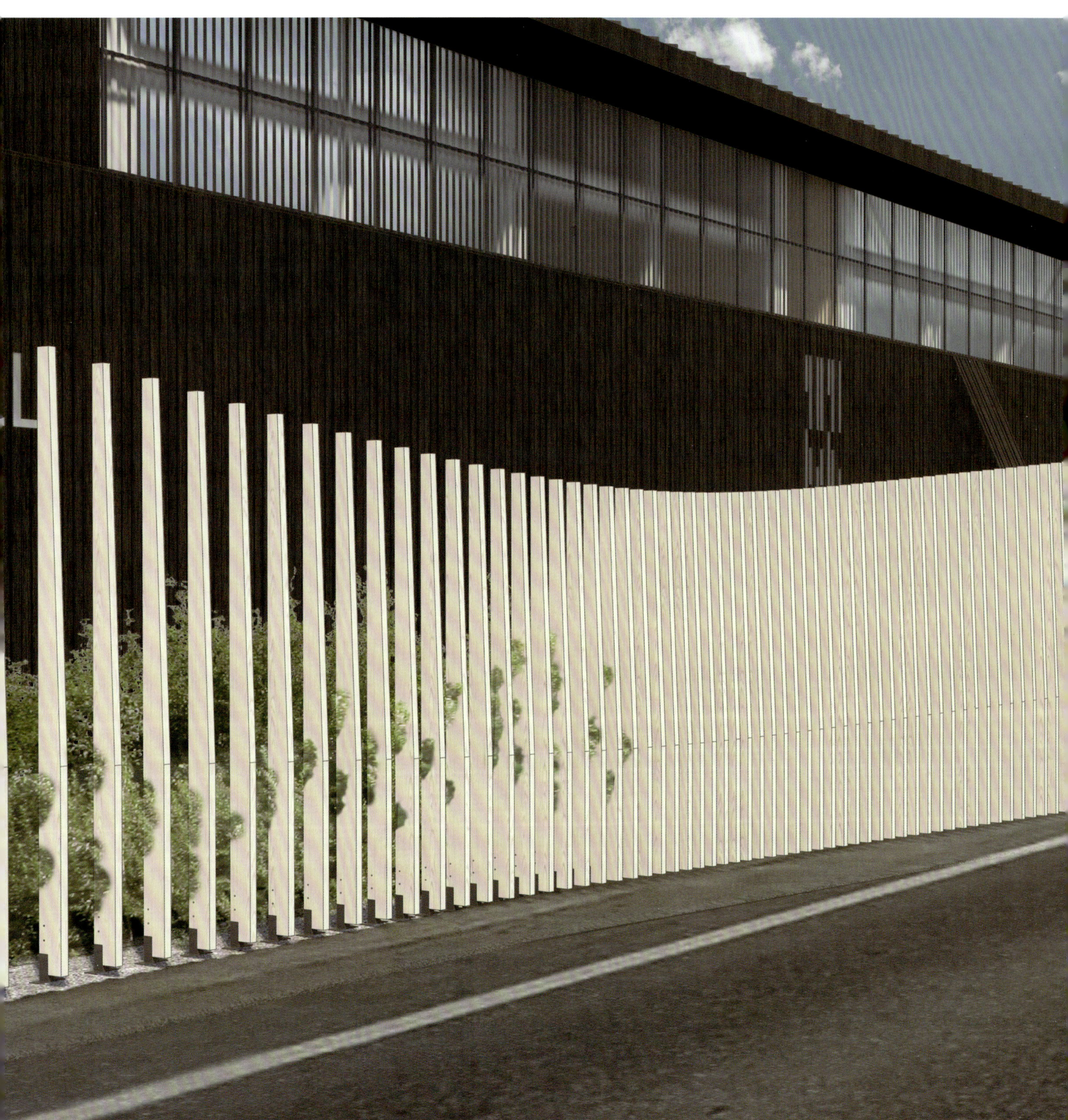

BONGO III

Site	Chicago, IL, United States	Status	Conceptual Design	Program	Residential · Commercial	Client	Novack Construction and Development

SILVER TOWER

Site plan

Silver Tower instigates new ecological design strategies in architecture by investigating the engineering factors of wind, seismic, and structural loading in relation to biological materials. Its floor plates shift horizontally to produce a variety of program configurations. The tower skin likewise shifts, bending and folding along the vertical axis. With its design rooted in structural experimentation and urban research—of streets, spaces, axes, monuments, patterns, and landscape—the tower interacts dynamically with the existing context. The massing of the tower responds to view corridors and frames key urban vistas. This visual dialogue differentiates horizons that appear within the shifting mass of the tower. At the same time, the form of the building produces connections between the tower and its local conditions while also enhancing its environmental performance. Climatic conditions vary throughout the tower's vertical strata as it cuts across multiple microclimatic zones. The bending and folding of the massing respond by decreasing the energy consumption in the tower and reducing solar heat gain.

The perforated silver skin of Silver Tower encases bioengineered moss that filters polluted air and rainwater to enhance its biological performance. The design of the tower is shaped by calculating the wind and air buoyancy for natural ventilation; meanwhile, rainwater is filtered through the silver façade for water recycling purposes. Silver Tower showcases urban remediation strategies that enhance microclimatic environments and increase public engagement around the city's streetscapes. In contrast with developers' tendency to maximize floor plates to increase profit, Silver Tower's floors are cut and fissured to reveal voids that can be used as public space within the vertical dimension. These articulated and diverse floor plates increase the number of microclimatic zones and decrease the immense carbon output for a high-rise building typology.

Site diagram

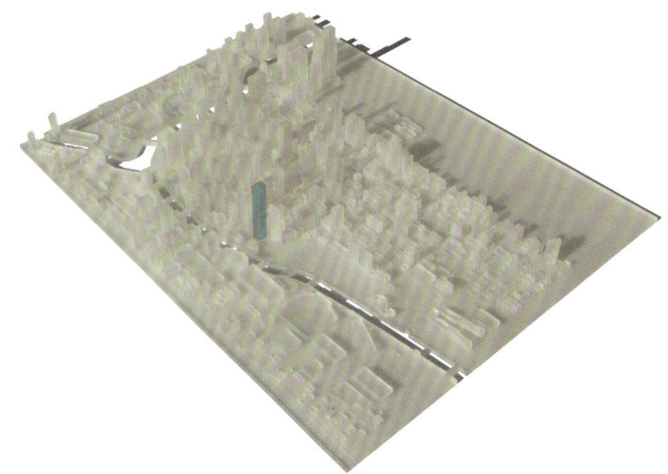

Urban context model

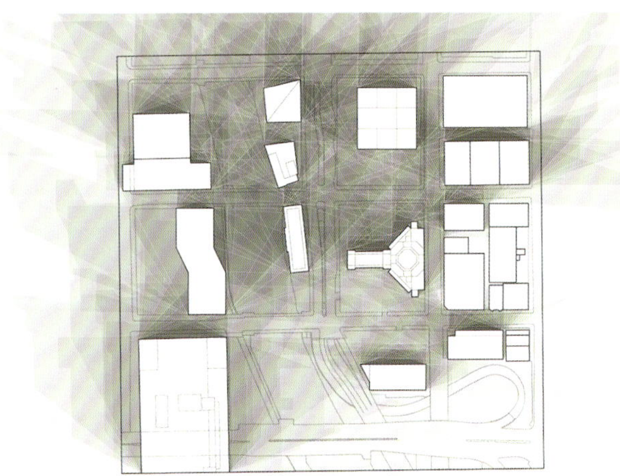

Sun study diagram

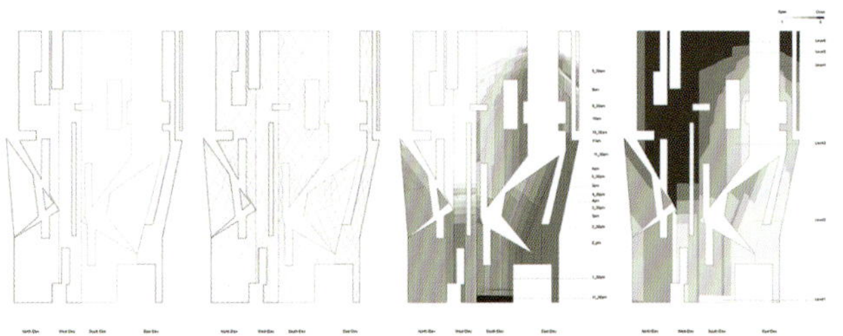

Shadow study diagram

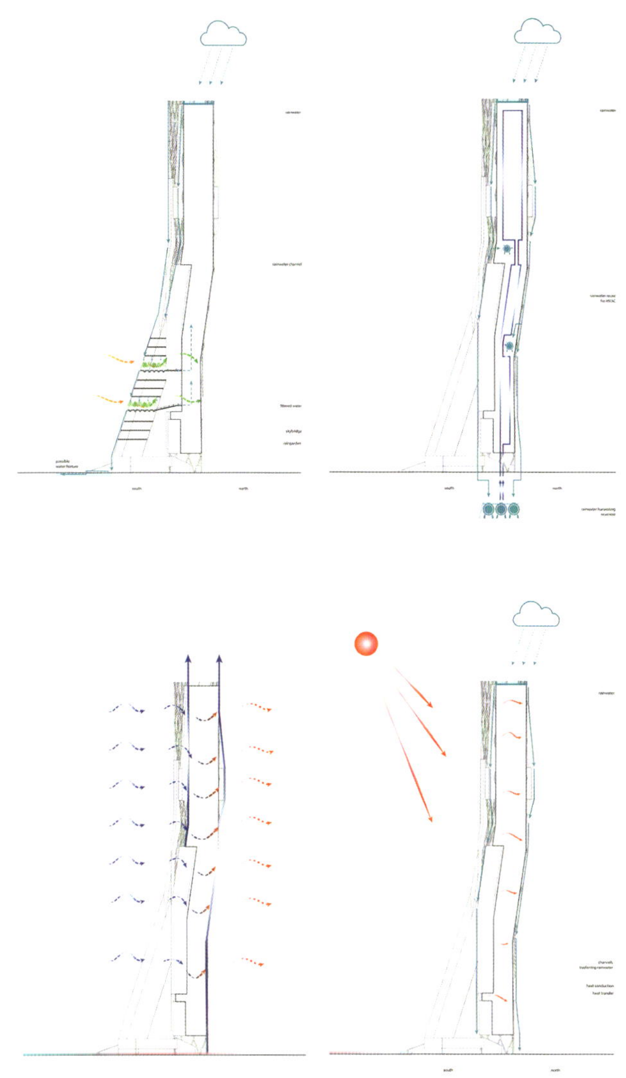

Systems diagram, biofiltration, heating thermal mass, cooling retention system (clockwise from top left)

Massing study models

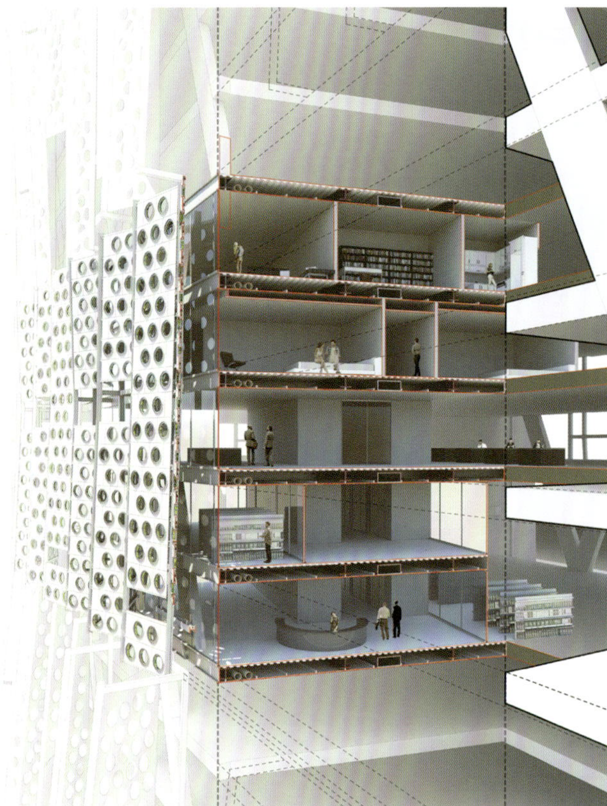

Façade and floor assembly diagram

Components of a module

1.Connection
2.Front-panel
3.Plastic joint
4.Screw
5.Stator container
6.Frame
7.Stator coil
8.Circuit
9.Wirecable
10.Moss cultivation
11.Rotor magnet
12.Irrigatior
13.Irrigation pipe

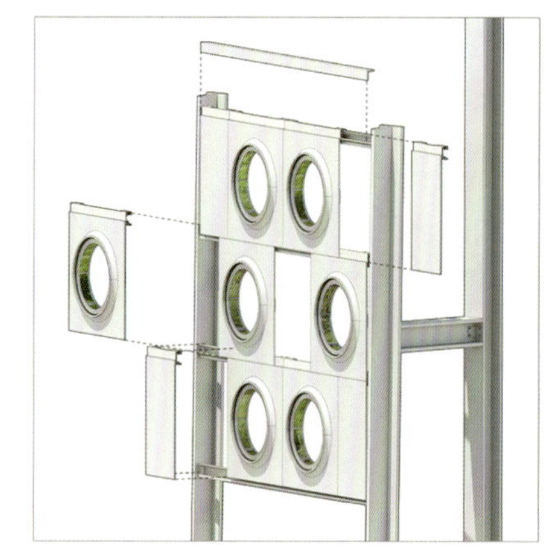

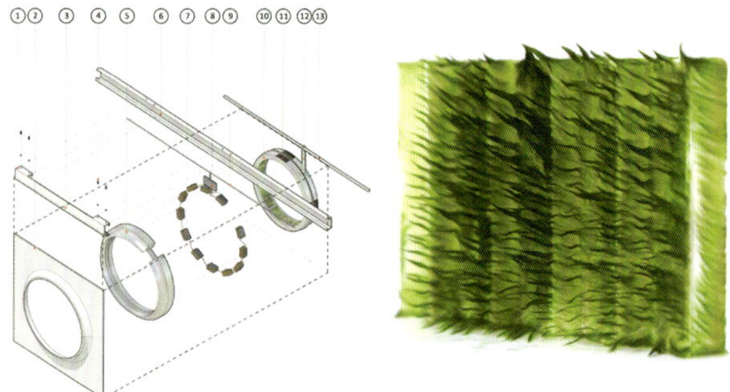

Bioengineered moss housing system assembly

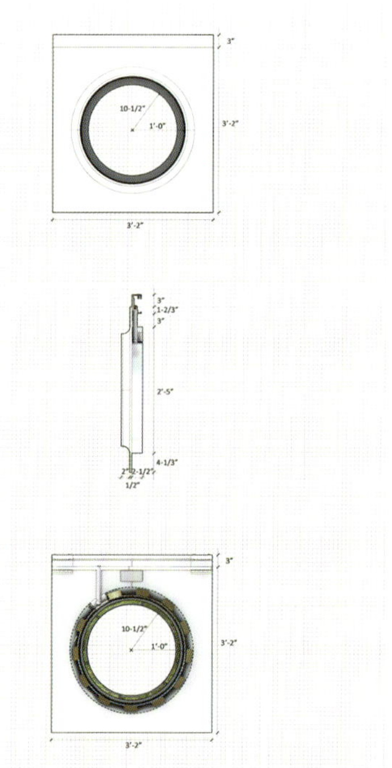

Silver skin detail

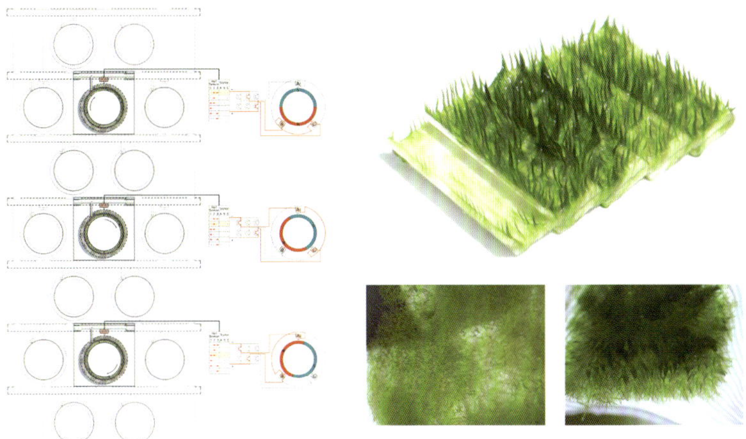

Bioengineered moss housing electrical magnetic system

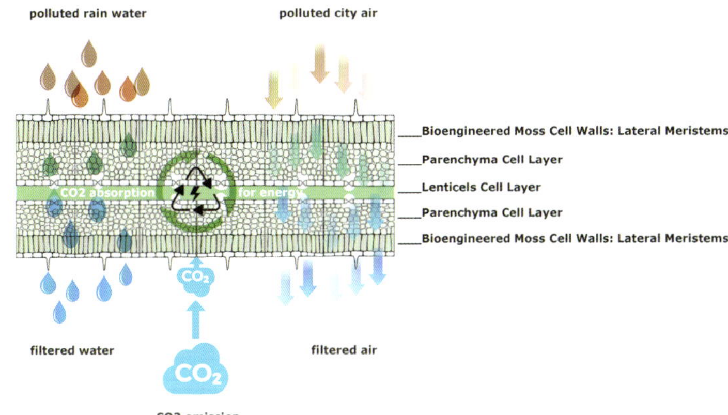

Bioengineered moss sectional anatomy diagram

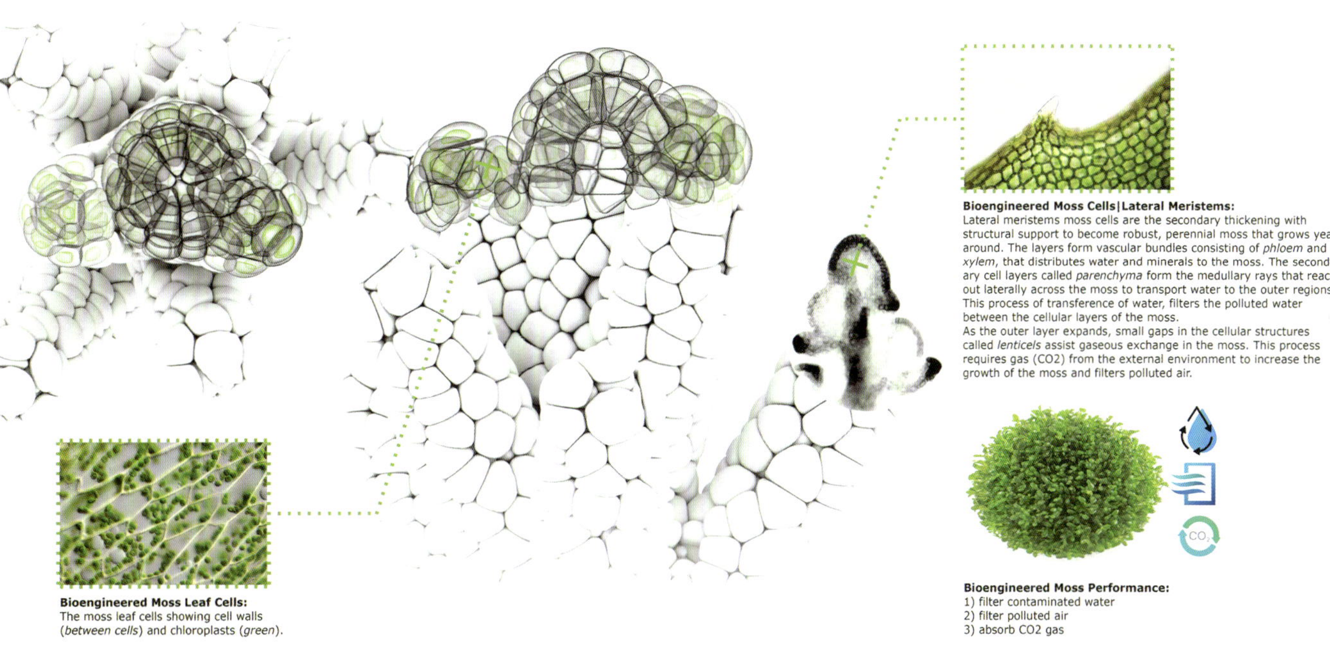

Bioengineered moss model and diagram

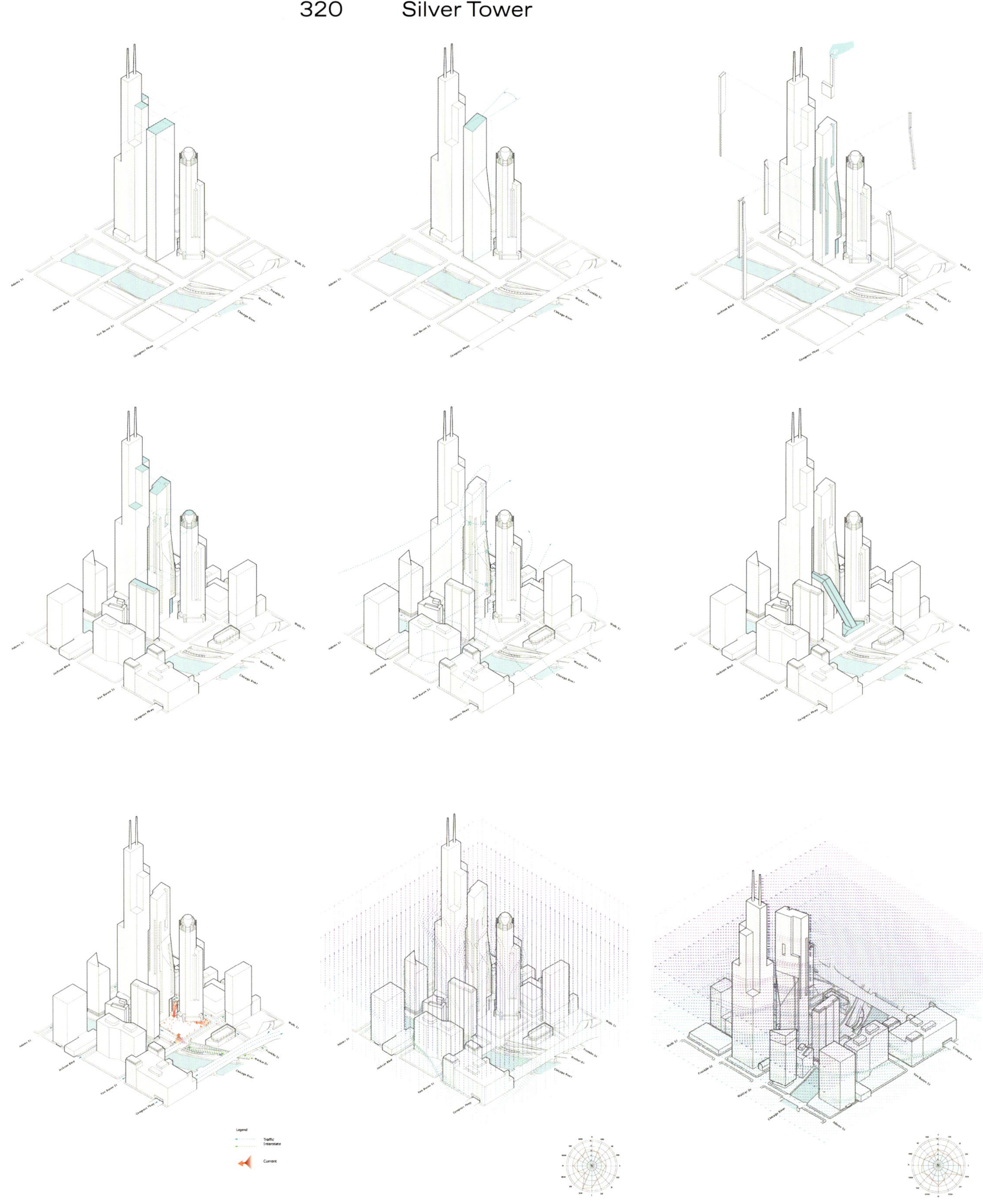

Public space transformation diagrams: height references, view references, void references, context references, windflow references, structural tripod, public and civic flows, vertical wind flows, horizontal wind flows (clockwise from top left)

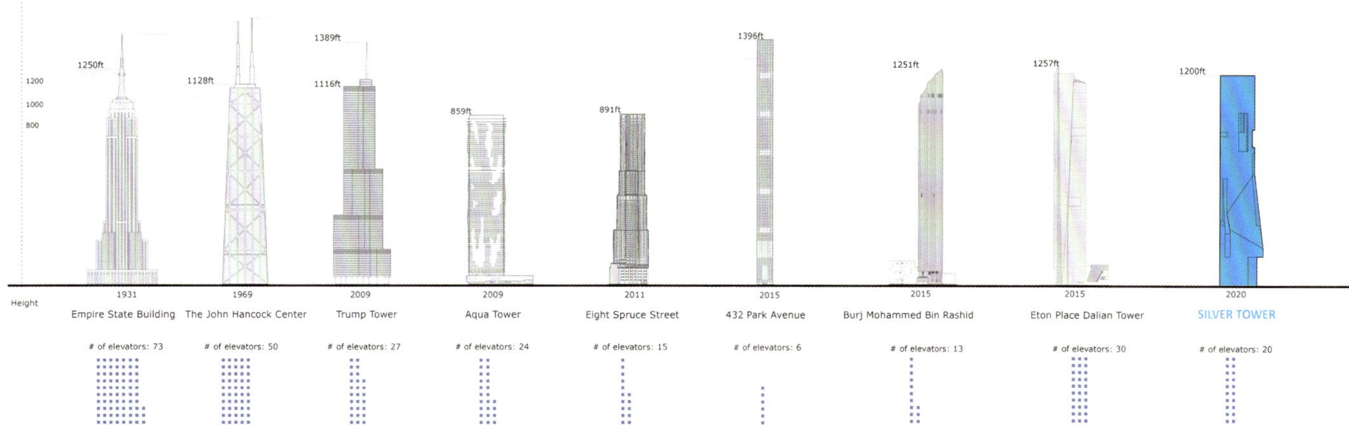

Elevator reference diagram

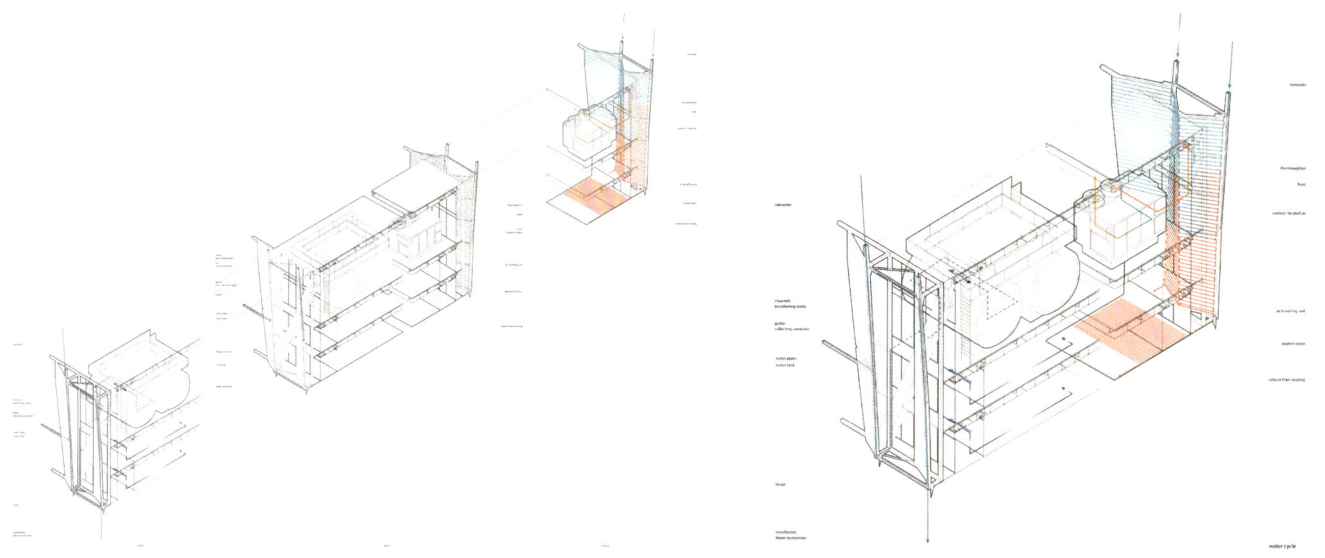

Water retention systems diagram

Cooling and heating systems diagram

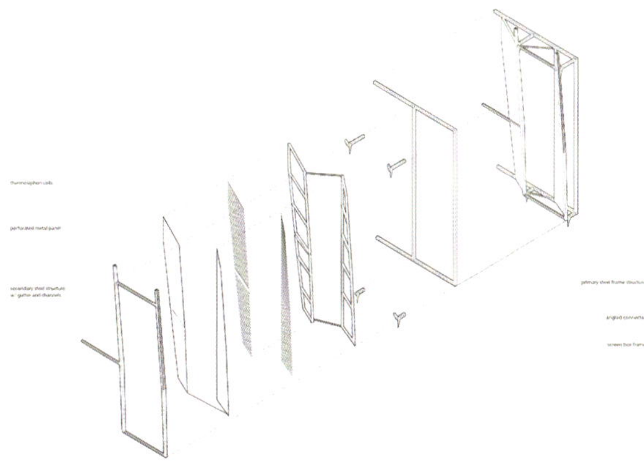

Skin arrangement

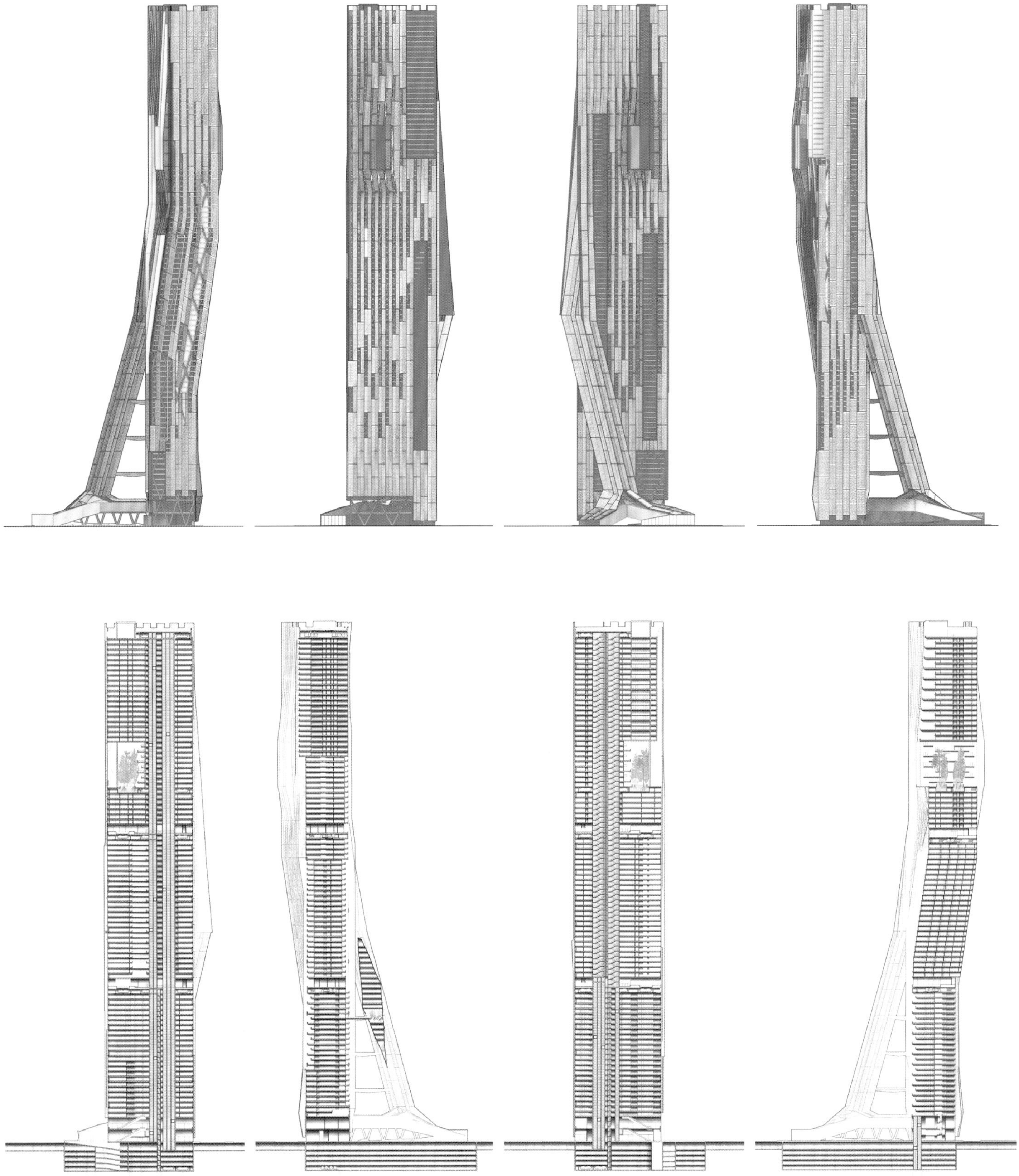

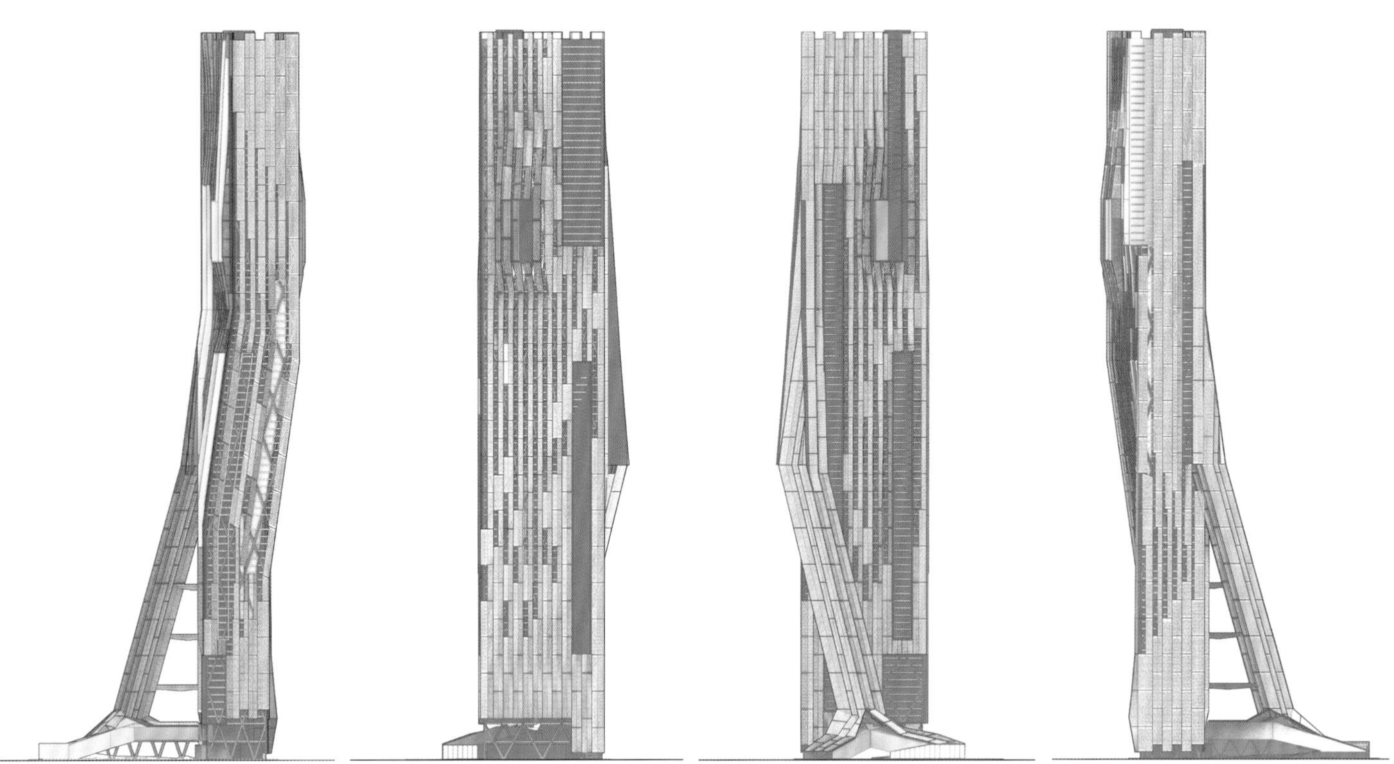

East, north, south, and west elevations (above, left to right) with north view, west view, south view, and east view sections (below, left to right)

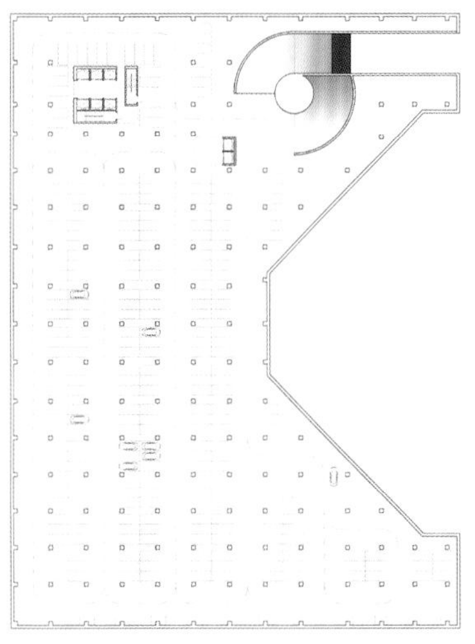

Parking floor plan

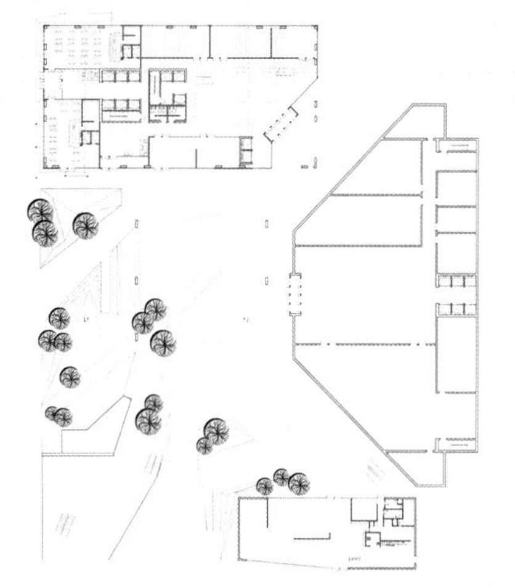

Ground floor plan

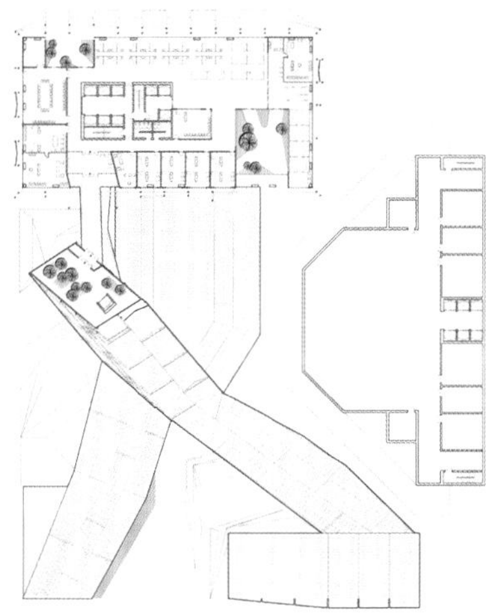

Office floor plan

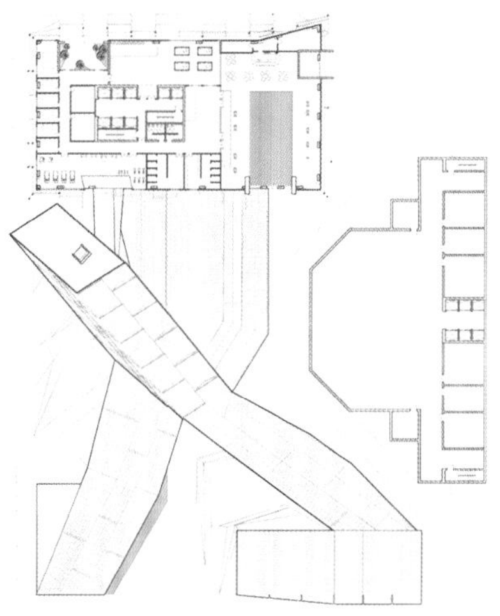

Hotel lobby floor plan

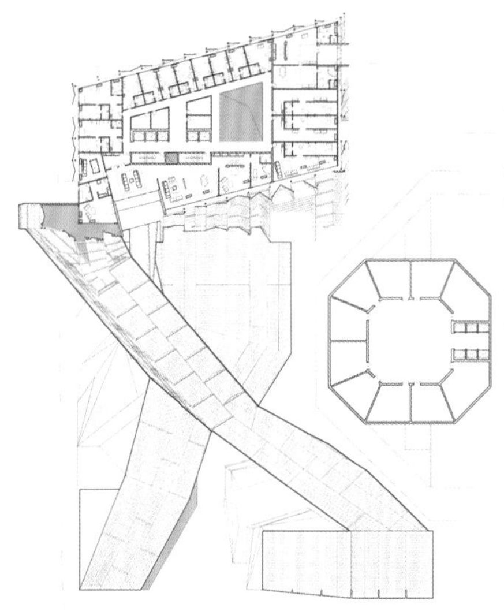

Hotel floor plan

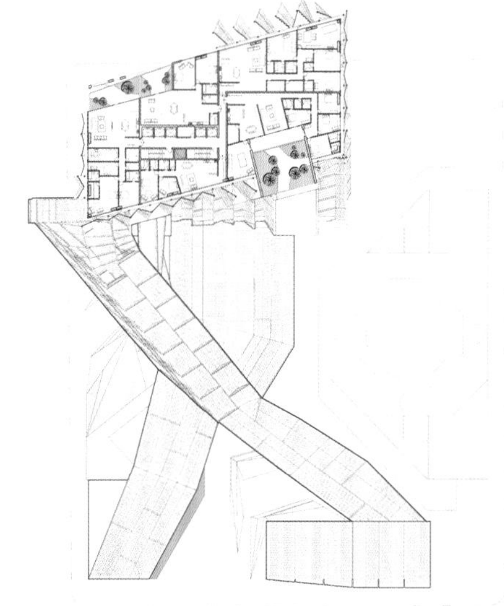

Apartment floor plan

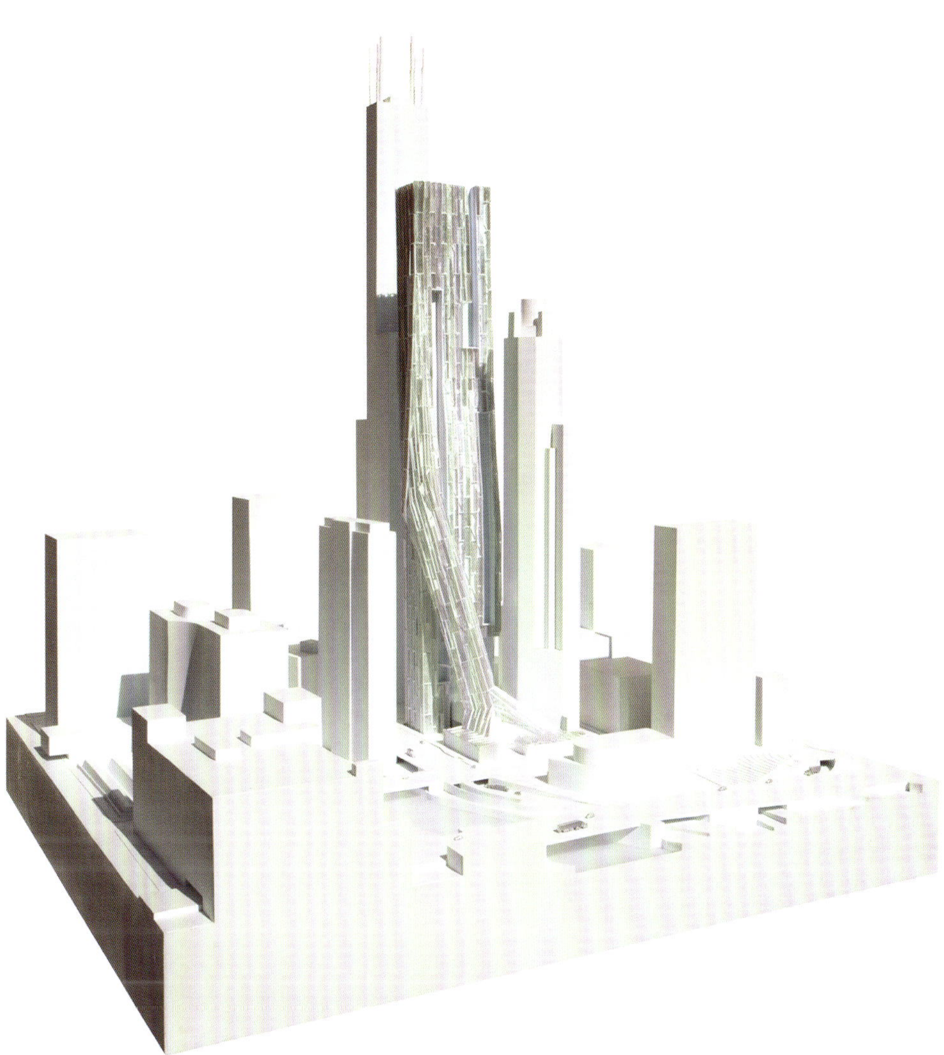

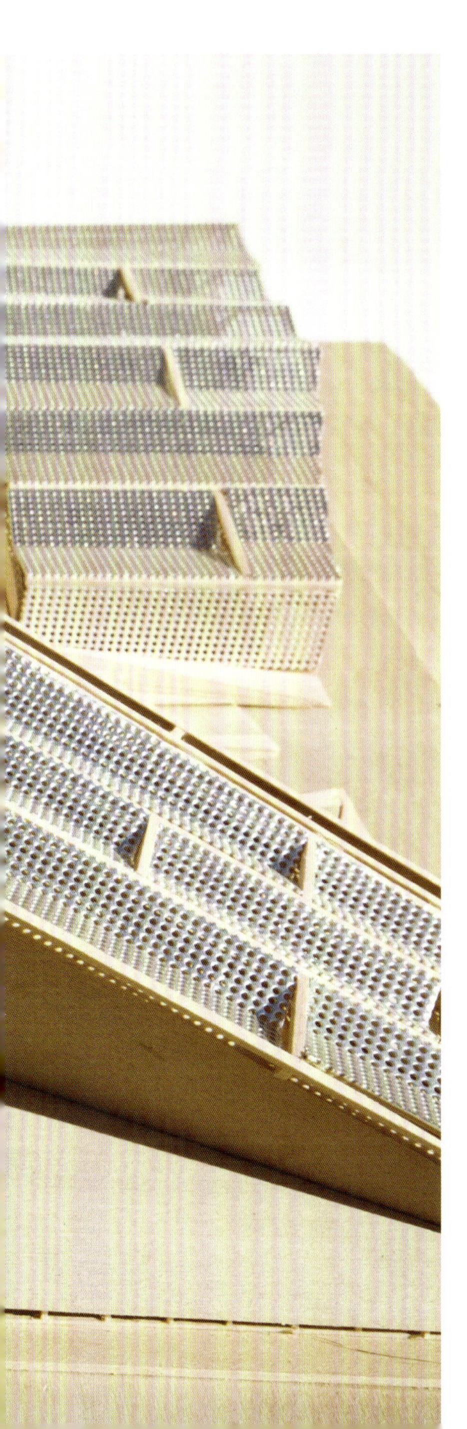

Site Senegal, Kafountine

Status Conceptual Design

Program Educational

Client Village of Kafountine

STRATIFICATIONS SCAPES

Paul Klee's watercolor painting *Monument in Fertile Country* (1929) depicts the stratification of landscapes, articulated by the complex layering of grounds. The Kafountine, Senegal Secondary School is inspired by the notion that architecture with multiple layers of strata can act as a generative ecology for the landscape and the community. The local community will construct the school using local building materials such as earthbags, translucent plastic roofs, woven bamboo canopies, simple metal structures, and concrete foundations. The school's architecture also calls for passive strategies, including solar panels for powering the water pumps and a layered roof and canopy with apertures that ventilate the building.

The *canopy/carpet* is a woven bamboo stratum that flows above the classrooms, offices, and multi-functional hall structures. This mediating roof stratum acts as a secondary element that carpets the entire school as a shading mechanism. The *roof/ceiling* is a translucent plastic stratum with articulated openings that passively ventilate classrooms for cooling and comfort. The *landscape/foundation* is an earth and concrete stratum that, as a heat sink, absorbs and dissipates heat on campus. The foundations of the school's entry rise up to form staggered sections, creating gardens that control the flow of people and choreograph a sequence of thresholds and movements on the ground. Assembled together, the stratifications and landscapes create an innovative spatial experience for educational events that unify the community.

The *canopy/carpet*, window shading, and door design accumulate into an abstract pattern that produces movement through lines, angles, spaces, and textures. The interlocking pattern represents balance, rhythm, proportion, and unity. Green color tones stand for renewal and growth, representing the birth and emergence of a new generation. The textile design deploys weaving techniques—strips of bamboo, an essential building material in Senegal, bound together—to create continuous woven surfaces.

Using these different strata, the Kafountine, Senegal Secondary School is a project that interfaces with the local economy through developing education in agricultural business. The colors and patterns of its architecture, meanwhile, create a symbol of local culture and equity in Senegal. This architecture creates a gathering space for the community and a haven for the next generation of Senegalese students.

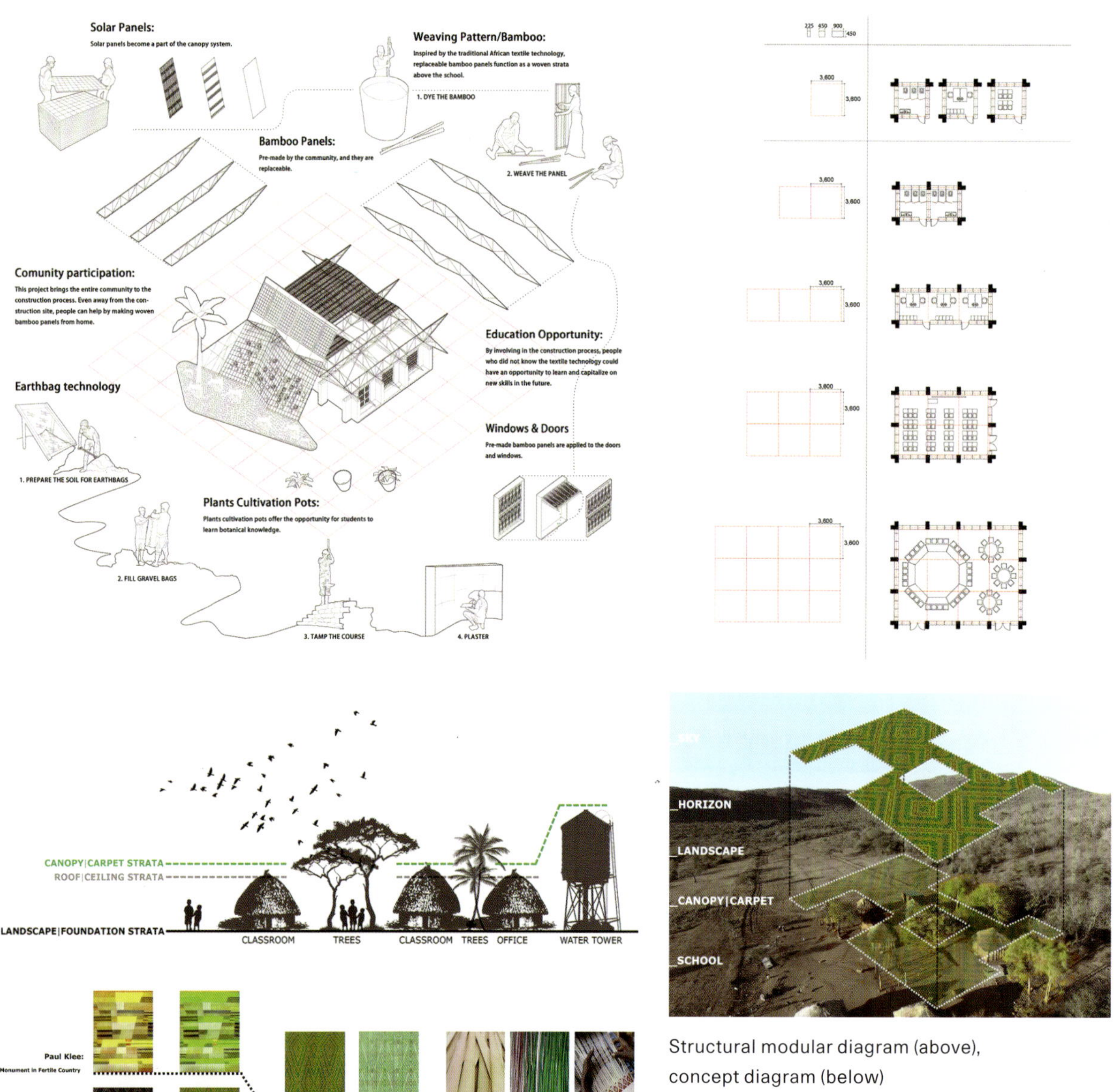

Structural modular diagram (above), concept diagram (below)

Community activitism diagram (above), architectural concept diagram (center), canopy ideogram (below)

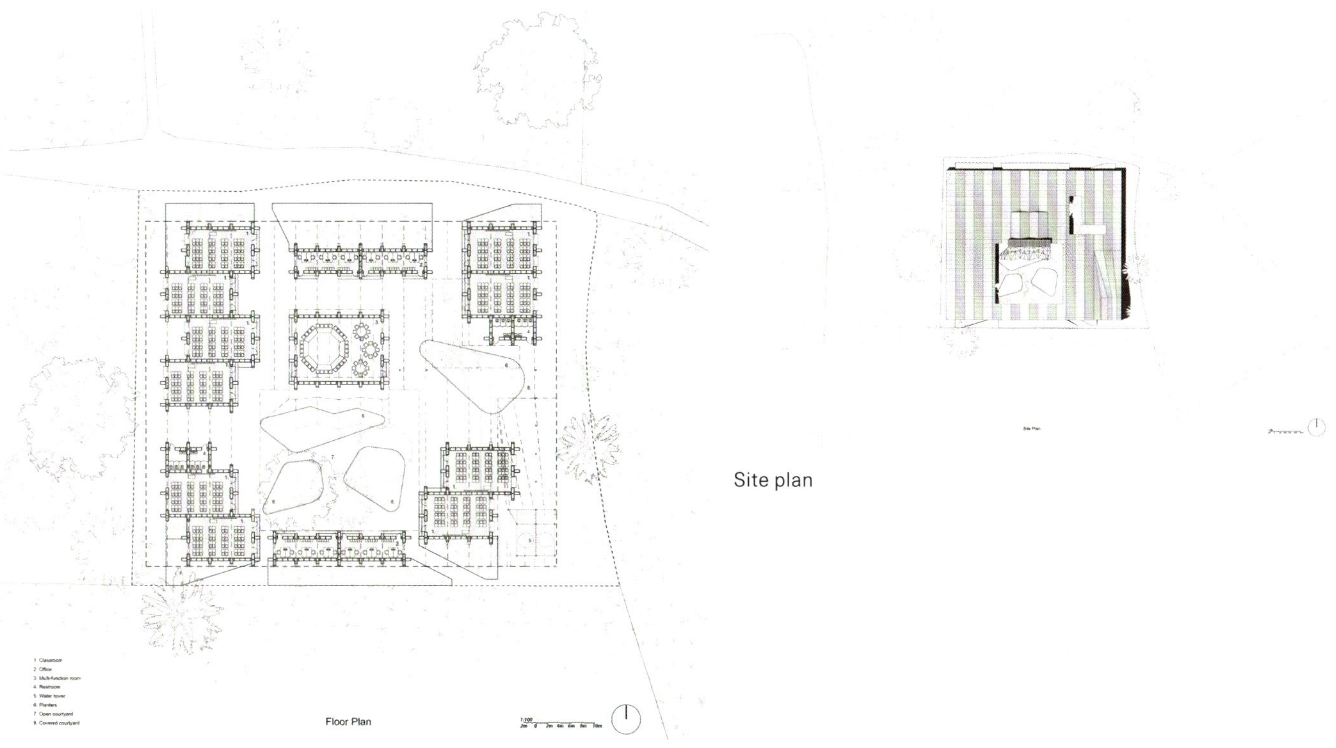

Site plan

First-floor plan

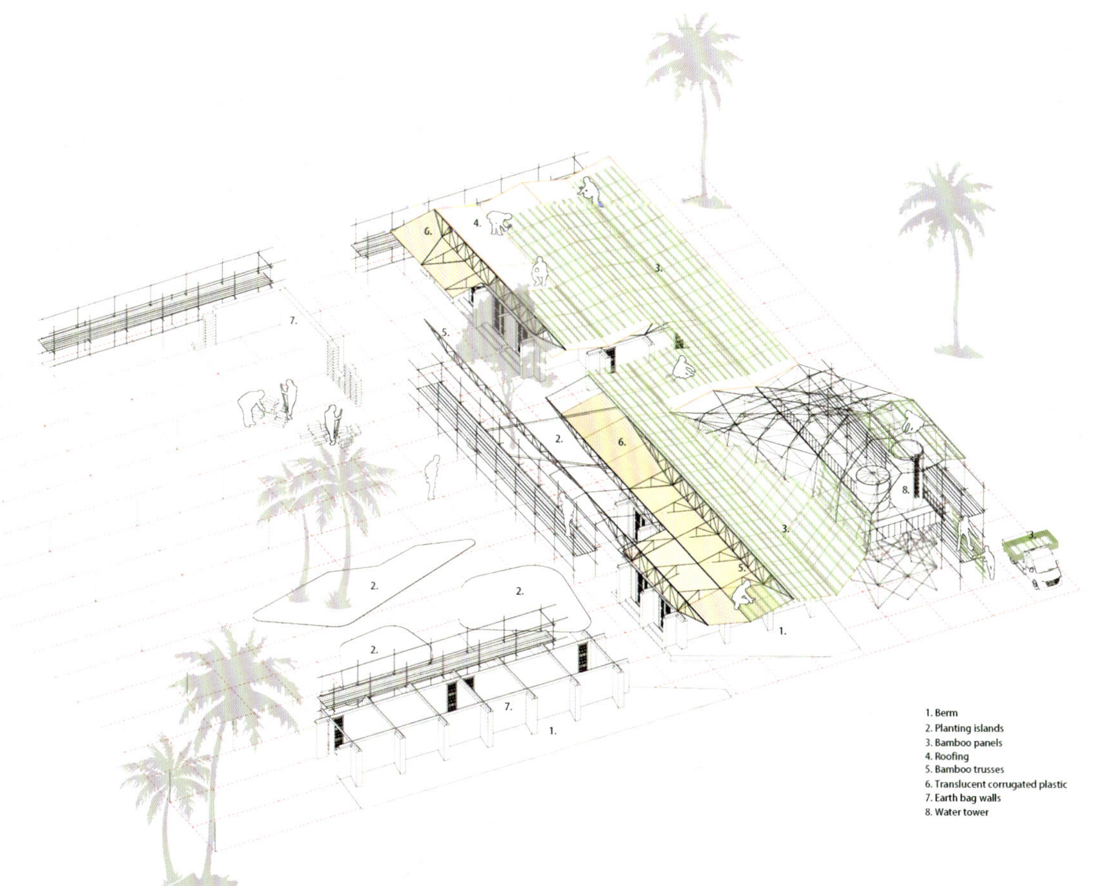

Construction assembly diagram

Transverse perspectival section

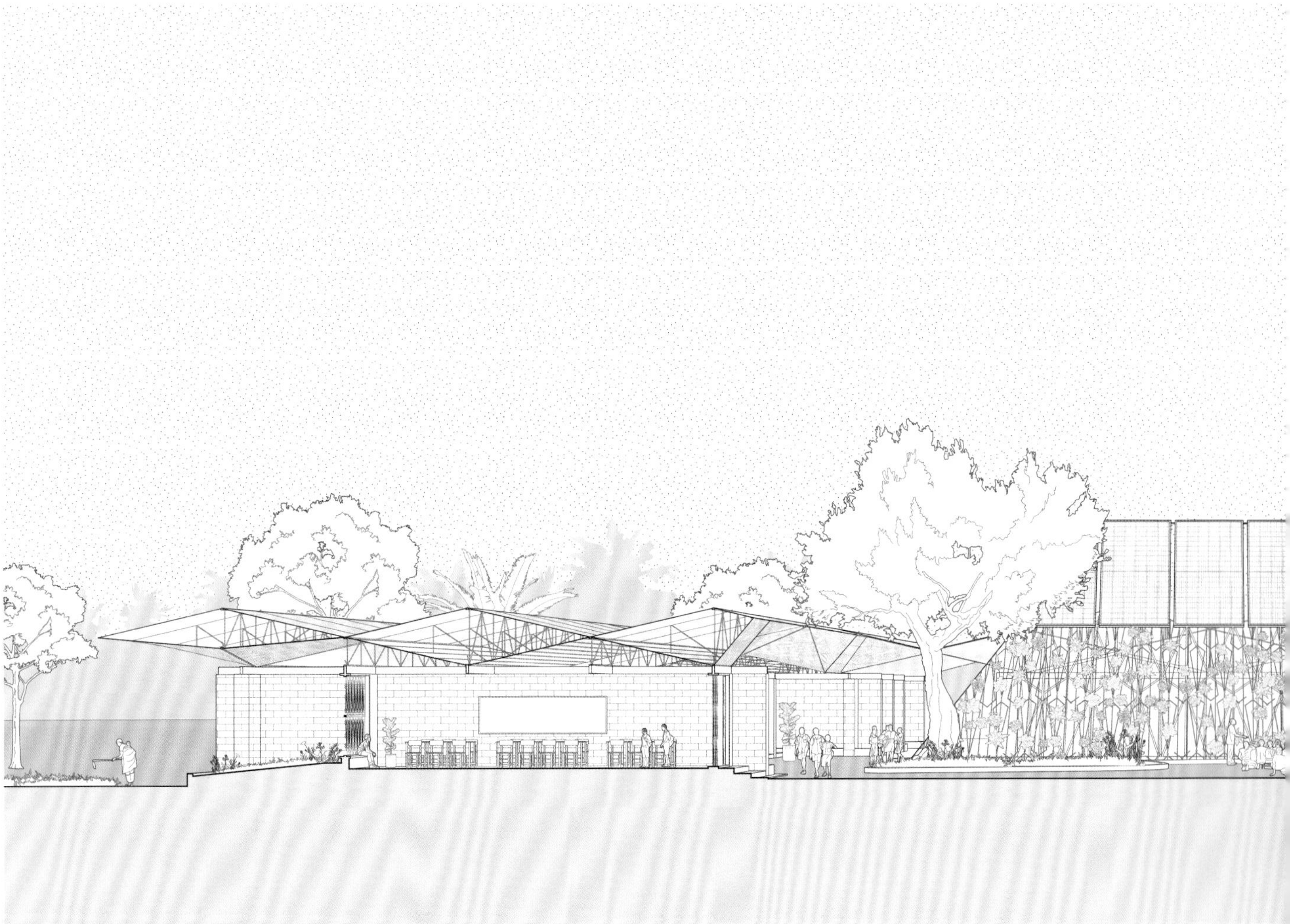

Longitudinal perspectival section

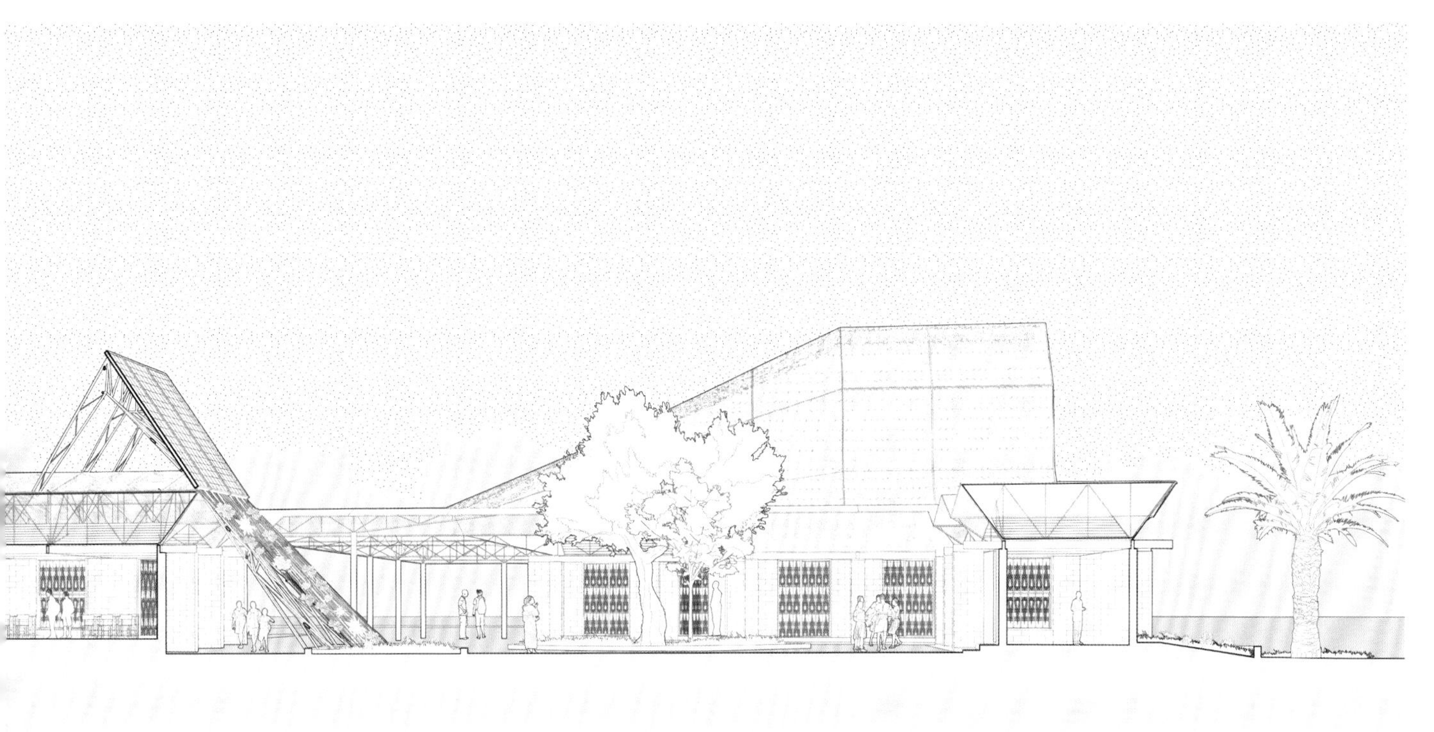

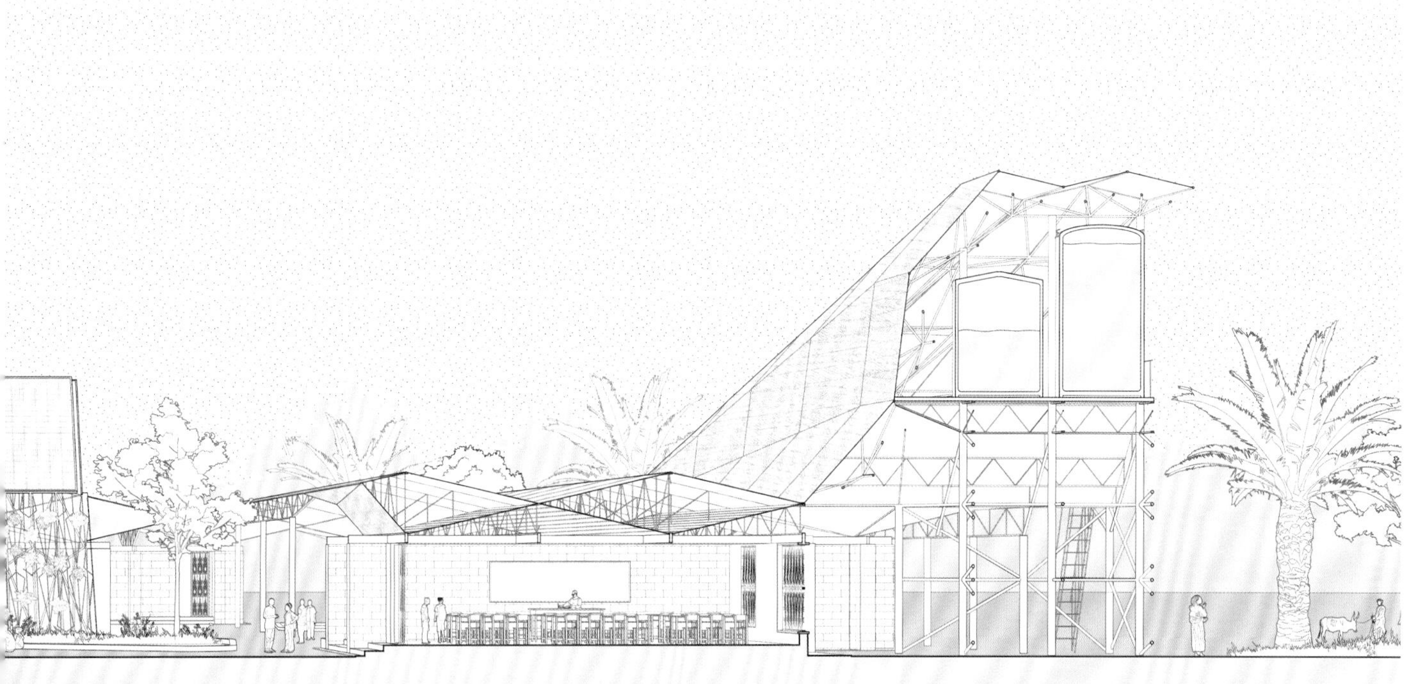

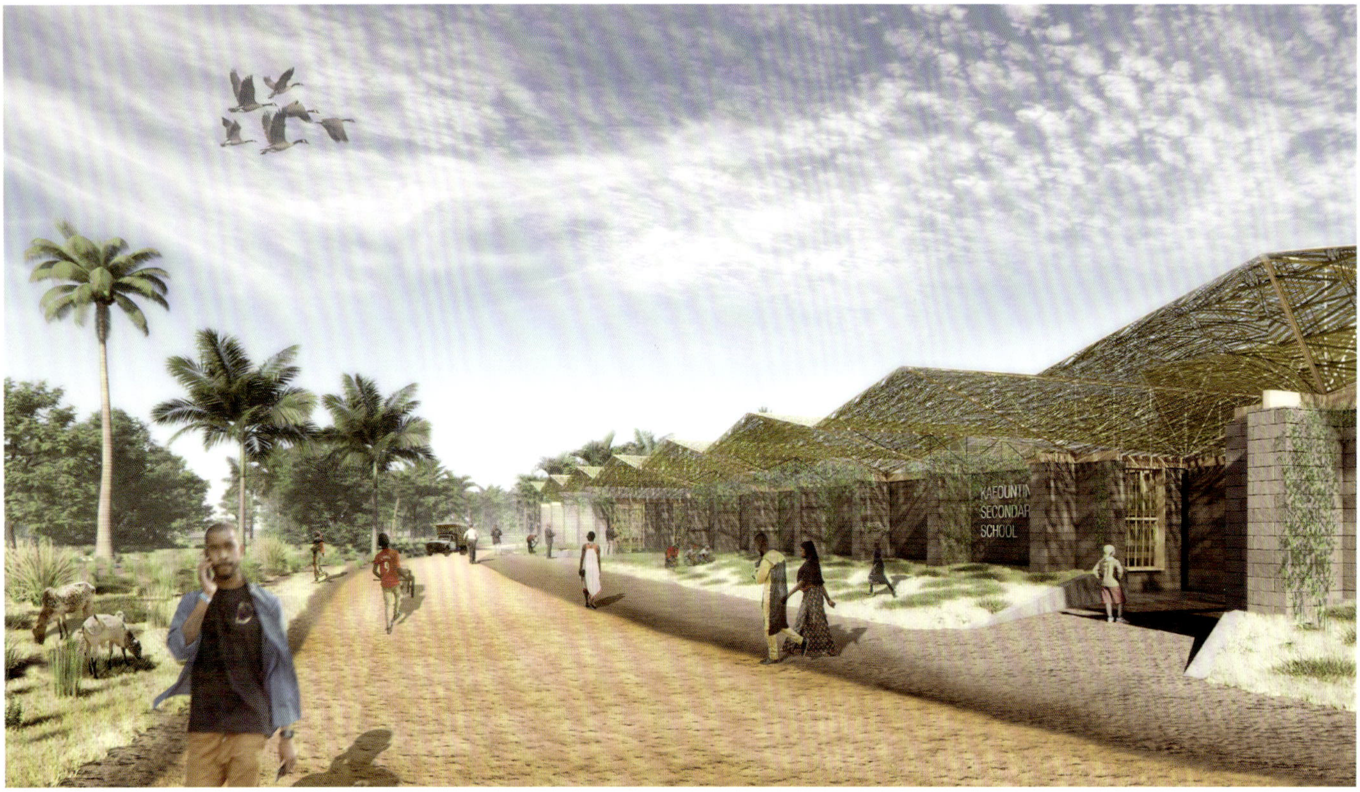
KAFOUNTIN
SECONDAR
SCHOOL

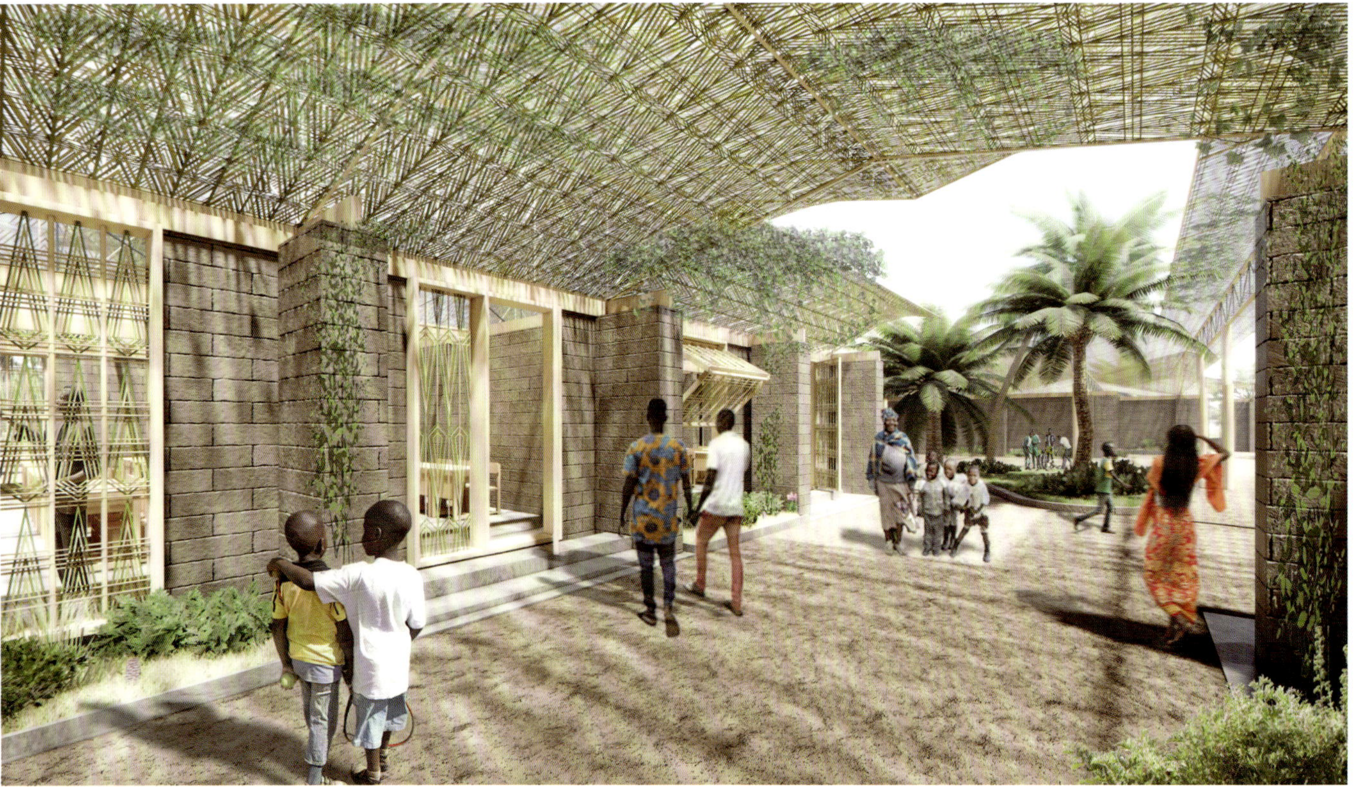

EPILOGUE

Jesse Reiser and Nanako Umemoto
with Julian Harake

It's one thing to speak of architecture's ability to directly engage the many complicated facets of society and another thing altogether to convince clients to remain within budget, meet local regulations, and maintain authorial integrity. As demonstrated through their work, Axi:Ome has found a delicate mode of practice often rejected by too many architects. Their projects push against preexisting models of building design as opposed to rejecting them outright. Less a compromise or blind acceptance of conventions, we take this as a formal realpolitik. Our own administrative experiences with clients corroborate this. What this does is grant their practice social and cultural relevance, often absent from the practices of many speculative or academically-oriented architects, while maintaining the architectural integrity missing from more normative offices. By straddling these two roads, they do things the harder way.

Invisible ideas cannot cut stone. Previously, they were not misperceived so. The outlines of St. Peter's were drawn directly on the ground at full scale, such that architecture's ideation through drawing was once a physical act of scratching away at the earth. As stereotomy precedes descriptive geometry, similarly went the full-scale drawings used by masons. Buildings required experience and sensitivity more than ideas, which is not to say they weren't intelligent, but rather that intelligence was more readily perceived as embedded in craft, making, and working with one's hands. We hope this is still the case now. Our graphite-tainted clothes attest to a more recent period—within our very lifetimes—when drawing was a more physical activity, engaging our hands as well as our eyes and intuitive senses (and lungs). Against the perceived smartness of ideas, matter was seen as somehow less dumb, and in that sense seemed to have ideas of its own worth exploring and cultivating through work.

This is a fundamental task of architecture—or should be today. As the ideation of invisible ether was in error, so too was the ethereality of ideas. Lest our world fails to be anything at all, or anything worth looking at: unmovable, ungraspable, unchangeable, and ultimately inert. Less complaints, these are impetuses for our work; less representations of ideas, cultures, economics, or politics but the direct manipulation of those societal facets as instigated by material organization. Rather than represent a political stance or set of ideas, our large institutional projects are the products of political maneuvering by elected officials and pragmatically-minded consultants. The pyramids of Egypt did more than represent the god-like powers of the pharaoh, they made him god-like through the subjugation of laborers as engendered by colossal built-works. More optimistically, Victor Horta's Maison du Peuple, commissioned by the Belgian Worker's Party, was built by, of, and for the people and causes it served. They would have been otherwise impossible. The architecture attests, as one shapes the world by shaping a stone, the architect must be literal.

What we might take from Axi:Ome is this: the dichotomy between professional practice and speculative architecture is unhelpful. This appears most frequently when architecture is taken en masse as a symbol rather than an object in itself and when it is reduced to little more than the power structures and material resources which bring it into being. This generalizing mode is ascendant today, aimed at practices like Axi:Ome from both the profession and the academy. What is lost are the specifics of the architectural artifact. Amidst its frequent vilification, we risk the ability to perceive architecture. On the contrary, Axi:Ome formally and architecturally reconciles these two spheres. Form is less manipulated than carefully shepherded from preexisting models and, through that process, becomes seemingly more embedded in the world and in tune with administrative realities and conventions of building. As speculative architecture struggles to maintain relevance and visibility, theirs is a compelling model for the future, for architecture matters when it ventures beyond its own orbit and extends beyond the representations and rhetoric too often mistaken as an end. Of this, both academics and professionals have been guilty.

As Axi:Ome's work seeks to remedy these errors, it deserves serious consideration. By bridging the academy and professional practice while succumbing to neither, a surprisingly novel, more visible, and more relevant mode of practice emerges.

REFLECTIONS ON THE INVISIBLE

Michelle L. Hauk

Axi:Ome's oeuvre raises the question of what it means in practice for architecture to be "invisible," a term Merriam-Webster defines as that which is "incapable by nature of being seen" or "not perceptible by vision." Many familiar phenomena are invisible to the human eye: oxygen, radio waves, germs, and music, to name a few. But architecture arises from material and spatial forms of creative expression that are inherently visible, even in their speculative or imaginary manifestations. Architecture is a visual art. Axi:Ome's conceptualization of the invisible proposes a metaphorical challenge to this maxim. Their body of work suggests that, despite its concreteness, architecture has the potential to become inconspicuous by functioning as one of many parts of a landscape rather than dominating it. Although still perceptible, it does not have to make itself known or proclaim its presence in such a way that it overpowers everything around it. To put it another way, architecture, when executed well, can belong.

A methodology of belonging seeks the invisible not through the negation of concrete form but through architecture's integration with its social and cultural context. The massing of Axi:Ome's COCA expansions, for example, respond equally to the residential neighborhood surrounding this beloved institution and to the heritage of the existing Mendelsohn building. Taken together, the old and new form a whole. The careful selection of materials—brick in this case—together with the complex's low profile further promote COCA's connectivity with the surrounding neighborhood of two- to three-story brick-clad apartments and single-family homes. At the same time, COCA's parking garage invites the neighborhood into the institution using hybrid-style spaces that create opportunities for community engagement. This sensitivity to what Nader Tehrani describes in the preface of this book as "connectivity, transparency, and continuity" (20) appears in other works as well, including the Olive Street Redevelopment project and the Wolfner Library.

Axi:Ome's careful integration of its projects into neighborhood and regional contexts does not, however, require aesthetic erasure. The Silver Tower, for example, rises confidently to 1,200 feet, its form subtly sculpted by the urban block's sun and wind patterns, themselves influenced by skyscrapers already existing on site. The tower's perforated façade also promises a striking effect both inside and out by both filtering and reflecting sunlight through a skin that doubles as an air and rainwater filter. Woofter and Kim's careful attention to the microclimates created by the building ensures that it will function as a member of a rich urban ecosystem. Likewise for the Secondary School proposed for Kafountine, Senegal, which has an undulating bamboo canopy that both distinguishes the building visually while also providing continuity with the ecology and cultural context of the site. It is this careful balance between presence and belonging that marks Axi:Ome's body of work.

If architecture is to be invisible then, it is not by becoming imperceptible by vision but rather by deploying a visual and spatial language that allows it to be perceived as a part of a larger whole. It is this language toward which Axi:Ome's practice aims. In doing so, Woofter and Kim's projects, both built and speculative, point to a future where architecture bridges the gap between human communities and the technologies that so often do just the opposite by alienating communities and the individuals within them. Theirs is a practice that seeks to create space for the invisible, but no less important, elements of design that bring architecture to life—compassion, empathy, community, and belonging—and in doing so, heal the landscapes and ecosystems that help us thrive.

CONTRIBUTORS

HEATHER WOOFTER received a Bachelor of Architecture from Virginia Polytechnic Institute ('91) and a Master of Architecture from the Graduate School of Design at Harvard University ('98). Woofter was a project architect and manager at Bohlin Cywinski Jackson (Wilkes-Barre, Pennsylvania), Marks Barfield (London), and Robert Luchetti Associates (Cambridge, Massachusetts) and is a registered architect in Pennsylvania and Missouri and has completed the Royal Institute of British Architects Part I and Part II qualifications. Woofter has taught at the Harvard Graduate School of Design Career Discovery Program, Boston Architectural College, and Roger Williams University. She has also served as an assistant professor at Virginia Polytechnic Institute and a visiting professor at Aristotle University of Thessaloniki in Greece and Konkuk University in Seoul, Korea. At Washington University in St. Louis, Woofter was the Sam and Marilyn Fox Professor and the director of the College of Architecture and Graduate School of Architecture & Urban Design. She is currently the dean of the School of Architecture at the University of Texas in Austin. Woofter is the owner and co-director of Axi:Ome, which she co-founded with Sung Ho Kim in 2003.

SUNG HO KIM received a Bachelor of Fine Arts and Bachelor of Architecture from the Rhode Island School of Design ('94) and an AA Diploma from the Architectural Association of London ('96), where he completed the Royal Institute of British Architects Part I and Part II qualifications. He also received a Master of Science in Architecture Studies from Massachusetts Institute of Technology ('98). Kim worked as a project designer for Nasrine Seraji (Paris) and Wellington Reiter (Cambridge, Massachusetts) and was a principal researcher for the Interrogative Design Group at the Center for Advanced Visual Studies at MIT between 1997 and 2001. Kim has taught at the Rhode Island School of Design and was an assistant professor at Northeastern University and a visiting professor at Aristotle University of Thessaloniki in Greece and Konkuk University in Seoul, Korea. At Washington University in St. Louis, he was the Raymond E. Maritz Professor of Architecture and engaged in multidisciplinary research with the Biology and Computer Science Departments. Currently, he is the director of Architecture and Urban Design at Kent State University. Kim is a co-director of Axi:Ome, which he co-founded with Heather Woofter in 2003.

NADER TEHRANI received a Bachelor of Fine Arts ('85) and a Bachelor of Architecture ('86) from the Rhode Island School of Design. He has also completed a post-graduate program in history and theory at the Architectural Association and received his Master of Urban Design from the Graduate School of Design at Harvard University ('91). Tehrani is a professor at the Irwin S. Chanin School of Architecture at the Cooper Union and is its former dean. He is also principal of NADAAA, a multi-disciplinary practice with projects in architecture, urbanism, and planning. Tehrani has also served as the Gehry Chair at the Daniels Faculty in the University of Toronto, The Ventulett Chair at Georgia Tech, and will serve as the upcoming Saarinen Chair at Yale University. Tehrani has been the recipient of multiple prizes, including the 2020 Arnold W. Brunner Memorial Prize of the American Academy of Arts and Letters, and the 2022 Design Visionary Award from Cooper Hewitt, Smithsonian Museum of Design, and was recently elected to the American Academy of Arts and Sciences. He also served as the 2017–2018 William A. Bernoudy Architect in Residence at The American Academy in Rome.

ALAN BALFOUR received a diploma in architecture from Edinburgh College of Art ('61) and a Master of Fine Arts from Princeton University ('65). He is an emeritus professor and the former dean of the College of Architecture (now called the College of Design) at Georgia Institute of Technology. He has also taught at MIT, Rensselaer Polytechnic Institute, Rice University, and the Architectural Association (London), programs in which he has held numerous leadership positions. Since 2014, he has held the position of advisory professor at the College of Architecture and Urban Planning at Tongji University in Shanghai. In 2000, Balfour received the Topaz Medal, the highest recognition given in North America to an educator in architecture. Balfour has published several works, including *Rockefeller Center: Architecture as Theater* (1978); *Berlin: The Politics of Order, 1737–1989* (1990); and more recently *The Walls of Jerusalem: Preserving the Past, Controlling the Future* (2019).

ERIC PAUL MUMFORD received a Bachelor of Arts from Harvard University ('80), a Master of Architecture from Massachusetts Institute of Technology ('83), and a Doctor of Philosophy degree in architecture at Princeton University ('96). Mumford is the Rebecca and John Voyles Professor of Architecture in the Sam Fox

School of Design & Visual Arts at Washington University in St. Louis. His books and edited volumes include: *The CIAM Discourse on Urbanism, 1928–1960* (2000; second edition forthcoming); *Defining Urban Design: CIAM Architects and the formation of a discipline, 1937–1969* (2009); *Designing the Modern City: Urbanism Since 1850* (2018); *Ando and Le Corbusier*, volume 2: Le Corbusier (2021); and *Design Agendas: Modern Architecture in St. Louis, 1930s–1970s* (forthcoming).

JENNIFER YOOS earned her Bachelor of Architecture from the University of Minnesota ('91) and an AA Graduate Diploma from the Architectural Association of London Design Research Lab ('98). She was a recipient of Harvard's Loeb Fellowship in Urban and Environmental Studies for 2002–2003 and in 2013, was inducted into the American Institute of Architects College of Fellows in the category of Design. She has previously taught as the NADAAA visiting professor at the Cooper Union, the Ruth and Norman Moore visiting professor at Washington University in St. Louis, the John G. Williams Distinguished Professor at the University of Arkansas, and as a faculty member at the University of Minnesota, where she is now professor and head of the Schools of Architecture, Landscape Architecture, and Interior Design. Yoos is also a principal and CEO of VJAA, a Minneapolis-based firm known for its highly-crafted buildings and its research-based, experimental, and contextual approach to architectural practice and environmental design. She is co-author, with partner Vincent James, of the book *Parallel Cities* (2016) and a monograph on the work of their practice.

JESSE REISER received his Bachelor of Architecture from the Cooper Union in New York and completed his Master of Architecture at the Cranbrook Academy of Art. He was a fellow of the American Academy in Rome in 1985 and has worked for the offices of John Hejduk and Aldo Rossi. Reiser has taught at schools throughout the United States and Asia, including Columbia University, Yale University, Ohio State University, Hong Kong University, and the Cooper Union. He is currently a professor of Architecture at Princeton University and an honorary fellow at the University of Tokyo's School of Engineering. Reiser is a principal at the internationally recognized, multidisciplinary design firm Reiser + Umemoto, which he formed with Nanako Umemoto in 1986. The firm has received numerous international honors and published a number of books, including the *Atlas of Novel Tectonics* (2006).

NANAKO UMEMOTO received her Bachelor of Architecture from the Cooper Union in New York ('83), following studies at the School of Urban Design and Landscape Architecture at the Osaka University of Art. Umemoto has taught at various schools in the U.S., Europe, and Asia, including Harvard University, the University of Pennsylvania, Columbia University, EPFL in Lausanne Switzerland, Hong Kong University, Kyoto University, and the Cooper Union, and is currently a Professor of Practice at Washington University in St. Louis. Umemoto is a principal at the internationally recognized, multidisciplinary design firm Reiser + Umemoto, which she formed with Jesse Reiser in 1986. The firm has received numerous international honors, including an AIA design award, and published a number of books, most recently *The Projects and Their Consequences* (2019).

JULIAN HARAKE received his Bachelor of Arts in architecture from the University of California at Berkeley ('13) and a Master of Architecture from Princeton University ('16). He is an architect and artist and has exhibited in various galleries in New York and has worked at the firms of Guy Nordenson and Associates (2016–2018) and Reiser + Umemoto (2019–2022). Harake has also taught at Barnard College, Syracuse University, Princeton University, the University of California at Berkeley, and the Parsons School of Design. His essays and criticism have been featured in *Dispatches Magazine*, the *New York Review of Architecture*, *Pidgin*, and *See/Saw*, as well as several published books.

MICHELLE L. HAUK received her Bachelor of Arts from Kalamazoo College ('07) and a Master of Architecture and Master of Science in Architectural Studies from Washington University in St. Louis ('15). She completed her Doctor of Philosophy in Japanese history at Columbia University ('23). Her research examines the cultural and social history of water in twentieth-century Japan through the lens of architecture, technology, and design. She is currently a postdoctoral fellow at the Reischauer Institute of Japanese Studies at Harvard University and will join the faculty at the Sam Fox School of Design & Visual Arts at Washington University in St. Louis as assistant professor of Architectural History and Theory in the fall of 2024.

PROJECT CREDITS

44

COCA EXPANSION II

Design Architect: Axi:Ome LLC
Design Directors: Heather Woofter and Sung Ho Kim
Project Coordinator: Jaymon Diaz
Project Team: Joe Boudreau, Mingchen Cui, Tim Scolarici, Yuxiang Wang, Wenqian Wen, Jiacheng Ye, and Yijin Zhao
Architect of Record: Christner Architects
Structural Engineering: Optimal Engineering Solutions
Mechanical, Electrical, Plumbing, Engineering: Buro Happold Engineering
Acoustical Engineering: Kirkegaard Associates
Theater and Lighting Engineering: Schuler Shook

54

COCA EXPANSION III

Design Architect: Axi:Ome LLC
Design Directors: Heather Woofter and Sung Ho Kim
Project Coordinator: Cassandra Cook
Project Team: Daniel Aguilera, Haoyi Chen, Yiming He, Taokai Ma, Dara Smyth, Jeong Min Wui, and Yi Zhou
Architect of Record: Christner Architects
Structural Engineering: Optimal Engineering Solutions
Mechanical, Electrical, Plumbing, Engineering: Buro Happold Engineering
Acoustical Engineering: Kirkegaard Associates
Theater and Lighting Engineering: Schuler Shook

74

COCA PARKING

Architect: Axi:Ome LLC
Design Directors: Heather Woofter and Sung Ho Kim
Project Coordinator: Jaymon Diaz
Project Team: Christopher Liao, Timothy Scolarici, and Jiacheng Ye

82

WUNDERLAND STAGE SET

Architect: Axi:Ome LLC
Design Directors: Heather Woofter and Sung Ho Kim
Project Coordinator: Jae Bum Byun
Project Team: Kevin Mojica and Yulia Morina

88

LITTLE DANCER STAGE SET

Architect: Axi:Ome LLC
Design Directors: Heather Woofter and Sung Ho Kim
Project Coordinator: Allen Liang
Project Team: Zitao Zhang

100

V9 DIGITAL

Architect: Axi:Ome LLC
Design Directors: Heather Woofter and Sung Ho Kim
Project Coordinator: Cassandra Cook
Project Team: Li Gong, Tim Scolarici, and Yi Zhou

106

NINE NETWORK MASTER PLAN

Architect: Axi:Ome LLC
Design Directors: Heather Woofter and Sung Ho Kim
Project Coordinator: Cassandra Cook
Project Team: Daniel Aguilera, Jae Bum Byun, Yiming He, Dara Smyth, Sheng Yan, and Yi Zhou

124

HAN HOUSE

Architect: Axi:Ome LLC
Design Directors: Heather Woofter and Sung Ho Kim
Project Coordinator: Jaymon Diaz
Project Team: Jae Bum Byun, Josh Chan, Tim Scolarici, Modupeola Thomas, and Xuanchen Zhang

132

OLIVE STREET REDEVELOPMENT

Architect: Axi:Ome LLC
Design Directors: Heather Woofter and Sung Ho Kim
Project Coordinator: Jaymon Diaz
Project Team: Joseph Boudreau, Timothy Scolarici, Jiacheng Ye, and Yijin Zhou

158

WOLFNER LIBRARY REDEVELOPMENT

Architect: Axi:Ome LLC
Design Directors: Heather Woofter and Sung Ho Kim
Project Coordinator: Cassandra Cook
Project Team: Daniel Aguilera, Jae Bum Byun, Yiming He, and Dara Smyth

166

LENS BRIDGE and URBAN DECK

Architect: Axi:Ome LLC
Design Directors: Heather Woofter and Sung Ho Kim
Project Coordinator: Jae Bum Byun
Project Team: Haoyi Chen, Cassandra Cook, Jackson Feinknopf, Allen Liang, Yifan Luo, Patrick Murray, Mason Radford, Jeong Min Wui, and Guangdi Yao

186

NORTHWOOD RENOVATION

Architect: Axi:Ome LLC
Design Directors: Heather Woofter and Sung Ho Kim
Project Coordinator: Jae Bum Byun
Project Team: Madeline LaPointe and Allen Liang
Structural Engineering: Upright Design Consulting and Engineering
Mechanical, Electrical, Plumbing, Engineering: Mann Architectural Engineering

196

MAISON FELINE

Architect: Axi:Ome LLC
Design Directors: Heather Woofter and Sung Ho Kim
Project Coordinator: Cassandra Cook
Project Team: Jae Bum Byun, Madeline LaPointe, and Allan Liang

210

FERRY TERMINAL THE CLOUD

Architects: Axi:Ome LLC with Javier Maroto of SOLID ARQUITECTURA and MAREMOTO PAISAJES
Design Directors: Heather Woofter and Sung Ho Kim
Project Coordinator: Daniel Aguilera
Project Team: Li Gong, Taokai Ma, Uros Stanojevic, and Yi Zhou with Teresa Maraca and Mónica Thurne of SOLID ARQUITECTURA and MAREMOTO PAISAJES

218

CRYSTAL ARMATURE

Architect: Axi:Ome LLC
Design Directors: Heather Woofter and Sung Ho Kim
Project Coordinator: Jaymon Diaz
Project Team: Joshua Chan, Ran Gu, Collen Qiu, Timothy Scolarici, Borislav Tchatalbachev, Modupeola Thomas, Jessica Ye, Meo Zhang, Michelle Zhang, Tianyi Zhang, Xuanchen Zhang, Yi Zhou, and Zhaoyu Zhu

234

ALBANY HOUSING I FLOATING POOL

Architect: Axi:Ome LLC
Design Directors: Heather Woofter and Sung Ho Kim
Project Coordinator: Jaymon Diaz
Project Team: Joseph Boudreau, Yiming He, Timothy Scolarici, Jiacheng Ye, Yuelin Yu, and Xuanchen Zhang

244

ALBANY HOUSING II ELEVATED GROUND

Architect: Axi:Ome LLC
Design Directors: Heather Woofter and Sung Ho Kim
Project Coordinator: Jaymon Diaz
Project Team: Joseph Boudreau, Yiming He, Timothy Scolarici, Jiacheng Ye, Yuelin Yu, and Xuanchen Zhang

252

SILVERLAKE INTERNATIONAL HIGH SCHOOL

Architect: Axi:Ome LLC
Design Directors: Heather Woofter and Sung Ho Kim
Project Manager: Fei Xie
Project Coordinator: Cassandra Cook
Project Team: Daniel Aguilera, Jae Ho Ahn, Daniel Fernandez-Barbara, Siyu Huang, Taokai Ma, Mason Radford, Dara Smyth, Catty Dan Zhang and Yi Zhou
Landscape Architect: Hybridesign
Landscape Team: Yadan Luo

274

MICRO HOUSING I

Architect: Axi:Ome LLC
Design Directors: Heather Woofter and Sung Ho Kim
Project Manager: Ji Hoon Kim
Project Coordinator: Yuelin Yu
Project Team: Daniel Aguilera, Daniel Fernandez-Barbara, Ming He, Taokai Ma, Mason Radford, and Dara Smyth

280

MICRO HOUSING II

Architect: Axi:Ome LLC
Design Directors: Heather Woofter and Sung Ho Kim
Project Manager: Ji Hoon Kim
Project Coordinator: Yuelin Yu
Project Team: Daniel Aguilera, Daniel Fernandez-Barbara, Ming He, Taokai Ma, Mason Radford, and Dara Smyth

288

ROOFSCAPE HAUS

Architect: Axi:Ome LLC
Design Directors: Heather Woofter and Sung Ho Kim
Project Manager: Ji Hoon Kim
Project Coordinator: Taokai Ma
Project Team: Daniel Aguilera, Jae Ho Ahn, Daniel Fernandez-Barbara, and Mason Radford

302

FACTORY + FENCE

Architect: Axi:Ome LLC
Design Directors: Heather Woofter and Sung Ho Kim
Project Manager: Ji Hoon Kim
Project Coordinator and Team: Jae Bum Byun

314

SILVER TOWER

Architect: Axi:Ome LLC
Design Directors: Heather Woofter and Sung Ho Kim
Project Manager: Jaymon Diaz
Project Coordinator: Xun Wang
Project Team: Darwin Barnes, Cassandra Cook, Mingchen Cui, Li Gong, Yifan Luo, Mason Radford, Tim Scolarici, Angela Hye Rim Shim, Yufan Song, Yuxiang Wang, Wenqian Wen, Erin Wong, and Yepeng Zhang
Biology Research Principal Investigator: Dr. Ram Dixit
Biology Research Assistant: Daniel Adams
Moss Research: Dr. Pierre-Francois Perroud in Dr. Ralph Quatrano's Lab at Washington University in St. Louis

336

STRATIFICATIONS SCAPES

Architect: Axi:Ome LLC
Design Directors: Heather Woofter and Sung Ho Kim
Project Coordinators: Xun Wang and Lingyue Wang
Project Team: Mic Ma and Shangfeng Rao

Daniel Gass
Molly Gleason
Li Gong
Christos Gourdoukis
Dimitris Gourdoukis
Ran Gu
Cheng He Guan
Neena Gupta
Anthony Hahn
Michael Hahn
Maria-Anna Hatziliades
Yiming He
Ryan Headd
Michael Heller
Matt Horvath
Tyson Hosmer
Tianhui Hou
Yi Hou
Siyu Huang
Kyla Hygysician
Fiza Idrees
Adni Isakovic
Philip Jia
Daniel Katebini
Alex Kim
Dj Kim
Doh Young Kim
Ji Hoon Kim
Jin Kim
Nicole Kim
Steven Kim
Andrew Koh
Sarah Kott
Mikale Kwiatkowski
Jenny Kwon
Madeline LaPointe
Si Eun Lee
Lincoln Lewis
Allen Liang
Christopher Liao
Ruogu Liu
Geoff Loo
Seth Looper
Yifan Luo
Mic Ma
Taokai Ma
Matthew MacRaild
Pak-Kei Mak
Lauren Matrka
Nick McFadden
Lior Jacob Melnick
Hamis Mhando
Marisa Miller
Sam Moen
Kevin Mojica
Yulia Morina
Daniel Moroze
Greg Murphy
Kevin Myers
Ahsan Najmi
Mara Noble
Adam Novack
Hannah Novack
Sehzat Oner
Davis Owen
Rodrigo Pantoja
Kevin Park
Shin Young Park
Brandon Petrella
David Poeyamidjaya

–2023